In this book Peter J. Schraeder offers the first comprehensive theoretical analysis of US foreign policy toward Africa in the postwar era. He argues that though we often assume that US policymakers "speak with one voice," Washington's foreign policy is derived from numerous centers of power which have the ability to simultaneously pull policy in different directions. The book describes the evolution of policy at three levels: Presidents and their closest advisers; the bureaucracies of the executive branch; and Congress and African affairs interest groups. Most importantly, the evidence presented demonstrates that the nature of events on the African continent – ranging from routine to crisis and extended crisis situations – has itself affected the operation of the US policymaking process, and therefore the substance of US Africa policies. Drawing on over 100 interviews, and detailed case studies of US relations with Zaire, Ethiopia–Somalia, and South Africa, this book provides a unique analysis of the historical evolution of US foreign policy from the 1940s to the 1990s.

D0876844

UNITED STATES FOREIGN POLICY TOWARD AFRICA

INCREMENTALISM, CRISIS AND CHANGE

Cambridge Studies in International Relations is a joint initiative of Cambridge University Press and the British International Studies Association (BISA). The series will include a wide range of material, from undergraduate textbooks and surveys to research-based monographs and collaborative volumes. The aim of the series is to publish the best new scholarship in International Studies from Europe, North America and the rest of the world.

CAMBRIDGE STUDIES IN INTERNATIONAL RELATIONS

Series list continues after index

UNITED STATES FOREIGN POLICY TOWARD AFRICA
INCREMENTALISM, CRISIS AND CHANGE

PETER J. SCHRAEDER

Loyola University of Chicago

CAMBRIDGE
UNIVERSITY PRESS

Published by the Press Syndicate of the University of Cambridge
The Pitt Building, Trumpington Street, Cambridge CB2 1RP
40 West 20th Street, New York, NY 10011–4211, USA
10 Stamford Road, Oakleigh, Melbourne 3166, Australia

First published 1994
Reprinted 1995, 1996

A catalogue record for this book is available from the British Library

Library of Congress cataloguing in publication data

Schraeder, Peter J.
  United States foreign policy toward Africa:
Incrementalism, crisis and change / Peter J. Schraeder.
      p.   cm. – (Cambridge studies in international relations; 31)
Includes bibliographical references.
ISBN 0 521 44439 X
1. Africa – Foreign relations – United States.
2. United States – Foreign relations – Africa.
3. United States – Foreign relations – 1945–1989.
4. United States – Foreign relations – 1989–1993.
I. Title. II. Series.
DT38.W45 1993
327.7306 – dc20 93–21590 CIP

ISBN 0 521 44439 X hardback
ISBN 0 521 46677 6 paperback

Transferred to digital printing 2002

CE

To Mark "Spanks" Przybyla,
the best friend a person could ever have

CONTENTS

TABLES

PREFACE

The genesis of this book was a desire to write a systematic overview and analysis of United States foreign policy toward Africa that would be of interest not only to scholarly audiences and members of the policymaking establishment, but also to those Africans entrusted by their respective governments in negotiating the labyrinth of Washington's foreign policy establishment. As an Africanist with training in the fields of international relations theory and comparative foreign policy, I often have been frustrated by the paucity of scholarly research in these fields that addresses my particular interest in US relations with the African continent. Indeed, the study of Africa within the fields of international relations theory and comparative foreign policy historically has been a low academic priority. Studies that either focus on traditional security concerns, such as East–West relations and the nature of the Atlantic Alliance, or geographical regions of perceived greater importance, such as Southeast Asia, Central America, and, more recently, Eastern Europe and the Middle East, are given priority. Similarly, this attitude is found in official policymaking circles, as well as among segments of the general public.

The primary purposes of this book, therefore, are threefold. The first purpose is to address the lack of understanding and attention that Africa has received within the fields of international relations theory and comparative foreign policy. Although I have not argued, as have some of Africa's most passionate supporters, that the continent constitutes the region of greatest importance to US foreign policy, the fact remains that Africa is poorly understood by academia, the policymaking establishment, and the general public. Perhaps the greatest danger inherent in such a state of affairs is that poor understanding can foster poorly devised policies that ultimately are destined to fail. In this sense, our awareness and understanding of African issues must be heightened if the US is to play a positive, proactive role on the African continent.

The second purpose of this volume is to describe the roles played by various actors within the policymaking establishment devoted to US Africa policies. Although we often speak of a "United States" foreign policy toward Africa, one must remember that the US is not a monolithic actor that "speaks with one voice." Rather, Washington's foreign policy landscape is composed of numerous centers of power which have the ability to simultaneously pull policy in many different directions. One can (and should) find legitimate differences of opinion and intense rivalries for control of US Africa policies. For example, these rivalries not only come into play between the executive and congressional branches of government, as one would expect, but also within a particular branch (such as between the Department of State and the Department of Defense), as well as within individual bureaucracies (such as between the State Department's bureaus of African Affairs and European Affairs). This book thus focuses on three major levels of the policymaking process. The first and most obvious level is that of the White House, including Presidents and their most trusted foreign policy advisers (usually the Secretary of State and the National Security Adviser). A second important level of the policymaking process is composed of the national security bureaucracies of the executive branch. The relevant foreign policy actors at this level are the State Department, the Defense Department, and the Central Intelligence Agency (CIA), as well as each bureaucracy's separate bureaus devoted specifically to Africa. The final level of analysis is the arena of domestic politics, most notably the Africa subcommittees of both the Senate and the House of Representatives, the Congressional Black Caucus, and private interest groups, such as TransAfrica.

The third and most important purpose of this volume is to describe and explain continuity and change in US Africa policies during the post-World War II period. In order to achieve such an understanding, one must build bridges between the fields of international relations theory and comparative foreign policy. Specifically, the evidence presented in this study demonstrates that the nature of events on the African continent – ranging from routine to crisis and extended crisis situations – historically has affected the operation of the US policymaking process, and therefore the substance of US Africa policies. Bilateral relationships with various African regimes have not remained static, but instead have evolved as different portions of the foreign policy establishment have asserted their influence within the policymaking process at different points in time. Thus, by focusing on the interplay between the nature of events on the African continent and the operation of the policymaking process, one can gain a clearer understanding of continuity and change in US foreign policy toward Africa.

In order to facilitate our understanding of the processes affecting US Africa policies, emphasis here is placed on describing the historical evolution of US relations with several African countries over more than fifty years. Detailed comparative case studies include an overview and analysis of US relations with Ethiopia and Somalia (treated as one area), South Africa, and Zaire during the post-World War II era, inclusive of the Bush administration, but ending with the inauguration of President Bill Clinton on January 20, 1993. Although observers of different ideological backgrounds have often characterized US Africa policies as highly erratic, the analysis demonstrates that one can discern several dominant patterns of the US policymaking process. Whereas some of these are unique to US Africa relations, others are indicative of US foreign policy in general.

This careful blending of historical analysis with policy-relevant case studies contributes to our knowledge of the theory and practice of US foreign policy. In this regard, the book was written with several audiences in mind. The two most important audiences are scholars in the fields of international relations theory and comparative foreign policy, and Africanists both within and outside the policymaking establishment. The volume is also intended as a starting point for those Africans seeking to understand the nature and evolution of US foreign policy toward their continent. As Somali Chargé d'Affaires Abdi Awaleh Jama remarked at a meeting of the Northeast African Studies Association in 1989, the primary dilemma facing African diplomats assigned to Washington "is that the US government speaks with many voices, which oftentimes are contradictory." "In order to survive," he continued, "we African diplomats must learn to walk a precarious diplomatic tightrope, all the time concentrating on which voice, if any, predominates and thus serves as the proper guidepost for our initiatives."

ACKNOWLEDGMENTS

Some of the greatest joys of carrying out an extended research project are the numerous individuals that one meets along the way who are graciously willing to donate valuable amounts of their time to ensure the ultimate success of the project. The winding process that led to the completion of this book fostered contact with a wide variety of individuals, each of whom contributed in a different fashion to the final product. Although it is my distinct pleasure to acknowledge the special and much-appreciated roles played by these individuals, I accept sole responsibility for any remaining deficiencies embodied in this work.

First and foremost, I wish to thank the members of my dissertation committee, each of whom brought a special vision to the finished product which, in turn, became the basis for this book. Jerel A. Rosati served as the intellectual guide and inspiration for creating a project that combined my interest in the fields of international relations theory, comparative foreign policy, and African politics. Charles W. Kegley, Jr., an unparalleled scholar in the field of comparative foreign policy, fostered my interest in theory and empirical analysis. Anthony Lake, who can claim a unique combination of extensive experience within both the academic world and the policymaking establishment, most notably as Director for Policy Planning in the State Department under the Carter administration, as well as the recently appointed National Security Adviser of the Clinton administration, corrected the innumerable errors committed by an outsider dedicated to the study of US Africa policies. Janice Love, who initially inspired me to write about US foreign policy toward the Horn of Africa while working together with me in Mogadishu, Somalia, also cultivated my interest in US–South African relations and the evolution of the US anti-apartheid movement. Finally, although he did not serve on the committee in an official status, Mark W. DeLancey was there at the beginning, always helpful and encouraging to those, including myself, who share his love for Africa.

Other scholars helped to focus my arguments throughout the writing process by critiquing earlier versions of individual chapters, several of which were presented as papers at the annual conferences of the African Studies Association, the International Studies Association, and the Northeast African Studies Association. James J. Zaffiro, Joseph M. Scolnick, Donald L. Gordon, and Francis Kornegay, Jr. provided helpful comments on Chapters 1, 2, and 6 at the formative stage of the project. Similarly, each of the case studies benefited from the thoughtful comments of regional specialists. Among those who offered rigorous critiques were Patrick M. Boyle, John W. Harbeson, and Crawford Young (Chapter 3 – Zaire); Daniel Compagnon, Ali K. Galaydh, Abdi Awaleh Jama, David Laitin, I. M. Lewis, Terrence P. Lyons, and John H. Spencer (Chapter 4 – Ethiopia and Somalia); and R. Hunt Davis (Chapter 5 – South Africa).

Written critiques of individual chapters were further sharpened by dozens of presentations on the African continent as part of two summer lecture tours sponsored by the United States Information Agency (USIA) and its "American Participant" (AmParts) program during both 1990 and 1991. Among those African institutions which sponsored lectures and, in the process, opened up my research to the insightful comments of African scholars too numerous to list individually, were: Department of Political Science, National University of Benin; Department of Government, National University of Burundi; Faculty of Letters and Faculty of Education Sciences, Ruhengeri Campus, National University of Rwanda; Faculty of Social Sciences and Faculty of Public Administration, Butare Campus, National University of Rwanda; Department of History and Geography, Higher Institute of Pedagogy (Mozambique); Center for African Studies, Eduardo Mondlane University (Mozambique); Department of Political Science, Fourah Bay College, University of Sierra Leone; Department of Political Science and Legon Center for International Affairs, Legon University (Ghana); Department of Government and Institute of Diplomacy and International Studies, University of Nairobi (Kenya); Faculty of Arts, Kenyatta University (Kenya); Institute of Diplomacy, Somali Ministry of Foreign Affairs (Somalia); and Somali Institute for Development and Management (Somalia).

Several institutions also facilitated the research and writing process. Special thanks is first due to the University of South Carolina and the faculty and staff associated with the Department of Government & International Studies, the Institute of International Studies, and the International Studies Association. In addition to providing a uniquely creative and nurturing environment dedicated to the pursuit of knowledge, the University of South Carolina also provided a series of graduate fellowships and a 1987–88 West Foundation grant which enabled me to develop a dissertation topic. During 1989 and 1990, my status as a visiting scholar in residence with the African Studies Program at Northwestern University provided the perfect atmosphere in which to write a first draft. I will never forget the warm hospitality offered by Assistant Program Director Akbar Virmani, as well as my numerous discussions with Hans Panofsky, Senior Director of the Melville Herskovitts Library of African Studies who retired in 1991 – he will be sorely missed. In Washington, DC, special thanks is due to Kenneth Mokoena and the staff at the National Security Archive, a private foundation which allowed access to a wealth of declassified documents on US Africa policies, as well as the extremely able staff at the Library of Congress. Finally, my current position as an assistant professor in the Department of Political Science at Loyola University of Chicago continues to provide me with an exceptionally collegial and supportive workplace. Among those at Loyola who contributed to completion of the final product were Kate Ahrens, Judy Calix, Wendy Chiaramonte, Nicole Favreau, Phillips George, Bonnie Juettner, Miegan Lesher, Nancy Norman, Bruce Taylor, Michael Walsh and Bryon White.

The most important aspect of the research and writing process, however, was the loving support of my family and friends. Among those who never lost faith and provided constant encouragement were Ahmed and Fowzia Jirreh, Susan M. Lowry, Tom and Laura Montbriand, Mark "Spanks" Przybyla, and the entire Schraeder clan: Bill and Helen, Tom and Jorja, Bill and Laura, Max, Jerry, Jason, Paul, Phillip, and Tricia.

ACRONYMS

ACOA	American Committee on Africa
AFSC	American Friends Service Committee
ANC	African National Congress (South Africa)
APC	Armored Personnel Carrier
ASA	African Studies Association
BOSS	Bureau of State Security (South Africa)
CBC	Congressional Black Caucus
CIA	Central Intelligence Agency
CNL	Committee of National Liberation (Zaire)
CONACO	National Confederation of the Congo (Zaire)
CPSU	Communist Party of the Soviet Union
CRISP	Center for Research and Socio-Political Information (Belgium)
CRS	Catholic Relief Service
DCI	Director of Central Intelligence
DDI	Deputy Directorate of Intelligence
DDO	Deputy Directorate of Operations
DFSS	Democratic Front for the Salvation of Somalia (Somalia)
DIA	Defense Intelligence Agency
DONS	Department of National Security (South Africa)
ECOWAS	Economic Community of West African States
EPLF	Eritrean People's Liberation Front (Eritrea)
EPRDF	Ethiopian People's Revolutionary Democratic Front (Ethiopia)
ESF	Economic Support Fund
EURCOM	European Command
FIS	Islamic Salvation Front (Algeria)
FLNC	Front for the National Liberation of the Congo (Zaire)
FMS	Foreign Military Sales
FNLA	Frente Nacional de Libertaçao de Angola (Angola)
FSO	Foreign Service Officer
FY	Fiscal Year

GAO	General Accounting Office
GPO	Government Printing Office
ICCR	Interfaith Center on Corporate Responsibility
IGADD	Intergovernmental Authority on Drought and Development (Horn of Africa)
IMET	International Military Education and Training
IMF	International Monetary Fund
ISA	International Security Affairs
LIC	Low-Intensity Conflict
MAAG	Military Assistance Advisory Group
MAP	Military Assistance Program
MPLA	Movimento Popular de Libertaçao de Angola (Angola)
MSD	Marine Security Detachment
MSN	Mozambique Support Network
MTT	Mobile Training Team
NAACP	National Association for the Advancement of Colored People
NASA	National Aeronautics and Space Administration
NATO	North Atlantic Treaty Organization
NIF	National Islamic Front (Sudan)
NSC	National Security Council
NSSM	National Security Study Memorandum
OAU	Organization of African Unity
OLF	Oromo Liberation Front (Ethiopia)
PBS	Public Broadcasting System
PL 480	Public Law 480
PLA	Popular Liberation Army (Zaire)
PMAC	Provisional Military Administrative Council (Ethiopia)
RAF	Royal Air Force (Great Britain)
RENAMO	Mozambique National Resistance Movement (Mozambique)
SACP	South African Communist Party (South Africa)
SALT	Strategic Arms Limitation Talks
SNM	Somali National Movement (Somalia)
SPLA	Sudan People's Liberation Army (Sudan)
SPM	Somali Patriotic Movement (Somalia)
SWAPO	South West African People's Organization (Namibia)
TPLF	Tigrean People's Liberation Front (Ethiopia)
UDPS	Union for Democracy and Social Progress (Zaire)
UN	United Nations
UNITA	Uniao Nacional para a Independência Total de Angola (Angola)

USAID	United States Agency for International Development
USC	United Somali Congress (Somalia)
USIA	United States Information Agency
USIS	United States Information Service
USSR	Union of Soviet Socialist Republics
WCOA	Washington Committee on Africa
WIGMO	Western International Ground Maintenance Operation
WSLF	Western Somali Liberation Front (Ethiopia)

Map 1   Africa

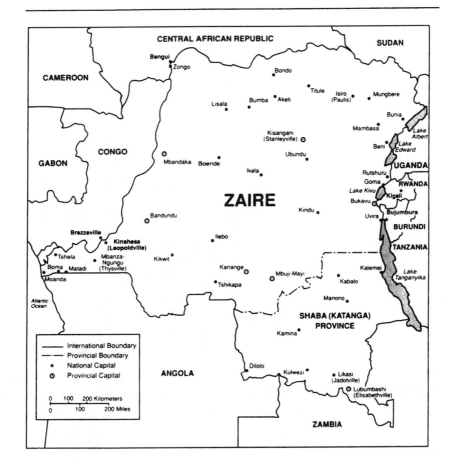

Map 2   Central Africa

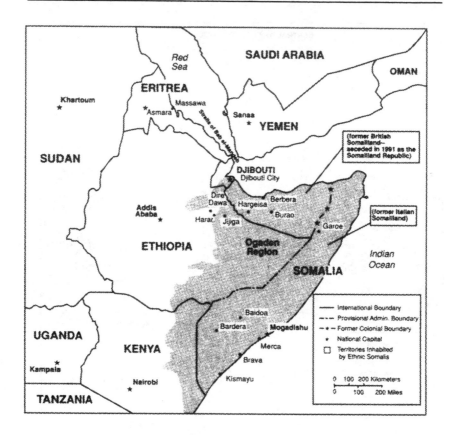

Map 3   Horn of Africa

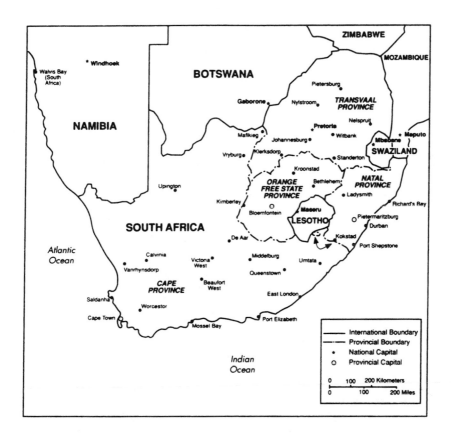

Map 4   Southern Africa

1 AN INTRODUCTION TO US FOREIGN POLICY TOWARD AFRICA

No other continent has been so consistently ignored by our policy-makers, and yet none but Europe has been so continually connected to important developments in America, from the founding of the Republic in the era of the Atlantic slave trade to the inauguration of training exercises for the new Rapid Deployment Force.[1]

Introduction

As the nationalist urges of independence movements swept the countries of Africa during the 1950s and these so-called "winds of change" marked the beginning of the end of European colonialism, two politicians of widely divergent political perspectives underscored the necessity of rethinking US foreign policy toward the continent. "For too many years," Vice President Richard M. Nixon noted in 1957 after returning from a twenty-two day tour of the African continent, "Africa in the minds of many Americans has been regarded as a remote and mysterious continent which was the special province of big game hunters, explorers and motion picture makers."[2] Recognizing the importance of an emerging Africa in the international scene – especially within the context of the East–West struggle – Nixon recommended that President Dwight D. Eisenhower authorize the creation of a separate Bureau of African Affairs within the State Department, an idea which reached fruition in 1958.

Also speaking out in 1957, Senator John F. Kennedy (D-Massachusetts) derided what he perceived as Washington's inability to come to grips with the question of colonialism and the growing forces of nationalism in Africa.[3] Kennedy later warned that the "only real question is whether these new nations [of Africa] will look West or East – to Moscow or Washington – for sympathy, help, and guidance in their effort to recapitulate, in a few decades, the entire history of modern Europe and America." In order to blunt what he perceived as the steady decline of US prestige in Africa at the expense of growing

Soviet influence, Kennedy concluded that "we must embark on a bold and imaginative new program for the development of Africa."[4]

The prescription offered by both Nixon and Kennedy was to upgrade Africa to a position of priority within the policymaking establishment in accordance with changing international realities. Yet despite important changes in US Africa policies which came about after these leaders voiced their opinions during the late 1950s, Africanists within both governmental and academic circles have continued to lament the low level of attention focused on African issues. The result is a general lack of understanding concerning the formulation and implementation of US Africa policies. Invoking the image of Christopher Columbus, former British Prime Minister James Callaghan placed this state of affairs in perspective in May 1978 when he chided disagreement within the US policymaking establishment over how to respond to the invasion of Zaire by exiles based in neighboring Angola. "There seem to be a number of Christopher Columbuses setting out from the United States to discover Africa for the first time," Callaghan began. "It's been there a long time."[5]

Unfortunately, the United States has had to "rediscover" Africa at several junctures during the post-World War II era. US policymakers have tended to ignore the African continent until some sort of politico-military crisis grabs their attention. One undesirable outcome of such an approach is that policy often becomes driven by events, as opposed to the more desirable outcome of policy shaping events. Perhaps the greatest danger in such a state of affairs is that poor understanding on the part of policymakers can foster poorly devised policies that ultimately are destined to fail. As the US prepares to enter the twenty-first century it will become increasingly important to shed its Christopher Columbus image and formulate effective policies that are proactive rather than reactive.

Africa as a foreign policy backwater

One of the earliest recorded incidents of North America's involvement with Africa took place in 1619 when a Dutch ship sold twenty Africans into slavery in the British North American colonies.[6] From this inauspicious beginning, the colonies eventually became part of a worldwide slave-trading network, the legacy of which nearly four centuries later would be over 30 million citizens – roughly 12 percent of the US population – claiming an African-American heritage.[7]

Despite historical and cultural ties between the US and the African continent, there exists no consensus within the policymaking

2

establishment over Africa's importance to US national security interests. Indeed, Africa's importance, like the proverbial perception of beauty, lies in the eyes of the beholder. For example, TransAfrica, the foreign policy lobbying apparatus for African-Americans, and the Congressional Black Caucus are quick to emphasize the importance of the racial link. Other members of Congress underscore the humanitarian or moral imperatives which link the US to Africa. Of particular concern are Western efforts to alleviate chronic drought and famine. The Department of Commerce, noting the potential market of nearly 600 million people for US goods and services, as well as significant imports of US oil and mineral imports from West and southern Africa, respectively, underscores the economic links of the relationship. The Department of State focuses on political linkages – most notably the weight of over fifty votes within the United Nations (UN) and the importance of the Organization of African Unity (OAU). The Department of Defense naturally focuses on military linkages, including Africa's geographical proximity to strategic "chokepoints" such as the Straits of Bab el-Mandeb in the Horn of Africa and the Cape of Good Hope in southern Africa.

Despite these linkages, Africanists generally agree that US Africa policies from the founding of the Republic in 1789 to the present have been marked by indifference, at worst, and neglect, at best.[8] Africa has been treated as a "backwater" in official policymaking circles, compared to the time and resources allocated to other regions considered to be of greater concern. A spirited exchange between Senator Jesse Helms (R-North Carolina) and Senator Daniel Patrick Moynihan (D-New York) as reported in 1987 by the *New York Times*, for example, underscores the gap of knowledge concerning Africa among some elected officials. The debate revolved around an amendment put forth by Helms who, concerned with perceived communist advances in Africa (most notably the presence of Soviet military advisers in Mozambique and Cuban troops in Angola), sought a ban on aid to any African country hosting foreign troops on its soil.

> But, Mr. Moynihan said, what of Chad, which is "fending off the Red armed hordes" with the help of the French? And what of Djibouti, which is doing the same? Mr. Helms was puzzled. Djibouti? Where is this Djibouti? Mr. Moynihan sprang to his feet, strode to the wall of the hearing room, clambered atop a chair and referred to a big map. He pointed to the Horn of Africa. "Communists to the left," he said, gesturing broadly. Another gesture: "Communists to the right." A stab of the finger on the map: "Djibouti – right in the middle." Mr. Helms appeared enlightened, even chastened. The amendment was defeated.[9]

Athough Moynihan is credited with enlightening Helms' knowledge of foreign troops stationed in Africa, his analysis of the situation at hand was not without error. The "Red armed hordes" that the French were credited with stopping in Chad were, in reality, Libyan troops under the leadership of Muammar Qaddafi, an independent African leader who has vilified communism and capitalism alike as poor models for African development.[10] Furthermore, the designation of Somalia as a communist country is somewhat misleading. It is true that Marxist rhetoric centering on the need to create a society based on social justice and individual freedom within a socialist framework filled oratorical speeches and official development plans of the Somali regime (1969–91) headed by General Siad Barre. However, in the aftermath of its rupture of relations with the Soviet Union in 1977 and defeat in the 1977–78 Ogaden War with Ethiopia (see Chapter 4), Somalia was a recipient of US aid and followed an export-oriented capitalist path of development.[11]

The lack of substantive knowledge of Africa is especially acute at the level of the mass public, which maintains what can be called a *National Geographic* image of the continent. Although topics, such as apartheid in South Africa and famine in the Horn of Africa, receive regular press coverage and have somewhat improved the public's awareness of African political and economic issues, the mention of Africa typically conjures up images of lush jungles and wild animals. Many citizens seem quite surprised to learn that Africa's jungles comprise only approximately 4 percent of the continent and that, each and every business day, African businesspersons dressed in Western-style suits report to offices in financial hubs, such as Abidjan and Nairobi.[12]

This *National Geographic* image is reinforced by the nature of US media programming and the safari tradition of US journalism. Media programming, when it does focus on Africa, usually concentrates on the sensationalistic and often negative aspects of the continent.[13] Hodding Carter, narrator of *Assignment Africa*, a Public Broadcasting System (PBS) documentary on the role of the press in Africa, notes that there is a difference between "the Africa you read about or see on your TV screen, and the other more complex Africa that is hidden from you."[14] Unless field reporters can produce a "hard" news story that can attract attention back home – such as interviews with US Marines detailing the hardships of being deployed in Somalia during the Christmas season as part of Operation Restore Hope – editors interested in what will sell make it difficult to achieve placement of a feature story in the press. Even the traditional crisis-oriented stories that usually make it into the Western press are often blocked. For example, despite the availability of excellent film footage documenting the emerging Ethiopian famine of 1983–85 – an event which ultimately would receive significant press coverage and produce an outpouring of Western aid – editors initially refused to air the material because they "thought that there was no news in another African famine."[15]

The safari tradition of US journalism – sending generalists to Africa on short-term assignments as opposed to those willing to make a long-term commitment to becoming authorities on Africa – reinforces the checkered view of what the public learns about the continent. Helen Kitchen, a former journalist and respected Africanist, notes that while much of the reporting by US newspaper and wire correspondents is informed and conscientious, follow-up is inconsistent. Kitchen laments that what one still gets from the US media is "discontinuous segments of the day-to-day history of Africa."[16] As another journalist poignantly notes, "The media's misunderstanding of African crises stems from a dearth of the kind of day-to-day coverage of the continent that would put extraordinary events like famines and coups into perspective."[17]

Finally, even the scholarly community has focused an inadequate amount of attention on US Africa policies.[18] Indeed, the study of Africa within the fields of comparative foreign policy and international relations theory has been relegated to a low-level status. Instead, studies that focus on traditional US security concerns, such as East–West relations and the nature of the Atlantic Alliance, or geographical regions of perceived greater importance, such as Eastern Europe or the Middle East, are given academic priority. It is for these reasons that scholars are hopeful that the substantial increase in African studies and African-American studies programs since the 1960s and 1970s will contribute to a greater exploration of African issues within academia.

Continuity or change?

One outgrowth of Africa's low status within the policymaking community, the public, and especially academia is the lack of understanding surrounding the nature and evolution of US Africa policies. Every few years it has been a ritual exercise for Africanists to ponder the continuities and discontinuities inherent in US Africa policies. In carrying out such exercises, the time-frame of analysis is usually the post-World War II period to the present, with 1958 – the year marking "official" recognition of Africa through the creation of the State Department's Africa Bureau – serving as a convenient starting point.

The fairly consistent conclusion of these studies is that US Africa

5

policies largely have been marked by continuity rather than by change. For example, in his remarks on the twenty-fifth anniversary of official relations between the US and Africa, former African Studies Association President Crawford Young noted that it was the "essential continuity" which stood out. Although Young added that "noteworthy fluctuations" have occurred, he concluded that "these variations have been above all of style, tone, and the subtler chemistry of policy articulation, and not its underlying substance."[19] Five years later, another scholar concurred, noting that US Africa policy "has demonstrated remarkable coherence and regularity despite the differences between Republican and Democratic administrations and the tenure of nine different Assistant Secretaries of State for African Affairs."[20] Finally, writing in 1992 from the vantage point of an Africanist who has witnessed the decline of communism and the fragmentation of the Soviet Union, Michael Clough, Senior Fellow for Africa at the Council on Foreign Relations, warns of the dangers associated with foreign policy continuity, and argues for abandoning traditional, government-to-government diplomatic approaches in favor of greater links at the local community level.[21]

Has US foreign policy toward Africa been marked by continuity, or is this much too simple a statement for summarizing the complexities involved in US relations with over fifty African countries? In the case of variations between Republican and Democratic administrations, for example, it has been noted that the Africa policies of the Kennedy administration constituted a significant departure from the anti-nationalist tendency of US foreign policy in the Third World.[22] I have argued elsewhere that President Jimmy Carter's policy of promoting majority rule in Zimbabwe – which inevitably meant supporting the Marxist Patriotic Front headed by Robert Mugabe – broke rank with yet another standard of US foreign policy. This standard is based on the belief that radical forces in Third World countries should be excluded from playing a major role in internal political and economic reforms.[23] Finally, others have noted that the Reagan administration's policy of "constructive engagement" – most notably its willingness to publicly upgrade ties with South Africa – also constituted a significant departure from past US foreign policy.[24]

The common thread linking all three of these examples is that they find discontinuity in US foreign policy toward Africa. Yet are these isolated cases, or are they indicative of significant changes brought on as new administrations with divergent beliefs replaced their predecessors? Crawford Young attempts to answer this question by asserting that, despite the fact that the Kennedy, Carter, and Reagan administrations all "entered office with an African policy project that diverged sharply from that of its predecessor," in each case "the actual change was far less than what appeared in prospect from the blueprints."[25] Indeed, proponents of the theme of continuity can note that, despite strong rhetoric denouncing Portuguese colonialism on the African continent and suppporting black majority rule, the Kennedy administration largely failed to move beyond this rhetoric. When US access to the highly valued and Portuguese-controlled bases in the Azores was called into question, Kennedy ultimately sided with the Europeanists in his administration who were in favor of the established status quo.[26] Similarly, despite a stated commitment to human rights and the need to decrease ties with authoritarian dictatorships, the Carter administration largely failed to follow through on this promise in 1977 in the case of Mobutu Sese Seko's Zaire (see Chapter 3). Rather, strong rhetoric in the first year of the administration ultimately gave way to inaction and acceptance of a consensus within the national security bureaucracies that Mobutu's fall would yield chaos and instability. Finally, it has been noted that the Reagan administration's strong anti-communist proclivities and stated intention of shoring up valued clients often were not realized on the African continent. For example, the administration's relationship during the 1980s with Somalia – an anti-communist client said to be threatened by formerly Marxist Ethiopia – initially followed the cautious, restrained path of the Carter administration (see Chapter 4).[27]

Who is correct? Those arguing continuity? Those arguing discontinuity? Or some combination of the two? Clearly there exist opposing interpretations depending on the particular cases emphasized. Yet one finds opposing interpretations even when scholars focus upon the same factual events. In the case of the Reagan administration's policy of constructive engagement, for example, some opponents branded the initiative as a radical departure from established policy toward the apartheid government of South Africa. At the same time, other opponents merely perceived the policy as the refurbishment or codification of the Nixon administration's tilt toward the white-ruled regimes in the region. Posing the dilemma in a more light-hearted manner, Crawford Young notes:

> Is it possible that Chester Crocker is simply Richard Moose by another name? Senator Jesse Helms apparently thinks so, but should we? Or, to put the matter more graphically, is it plausible that, despite the apparent rhetorical contrasts, United Nations Ambassador Jeane Kirkpatrick holds essentially the same views concerning

7

Africa as did her predecessors Andrew Young and Donald McHenry?[28]

Overview

The most important purpose of this book is to describe and explain continuity and change in US foreign policy toward Africa by identifying the dominant patterns of US interventionist practices on the continent during the post-World War II period. Specifically, the goal of this research is to clarify why Washington has strengthened or weakened security relationships with African regimes over time. (See Appendix A for a brief note on research method.) Several questions are key in this regard: Under what circumstances has the US become involved with a particular regime in Africa? Who have been the key actors within the foreign policy establishment? What role do foreign powers play in decisions to intervene? Do the beliefs and interests of US leaders play a major role in determining when to intervene? What effect do foreign events have on these decisions? What role has been played by African Americans in the foreign policy process? What does the end of the Cold War mean for the future of US Africa policies? The remaining five chapters of this book are devoted to exploring these questions.

Before proceeding with an overview, however, it is important to explicitly state what is meant in the context of this book by "intervention" – a term which is widely used and is potentially confusing, meaning many different things to many different people.[29] Intervention is defined, in a broad sense, as the calculated use of political, economic, and military instruments by one country to influence the domestic or the foreign policies of another country. Four important aspects of this definition stand out. First, intervention is seen as purposeful, underscoring the intentional nature of the act. Second, intervention entails a wide choice of instruments ranging from the extension of economic and military aid to economic sanctions, covert action, paramilitary interference, and, finally, direct application of military force. Third, attempts to influence a country's policies need not be restricted to efforts to change those policies but may also support a given regime in order to insulate it from change. Finally, intervention is not limited to affecting the domestic politics of a given country, but can be undertaken to affect that country's foreign policies, as well.

This broad definition is adopted to capture the entire range of US foreign policy toward Africa and how it affects the strengthening or weakening of security relationships with African regimes over time. The field of actions covered by this definition therefore includes such policies as President Lyndon B. Johnson's decision in 1964 to provide transport for Belgian troops to rescue and evacuate hostages and defeat the vestiges of a guerilla insurgency in northeastern Zaire; the State Department's growing advocacy during the 1960s of increased levels of economic and military aid to Ethiopian Emperor Haile Selassie in exchange for continued access to strategically important facilities; congressional adoption in 1986 of economic sanctions against South Africa in an attempt to force changes in that country's apartheid system; and the Defense Department's airlift in 1988 of military supplies to strengthen the Somali regime of General Siad Barre against an internal insurgency.

Chapter 2 is devoted to outlining a theoretical framework for analyzing the patterns and processes of US Africa policies during the post-World War II period. An important theme of this chapter is that US interventionist episodes – such as the four noted above – do not constitute isolated incidents, but rather are the result of identifiable trends. Some of these are unique to US Africa policies, while others are indicative of US foreign policy in general.

Chapters 3–5 constitute three case studies illustrative of broad trends in US foreign policy toward the African continent. Each chapter begins with an overview of US relations with a particular African country and ends with a short section summarizing the nature of that involvement. The bulk of each chapter is devoted to an assessment of why the US has strengthened or weakened its foreign policy relationship with a particular African country during the post-World War II period. Detailed comparative case studies include an overview and analysis of US foreign policy toward Zaire (Chapter 3), Ethiopia and Somalia (Chapter 4), and South Africa (Chapter 5). In each of these cases, the analysis ends with the inauguration of President Bill Clinton on January 20, 1993.

The final chapter of the book assesses the implications of the end of the Cold War on the future of US Africa policies. Among the major trends discussed are (1) the reinforcement of the historical tendency to treat Africa as a "back-burner" issue; (2) pressure to trim already reduced levels of economic and military aid; (3) the continuing importance of the national security bureaucracies as the primary driving forces of US Africa policies; (4) rising perceptions of the threat posed by the spread of Islamic fundamentalism; (5) Great Power involvement in the resolution of regional conflicts, particularly in cooperation with regional and international organizations; and (6) the rising debate over making multiparty democracy a precondition of closer US ties.

A final note about sources is in order. A significant portion of what is written in these pages is the result of nearly 100 interviews with members of the US foreign policy establishment, both past and present, who have been intimately involved in the conduct of US Africa policies. (See Appendix B for a brief review of the interview process.) Although several of these individuals made their comments for attribution, and are noted as such, the majority, requested anonymity due to legitimate concerns that "on-the-record" remarks could affect current or future standing within the policymaking establishment. This, of course, would pose a problem if the only sources tapped were oral histories. However, the discussion is also based on four additional sets of primary sources: (1) the vast government public record, including official speeches, statements, and proceedings, such as those published in the voluminous congressional record; (2) previously classified government documents, such as those held by the National Security Archive in Washington, DC; (3) public reporting of events in newspapers, such as the *New York Times*; and (4) the memoirs and autobiographies of relevant US officials, such as the insightful analysis of the US–Ethiopian relationship written by David A. Korn, former US Ambassador to Ethiopia.[30] All of these sources have been weighed against much of the substantial secondary material that has been written about US Africa policies during the last forty years.

2 PATTERN AND PROCESS IN US FOREIGN POLICY TOWARD AFRICA

The story of the blind men and the elephant is universally known. Several blind men approached an elephant and each touched the animal in an effort to discover what the beast looked like. Each blind man, however, touched a different part of the large animal, and each concluded that the elephant had the appearance of the part he had touched. Hence, the blind man who felt the animal's trunk concluded that an elephant must be tall and slender, while his fellow who touched the beast's ear concluded that an elephant must be oblong and flat. Others of course reached different conclusions. The total result was that no man arrived at a very accurate description of the elephant. Yet, each man had gained enough evidence from his own experience to disbelieve his fellows and to maintain a lively debate about the nature of the beast.[1]

Introduction

Thoughtful discussions among policymakers, scholars, and the informed public concerning trends in US Africa policies often parallel the story of the blind men and the elephant. Due to previous experiences or professional interests, Africanists inevitably focus on different episodes of Washington's relationships with the African continent to explain the nature of the beast – in this case continuity and change in US intervention. For example, those attempting to understand why economic sanctions were adopted against South Africa in 1986 may look to the pressure exerted on a politically attuned Congress by increasingly powerful and vocal anti-apartheid groups. Others wishing to explain the growing military commitment to Ethiopia during the 1960s may discount the role of Congress, and instead focus on the bureaucratic infighting waged by the State Department. Still others interested in covert intervention in the Angolan civil war during both the 1970s and 1980s may focus on the role played by the CIA. The list can go on. The net result – like the conclusion reached in the story of the blind men and the elephant – is that, although each explanation is partially correct, none is able to provide an accurate description of the elephant as a whole. Ultimately, these widely divergent conclusions contribute to continuing debate over the true nature of the beast.[2]

The purpose of this chapter is to shed some light on the nature of the proverbial elephant. This understanding begins with a clarification of the roles played by various members of the foreign policy establishment in the formulation and implementation of US Africa policies. Furthermore, by looking at the ways these government agencies interact, and by examining the patterns that have emerged as a result of these actions, we can describe and explain continuity and change in US intervention in Africa during the post-World War II period. The central theme of this chapter is that the nature of events on the continent historically has affected the operation of the US policymaking process, and therefore the substance of US Africa policies. The importance of the interplay between events in Africa and policy formulation is demonstrated by examining US Africa policies in light of three general patterns: routine situations and bureaucratic politics; crisis situations and presidential politics; and extended crisis situations and domestic politics.

Routine situations and bureaucratic politics

The tendency has been for the President to delegate day-to-day responsibility for overseeing US Africa relations, in the absence of any crisis, to those national security bureaucracies which primarily focus on the politico-military aspects of foreign policy relationships. They include the State Department, the Defense Department, and the CIA, as well as their specialized agencies devoted specifically to Africa.

Bureaucratic influence within the policymaking process

Three factors historically have contributed to bureaucratic influence within the policymaking process during the post-World War II era: the low level of attention typically paid to African issues by the President; the executive's traditional assumption that, due to their colonial heritage, the European allies should assume primary responsibility for Western interests in Africa; and, at least prior to the end of the Cold War, the East–West dimension of a particular situation.

(1) *Low level of attention paid to African issues.* "The President," John F. Kennedy noted, "is rightly described as a man of extraordinary powers."[3] Standing at the apex of an immense bureaucratic machinery,

the President as commander-in-chief, head of state, chief diplomat, and chief administrator embodies substantial powers allowing the White House to set the foreign policy agenda. "Yet it is also true," Kennedy continued, "that he must wield those powers under extraordinary limitations."[4] Among these are the impracticality of one person monitoring relations with over 150 countries (including over 50 in Africa) and the time constraints imposed by the elected term of office (four to eight years). In addition, the President often must contend with a Congress with a separate and different foreign policy agenda, an uncooperative bureaucracy, and lagging levels of public support. Newly elected Presidents therefore must balance the overwhelming urge to completely reorient the goals, priorities, and substance of foreign policy with a recognition of the time constraints involved. In short, Presidents are forced by necessity to select those countries, geographical regions, and functional issues which will receive priority attention by their administrations.

Although contacts between the US and Africa have expanded in both quantity and quality during the post-World War II period, Presidents from Harry S. Truman to George Bush traditionally have been the least interested in, and subsequently have paid the least amount of attention to, Africa, relative to other regions of the world. It is highly likely that this trend will continue under the Clinton administration, most notably due to President Clinton's desire to downplay the importance of foreign policy and instead focus primarily on US domestic economic concerns. Even under President Carter – recognized by Africanists as pursuing one of the most enlightened policies toward the continent during the post-World War II period – Africa ranked last in terms of foreign policy attention (see Table 2.1).[5] Whereas Africa accounted for nearly 11 percent of the Carter administration's foreign policy behavior in 1977, the continent still trailed all other regions of the world, and in fact decreased in importance by nearly 50 percent over the next three years. Indeed, the personal significance attached to Africa relative to other regions of the world by Carter is portrayed in his memoirs, which included only passing reference to Africa. "This is not a history of my administration but a highly personal report of my own experiences," Carter began, "I have emphasized those matters *which meant the most to me*, and particularly those events in which I played a unique part, such as the search for peace in the Middle East and the Camp David negotiations."[6]

This emphasis on the lack of presidential attention to Africa relative to other regions of the world is not meant to suggest that Presidents should be intimately involved in the day-to-day running of US Africa

13

Table 2.1. *Carter administration foreign policy behavior by region*[a]

Regions acted toward	1977	1978	1979	1980
Soviet Union & Eastern Europe	14.6	29.3	14.9	33.0
Western Europe & Japan	16.1	13.4	12.8	15.1
Middle East	11.7	14.6	30.5	27.4
China & Asia	16.8	15.8	19.9	8.4
Latin America	23.4	12.2	10.6	7.8
Africa	10.9	4.9	6.4	4.5
Global (no specific region)	6.6	9.8	7.8	3.9

[a] Numbers represent percentages of foreign policy acts. The table is derived from Jerel A. Rosati, "The Impact of Beliefs on Behavior: The Foreign Policy of the Carter Administration," in Donald Sylvan and Steve Chan, eds., *Foreign Policy Decision-Making* (New York: Praeger, 1984), pp. 158–91. See also Jerel A. Rosati, *The Carter Administration's Quest for Global Community: Beliefs and their Impact on Behavior* (Columbia: University of South Carolina Press, 1987).

policies – in essence conjuring up images of Presidents serving as de facto "desk officers" for African problems. Rather, the crucial theme is that the personal predilections of individual Presidents toward other regions of perceived greater concern, combined with the vast range of presidential responsibilities, yield outcomes which make US Africa policies, perhaps more so than those directed toward any other region of the world, subject to the influence of bureaucrats within the national security bureaucracies.

(2) *Assumption of European responsibility.* Africa's enduring relationship with Europe is a second element that reinforces the President's tendency to allow US Africa policies to be heavily influenced by the national security bureaucracies. All Presidents (although in varying degrees) traditionally have looked upon Africa as a special area of influence and responsibility of the former European colonial powers. Therefore, Presidents generally have deferred to European sensitivities and maintained a low profile during routine periods when one of these countries has taken the lead on a particular foreign policy issue.

In particular, White House recognition of European sensitivities prevailed prior to the 1960s when policymakers generally perceived European colonialism on the African continent as "progressive." Ultimately, the belief was that colonial rule would lead to modernization and political and economic stability.[7] When the strength of African nationalism and the inevitable process of decolonization and political independence became apparent during the 1960s, this position evolved. Policymakers attempted to walk a diplomatic tightrope between the potentially mutually exclusive goals of support for decolonization and the continued strength of the Atlantic Alliance.[8]

Yet when African demands clashed with policies considered crucial to US security relationships with Europe, Presidents ultimately decided in favor of the Atlantic Alliance.[9]

This European component, which results from a shared democratic political culture significantly strengthened through Allied cooperation during World War II, was best summarized in 1968 by George Ball, Under Secretary of State in the Kennedy administration. Ball noted that the US recognized Africa as a "special European responsibility" just as European nations recognized "our particular responsibility in Latin America."[10] Although these spheres of influence increasingly have become broached by both sides from the 1970s to the beginning of the 1990s, there is no disputing the fact that the White House continues to look to its European allies – especially France, Britain, and, to a lesser degree, Italy, Belgium, and Portugal – to take the lead in their former colonial territories.

(3) *East–West dimension of the situation.* The East–West dimension is the final, and perhaps most important, element that historically has influenced presidential attention to African issues. Since 1947 when George F. Kennan formulated the doctrine of containment and the Soviet Union and communism became the central concerns of US strategic thinking, policymakers have tended to view Africa from an East–West perspective. This view centered specifically on the threat posed by the Soviet Union and its allies to US interests. The importance of the Soviet threat was stated most vividly by the Kennedy administration at the height of the African independence movement during the early 1960s: "What we do – or fail to do – in Africa in the next year or two will have a profound effect for many years," noted a memorandum signed by Kennedy. "We see Africa as probably the greatest open field of maneuver in the worldwide competition between the [communist] bloc and the non-communist world."[11]

Although there were variations in the assessment of the Soviet threat and the utility of containment as originally conceived, all Presidents from Truman to Bush (at least prior to the decline of communism and the fragmentation of the Soviet Union in 1991) sought to limit Soviet influence in Africa.[12] The result was increased presidential attention to African issues when the former Soviet Union and its allies became significantly involved on the continent. Yet when the East–West element was lacking, there existed a high probability that the President would remain distant and uninvolved in African issues. The day-to-day responsibility for overseeing policy was left in the hands of the national security bureaucracies. As it became readily apparent in 1991 that, for all practical purposes, the Cold War officially had come to

15

an end, African scholars and policymakers increasingly began to worry that this state of affairs would result in the decline of already low levels of presidential interest in the African continent (and, thus, reinforce the influence of the national security bureaucracies in the policymaking process). As discussed in Chapter 6, some have even argued that growing US cooperation with Russia – the largest successor state of the former Soviet Union – entails even greater risks for Africa. For example, citing the traditional Swahili proverb, "When the elephants (superpowers) fight, the grass (Africa) suffers," one Africanist noted that, "When the elephants make love, the grass suffers just as much."[13]

Bureaucracies and organizational missions in Africa

The net result of bureaucratic influence within the policymaking process is that the Africa policies of the United States become fragmented, interpreted differently according to the established organizational missions of each bureaucracy that historically has been created to deal with a particular aspect of the foreign policy relationship. Subsequently, each fosters an institutional culture – what one observer aptly has described as a "curator mentality" – that both supports its mission and socializes individuals into working toward its attainment.[14] Although other sources of behavior are important, such as the substantive views and personal ambitions of the most influential bureaucrats, the critical theme of this section is that the latter often tend to interpret national security according to their agency's role and mission in the foreign policy establishment.[15]

The State Department was the first among the national security bureaucracies to recognize the importance of Africa through the creation in 1958 of a separate Bureau of African Affairs.[16] This bureau is headed by an Assistant Secretary of State for African Affairs who, in turn, is supported by a Senior Deputy Assistant Secretary, three Deputy Assistant Secretaries, as well as a host of regional offices staffed by country directors and desk officers who monitor day-to-day developments in sub-Saharan Africa. (Events in North Africa are monitored by the State Department's Bureau of Near Eastern and South Asian Affairs.)

The primary mission of the Africa Bureau is the maintenance of smooth and stable political relationships with all African governments. The emphasis is on quiet diplomacy and negotiated resolution of any conflicts that may arise. Career Foreign Service Officers (FSOs) within the bureau are usually the most willing of any members of the executive branch to place policies in alignment with the aspirations of

16

African nationalist leaders. Consequently, they are also more sensitive to the importance that African leaders attach to regional political associations, such as the OAU.[17] These same FSOs, when addressing the nature of conflict in a particular African country, also tend to balance the traditional impulse to attach blame to external powers – whether a communist Soviet Union of the 1980s or a "radical" Islamic fundamentalist Iran of the 1990s – with a well-grounded understanding of the conflict's internal cultural, economic, historical, and political roots.

The Africa Bureau, however, is but one of many regionally and functionally organized bureaus at the State Department which periodically become involved in African issues. Other bureaus, although generally in agreement over the necessity to pursue diplomatic options, have missions which can conflict with (or complement) those pursued by the Bureau of African Affairs. The Bureau of European and Canadian Affairs is naturally more concerned with European sensitivities when African issues arise, and thus serves to reinforce the executive branch's tendency to defer to European, as opposed to African, sensitivities. Similarly, the Bureau of Politico-Military Affairs, with its emphasis on US security policies throughout the world, tends to emphasize the centrality of Europe and the Atlantic Alliance and relegate Africa to its traditional place within the regional pecking order – last. The Bureau of International Organization Affairs, however, whose mission entails promoting a positive US image at the UN, often has been allied with the Africa Bureau in recognition of the African continent's substantial potential voting bloc in the UN General Assembly. Other State Department offices which include Africa specialists and may become involved in policy debate include the Policy Planning Staff and the Bureau of Human Rights and Humanitarian Affairs, as well as the offices of Refugee Affairs and Legislative Affairs.[18]

The CIA was the second among the national security bureaucracies to recognize the importance of Africa through the creation in 1960 of a separate Africa Division within the Deputy Directorate of Operations (DDO) that is responsible for mounting covert actions throughout the globe.[19] (Not to be confused with the Deputy Directorate of Intelligence (DDI) and its Africa-related Office of African and Latin American Analysis, or that portion of the CIA committed to providing the Director of Central Intelligence (DCI) and the White House with up-to-date summaries and analyses of gathered intelligence.) Even though it was created during roughly the same period as the State Department's Africa Bureau, the Africa Division's official mission and

17

outlook from the 1960s to the beginning of the 1990s was radically different: to carry the ideological battle against the Soviet Union and communism to the continent, in efforts that ranged from the cultivation of local agents to the mounting of covert operations.[20]

Subsequently, African aspirations and the internal causes of conflict on the continent historically have been downplayed by DDO officers. They usually have had the greatest tendency within the executive branch to view Africa as a strategic battleground and attribute instability in a particular African country to externally motivated aggression. Openly contemptuous of self-proclaimed Marxist regimes, "leftist" leaders and liberation movements, and, more recently, "radical" activists (such as Libya's Muammar Qaddafi) and religious movements (such as Islamic fundamentalism), the CIA prefers close liaison with the security services of European allies on the continent. In addition, the CIA traditionally has maintained close ties with the internal security services of friendly African regimes, such as Mobutu Sese Seko's Zaire, King Hassan II's Morocco, and, perhaps of greatest concern to Africanists, the Afrikaner-dominated regime of South Africa.

The Defense Department has been the relative latecomer among the national security bureaucracies in recognizing the importance of Africa.[21] Its Office of International Security Affairs (ISA) waited until 1982 before appointing a Deputy Assistant Secretary of Defense to head the newly created Office of African Affairs.[22] Leaning toward the globalist vision of the CIA, the Office for African Affairs tends to downplay local African concerns in favor of the continent's strategic position within the international military balance, focusing on paramount US interests in Europe, the Middle East, and, prior to the end of the Cold War, Eastern Europe and the former Soviet Union. Moreover, the domestic nature of an African regime is not necessarily perceived as an impediment to US military cooperation as long as that regime is pro-Western.

The primary mission of the Office for African Affairs is the coordination and facilitation of two major military objectives on the continent: maintaining stable, pro-Western governments through the transfer of military equipment and the training of local forces in its usage; and ensuring continued access to training facilities and strategically located bases and other facilities for responding to local crises and, most important, military contingencies in Europe or the Middle East. Subsequently, military objectives are carried out by the three major military services – the Navy, Air Force, and Army – each of which has its own particular bureaucratic mission on the African continent.[23]

Other components of the executive branch, of course, deal with the non-politico-military aspects of US Africa policies. The United States Agency for International Development (USAID) pursues economic development in African countries through a variety of projects and programs.[24] The Departments of Commerce and Treasury, with their emphasis on strengthening and expanding the US economy, seek inroads for trade and investment in the continent. Finally, the US Information Agency (USIA) promotes greater cultural understanding through, for example, exchange programs and goodwill missions.[25] Although each of these bureaucracies obviously plays an important African role, the emphasis in this discussion is on the politico-military aspects of US Africa policies.

The impact differing bureaucratic missions have on the implementation of US Africa policies is illustrated by a brief examination of the various bureaucratic representatives stationed as of 1987 at the US Embassy in Djibouti, a former French colony and current military base for approximately 3,500 French soldiers.[26] The Ambassador, John P. Ferriter (a career FSO), sought on behalf of the State Department to maintain a correct, low-profile approach in Djibouti that would augment, but not replace, traditional French interests. Great emphasis was placed on consultation with the French, avoiding any actions that might appear to undermine their influence. The representative of the Defense Department, Major Brian McMillan, was less concerned with the political aspects of the US–Djiboutian relationship than with this small country's strategic location adjacent to the Red Sea and the Indian Ocean. (Indeed, another military officer complained that the State Department's low-profile policy was too pro-French at the expense of US interests.) The CIA Chief of Station's concern was with Soviet bloc influence in Djibouti, especially from neighboring Ethiopia; he naturally worked extensively with the local French intelligence service to monitor perceived Soviet threats. Finally, the USAID representative, John Lundgren, eschewed both politics and questions of military-strategic interest, being primarily interested in Djibouti's economic development and its role in a regional development organization, the Intergovernmental Authority on Drought and Development (IGADD). In short, all four individuals were representative of, and assessed US policy interests according to, their respective bureaucratic cultures and missions.

An important aspect of differing bureaucratic approaches to US Africa policies is an often less than harmonious relationship among the national security bureaucracies within the executive branch. Indeed, bureaucracies do not run wild within a political void, but rather constitute part of a political process – in this case, bureaucratic politics.

19

To this end, they bargain and compromise, ultimately seeking to maximize their own positions within the policymaking establishment. For example, a certain amount of tension sometimes exists between overseas State Department personnel and their CIA counterparts who often are provided with an embassy "cover." One source of contention is the seemingly unlimited amounts of money available to the CIA Chief of Station as opposed to the relatively limited amounts under the control of State Department FSOs. "Altogether I had about $30,000 cash each year to dole out or spend to enhance my effectiveness," notes John Stockwell, former CIA Chief of Station in Burundi during the late 1960s, "The ambassador and three foreign service officers had a total of $2,000 between them, not enough to cover the Fourth of July reception" (one of the biggest annual events handled by all US embassies). According to Stockwell, the significance of this disparity is that the "extra money translates into greater social and operational activity," suggesting that the true center of power is the CIA and not the State Department. "Often the CIA man will even establish a direct contact with the chief of state, leading him to believe that through the CIA he has the more authentic contact with the American government," explains Stockwell. "At the same time, while the CIA station rarely produces significantly better or more timely intelligence than the embassy obtains through overt sources, it always represents a liability to the United States embassy as CIA officers scurry about with their semicovert operations, bribing and corrupting local officials." Stockwell rightly concludes that, although an ambassador strongly opposed to covert activities can make problems for the CIA chief of station, "any effort to evict a CIA station altogether is impossibly restricted by politics and bureaucratic inertia back in Washington."[27]

The primary theme of our analysis, however, is that bureaucratic influence within the policymaking process often yields a foreign policy outcome resulting from that bureaucracy's established organizational missions. The US response to ethnic strife in Burundi in 1972 provides an excellent example of how established organizational missions can affect the policymaking process in Washington.[28] Through the spring and summer of 1972, nearly 250,000 members of the Hutu ethnic group were killed by the ruling minority Tutsi regime headed by Colonel Michel Micombero. For reasons to be explained below, President Nixon and National Security Adviser Henry A. Kissinger remained largely uninvolved in this issue, allowing policy to be formulated and implemented by the State Department's Africa Bureau. The two officials recognized as responsible for the policy were Assistant Secretary of State for African Affairs David D. Newsom, and Country

Director for Central African Affairs Herman J. Cohen (who would serve as Assistant Secretary of State for African Affairs under the Bush administration).

The US response to the internal crisis is revealing both for what the Africa Bureau did and did not do. In accordance with standard operating procedures, quiet diplomatic efforts were initiated to enlist the support of Burundi's regional neighbors and the OAU to pressure the Micombero regime to stop the killings. However, it soon became apparent that most African countries – themselves beset by the delicate political problem of how to deal with their respective minority populations – were opposed to this policy. Moreover, it was feared that further actions would run the risk of damaging US relations with Burundi and other countries on the continent. Thus, policymakers chose a course of inaction. Indeed, despite the fact that the US imported nearly 75 percent of Burundi's primary export of coffee, potentially viable options, such as economic sanctions, were dismissed.

The Africa Bureau even suggested that Washington refrain from publicly denouncing the Micombero regime, although such inaction clearly would have been in direct opposition to international human rights conventions and the frequently invoked US commitment to human rights. The reason behind the decision, according to a group of specialists that included former State Department personnel, was simple: "For a bureaucracy which conceived its day-to-day job as the maintenance of untroubled relations with African governments, an independent American response to the Burundi killings threatened that mission."[29] As an official of the Africa Bureau noted afterwards: "If we'd involved ourselves in this, we'd be creamed by every country in Africa for butting into an African state's internal affairs. We don't have an interest in Burundi that justified taking that kind of flack."[30]

Bureaucracies and maintenance of the status quo

The Africa Bureau's tendency to rely on previously established ways of thinking in formulating policy toward Burundi underscores an important aspect of bureaucratic cultures. A fundamental resistance to change, or a predilection toward the maintenance of the status quo, has been long recognized by both policy analysts and practitioners alike. Among the most important factors contributing to bureaucratic conservatism are the safety of relying on established, standard operating procedures, as well as the realization that undue risk-taking may permanently damage one's career by effectively blocking upward mobility through the ranks.[31] The net result, according to Morton

21

H. Halperin, a respected scholar on bureaucratic politics and US foreign policy, is that the "majority of bureaucrats prefer to maintain the status quo, and only a small group is, at any one time, advocating change."[32] Subsequently, members of a bureaucracy – especially its head – will often put up a fierce fight rather than submit to changes that they perceive as infringing on their "turf," or threatening the integrity of their organization's mission.[33]

The importance of entrenched bureaucratic missions in contributing to the maintenance of the status quo is portrayed by the fierce struggle waged during the first two years of the Kennedy administration over how to respond to Portugal's colonial policies in Africa, most notably Angola. Prior to 1961, Washington consistently supported Portugal's assertion that the management of its colonies was an internal affair, subsequently voting against (or at least abstaining) when the issue of self-determination was brought before the UN. Speaking with one voice, the various bureaucracies placed Portugal's membership in the North Atlantic Treaty Organization (NATO) alliance and the 1951 joint US–Portugal defense treaty – which allowed US access to a highly valued military base on the Azores Islands – above the demands of African nationalists.

However, in the aftermath of Kennedy's inauguration in 1961, this policy changed. Appealing to the President's personal commitment to support the independence aims of African nationalist movements, two political appointees, Assistant Secretary of State for African Affairs G. Mennen Williams and US Ambassador to the UN Adlai A. Stevenson, outmaneuvered the Europeanist elements within the executive branch and succeeded in altering the once cozy Washington–Lisbon relationship: restrictions were placed on Portugal's practice of diverting US–supplied NATO weaponry to counterinsurgency efforts in Africa; the CIA and other components of the administration were directed to establish contacts with nationalist elements in Angola; and, perhaps most significant, the US for the first time cast a vote at the UN in favor of a resolution calling upon Portugal to make progress toward independence for Angola."[34]

This shift in policy, although denounced by proponents of the former status quo, did not galvanize opposition within the executive branch until significant bureaucratic missions were threatened or called into question. In a statement referring to what the Defense Department considered to be one of the most important US military assets in Africa, Portuguese President Antonio de Oliveira Salazar threatened to refuse renewal of the 1951 agreement allowing US access to the Azores military base – due to expire at the end of 1962 – unless interference in Portugal's Africa policies was terminated. The Defense Department, led by the Joint Chiefs of Staff, strongly argued that the Azores base was indispensable to US security concerns in Europe and the Middle East, and therefore should not be compromised in order to curry favor with African nationalists.[35]

The military rationale was reinforced by political arguments underscoring the importance of maintaining the integrity of the Atlantic Alliance. For example, Dean Acheson, the vocal Secretary of State under Truman, argued that continued US interference not only risked US access to the Azores base, but would inevitably lead to greater instability in Portuguese Africa and even revolution in Portugal itself.[36] The pro-Portuguese sentiments of both the military and political groups were ultimately supported by Secretary of State Dean Rusk and National Security Adviser McGeorge Bundy. The net result of this debate was a gradual return in late 1962 to the status quo policy of favoring Portuguese interests, and thus a reversal of the shortlived victory by Stevenson and Williams in placing policy in greater alignment with African nationalist concerns.[37]

Bureaucratic incrementalism

The inherently conservative nature of bureaucracies prompts resistance to change. In turn, the self-interested nature of these agencies propels members to seek to widen the role of their own organization within the policymaking establishment. The primary means of doing this, of course, is through greater amounts of economic and military aid, and by the expansion of activities within the host country. Other ways of achieving closer ties include the Africa Bureau's pursuit of White House visits for African Heads of State, the Defense Department's growing interest in joint military maneuvers with African regimes, and the CIA's willingness to share intelligence findings with friendly and trusted leaders. Regardless of the strategy pursued in strengthening ties with a country, the term "incrementalism" best captures the resulting process of change: once a foreign policy relationship is established, the self-interested nature of bureaucracies often contributes to the gradual enhancement of relations with that country.[38]

US citizens posted abroad in an official government capacity are usually the most vigorous proponents of their host country's interests, regardless of whether they are State Department FSOs, Defense Department military attachés, or CIA case officers. The reason behind this advocacy – derisively termed "clientitis" by those who claim to be

23

looking at the "big picture" in Washington – are threefold. First, an individual's perception of a country's worth almost always rises once he/she lives there and gets to know the people.[39] Second, the representative often is responding to constant pressure exerted by the host government to enhance the nature of the relationship. As a former military attaché to Zaire explained, "If you're beaten up every day for greater amounts of military aid, you will inevitably push for it in Washington, if only to get your in-country counterpart off your back."[40] Most important, however, is that advocacy is inherent in the field officer's job. "Because Americans measure success in terms of accomplishing something during their two-to-four-year term in-country," the attaché continued, "field officers are driven to get something tangible to leave behind for the host government as proof of their success; the greatest inclination is to seek greater levels of aid."[41] The rationale for such an approach is simple: By leaving behind a successful legacy, the officer hopes to obtain the best of both worlds – good reviews with the in-country elite, as well as with superiors back in Washington.

Returning to our discussion of Djibouti, one finds that US officials in the field (like their predecessors) attempted in 1987 to increase aid levels according to their perceived bureaucratic missions. The US Ambassador, for example, in efforts backed by the CIA Chief of Station, argued that increased levels of economic aid were necessary to ensure Djibouti's political stability and pro-Western path. Even though this small state was not perceived to be threatened with instability at the time, the rationale given was that additional aid would act as an insurance policy against possible negative future trends. The representative of the Defense Department, noting Djibouti's strategic location in a region marked by growing instability, sought more military aid, doubtless bearing in mind that increased unrest in Somalia would result in the termination of US access to military facilities in that country. Finally, the USAID officer, who perhaps pushed the strongest for greater amounts of development aid, noted that support for IGADD was of crucial importance to the long-term economic health and vitality of Djibouti.

Although congressional passage of the Gramm-Rudman-Hollings Deficit Reduction Act in 1986 served as an important brake on increased levels of aid to Djibouti in 1987, pressures emanating from the national security bureaucracies nonetheless had contributed to an increase in aid levels from a meager $1.1 million in 1978, to $3.8 million in 1982 and $7.8 million in 1986.[42] This should not imply, however, that aid automatically increases due to bureaucratic advocacy. (In 1986, for

24

example, despite Embassy pressures to the contrary, USAID decided to withdraw its representative from Djibouti and place ongoing projects under the authority of a regional office in Nairobi, Kenya.) Rather, the primary point is that established bureaucratic missions serve as important barriers against attempts to downgrade an already established relationship. Indeed, whether relations with an African country are improving or deteriorating, the bureaucratic impulse is usually to request greater amounts of aid. The rationale is quite simple: greater amounts of aid, it is argued, will either consolidate already close ties or prevent the further slippage of what is perceived to be a deteriorating relationship.

The process of incrementalism helps explain why it is rare for there to be a significant change in the majority of US Africa policies even when a new administration has seemingly different beliefs than its predecessor. For example, the Carter administration, despite a stated commitment to human rights and the need to decrease ties with authoritarian dictatorships, largely failed to move beyond rhetoric in 1977 in the case of Mobutu Sese Seko's Zaire (see Chapter 3). As noted earlier, the time constraints of a four-year term of office, coupled with the traditionally low level of attention paid to African issues by the President, favors bureaucratic influence, and therefore general support of the status quo, within the policymaking process. Perhaps the most significant barrier to change, however, is that the numerous activities of the bureaucracy simply do not fall under the realm of presidential action. As Rusk commented after Nixon had replaced Johnson:

> A transition is not so earth-shaking. Of the thousand or so cables that go out of here every day, I see only five or six and the President only one or two. Those who send out the other 994 cables will still be here. It is a little bit like changing engineers on a train going steadily down the track. The new engineer has some switches he can make choices about – but 4,500 intergovernmental agreements don't change."[43]

Although somewhat exaggerating the importance of bureaucracies during presidential transitions, Rusk's train metaphor correctly suggests that established bureaucratic missions greatly strengthen the possibility that US Africa policies will continue to chug along in established tracks until the White House and/or other domestic actors are faced by some kind of crisis that may precipitate a reassessment. In the absence of such a catalyst, the attention of the White House is usually focused elsewhere, as policies continue to be maintained and strengthened by the bureaucratic freight train.

Crisis situations and presidential politics

The President plays a potentially pivotal role in reorienting US Africa policies regardless of what happens in the continent. If a bureaucratic rift during a routine (i.e. non-crisis) period cannot be decided at the level of the Secretary of State or the Secretary of Defense, for example, the issue, by necessity, may be pushed to the White House for resolution. Similarly, general policy reviews, especially at the beginning of a new administration, as well as the internal processes that lead to the drafting and subsequent interpretation of influential documents and speeches, also offer unique opportunities for a more active stance to be adopted by the President. However, a major thesis of this analysis is that Africa's low standing relative to other regions of the world ensures that presidential involvement is rare and episodic. It is generally only when the White House is confronted by a crisis situation in Africa that a formerly obscure country becomes the focus of the President and his closest advisers. If an African issue is perceived to be of such importance, then the departmental bureaucracies are likely to find that the White House is asserting control over the policymaking process.

Crisis and presidential attention to US Africa policies

The triggering mechanism for sustained presidential attention to African issues is usually the occurrence of some type of intense politico-military conflict, such as the 1977–78 Ogaden War between Ethiopia and Somalia. It is the foreign dimension of an African conflict, however, which constitutes the critical aspect of whether that conflict becomes a *crisis* in the eyes of the President.[44] Specifically, crisis situations, at least prior to the end of the Cold War at the beginning of the 1990s, generally evolved due to White House perceptions of the involvement of two key sets of foreign actors: Washington's European allies and the former Soviet Union and other "radical" powers (particularly Cuba and East Germany).

Crisis and the role of European powers. US Presidents have generally recognized European spheres of influence within former African colonies, in essence relying upon their allies to maintain Western interests on a day-to-day basis. Similarly, US reaction to a crisis in Africa is generally peripheral when a European power is embroiled. Specifically, if it is perceived that a European power can handle the crisis situation, the tendency has been for the White House to defer to European intervention, essentially producing little if any change in policy.

Historical examples of peripheral presidential attention to African crises due to significant European involvement include the British struggle against the Afrikaners in South Africa from 1899 to 1902 and French counterinsurgency efforts against Algerian nationalists during the late 1950s. In more recent cases, despite the growing level of US politico-military ties with Africa, Presidents consistently have sought to keep European allies responsible for, and in the forefront of, crisis-related initiatives. President Carter, for example, despite an interest in pursuing a negotiated end to Zimbabwe-Rhodesia's growing guerrilla war and white minority rule, felt that the British should play the primary role, with the State Department's Africa Bureau playing a secondary, but strongly supportive role.[45] Similarly, President Reagan is said to have bluntly stated to French President François Mitterand during the August 1983 crisis in Chad that any needed interventionist measures were "France's historic responsibility."[46]

The initial US response to the 1967–70 Nigerian civil war provides an excellent illustration of White House sensitivity to European preferences in a crisis situation. After a year of spiraling ethnic violence, the Ibo-dominated province of Eastern Nigeria proclaimed itself the Republic of Biafra on May 30, 1967.[47] While Britain, the Soviet Union, and the majority of African countries supported the Nigerian federal government when, nearly two months later, it launched a military attack to end the secession by force, France, Portugal, South Africa, Tanzania, Côte d'Ivoire, Gabon, and Zambia provided Biafra with economic and military support. Despite Nigeria's significance in the West as Africa's most populous country, a major producer of oil, and one of the continent's avid supporters of a capitalist path of development, the US embargoed the sale of arms to both sides and maintained a low profile. Characteristic White House sensitivity to British policy preferences was one of the major reasons for keeping out of the conflict, despite a variety of sympathies in the Johnson and Nixon administrations, as well as repeated requests by the Nigerian government to purchase armaments. "It had been suggested by the British government that Britain should supply all the arms needed by Nigeria since Nigeria was a British sphere of influence," notes F. Chidozie Ogene, a former member of the Nigerian Diplomatic Service, "The US, according to the British proposal, should not supply arms [but] was required to give full support for the British position in Nigeria."[48]

In sharp contrast, when there is a politico-military power "vacuum" in Africa – historically due to the inability or refusal of a weakened and withdrawing colonial power to maintain order – the tendency has been for the White House to take a much more active role, sometimes transforming US foreign policy toward the country in question. For example, prior to 1974, Angola remained a low priority for the White House, with Presidents Truman to Nixon ultimately deferring to Portugal's efforts to maintain its colonies in Africa. US policy continued to be dominated by traditional political and military arguments over the need to maintain access to military bases in the Portuguese-controlled Azores islands. However, the overthrow of the regime headed by Marcello Caetano set off warning bells in Washington.[49] The *coup d'état* was carried out by a group of young Portuguese military officers determined to end failing, and increasingly costly, counterinsurgency efforts in Africa by granting independence to Portugal's colonies – all of which were confronted by guerrilla insurgencies supported by the Soviet bloc. As discussed more fully below, the potential for instability created by the voluntary withdrawal of Portuguese colonial rule ensured that Central Africa, and particularly Angola, would become top priorities of the White House.

The US tendency to fill power vacuums is not limited to Africa, but instead is the result of a historical trend in which an increasingly powerful United States has taken the place of declining colonial empires and withdrawing European power and influence throughout the Third World. During the nineteenth century, the Monroe Doctrine served as the basis for asserting US hegemony in Latin America in the face of gradual European withdrawal from the hemisphere. In 1947, the Truman Doctrine sought to stem instability in Greece and in Turkey due to Britain's withdrawal from southern Europe. Similarly, promulgation of the Eisenhower Doctrine in 1958 was in response to British and French withdrawal from the Middle East, while French withdrawal from Southeast Asia presaged US entry into the debilitating nationalist struggles of the region, most notably the Vietnam War.[50] Indeed, as the politico-military power of the former European colonial powers has declined, the geographical realm of US intervention in the Third World evolved from the relatively constrained Western Hemisphere focus of the Monroe Doctrine during the nineteenth century to the worldwide embrace of the Bush administration's "new world order" as the twentieth century draws to a close.

Crisis and the role of the former Soviet Union and other "radical" powers. The Soviet Union's involvement in a crisis situation on the African continent constituted, perhaps, the most important factor in determining the level of presidential involvement in the Africa policymaking process during the Cold War era. In those crisis situations in which an East–West dimension was lacking or somehow neutralized, the White House generally would avoid involvement in the conflict, resulting in foreign policy continuity – incrementalism prevailed. For example, returning to the example of ethnic strife in Burundi in 1972, it has been documented that the Nixon White House, although aware of the situation, left the formulation and implementation of the US policy response to the Africa specialists in the State Department's Africa Bureau, almost certainly because the massacres in a region of little strategic concern lacked any hint of communist involvement.[51]

White House inaction in Burundi starkly contrasts with the marked degree of attention focused on Angola after the 1974 Portuguese *coup d'état*. One of the primary differences was that the Soviet Union and Cuba were the primary backers of Agostinho Neto's Movimento Popular de Libertaçao de Angola (MPLA); the other two guerrilla groups vying for power were Holden Roberto's Frente Nacional de Libertaçao de Angola (FNLA), supported by the People's Republic of China (PRC) and Zaire, and Jonas Savimbi's Uniao Nacional para a Independência Total de Angola (UNITA), backed by China and South Africa. Ignoring the advice of those in several State Department bureaus who argued against assisting any of the guerrilla factions seeking supremacy,[52] President Gerald R. Ford, at the urging of Secretary of State Kissinger and the CIA, decided to intervene covertly on the side of the FNLA.[53] According to John Stockwell, the CIA Chief of the Angola Task Force who managed the covert operation to assist the FNLA, Soviet involvement on the side of the MPLA was the primary factor guiding White House policy: "Kissinger saw the Angolan conflict solely in terms of global politics and was determined that the Soviets should not be permitted to make a move in any remote part of the world without being confronted militarily by the United States." "Uncomfortable with recent historic events, and frustrated by our humiliation in Vietnam," continues Stockwell, "Kissinger was seeking opportunities to challenge the Soviets."[54]

The importance of Soviet involvement in influencing White House policy is captured by a House Select Committee on Intelligence hearing in mid-December 1975.[55] Asked about the differences between the three guerrilla groups vying for power in Angola, CIA Director William Colby noted that in reality they were all quite similar: "They are all independents. They are all for black Africa. They are all for some fuzzy kind of social system ... without really much articulation, but some sort of 'let's not be exploited by the capitalist nations.'" The natural response on the part of the committee members to Colby's answer was confusion over why different countries, including the US, were supporting one or more guerrilla factions if they were all so similar in outlook.

CONGRESSMAN LES ASPIN: And why are the Chinese backing the moderate [FNLA] group?

COLBY: Because the Soviets are backing the MPLA is the simplest answer.

ASPIN: It sounds like that is why we are doing it.

COLBY: It is.[56]

In short, the crucial element driving US involvement in the Angolan civil war was not identification with the aims of a particular guerrilla group, or even an interest in Angola. Rather, the fact that the Soviet Union aligned itself with one of the guerrilla factions was the deciding factor in turning the Angolan conflict into a crisis, and therefore paving the way for US support for the FNLA and UNITA.

The end of the Cold War, however, does not mean that African conflicts will cease to attract the attention of the White House. Indeed, although the end of the Cold War offers tremendous opportunities – particularly the possibility of replacing superpower confrontation with a greater sensitivity to a host of development problems in Africa – it has also ushered in an altered international system replete with problems as old as history itself, such as rising ethnic conflict, religious fundamentalism, and economic nationalism, as well as a variety of more recent but equally threatening problems: nuclear proliferation, chemical weapons production, and the spread of international drug cartels. Most important, as discussed in Chapter 6, there appears to be a growing perception at the highest levels of the policymaking establishment that Islamic fundamentalism is a threat to US interests on the African continent. Many officials privately note, for example, that the decline of the Soviet Union and communism have created a power vacuum on the African continent that could easily be filled by "radical" forms of Islamic fundamentalism, particularly the "shia" variant espoused by Iran. In a sense, the anti-communist logic of containment of the Soviet Union during the Cold War era may be in the process of being replaced by an anti-Islamic variant focused specifically on the variety of fundamentalist regimes in the Middle East and North Africa. In this regard, conflicts perceived as being manipulated by "radical" agents of fundamentalism may possibly become the triggers of sustained presidential attention in the emerging post-Cold War international system.

Crisis and the impact of administration worldviews

The process of bureaucratic incrementalism suggests that, in the absence of crisis, many of the Africa policies of a previous administration are likely to continue, even though they may differ from the perceptions of the nature of the world held by the new President and his most trusted foreign policy advisers (usually the Secretary of State and the National Security Adviser), which subsequently form the basis of their foreign policy initiatives. The reason behind this discrepancy between the "worldview" of an administration and its foreign policy behavior is the traditionally low level of interest accorded to African issues by the White House. Thus, despite the inauguration of an administration with widely varying beliefs from its predecessor, policies often are continued in accordance with established guidelines.

Indeed, Africa's lower priority relative to other regions of the world sometimes makes US Africa policies particularly susceptible to White House domestic political considerations. For example, as already noted, despite Kennedy's strong anti-colonial beliefs, his administration largely failed to move beyond rhetoric in the case of Portuguese-ruled Africa. Although it was argued that established bureaucratic missions played the major role in ensuring policy continuity, domestic political considerations also influenced Kennedy's decision to decide in favor of the pro-Portuguese forces within the administration. He allegedly feared that a rift in the NATO alliance (threatened by Portuguese leaders if the US continued to interfere in its colonial affairs) would alienate security-minded Republicans in the Senate, and thus doom any chances of congressional ratification of a much-desired US–Soviet test ban treaty.[57] According to Arthur M. Schlesinger, Jr., Kennedy also was looking ahead to the 1964 elections, and "had to take into account the possibility that the loss of the Azores, on top of a test ban, might open the way to a Republican attack on the administration for alleged neglect of vital national interests."[58]

Yet bureaucratic factors and domestic influences weigh considerably less when crisis situations prompt the White House to critically examine and review – often for the first time – the nature and goals of US foreign policy toward a particular African country. In addition, crisis situations also serve as natural opportunities for the President to shape public opinion, and to make the parochial policies of individual bureaucracies more consistent with each other, as well as with that administration's worldview.[59] During the Cold War era, the most important element of any administration's worldview – from which all other assumptions derived – was the collective perception of the Soviet Union and its ability to create instability in the Third World.

Administration worldviews from Truman to Clinton. The Truman administration's worldview, which gave birth to the policy of containment of the Soviet Union, became the basis for an active policy of US intervention in Africa during the post-World War II period. Truman's worldview, as shared by his most trusted foreign policy adviser, Secretary of State Dean Acheson, rested on two major premises.[60] The first premise, resulting from Truman's interpretation of the Greek civil war (1946–49), was that revolutionary upheaval and conflict were due to external communist pressures and subversion.[61] The internal causes of revolutionary upheaval were downplayed in favor of the communist bloc's ability to export revolution. The second premise, which in the eyes of policymakers was confirmed in 1950 by North Korea's invasion of South Korea, was that communism led by the Soviet Union represented a monolithic force bent on world domination.[62]

The Truman–Acheson premises of containment were firmly embraced by President Eisenhower and his Secretary of State, John Foster Dulles.[63] In the worldview of Dulles, however, anti-communism became a moral imperative which divided the world into black-and-white categories of pro-US and pro-Soviet countries. The growing forces of African nationalism were dismissed as of little importance and special disdain was reserved for those African elites espousing the "immoral and shortsighted conception" of neutralism.[64] African governments, according to Dulles, were either with the US or against it; there was no middle ground. Both Eisenhower and especially Dulles felt that mere containment was too static a policy, in essence leaving the Soviet Union secure in its successes and ceding the field of maneuver to the communist bloc countries. The Eisenhower–Dulles worldview thus incorporated the vision of "rolling back" perceived communist gains, but only when such a policy could avoid direct military conflict with the Soviet Union.

The Kennedy administration entered office with a worldview that was split between the so-called "New Frontiersmen," such as Chester Bowles, who favored a less confrontational approach to the Soviet Union, and those individuals, such as Secretary of State Dean Rusk, who continued to favor a more cautious, traditional approach.[65] The New Frontiersmen, although strongly anti-communist, disagreed with the traditionalists over the proper tactics for ensuring the containment of the Soviet Union and maintaining US preeminence in the emerging independent countries of Africa. For example, the New Frontiersmen had greater sympathy and understanding for the potent force of African nationalism and were more willing to construct positive relationships with avowed neutralists, such as Ghana's Kwame Nkrumah. Yet the anti-communist impulse still seemed to overshadow the supposedly "fresh thinking" of this group's worldview. For example, although Kennedy – who philosophically leaned toward the arguments of the New Frontiersmen – acknowledged that many of the conditions that gave rise to insurgency were internal to the countries themselves, he still believed that internally bred dissent could be manipulated by external communist forces, and therefore required a vigorous US response. Competition between the two groups largely was resolved in favor of the traditionalists when, in the wake of Kennedy's assassination in 1963, President Johnson recognized National Security Adviser Walt Rostow as chief foreign policy adviser.[66]

The Nixon (and later Ford) administration's worldview departed from the Cold War image integral to the Truman, Eisenhower, Kennedy, and Johnson worldviews of the Soviet Union as the leader of a monolithic communist bloc bent on world domination. An alternative *realpolitik* worldview, most notably held by National Security Adviser (and later Secretary of State) Kissinger, instead regarded the Soviet Union as a traditional great power with which the US could negotiate.[67] An important element of this worldview – which rested on the twin themes of détente and the Nixon Doctrine – was the necessity of maintaining and regulating the existing balance of power between the US and the Soviet Union to avoid superpower conflict in Africa. Nixon and Kissinger believed that a policy of détente, which relied on the crafting of political and economic ties between the superpowers, would transform the Soviet Union into a status quo country willing to join Washington in maintaining an orderly and stable world. Until that point was reached, the Nixon Doctrine would serve as the means for containing a still expansionistic Soviet Union. The Nixon Doctrine signaled an important departure from past containment policies in that it entailed a retrenchment of US forces and disavowed direct intervention in Africa. Rather, pro-US African client states, such as Emperor Haile Selassie's Ethiopia and Mobutu Sese Seko's Zaire, theoretically would bear the brunt of responsibility for maintaining the regional status quo, and therefore US interests, in Africa.

The Carter administration's worldview, most notably its emphasis on human rights, offered to open a new chapter in US foreign policy that went beyond traditional preoccupations with anti-communism and containment.[68] Yet this worldview was split between two competing visions as manifested by the conflict between Carter's two closest foreign policy advisers, Secretary of State Cyrus Vance and National Security Adviser Zbigniew Brzezinski.[69] Brzezinski's worldview emphasized the traditional US proclivity to view African issues – and especially conflict there – through the lens of the overall US–Soviet strategic relationship. In the so-called "arc of crisis" ranging from Asia to southern Africa, for example, the Soviet Union was perceived as exploiting instability according to a well-defined grand strategy. Although détente, according to this worldview, was desirable, the inherently expansionistic nature of the Soviet Union made such US–Soviet cooperation highly unlikely; containment, thus, remained the norm. Vance's worldview, although not denying the necessity to take into account the impact of the Soviet Union, deemphasized the East–West dimension of conflicts in Africa in favor of their internal cultural, economic, and historical origins. Reminiscent of the New Frontiersmen, this "regionalist" worldview underscored the importance of African aspirations and the potent force of African nationalism. Unlike the New Frontiersmen, however, African nationalism was perceived as an important barrier to the successful intervention of both the US and the Soviet Union in Africa.[70]

The Reagan administration completely cast aside any consideration of regionalist logic and harkened a return to the Cold War beliefs embodied in the Truman and Eisenhower worldviews.[71] In language reminiscent of John Foster Dulles, Reagan characterized the Soviet Union as the "evil empire" which was the primary source of instability in Africa. "Let us not delude ourselves," Reagan declared in 1982, "The Soviet Union underlies all the unrest that is going on. If they weren't involved in this game of dominoes, there wouldn't be any hotspots in the world."[72] Yet inherent in the Reagan administration's worldview was a split over how best to deal with the Soviet Union. The far right wing of the administration, as embodied in the beliefs held by National Security Adviser William Clark, supported a hardline policy which went beyond mere containment and included the roll-back of communist advances in Africa.[73] This view resulted in the Reagan Doctrine: a comprehensive, ideologically based program for arming insurgents intent on overthrowing self-proclaimed, communist regimes in the Third World. The more pragmatic side of the Reagan administration worldview (such as that held by Secretary of State George P. Schultz) alternately pressed for greater attention to diplomatic negotiations with the Soviet Union. Central to this worldview was that US–Soviet negotiations, which resulted in four superpower summits in the latter half of the 1980s, could reduce US–Soviet tensions throughout the world and serve as the basis for resolving regional conflicts.

The Bush administration's worldview, as shared by President Bush, Secretary of State James A. Baker III, and National Security Adviser Brent Scowcroft, represented a departure from the ideological views of the Reagan administration, and instead embraced a *realpolitik* vision reminiscent of the Nixon administration.[74] Confronted with the decline of communism in Eastern Europe and the eventual fragmentation of the Soviet Union into several smaller, non-communist republics, the Bush administration described its primary goal as "moving beyond containment, to seek to integrate the Soviets [and, subsequently, Russia] into the community of nations, to help them share the rewards of international cooperation."[75] The Bush administration also perceived the end of the Cold War as allowing the US to craft a "new world order" that would be based on the global diplomatic and military engagement of the US as the sole remaining superpower. According to this *realpolitik*-inspired vision of the international system, power politics, military preparedness, and a resolve to intervene remained essential components of US foreign policy in the post-Cold War era. However, the Bush administration tempered its *realpolitik* vision with a pragmatic desire to enhance the role of regional and international institutions within the international system, albeit as instruments for the promotion of US security interests.

Although it remained unclear as of January 1993 what would serve as the unifying themes of the Clinton administration's worldview, campaign rhetoric suggested close parallels with the Bush administration's themes of moving beyond containment in the post-Cold War era and creating a new world order based on US leadership as the sole remaining superpower. However, President Clinton's selection of Anthony Lake as National Security Adviser and Warren G. Christopher as Secretary of State suggested a return to the regionalist policies reminiscent of the Carter administration. As a result, the administration can be expected to downplay the foreign dimensions of conflicts in Africa in favor of their internal roots, and recognize the potent force of African nationalism as a constraint on intervention by foreign powers, including the United States.

The Angolan crisis and the Nixon worldview. For a notable example of the importance of the administration's worldview in contributing to a particular policy outcome during a crisis situation, we need only return to our ongoing discussion of the civil war in Angola. In March 1975, US policymakers faced a crucial turning point in Angola when the FNLA attacked the MPLA and a latent power struggle erupted into what would become an escalating civil war among the three competing guerrilla factions.[76] The uncertainties created by Portugal's abrupt withdrawal from the region, as well as Washington's perception of the Soviet Union's willingness to profit from the situation (Moscow sent nearly 100 tons of arms to the MPLA from March to July), prompted the White House to become more involved in the crisis. Kissinger (after receiving final approval from Ford) is recognized as the key architect of the interventionist response.

Conflict had arisen among the national security bureaucracies, primarily between the CIA, which pushed for an increase in aid to the MPLA (as well as for the initiation of assistance for UNITA), and the State Department, especially the Africa Bureau, which argued against aiding any of the guerrilla factions. Although Secretary of State at the time, Kissinger dismissed the opinions of the State Department and leaned instead toward the CIA's policy of providing greater amounts of covert aid to the FNLA (and, shortly thereafter, to UNITA). An important element of defeating the MPLA on the battlefield was Washington's reliance on funneling significant amounts of covert aid through both South Africa and Zaire, as well as tacit support for those two countries to introduce their regular forces onto the Angolan battlefield. The net result was a significant change in policy as the White House became heavily involved in the civil war.

The critical aspect of this case is that the dramatic change in policy was the result of the worldview held by Kissinger, who perceived the Soviet Union as a traditional great power with which the US could negotiate. "We have sought – and with some successes – to build more constructive relations with the USSR," Kissinger noted in testimony before the Senate Subcommittee on Africa, "to reduce tensions in areas where our vital interests impinge on one another; to avoid destabilizing confrontations in peripheral areas of the globe – such as Angola." However, constructive relations hinged on the Secretary of State's perception of the need to maintain and regulate the existing balance of power between the two superpowers in Africa. According to Kissinger, this was upset by the arrival of Soviet-backed Cuban troops to assist the MPLA regime: "Let there be no mistake about it – the culprits in the tragedy that is now unfolding in Angola are the Soviet Union and its client state Cuba." His concern, however, was not for Angola, described as of "modest direct strategic interest," but the greater East–West issues of global stability and US credibility. "If the United States is seen to emasculate itself in the face of massive, unprecedented Soviet and Cuban intervention," explained Kissinger, "what will be the perception of leaders around the world as they make decisions concerning their future security?"[77]

Most important, by denigrating the internal aspects of the conflict in favor of its East–West dimension, US intervention became justified, if not necessary, to contain perceived Soviet expansionism. In accordance with the Nixon Doctrine and the constraints imposed by the Vietnam War on direct military involvement in the Third World, the proper means of intervention was indirect support of regional proxies (such as the FNLA in Angola) as aided by local client states (such as South Africa and Zaire).

Extended crisis situations and domestic politics

The longer an African crisis continues, the greater is the likelihood that more factions outside the executive branch will become involved in the formulation of policy as debate eventually spills over into the public domain. This often leads to a situation in which domestic politics, generally played out within a congressional context, increases in importance as a determinant of policy. Although public opinion and the activities of interest groups theoretically can directly influence the deliberations of the President, the most common pattern is one in which Congress, either acting independently or as the result of public opinion and organized interests, takes the initiative away from the executive branch and asserts its influence within the policymaking process.

Congressional involvement in the policymaking process

Congress historically has played a limited role in the realm of foreign policy, particularly with respect to Africa.[78] Among the most important reasons are the benign neglect of African issues by both the Senate and the House of Representatives, as well as the limited powers of Congress relative to the executive branch.

Benign neglect of African issues and subcommittee activity. Reelection pressures and time constraints imposed by elected terms of office (two years for Representatives and six years for Senators) force members of Congress to give priority to those domestic and international issues which will receive their attention. Since the primary objective of most members is to be reelected, and since most voters know or care very little about the African continent, conventional wisdom suggests that it is politically smart to avoid unpopular issues.[79] The rationale for such a perspective, is presented in its most cynical form: "If my constituents don't care, why should I?"[80]

The desire for career advancement is also relevant. For example, due to their limited financial and staff resources relative to other subcommittees, the Africa subcommittees of both the House and the Senate are usually not held in high regard by those aspiring for a more influential forum,[81] and some just use their membership as a "launching pad" for more prestigious appointments, such as those relating to

37

Europe or Japan.[82] As explained by Charles C. Diggs (D-Michigan), former chairperson of the House Subcommittee on Africa: "As soon as somebody on the Foreign Affairs Committee becomes eligible for a subcommittee, that person is usually given Africa," yet "as soon as they can ....they move on to something else."[83]

A brief analysis of the evolution of activity within the House and Senate Subcommittees on Africa underscores both the historical neglect of the continent within Congress, as well as a growing (although still small) voice for increased congressional attention to African concerns. Although established by the Foreign Relations Committee in 1959, the Senate Subcommittee on Africa suffered from a rapid succession of chairpersons, and did not become really active until 1975 (over sixteen years after its creation) under the leadership of Senator Dick Clark (D-Iowa).[84] But his successor in 1979, Senator George McGovern (D-South Dakota), avoided controversial issues on Africa because of waning popularity at home. Even Senator Nancy Kassebaum (R-Kansas), an extremely active subcommittee chairperson during the 1980s, originally did not want to focus on Africa and instead sought to head the Subcommittee on Latin America.[85] Finally, the chairperson since 1987, Senator Paul Simon (D-Illinois), has sought to place the subcommittee in the forefront of such high profile issues as the US military operation in Somalia known as Operation Restore Hope, but is perceived by some of his peers as lacking the necessary interest to make the subcommittee effective.[86]

In sharp contrast, the House Subcommittee on Africa has boasted a relatively stable leadership of six chairpersons from 1959 to 1993 (as opposed to eleven for the Senate Subcommittee during the same period), becoming an active and aggressive challenger of administration policies in Africa, beginning in 1969 with the tenure of Diggs,[87] and continuing under his successor, Stephen J. Solarz (D-New York), until he left in 1981 to lead the more prestigious Asia and Pacific Subcommittee. During the next ten years, Howard Wolpe (D-Michigan) not only brought distinguished Africanist credentials to the position of chairperson, but earned high marks among numerous knowledgeable groups for his active oversight of executive branch policies. However, in the aftermath of Wolpe's departure from Congress in 1991, continuity in leadership has become more tenuous. Specifically, Mervyn Dymally (D-California), a distinguished member of the Congressional Black Caucus, only served from 1991 to 1993, and has been replaced by Harry Johnston (D-Florida), a relatively junior Representative who has very little experience in African affairs.

Yet it is important to remember that both subcommittees, even with highly motivated chairpersons and members, face an uphill task in pushing African issues to the forefront of congressional debate. As Wolpe once noted, the House Subcommittee on Africa represents only ten members of Congress "who must seek the support of a majority of their 435 colleagues in the House if their efforts are to have their fullest impact."[88] Even if legislation originating in the House Subcommittee on Africa is voted out of the House Foreign Affairs Committee and passes the full House, inevitable differences with a Senate version must be overcome. (Assuming, of course, a similar bill has been adopted by the Senate Subcommittee on Africa, the Senate Foreign Relations Committee, and the full Senate.) Although all bills must follow this legislative process, congressional neglect and indifference regarding African issues make it very difficult to secure the needed enactments.

Powers of Congress relative to the executive branch. The twin themes of political survival and career advancement have not only fostered congressional apathy about Africa, but have ultimately reinforced the already limited constitutional role of Congress in framing US Africa policies, generally restricted during non-crisis periods to four realms:

(1) *Confirmation of presidential appointees.* In one of its most basic but vital legislative roles, Congress confirms numerous presidential appointees who will carry out executive branch policies in Africa, including the Assistant Secretary of State for African Affairs and designated Ambassadors. Although congressional approval for Africa-related appointments has rarely been denied, this power has enabled members of the Senate Foreign Relations Committee to temporarily frustrate the wishes of the President. For example, deeply opposed to the Reagan administration's policies of constructive engagement with South Africa and the fostering of closer ties with the formerly Marxist regime of Mozambique, Senator Helms attempted to derail both policies by holding up confirmation of Chester Crocker as Assistant Secretary of State for African Affairs and Melissa Wells as the Ambassador to Mozambique. Although both attempts ultimately failed, each delayed final Senate confirmation by six and eleven months, respectively.

(2) *Convening of hearings.* Other congressional oversight responsibilities include the sponsorship of fact-finding missions to Africa, meetings with visiting heads of state and other dignitaries, and the conducting of hearings on African issues, which increased dramatically in the late 1970s and early 1980s. Able to request testimony from knowledgeable persons, including those responsible for any decisions being taken or planned in the continent, hearings serve to broaden

congressional awareness and understanding of the administration's policies, as well as provide the basis for informed debate.

(3) *Authorization and appropriation of aid.* A more significant aspect of the power of Congress is its constitutionally mandated role of authorizing and appropriating all military and economic aid requested by the executive branch.[89] Congress and the executive branch traditionally have been less willing to do battle with each other over aid priorities in Africa as opposed to other regions of greater concern. In addition, the combination of executive branch priorities and the traditional congressional reflex to cut levels of foreign assistance has led to Africa finding itself placed last in the hierarchy of foreign aid. (During 1992, for example, Africa received roughly 7.6 percent of all US economic and military foreign assistance.)[90] The congressional impulse to limit aid levels in general (and aid to Africa in particular) is based on the simple reality that "foreign" aid is simply not a popular issue with the "domestic" voting public.[91] Indeed, due to Africa's low status in the eyes of most policymakers, aid to the continent is especially hard hit during times of tight budgetary restrictions, as in the aftermath of the passage of the 1986 Gramm-Rudman-Hollings Deficit Reduction Act.

(4) *Legislation.* Finally, Congress can affect US Africa policies by passing bills on issues of particular importance. Although such enactments ostensibly offer an almost unlimited avenue for Congress to assert its influence within the policymaking process, in order to be successful, the efforts must transcend the innumerable partisan and ideological splits both within and between the Senate and the House of Representatives. Historically, these differences have limited the ability of Congress during non-crisis periods to pass legislation either independent of, or counter to, the established Africa policies of the executive branch. Even one often-cited exception to this tendency – the successful congressional effort in 1971 to modify US sanctions against Southern Rhodesia – underscores the limits of congressional activism and the inherent powers of the executive branch.

After Southern Rhodesia's white minority leadership unilaterally declared the territory's independence from Great Britain in 1965 (and rejected any movement toward majority black rule), US policy followed Britain's lead by imposing UN-mandated economic sanctions.[92] White House support of sanctions was formalized through President Johnson's discharge of executive orders in 1968. Although this pro-British policy was defended vigorously by the State Department's bureaus of African and European affairs, a small group of Senators led by Harry F. Byrd (D-Virginia) were vehemently opposed to sanctions against the white Southern Rhodesian regime of Ian Smith. The pro-

Southern Rhodesian forces scored a victory in 1971 when Congress, through passage of the Byrd Amendment, partially lifted US economic sanctions by allowing the importation of Southern Rhodesian chrome and seventy-two other minerals of perceived strategic importance to the US economy.

While the partial repeal of sanctions represented a significant change in policy, this act was neither the result of broad-based congressional activism nor the defeat of executive branch policy. "The fact is," notes Anthony Lake, National Security Adviser under the Clinton administration, "that the Byrd Amendment intruded little into the consciousness of most members of Congress." Instead, repeal of sanctions was due to the efforts of a small group of Congresspersons – acting partially in the interests of private US mining companies – who were able to frame the debate in such a manner that a majority of uninterested Senators voted in their favor. The primary argument which seemed to sway most undecided Senators was that sanctions threatened the national security by making the US dependent on the Soviet Union – the only other producer of chromium – for strategic minerals. "Public indifference," Lake concludes, "allowed most Congressmen and the White House to treat the Byrd Amendment as a minor issue deserving of little study and the expenditure of less political capital."[93]

However, the most significant lesson of the Southern Rhodesian episode is that the issue of scaling back sanctions was not considered important enough by the Nixon White House to take a stand either for or against repeal. Indeed, policy guidance offered by the White House is especially important to the success or the defeat of important legislation during non-crisis periods. As Stephen R. Weissman, former Staff Director of the House Subcommittee on Africa, points out, the executive branch enjoys several "natural advantages" in the realm of foreign policy. Among these are its veto power (which can only be overriden by a two-thirds vote in each house), superior organizational capacity, and the political clout of Senators, Representatives, and interest groups aligned with the incumbant President.[94] The executive branch's natural advantage is further enhanced by the large degree of apathy among the majority of Congresspersons concerning Africa. In the case of sanctions against Southern Rhodesia, for example, it is extremely doubtful that the Byrd Amendment would have been passed had the White House publicly declared itself in opposition.[95] Indeed, the lack of genuine commitment to the Byrd Amendment by the majority of Congresspersons ensured that, even if the bill initially passed, the requisite forces for overturning a presidential veto did not exist.

Interest groups and the role of African Americans

Defined as individuals "who share some common attitudes and orientation toward the political process,"[96] interest groups have traditionally attempted to get their views articulated in both the Senate and the House of Representatives. The potential for influencing Congress is especially great in that the majority of members do not exhibit much knowledge and/or concern about the continent, and hence are potentially responsive to any highly organized and articulate "lobby" in this field. Even more important, this responsiveness increases when the views of the interest group are shared by constituents in an elected official's congressional district.

As Congress has increasingly involved itself in matters of foreign policy from the mid-1970s onward, the potential has grown for interest groups to be taken seriously in the formulation of policy.[97] Among those that have sought to influence the substance of US Africa policies are *academic organizations,* such as the African Studies Association (ASA); *non-profit organizations,* such as the New York-based Rainbow Lobby (a citizen's group dedicated to civil and human rights); *relief organizations,* such as the Mennonite Central Committee; *foreign lobbyists,* such as Fenton Communications, a Washington, DC based company which has served as an agent of the Angolan regime; *private institutions,* such as the Carnegie, Rockefeller, and Ford Foundations, each of which actively has been involved in funding a variety of Africa related programs; *private corporations,* as exemplified by Foote Mineral's active lobbying in pursuit of the repeal of sanctions against Southern Rhodesia in 1972; and, finally, *human rights organizations,* including those with a general international focus, such as Amnesty International and the Lawyers Committee for Human Rights, as well as more Africa focused groups, such as the London-based Africa Watch.

An equally important aspect of domestic politics is the nature of public opinion. As discussed in Chapter 1, most US citizens remain largely unaware and disinterested in US Africa policies, with what can best be described as a *National Geographic* outlook on the continent: lush jungles, exotic animals, and, more recently, the human suffering associated with drought and famine. These images are reinforced by a popular press which highlights the negative and sensationalist aspects of African politics, as well as the "safari tradition" of US journalism: sending generalists on short-term assignments, as opposed to those willing to make a long-term commitment to becoming authorities on Africa.

Practitioners from all sections of the ideological spectrum in the US agree that the 30 million African Americans are potentially the most important lobby for African interests, not least because they comprise roughly 12 percent of the electorate. Anthony Lake, for example, while focusing specifically on the evolution of US–South African relations, noted in 1976 that the direction of US foreign policy will "depend heavily" on the African-American community. "It is the only American group with both the inherent motive and the political means of forcing such a shift," explained Lake, "The development of black consciousness about African issues will be a key in deciding the pace of pressure on the government."[98] Five years later, Chester Crocker, despite a significantly different vision about what should constitute a proper US–South African relationship, largely concurred with Lake over the potential influence to be wielded by African Americans. "For the past twelve years since black pressure was successful in obtaining the cancellation of the Cape Town visit of the aircraft carrier USS John F. Kennedy," explained Crocker, "there has been a steady if gradual expansion in black focus on Africa. South Africa is the most emotive and sensitive issue in Africa for these groups." Crocker concluded that, although one cannot accurately predict the influence of specific groups, "there is little question that the black voice in African policy issues will continue to grow."[99]

Yet the "black voice" in US Africa policies has historically been very weak and non-influential, especially when compared to the strength of other ethnic groups in support of their "homelands," most notably Jewish Americans. One of the primary reasons for this lack of influence has been the absence of an organized constituency capable of effectively working within the US policymaking establishment.[100] "Blacks as blacks may identify with Africa," noted Martin Weil in a prescient article in 1974, "but it is only as Americans that they can change US foreign policy in Africa." If African Americans ever "gain leverage," he continued, "it will be those black politicians who are most successful *within* the system who will do so – those who can command the respect of their black constituents and reassure white America at the same time."[101] The establishment and evolution during the 1970s and 1980s of the Congressional Black Caucus and TransAfrica are indicative of efforts by African-American elites to increase their leverage on US Africa policies.

The Congressional Black Caucus. The CBC was formed in 1971 by thirteen members of the House of Representatives who were determined that Congress should make the domestic plight of African Americans, and US Africa policies, issues of greater concern within Congress as a whole. Yet at the time, most CBC members were lacking in seniority (and, therefore, power) in the House and, perhaps of greater significance, were willing to leave issues concerning Africa largely in the hands of Diggs, who chaired not only the CBC but the House Subcommittee on Africa. It would not be until Diggs had left Congress, in the late 1970s, that more members would assume greater responsibility for African issues.[102] Most important, by the beginning of 1993 the membership of the CBC had tripled in number to thirty-nine members, inclusive of the historic event of Carol Moseley-Braun (D-Illinois) becoming the first female African American to assume a seat in the Senate, and its membership throughout the 1980s and the 1990s had steadily risen in seniority and power. Not only did Democratic Caucus Chairperson William H. Gray III (D-Pennsylvania) assume the office of Majority Whip (one of the most powerful positions in the House) in 1989 (although he resigned from Congress in 1991), and Ronald V. Dellums (D-California) acquired the prestigious position of chairperson of the House Armed Services Committee in 1993, but two other full House committees and thirteen subcommittees as of 1993 were also chaired by CBC members. As Bob Brauer, Special Counsel to Dellums, once proudly noted: "The power of the CBC is disproportionate to its numbers. We now have a significant constituency in the House."[103] Despite such glowing reports, CBC members are quick to note that their primary responsibility will continue to be the *domestic* plight of African Americans.

The TransAfrica lobby. Whereas the CBC is constantly organizing support within the House of Representatives, the strategy of Trans-Africa – a political lobby for a broad range of issues concerning Africa and the Caribbean – is to mobilize the African-American electorate. "There must be as many as 100 congressional districts across the country in which we can make a significant difference in the voting patterns of congressional members," notes Randall Robinson, Executive Director of TransAfrica, and "Our efforts are focused on those people in those districts."[104] The commitment to forge this political lobby emerged from the Black Leadership Conference convened by Diggs and Andrew Young in September 1976 in opposition to the Ford administration's policies in southern Africa. Incorporated as a political lobby in July 1977, TransAfrica as of 1993 boasts over 15,000 members located in fifteen chapters throughout the country.

Although the CBC and TransAfrica constitute a powerful lobbying apparatus potentially able to mobilize a growing African-American electoral voice, the fact remains that they rarely have the power to significantly alter US Africa policies during routine periods.[105] Like both the House and Senate subcommittees on Africa, members of the

CBC and TransAfrica face an uphill battle in any attempt to persuade the largely uninterested majority in Congress that changes are needed. Part of a "critical mass" of individuals that coalesced during the late 1970s, these two groups are nonetheless regularly concerned about Africa, and can be counted on to make their voices heard in Congress.[106] For example, they helped to defeat the conservative elements that attempted in 1979 to repeal the sanctions against Southern Rhodesia that had been reinstated two years previously by Congress at the request of the Carter administration.[107] In this sense, the CBC and TransAfrica have an important "watchdog" role to play in defending established policies which they perceive as beneficial to US interests in Africa.

Extended crisis and domestic politics

The combination of congressional and popular neglect of African issues relative to the more extensive and consistent involvement of the executive branch, and particularly the national security bureaucracies, has two conclusive results. First, a relatively disinterested Congress, in the absence of crisis, will generally not support the efforts of small groups within that body, or among the general public, to alter existing US Africa policies significantly. Second, even during short-term crises when an issue may attract the attention of many members of Congress, as well as a variety of interest groups and portions of the general public, control of the policymaking process naturally flows to the President and the bureaucracies of the executive branch. A typical aspect of such situations is that the President is generally able to rally public and congressional support for the administration's foreign policy objectives. As Anne Forrester Holloway, another former Staff Director of the House Subcommittee on Africa, notes: "If the larger public interest does not force a congressional reaction, then the executive branch looks to coopt legislative support for its traditional 'crisis management' policy response."[108]

The longer a crisis continues, however, the greater is the possibility that the extent of US involvement in a particular African country will become the concern of more and more members of Congress, and of other interested individuals outside of the administration. This is especially true if an issue becomes the focus of popular opinion. When executive branch policy veers too sharply away from mainstream congressional opinion – which tends to mirror that generally held by the public – the combination of extended crisis and popular pressure may result in congressional attempts to alter administration policy. In this regard, the media often plays a crucial role in determining whether a previously ignored aspect of US Africa policies is transformed into a mainstream domestic political issue. Specifically, the mobilization of sympathetic public support for a more activist role by Congress is generally fed by extensive media coverage of a particular event – a phenomenon which, in turn, is fueled by extended crisis situations and their ability to sell newspapers. US involvement in the latter half of the 1967–70 Nigerian civil war offers an early example in which popular opinion successfully prompted members of Congress to seek a change in policy.[109]

Even though Washington supported Nigeria's federal policy and opposed Biafra's secessionist demands, US policy in the initial stages of the conflict (1967–68) was one of sympathetic neutrality as the Johnson administration acceded to British requests not to provide arms to the Nigerian federal government. As the crisis dragged on, it became widely reported in the US press that Washington's neutrality indirectly was supporting the Nigerian government's effective starvation methods designed to bring the secessionist Biafrans to their knees. Popular US opinion, most notably expressed by thousands of letters denouncing the Nigerian government received by congressional representatives, led to increasingly vocal congressional demands in 1968 that the White House end its neutrality and provide, at a minimum, humanitarian relief for the starving Biafrans. Moreover, public concern prompted the Biafra issue to become an election year issue in which both the Democratic and Republican candidates pressed for the provision of humanitarian aid. The net result of public concern was an altered White House strategy from mid-1968 until the end of the war in 1970 – over the strong objections of the State Department – in favor of providing significant levels of humanitarian aid to the Biafrans. "Without adequate pressure from non-governmental groups and from public opinion," notes F. Chidozie Ogene, a former member of the Nigerian Diplomatic Service, "congressional and White House reaction to the political and relief crisis would not have been different than the near indifference and quietude of the first year of the war."[110]

The combination of congressional pressure and public opinion, however, did not fundamentally change US foreign policy toward the Nigerian civil war. This essentially remained pro-federal and fostered a pro-humanitarian relief foreign policy orientation that both the Johnson and Nixon administrations were willing to accept. In this sense, public opinion has been influential in prompting Congress to respond to other humanitarian related crises in Africa regardless of the ideology of the regime in question. The most notable example, of course, was the tremendous outpouring of US popular support for drought and famine aid to Ethiopia in 1983–85 despite the pro-Marxist, pro-Soviet nature of the ruling regime (see Chapter 4). Apart from such humanitarian-related efforts, it was not until 1975 that Congress for the first time overturned a major foreign policy initiative of the White House in Africa, and therefore played a significant role in affecting US intervention in the continent. The case in question is our ongoing discussion of US involvement in Angola's 1975–76 civil war.[111]

The Ford administration, under the personal direction of Kissinger, originally intended to shield its covert operation in Angola from what almost certainly would have been congressional disapproval. Decisions concerning the ever-expanding US commitment to the FNLA – from $300,000 in January 1975 to $30 million six months later – were made within the restricted policymaking circles of either the administration's "40 committee" or the National Security Council (NSC).[112] Yet the visibility that inevitably accompanies rapidly expanding covert operations led to accusations in the press that the Ford administration was actively intervening in Angola with Zaire's assistance.

The initial response by members of Congress to growing allegations of US intervention provides an illustration of their general lack of interest in African issues. Only one Senator attended any of the hearings conducted by the Subcommittee on Africa in June and July 1975, namely its chairperson, Dick Clark. As newspaper accounts continued to mount, the Senate Foreign Relations Committee held a closed meeting on November 6, 1975, at which witnesses for the White House admitted that the administration had authorized a covert operation in Angola. Yet Congress continued to acquiesce due to the secrecy requirements surrounding these executive branch initiatives, and the fact that most members were neither attuned to, nor interested in, distant Angola. In the ensuing weeks, however, a series of leaks to the press led to numerous newspaper articles being published and, finally, Kissinger's public acknowledgement of US covert intervention in Angola. This admission was extremely important, according to Gerald Bender, because it "not only ignited a major debate in the media and among the public but also lifted restrictions from Congressmen who had been unable to introduce legislation (to cut off US participation) on the grounds that it was not a 'public' matter."[113] In the wake of Vietnam and fearful of the US being mired in another distant civil war, the Senate voted in December 1975 to cut off all aid to any guerrilla faction in Angola by adding the Clark Amendment to the 1976 Foreign Assistance Act. Although this was vetoed by Ford in an effort to stem congressional influence, the Senate responded on December 19, 1975, by successfully attaching the Tunney Amendment – which cut off all covert aid to Angola – to the 1976 Defense Appropriations Bill.

Three aspects of the Angola episode are worth noting. First, Congress asserted its influence within the policymaking process by passing legislation that effectively terminated an unpopular, but staunchly defended, White House policy. Equally significant is that congressional action reflected the public's desire in the wake of Vietnam to avoid any commitment in distant civil wars. "The country's mood," Bender explains, "indicated that the American public, embittered and disillusioned by recent American losses in Southeast Asia, would not support even minor involvement in another remote and confusing conflict.[114] A nationwide Harris poll released on November 21, 1975, confirmed this underlying sentiment. According to this poll, 72 percent of those interviewed believed that the US "should avoid involvement in all guerrilla-type wars in the future when it appears the US is participating in the civil war of another country."[115] Indeed, public weariness with the prospects of US soldiers dying on an obscure battlefield in Africa reinforced a growing anti-interventionist consensus within Congress – despite the Ford administration's simplistic attempts at manipulating public opinion by painting the conflict as an extension of the Cold War competition between the US and the Soviet Union.[116]

Most important, the Angola episode served as an important indicator of a more activist Congress – regardless of the nature of the situation in Africa or in any other region of the world – in the aftermath of the highly controversial and politically divisive Vietnam War. In addition to mirroring rising public dissatisfaction with that war, attempts to reassert the role of Congress within the foreign policy process were sparked by disclosures of ill-conceived foreign covert operations[117] and domestic excesses by the Nixon administration (which, opponents argued, contravened US law),[118] and, most important, by general perceptions of an "imperial presidency" increasingly at odds with the constitutional precept of "checks-and-balances."[119] Despite the gradual increase in congressional influence during the post-Vietnam era, it is nonetheless usually during times of extended crisis that Congress continues to play its greatest role in the policymaking process.

Patterns and process in perspective

It is necessary to go beyond the individual conclusions reached by the blind men in their quest to determine the true nature of the beast in

Table 2.2. *Pattern and process in US Africa policies*

External environment			US domestic environment		Continuity and change	
	Levels of foreign involvement					
Local situation	"radical" powers	European powers	Policy process	Policy determinants	Outcome	Chance for change
Routine	Low	High	Bureaucratic politics	Organizational missions	Incrementalism	Low
Crisis	High	Low	Presidential politics	Administration worldview	Uncertainty	High
Extended crisis	High	Low	Domestic politics	Societal interests	Uncertainty	High

order to fully understand continuity and change in US intervention in Africa during the post-World War II era. Hence the need to analyze the nature of events which historically have affected the operation of the policymaking process. Although this cannot be neatly divided into mutually exclusive categories of either bureaucratic, presidential, or domestic influence – indeed, the often "messy" politics of policy formulation and implementation is inherently blurred – the evolution of US Africa policies has followed three general patterns, as outlined in Table 2.2.

(1) *Routine situations and bureaucratic influence within the policymaking process.* Due to the historic neglect of the continent by both the White House and Congress, US Africa policies – perhaps more so than those directed toward any other region of the world – are best explained by focusing on the character of the bureaucracies concerned and the evolution of bureaucratic politics. Specifically, policies during routine periods tend to be driven by the established organizational missions of the national security bureaucracies comprising the executive branch, including the State Department, the Defense Department, and the CIA, as well as their specialized offices devoted to Africa. The net result of bureaucratic preeminence in the policymaking process is an incrementalist outcome in which the potential for change in interventionist practices is extremely limited. In fact, the best predictor for future policy is current policy.

(2) *Crisis situations and presidential influence within the policymaking process.* When situations in Africa change from routine to crisis, the likelihood increases that the African affairs bureaucracies will lose control of policy as Presidents and their most trusted foreign policy advisers will assert White House control over the policymaking

process. The most important determinants of whether a situation took on a crisis atmosphere – at least prior to the end of the Cold War at the beginning of the 1990s – historically have been the nature of European involvement, as well as that of the former Soviet Union and its allies. Crisis situations not only prompt the White House critically to examine and review the nature and purposes of US foreign policy toward a particular African country, but also serve to make the parochial policies of individual bureaucracies more consistent with each other, as well as with the worldview of the administration. The net result of presidential involvement in the policymaking process is an uncertain policy outcome in which the possibility for change in interventionist practices is extremely great.

(3) *Extended crisis situations and domestic influence within the policymaking process.* Finally, the longer that a crisis situation continues, the greater the possibility that more groups and individuals outside of the executive branch will become involved in the policy process as debate spills over into the public domain. This spill-over effect can lead to a situation marked by domestic politics in which Congress, acting either independently or as a result of public pressure, removes the initiative from the executive branch and takes the lead in formulating policy. Although the possibility for change in US Africa policies under such situations is significant, congressional ability to influence events dramatically decreases in the absence of crisis as traditional partisan and ideological rivalries prevent the Senate and the House of Representatives from taking unified action.

Together these three patterns capture the dynamic nature of US Africa policies, and provide the framework for analyzing the evolution of US foreign policy toward the case studies of this book. US relations with various African regimes do not remain static over time, but instead evolve as different portions of the foreign policy establishment assert their influence within the policymaking process at different points in time. One can therefore conceive of intervention as a sort of continuum in which periods of bureaucratic influence are briefly interrupted by episodes of presidential and domestic involvement during crisis and extended crisis situations. Yet even if changes have consequently occurred in a given relationship due to presidential or domestic politics, once the crisis situation subsides, policy usually soon falls under the realm of the national security bureaucracies, and the process of routine incrementalism again prevails, albeit in an altered form.

3 US FOREIGN POLICY TOWARD ZAIRE

> Zaire is among America's oldest friends and its President – President Mobutu – one of our most valued friends [on the] entire continent of Africa.... One of Africa's most experienced statesmen, President Mobutu has worked with six US Presidents. And together, they and we have sought to bring to Zaire, and to all of Africa, real economic and social progress, and to pursue Africa's true independence, security, stability as the bases for that development.
>
> Remarks made by President George Bush, White House meeting with Zairian President Mobutu Sese Seko, June 29, 1989.[1]

Introduction

Spanning more than three decades and the administrations of nine US Presidents, the US–Zairian "special relationship" was forged in the Cold War atmosphere of the early 1960s as the Eisenhower administration mounted a large-scale covert operation to maintain the territorial integrity and the pro-Western orientation of this formerly Belgian-ruled colony.[2] In the aftermath of what would be the first of many interventionist episodes in Zaire, US Presidents from Kennedy to Bush identified US interests with the continued stability of that country. In particular, since 1965, Presidents publicly have reiterated Washington's special relationship with Zairian leader Mobutu Sese Seko. In a notable example of these close ties, Mobutu was the first African head of state to be invited by the Bush administration to come to Washington for an official state visit. During that visit, Bush underscored the "excellent" nature of the US–Zairian bilateral relationship and praised Zaire as one of Washington's "oldest" and "most valued" friends on the African continent.[3]

The Belgian Congo as a bureaucratic backwater (prior to July 1960)

The Belgian-ruled colony of Zaire historically constituted a backwater for senior US policymakers in which the State Department's Bureau of

European Affairs took the lead in suggesting the proper course of US–Zairian relations. In January 1960, five months prior to when Zaire was to receive its independence, an NSC review of US foreign policy toward the region reflected the low-key, Euro-centric nature of this policy approach. Noting the "negligible" levels of communist influence and the "relatively modest" levels of US economic interests in the region (aside from those in South Africa), the document called for a policy of "encouraging and, to the extent feasible, relying on Western European nations to influence and support their respective dependent and recently independent areas" in Africa. In policy guidance directly relevant to Belgian-ruled Zaire, policymakers were instructed to "consult" with colonial powers concerning any US initiatives within dependent territories and to "avoid" any actions "likely to cause serious misunderstandings" between Washington and the European metropoles.[4]

Several dimensions of the US–Zairian relationship demonstrate how policy effectively reflected the European Bureau's predilection to favor Belgian sensitivities when dealing with colonial issues in Africa.[5] First, African Americans were barred from serving in Zaire to avoid both upsetting Belgian racial concerns and setting an example that could lead to independence demands among the Zairian population. Second, in deference to Belgian demands that Western consulates maintain their distance from the Zairian population, the US Consul-General in Leopoldville (Kinshasa) restricted US intelligence activities in the territory, instead relying on intelligence reports from Belgian sources. Third, limited technical aid plans were developed in close cooperation with the colonial authorities to supplement Belgian priorities and programs. Finally, the State Department even permitted Belgian authorities to compile the guest list for those Zairian leaders who would be invited to visit Washington one month before independence. Although this Europe-centric approach to the African colonies was firmly entrenched throughout the US policymaking establishment, the European Bureau's special interest in currying favor with Belgium and the other European colonial powers made that office particularly attentive to European preferences in Africa.

Washington's expectations for a smooth transition to a moderate, pro-Western Zaire were signaled by the perfunctory, congratulatory message sent by the State Department in Eisenhower's name to Zairian President Joseph Kasavubu on June 30, 1960, the day of his country's independence: "The independence of the Republic of the Congo is a source of deep satisfaction to the United States, especially since this freedom was achieved in friendly cooperation with

Belgium." The message concluded on a positive note that "the Government and people of the United States look forward to close and friendly relations with the Government and people of the Republic of the Congo."[6]

Crisis and resort to covert initiatives (July 1960–January 1961)

Western assumptions of an orderly transition of power were shattered on July 5, 1960, five days after independence, when Zairian soldiers of the 25,000 strong Force Publique mutinied against their white Belgian commanders at a garrison roughly 90 miles from Zaire's capital of Kinshasa.[7] Initiated by soldiers who were seeking the fruits of independence (most notably higher pay and positions of authority), the mutiny quickly spread and resulted in an increasing number of riots in Kinshasa and other areas of the country in the days that followed.

As thousands of Europeans (primarily Belgians) fled across the Congo River to the neighboring capital of Brazzaville, Belgian armed forces – without the prior approval of either Zairian Prime Minister Patrice Lumumba or Kasavubu – reinforced garrisons in Zaire and unilaterally intervened throughout the country ostensibly to restore order and protect Belgian lives. Rather than pacifying the mutinous troops, Belgian intervention severely exacerbated an already tense situation. To make matters worse, the fragile territorial integrity of this multiethnic country suffered a major blow when the wealthiest province, Katanga (Shaba), declared its independence on July 11 with the tacit support of Belgian economic interests. Similar action was taken in August by the diamond-rich province of South Kasai (which currently comprises one portion of East Kasai). Faced with what amounted to be a reoccupying colonial army and the territorial disintegration of the country, Lumumba and Kasavubu made direct appeals to the UN to provide troops "to protect the national territory" of Zaire "against present external aggression" (in other words, Belgium).[8]

As a result of Belgium's historic colonial role and apparent willingness to maintain order, the White House remained inattentive to the disturbances in Zaire, and thus deferred the fashioning of a proper US policy response to the specialists in the national security bureaucracies. Despite the CIA's significant expansion of the recently created Kinshasa station and the Defense Department's preparation of contingency plans for the possible evacuation of US citizens, the State

Department emerged as the primary bureaucratic player in determining the proper US policy response. Hoping to forestall superpower confrontation while at the same time placating the interests of both the Zairian and Belgian governments, the State Department successfully sought the creation of a multilateral UN military force which precluded involvement by contingents of the US, the Soviet Union, and the major Eastern and Western bloc powers. Such an arrangement, reasoned State Department FSOs, not only would preempt possible direct Soviet involvement, but would offer the necessary diplomatic breathing space to defuse a growing conflict between Belgium and Zaire. As Clare T. Timberlake, US Ambassador to Zaire, colorfully remarked in a cable to Secretary of State Christian A. Herter: "This should keep bears out of the Congo caviar. I assume most Americans have not yet developed a taste for it either."[9]

Two important events significantly altered White House inattention to Zaire. On July 14, 1960, Lumumba and Kasavubu broke diplomatic relations with Belgium and hinted that they would request Soviet intervention if the UN forces scheduled to arrive the following day were unable to force a Belgian withdrawal from Zaire. Three days later, after it became apparent that the Belgians had little intention of leaving, these same leaders issued a written ultimatum. Either all Belgian troops were to be withdrawn by midnight of July 19 or the Zairian government would request unilateral Soviet intervention. In a classic example of how conflict in a formerly obscure African country suddenly became transformed into a crisis situation, the very real threat of Soviet intervention served to push an already brewing debate in Washington over the ability to deal with the existing government in Zaire to the highest levels of the policymaking establishment.

Debate among policymakers revolved around the potential threat to Western interests posed by Lumumba, the militantly nationalist Prime Minister of Zaire. In contrast to negative views of Lumumba held by Belgians during the period immediately preceding Zaire's independence, the State Department's Africa Bureau and the US Embassy in Kinshasa were impressed by his political talents and felt he would wield most influence in an independent Zaire.[10] Even after Lumumba's threats of mid-July, senior State Department officials, including Herter and Under Secretary of State C. Douglas Dillon, continued to believe that they could exert a moderating influence on the Prime Minister. A cable sent to Washington by the US Embassy in Kinshasa underscored this optimistic outlook: "Lumumba is an opportunist and not a communist. His final decision as to which camp he will eventually belong will not be made by him but rather will be imposed upon him by the outside."[11]

The State Department's European Bureau and the US Embassy in Brussels, which naturally focused on Belgian sensitivities, adopted a much more sober view of Lumumba's intentions. For example, the US Ambassador to Belgium, William Burden, recommended in a July 19 cable that the US should attempt to remove Lumumba from power.[12] The CIA shared this hardline view, as noted by CIA Director Allen Dulles' description of Lumumba as a "Castro or worse."[13] The fear among this latter group was that, even if Lumumba was not a closet communist, his erratic behavior and growing reliance on "radical" advisers made Zaire a perfect target for communist subversion.

Since Soviet intervention had not yet become a reality, the State Department's desire for the diplomatic resolution of the brewing crisis prevailed as demonstrated by an invitation for Lumumba to visit Washington in late July. Rather than improve US relations with the Zairian government, however, the visit turned out to be a political disaster for the young Prime Minister. For example, Dillon remarked that Lumumba had left the "very bad" impression with almost all concerned that he was "an individual whom it was impossible to deal with." Moreover, Herter emerged from a meeting with Lumumba thinking that he constituted an "irrational, almost 'psychotic' personality."[14]

Although Lumumba's visit to Washington convinced some formerly hopeful policymakers in the State Department that the US could not effectively deal with the Prime Minister, the key turning point in US relations with Zaire occurred when Lumumba formally broke with UN Secretary-General Dag Hammarskjold on August 14 over the issue of Shaba. Completely exasperated over Hammarskjold's refusal to use military force to defeat the Shaba secession, Lumumba threatened the viability of the UN operation by calling for the withdrawal of all white UN troops from Zaire. To the great consternation of US officials, this demand was followed by the arrival in Zaire of 100 Soviet bloc technicians and substantial Soviet bloc matériel – including a squadron of seventeen Ilyushin transport planes – apparently destined for use by Lumumba's forces to invade Shaba.

In an NSC meeting convened on August 18 and attended by Eisenhower, Dillon voiced the concern that was on everyone's mind: Lumumba's success in forcing out the UN forces most likely would pave the way for a more direct Soviet role within the region. Convinced that Lumumba "was working to serve the purposes of the Soviet Union," Dillon argued that such a "disaster" surely constituted but the first step to eventual communist domination of Zaire.[15] According to an alarmist cable received that very day from Lawrence Devlin, the CIA Chief of Station in Kinshasa, such a course of events already was playing itself out:

> Congo experiencing classic communist takeover.... Although difficult determine major influencing factors to predict outcome struggle for power, decisive period not far off. Whether or not Lumumba actually commie or just playing commie game to assist his solidifying power, anti-West forces rapidly increasing power Congo and there may be little time left in which take action avoid another Cuba.[16]

The consensus which emerged from the NSC meeting was that Lumumba had to go. Any remaining State Department feelings that a diplomatic option was still feasible were pushed aside as the CIA became the preeminent bureaucratic player and covert action the preferred means of intervention.

The deciding factor in the White House's resort to more drastic measures was Eisenhower's firm belief that radical Third World leaders who looked to the Soviet bloc for military aid and support threatened US interests in an increasingly turbulent Third World.[17] As discussed in Chapter 2, Eisenhower's beliefs leaned toward the highly ideological vision of neutralism espoused by his former Secretary of State, John Foster Dulles, who divided the world into black-and-white categories of pro-US and pro-Soviet regimes. There was little or no inbetween. Since containment was perceived as too static a policy – in essence leaving the field of maneuver to the communist bloc – the administration's worldview incorporated the vision of "rolling back" perceived communist gains, but only when such a policy could avoid direct military conflict with the Soviet Union. Covert action implemented by the CIA therefore became the preferred means of intervening in Zaire.

In true bureaucratic fashion, the CIA already had prepared a covert action plan to depose Lumumba in favor of pro-Western elements, apparently only waiting for presidential approval. On August 19, the day following the NSC meeting, CIA Deputy Director for Plans Richard Bissell sent the following cable to Devlin: "You are authorized proceed with operation." Any confusion over what the "operation" ultimately could entail was clarified by a meeting on August 25 of the NSC's Special Group, or that subcommittee which oversaw the planning of covert operations.[18] After Special Assistant for National Security Affairs Gordon Gray underscored that "his associates" – a euphenism for Eisenhower designed to maintain "plausible deniability" on the part of the White House – desired "very straightforward action," the group agreed that CIA planning should not rule out "any particular kind of activity which might contribute to getting rid of Lumumba."[19] In short, a covert action program was approved which included the most coercive measure of all: assassination of Lumumba.

Covert efforts initially bore fruit on September 5 when the CIA-cultivated Kasavubu heeded US concerns and ordered the dismissal of Lumumba and his cabinet from the government.[20] In response, Lumumba declared the decree illegal, branded Kasavubu a traitor to the Zairian nation, and, in turn, announced his dismissal. As political paralysis threatened to spiral into civil war, Colonel Mobutu, another CIA-cultivated leader, temporarily assumed power through a military *coup d'état* on September 14 and gave the Soviet and other socialist embassies forty-eight hours to leave the country.[21] Any lingering doubts among US policymakers as to whether the young military leader would seek some sort of accommodation with Lumumba – as had been his inclination in the past – were laid to rest after the CIA played an instrumental role in thwarting Mobutu's assassination on September 18 by pro-Lumumbist elements. Cautioned by Devlin that more assassination plots were in the works and that the best way to counter such efforts was to seek the "permanent disposal" of Lumumba, Mobutu ordered the arrest of Lumumba and several of his associates on September 18.[22]

However, the twin goals of the CIA's bureaucratic mission in Zaire – the permanent disposal of Lumumba and the creation of a pro-Western military government capable of maintaining stability – were initially thwarted by the arrival of Rajeshwar Dayal, the new Special Representative of UN Secretary-General Hammerskjold. Unwilling to be as subvervient to Western demands as was his predecessor, Dayal placed Lumumba under UN protective custody and resisted all attempts by Mobutu's forces to place him under arrest. Of particular distress to US policymakers was Dayal's refusal to recognize the legitimacy of Mobutu's military rule, as well as his adamant belief that any lasting political solution by necessity had to include Lumumba. The irony of Dayal's postion was that, whereas Lumumba's break with the UN prompted the Eisenhower adminstration to seek his removal through covert means, the UN was now serving as a brake on that very program.

Dayal's actions contributed to a bureaucratic rift within the national security bureaucracies as the State Department and the CIA pursued contradictory policies. Intent on avoiding further conflict with the UN and fostering international acceptance of a pro-Western Zairian regime, the State Department sought to legitimize Mobutu's military rule with the "fig leaf" of a civilian government. An important element of this strategy, which focused on the reconvening of the Zairian parliament to confirm the pro-Western Joseph Ileo as Prime Minister, was that "Lumumba's presence" in parliament "would have to be accepted" (under the assumption, of course, that his influence could be mimimized).[23] In contrast, the CIA argued that any hopes of attaining stability through a civilian alternative constituted wishful thinking, preferring instead wholehearted support for a Mobutu-led military regime. According to this viewpoint, Lumumba needed to be permanently eliminated from the Zairian political scene.[24]

The more hardline position of the CIA prevailed a few months later when Lumumba was killed on January 17, 1961, just three days prior to Kennedy's assumption of the presidency. In the weeks immediately preceding this eventful day, the civilian alternative briefly sought by the State Department had fallen by the wayside as growing conflict in Zaire had threatened Mobutu's tenuous hold over power. The most significant threat occurred when Deputy Prime Minister Antoine Gizenga, a loyal proponent of Lumumba, established an alternative government in Stanleyville (Kisangani) – the capital of Lumumba's eastern political stronghold of Orientale Province (Haut-Zaire). Having left UN protective custody on November 27 to link-up with Gizenga, Lumumba was captured a few days later by Mobutu's forces with the support of the CIA and transferred to a Zairian prison at Thysville (Mbanza-Ngungu).[25] Yet when a mutiny at the prison on January 13, 1961, resulted in Lumumba's liberation for a few hours, a concerned CIA station cabled Washington that the refusal "to take drastic steps at this time" would eventually lead to the defeat of US policy in Zaire. The meaning of "drastic steps" became clear when, four days later, Lumumba was transferred to the authority of his "bitterest enemies" in Elisabethville (Lubumbashi) – the capital of the Shaba secessionist forces – where it was obvious what type of fate awaited the Prime Minister.[26]

This initial period of US intervention in Zairian domestic politics clearly underscored the importance of a crisis situation in significantly altering US Africa policies. During the initial stages of the conflict when Soviet involvement was minimal and it appeared that Belgium would be able to maintain order, policy largely remained in the hands of the State Department, most notably the Bureau of European Affairs. As a result, the US response constituted a diplomatic approach which sought to win over Lumumba by ensuring his inclusion in a government dominated by moderate, pro-Western elements. Yet once it became clear that Belgian military capabilities were insufficient to counter what was perceived in Washington as increased Soviet military intervention in an extremely volatile situation, rising debate within the administration was resolved by Eisenhower. As a result, the more hardline vision of the CIA found favor with an administration whose worldview strongly favored the removal of radical Third World leaders through covert means. Despite the absence of a "smoking gun" directly linking the CIA to the final death of Lumumba, the outcome clearly reflected the culmination of covert efforts authorized by Eisenhower in mid-August.[27]

Continuing crisis and the "New Frontier" (January 1961–May 1963)

The newly elected Kennedy administration found itself in the midst of a "howling crisis" when the international community learned on February 14, 1961, that Lumumba had been killed.[28] Protests and demonstrations throughout the world culminated in numerous countries – most notably those within the communist bloc – recognizing Gizenga's government in Kisangani as the sole legal authority of Zaire. Most important, in what appeared to be support for a "war of national liberation" against the Kasavubu–Mobutu regime, the Soviet Union announced that it was "prepared, together with other states friendly" to Zaire, "to render all possible help and support" to the Kisangani government.[29] Similar to events during the Eisenhower administration, the threat of unilateral Soviet military intervention ensured the attention of the highest reaches of the administration.

Kennedy's initial response reflected two important elements of his administration's worldview: containment of the Soviet Union and the cultivation of Third World nationalists. In a nationally televised press conference on February 15, Kennedy underscored his firm commitment to the UN presence in Zaire and warned that "any government" taking the "dangerous and irresponsible" step of unilateral intervention would face the "risks of war."[30] These tough words were backed up by the positioning of a US Navy task force off Zaire's coast. This traditional anti-Soviet reflex so common within the policymaking establishment was nonetheless tempered by Kennedy's willingness to accept the passage of an extremely controversial UN Security Council resolution. Designed to win favor with the African–Asian bloc, support for the resolution marked a significant departure from the policies of the Eisenhower administration and incurred the wrath of both the Belgian and Kasavubu–Mobutu governments. Among the primary components of the resolution were the strengthening of the powers of the UN forces in Zaire, a demand for the withdrawal of Belgian (and other foreign) military personnel, and the reconvening of the Zairian parliament.

The most controversial element of Kennedy's new approach was the reconvening of the Zairian parliament, inclusive of Gizenga's radical parliamentarians, in order to create a civilian-based coalition regime. The success of the plan, which sought to strengthen Zaire's moderate political center, was based on ensuring the parliament's continued support for Kasavubu as President and selection of Cyrille Adoula, a respected nationalist, as Prime Minister. This strategy rested on the strong beliefs of Kennedy and the so-called "New Frontiersmen" in the administration that nationalist and neutralist regimes could constitute important barriers to communist expansion and that coalition governments, if based on a strong nationalist center (Adoula and Kasavubu), could hold radical (Gizenga) partners in check. The most prominent supporters of such an approach, which signaled the rising preeminence of a new coalition of bureaucratic forces sympathetic to African issues, included Assistant Secretary of State for African Affairs G. Mennen Williams (and his deputy, Wayne Fredericks), Under Secretary of State Chester Bowles (who eventually would be replaced by George Ball), and Adlai A. Stevenson, US Ambassador to the UN.

Opposition to the coalition policy not surprisingly was found among those bureaucratic players who had advanced a more hardline policy during the Eisenhower administration. Advancing views supported by both the CIA and the Pentagon, Ambassador Timberlake argued in several cables to Washington that convening the parliament not only ran the risk of Gizenga's emerging as Prime Minister of the coalition, but that any role reserved for Gizenga and his radical allies could lead to subversion from within, compounding rather than solving Zaire's problems.[31] Clearly out of step with the prevailing voices of the new administration, Timberlake was recalled and replaced by Edmund A. Gullion, a career FSO who strongly favored a coalition government of national unity.

The policy prescriptions of the hardliners were not completely ignored by the new administration. Although Kennedy's belief in the strength of nationalism led him to seek greater ties with neutralist regimes, his equally strong anti-communist beliefs led him to oppose radical nationalists with strong Soviet ties. In the case of Zaire, these conflicting beliefs led to a policy which in some ways bridged the bureaucratic conflict within the administration: a coalition government would be acceptable only if the moderate forces prevailed and the radicals were excluded from exerting a major influence. This was to be achieved by preventing the radicals from winning the position of Prime Minister. Toward this end, Kennedy ordered the CIA to mount a covert action campaign to ensure the victory of the Kasavubu–Adoula ticket at a July 1961 parliamentary conference held at the Lovanium, the predecessor of the University of Kinshasa.[32]

Having never ceased to pursue its "king-making" role in Zaire in the aftermath of the 1961 presidential transition, the CIA discovered an underground tunnel which led into the supposedly isolated group of legislators at Lovanium while they voted on Zaire's political future. This tunnel became the primary means whereby millions of US dollars made their way into the hands of numerous parliamentarians who appeared willing to sell their vote to the highest bidder.[33] Although the administration's fallback position reportedly was to support a military *coup d'état* by Mobutu if the Gizengists captured the position of Prime Minister,"[34] such action became unnecessary when, as expected, Kasavubu was confirmed President, Adoula was elected Prime Minister, and Gizenga was offered the largely powerless position of Deputy Prime Minister. Without minimizing the importance of CIA vote-rentals in contributing to the "moderate" political solution favored by the Kennedy White House, the internal alignment of Zairian political coalitions was equally if not more important. For example, not only did Adoula's selection constitute a genuine compromise widely acceptable to a plurality of Zairian politicians, Gizenga's candidacy essentially was doomed due to the bitter opposition of a fraction of those same political leaders.[35] As such, CIA intervention at best served to push Adoula over the top in a contest that he most likely would have won regardless of US actions.

The Kennedy administration's success in bolstering a centrist coalition that coopted radical political elements was clouded by the refusal of Moise Tshombe – the conservative leader of Shaba province who had aspirations of national leadership – to send representatives to the parliamentary proceedings and to renounce the secessionist activities of his province. Shaba posed a unique dilemma because Tshombe enjoyed powerful support in conservative US and Belgian circles that the White House preferred not to offend. In US circles, Tshombe's staunch anti-communism and US missionary education served as perfect rallying points around which a growing and well-financed Katanga Lobby mobilized US conservative opinion.[36] The Katanga Lobby enjoyed the strong support of several conservative US Senators inclusive of prominent figures within the President's own Democratic Party, such as Thomas Dodd (D-Connecticut).[37] In the case of Belgium,

Tshombe's support derived from the importance of mineral-rich Shaba as the focal point of considerable Belgian economic investment in Zaire. Among the most powerful of these Belgian economic interests was the Société Générale de Belgique which reportedly controlled nearly 70 percent of the Zairian economy.[38]

Since a Zaire without Shaba threatened the stability of the Adoula–Kasavubu regime, bureaucratic debate – reflecting a growing Europeanist–Africanist split within the administration – focused on whether the US should build up UN forces in Zaire and seek the forceful return of the secessionist province to central government control.[39] Mindful of Belgium's desire to maintain Tshombe as a buffer to instability in other portions of Zaire, Assistant Secretary of State for European Affairs William R. Tyler opposed any build-up of UN forces that could possibly lead to military conflict in the province. The Africanist coalition, led by Williams, instead focused on the warnings of Gizenga and other radicals in the Adoula government that they would abandon the coalition unless military steps were immediately taken to end the Shaba secession. The Africanists worried that Tshombe's refusal to negotiate ultimately would set in motion a negative chain of events in which the only victors would be the radical nationalists and the Soviet Union. Specifically, the Africanist coalition feared that the example of Shaba would lead to further separatism on the part of other provinces which, in turn, would be followed by the fall of the moderate Adoula–Kasavubu government and, finally, civil war.

The lack of an immediate threat to the Adoula–Kasavubu government worked against the more activist military approach sought by the Africanist coalition. In a clear example of the relationship between the nature of events in Africa and the operation of the US policymaking process, the lack of a crisis situation favored the continuation of established policy. As long as there was a chance that the dispute between the Adoula–Kasavubu government and Tshombe could be resolved peacefully, the White House would not implement a controversial new initiative that clearly went against Belgian wishes and, most important, ran the risk of alienating a conservative coalition in Congress whose support was crucial to other presidential initiatives.

However two events in late 1961 served to strengthen the voices of those arguing for more coercive military measures. First, the growing fragility of the US-backed Adoula–Kasavubu regime was underscored when, under mounting pressure from radical members of parliament to end the secession, Adoula ordered a series of military actions – Operations "Rumpunch" and "Morthor" – against the Shaba province which ended in disaster.[40] Second, Gizenga left the central government and returned to his stronghold at Kisangani. This action marked the decline of the coalition government and revived the threat of civil war and an eventual communist victory as predicted by Williams.

The Africanists within the administration, led by Ambassador Gullion, skillfully used the threat of a possible communist victory to convince Kennedy of the need for more forceful action as favored by the African–Asian bloc.[41] Toward this end, Kennedy instructed Stevenson to vote for a November 24 Security Council resolution which permitted UN troops, if necessary, to employ "a requisite measure of force" to expell foreign mercenaries and advisers from Shaba.[42] After a bruising NSC meeting during the first week of December in which the Africanist position prevailed, Kennedy also ordered the Defense Department to place twenty-one transport planes at the disposal of the UN command to facilitate a major airlift of military equipment and personnel.[43] However, rather than achieving a quick victory over Tshombe's forces, the long-awaited UN offensive quickly bogged down in the face of strong ground resistance.

As originally feared by White House policymakers opposed to military intervention against Tshombe, the White House almost immediately found its new activist policy under attack by its European allies and domestic critics. Reportedly "infuriated" that the administration had not consulted with them before authorizing the UN to proceed with its military operations, the European allies demanded an immediate cease-fire and the resumption of diplomatic negotiations to end the conflict.[44] Of even greater concern to the White House was the growing domestic outcry orchestrated by the skillful activities of the Katanga Lobby. In the Senate, Kennedy was facing a revolt by the conservative wing of his own Democratic Party.[45] In the media, conservative columnists blasted what they perceived as a misguided attack on a staunch anti-communist bastion in Africa. These vocal attacks were accompanied by a "small flood" of right-wing mail and the appearance on December 14 of a full-page advertisement in the *New York Times*, "Katanga is the Hungary of 1961," both of which constituted the opening salvo of the "American Committee For Aid to Katangan Freedom Fighters," a newly created pro-Tshombe organization which quickly expanded by building upon the anti-communist and anti-UN beliefs of conservative citizens and organizations throughout the United States.[46]

In the face of international and domestic pressures, Kennedy overruled the objections of the Africanist coalition and backed away from the use of force. Although it is doubtful that conservative critics in Congress could have mustered enough votes to force the Kennedy administration to back down from its military strategy in Zaire if the White House chose to fight, this episode nonetheless demonstrated how a drawn-out crisis situation led to successful congressional demands for a change in policy. Among the factors which contributed to the Kennedy administration's decision to avoid a battle with Congress were a core group of congresspersons willing and able to bring the issue of Shaba before the House and the Senate, extensive positive media coverage of the seemingly embattled Tshombe, and the mobilization of growing popular support due to the activities of the Katanga Lobby. As a result, the White House adopted a diplomatic strategy which simply sought to deflect conservative charges that the administration was backing a radical central government at the expense of the anti-communist Tshombe. In addition to prompting a willing Adoula to arrest and jail the secessionist Gizenga, Kennedy invited the Prime Minister to come to Washington in February 1962 for an official head-of-state visit. (Similar requests on the part of Tshombe were refused.) The visit turned out to be a public relations boon for Adoula who is said to have "won praise from even the most confirmed [congressional] detractors of the administration's policy.[47]

Once the executive-congressional debate over military intervention in Shaba had been resolved, the lack of crisis, compounded by Kennedy's political desire to avoid further conflict with domestic critics and the European allies, led to bureaucratic drift. As a result of the lack of presidential leadership, the first eleven months of 1962 were marked by growing debate over the proper course of US foreign policy toward Zaire. In a unique balancing act, Devlin not only began preparing a military alternative to the Adoula–Kasavubu regime in case the civilian experiment failed, he also strengthened US links with the anti-communist Tshombe in preparation for a worst case scenario – the takeover of the central government by the radical Gizenga forces. The CIA's support for Tshombe was complemented by Under Secretary for Political Affairs George McGhee's continued pressure for a negotiated settlement of the Shaba secession, a status quo policy which, in turn, was supported by the State Department's European Bureau and the Joint Chiefs of Staff. In sharp contrast, the Africanist coalition continued to press for a more activist policy. Ideally preferring that the secession be settled once and for all by the use of military arms, the Africanists were willing to settle for less coercive economic measures (i.e., economic sanctions) to achieve the same result. Finally, Under Secretary of State George Ball, supported by White House advisers Carl Kaysen and Ralph Dungan, sought the most radical policy of all – complete US disengagement from the UN effort.[48] As is generally the case during non-crisis periods, the lack of presidential attention ensured that both the activists and the disengagers who were seeking policy changes would be stymied by the established bureaucratic status quo; in this case, the politically safe policy of continuing diplomatic negotiations.

Events once again intervened to push the Kennedy administration toward considering the use of force to end the Shaba secession. By the end of November 1962, Adoula's already shaky regime was facing the combined forces of Tshombe and Gizenga who had joined together in a parliamentary strategy designed to overthrow the government. The threat posed by this strange marriage of convenience was underscored when Adoula, only through "profuse" bribery on the part of the CIA and some last minute concessions, barely survived a November 24 vote of censure within the Zairian parliament.[49] Of even greater concern was the arrival in September 1962 of Sergei S. Nemchina, the first Soviet Ambassador to be accredited to Kinshasa since Mobutu expelled that country's delegation in September 1960. To the great distress of US policymakers, Nemchina made it clear to the desperate Adoula that the Soviet Union was prepared to offer the necessary types of aid to seek both a political accommodation with Gizenga and a quick military solution in Shaba.[50]

Adoula's impending fall and the possibility of a communist takeover galvanized the competing voices of the national security bureaucracies to finally agree with the Africanist coalition that more coercive measures were essential in order to avoid a major disaster in Zaire. This consensus was reinforced by Belgian Foreign Minister Paul-Henri Spaak's surprise announcement on December 11 that, even if military force was required, he would be willing to support the UN's efforts in Shaba.[51] Taking advantage of the unique combination of Belgian support and an interventionist consensus within the national security bureaucracies, Kennedy on December 17 authorized the delivery of a variety of military weaponry requested by UN Secretary-General U Thant in preparation for a likely military showdown with Tshombe.[52]

The expected showdown began on December 28 when UN forces initiated phase one of a military plan code-named "Grand Slam" and quickly achieved control of Shaba's capital of Lubumbashi the following day. Still sensitive to the negative political repercussions that most likely would accompany another bruising confrontation with Tshombe's conservative political supporters in the US, Kennedy sought a cease-fire and an immediate resumption of diplomatic talks designed to reach a political agreement with Tshombe. Yet UN forces already had begun attacking Jadotville (Likasi) – the principal target of phase two of the military plan – which was captured on January 3, 1963. With UN troops now moving toward Tshombe's final redoubt in the strategic city of Kolwezi, White House policy was overtaken by events and expeditiously became one of full support of the UN advance. European pressures for Tshombe to peacefully surrender proved the final straw. Accepting the inevitable, Tshombe personally welcomed the UN troops into Kolwezi on January 21, 1963, less than four weeks after the beginning of the UN operation. The Shaba secession, after nearly two-and-a-half years, was finally over.

So as to ensure the continued stability of Zaire in the aftermath of the inevitable withdrawal of UN forces, Kennedy approved US involvement in a military program that entailed the training of the Zairian Armed Forces by six Western nations. The original intention of the so-called "Greene Plan" was to seek UN approval and coordination of the training effort while at the same time rejecting any involvement by Soviet bloc countries.[53] In short, the plan sought a UN "cover" for a Western military aid program designed to keep a pro-Western regime in power.[54] When Thant rejected the plan due to pressures from the African–Asian and communist bloc countries, Kennedy, along with the leaders of Belgium, Israel, and Italy, decided to sign bilateral military agreements with Zaire and proceed as originally planned.

Taken less than one month after the resolution of the Shaba crisis, Kennedy's decision was extremely important for three reasons. First, the decision marked a growing recognition that Washington would assume an important responsibility for the continued stability of Zaire. Second, the decision marked the strengthening of a bilateral military relationship in which the Defense Department became more intimately involved in maintaining the integrity of any future Zairian regime. Traditionally wary of placing its advisers (and therefore its credibility) under the command of even a US-dominated multilateral UN force, the Defense Department preferred dealing directly with the Zairians on a bilateral basis.[55] Most important, the decision signaled the beginning of a movement away from the Africanist coalition's ideal of fostering a moderate and democratic civilian regime in favor of the CIA's preference for a military strongman capable of ensuring stability.

The Zairian personality who seemingly was being groomed for this spot was none other than Mobutu. A hint of Mobutu's rising importance as the designated key to US foreign policy in Zaire was offered by his May 1963 visit to Washington – less than four months after the defeat of Tshombe's forces – in which he was treated like a visiting head-of-state. "Although it appears General Mobutu would like to remain apart from politics," began a classified internal memorandum from the Pentagon to the White House, "his stature and position as commander-in-chief of the army are not likely to allow him to do so." A biographical addendum concluded that Mobutu's army, "either as a whole or in part," would "of necessity be involved in any violent changes in the composition" of the Zairian government.[56] Of greatest significance, however, was Mobutu's private meeting with Kennedy at the White House on May 31, 1963. Kennedy extolled Mobutu's crucial behind-the-scenes role in the Cold War struggle against communism in Zaire: "General, if it hadn't been for you, the whole thing would have collapsed and the communists would have taken over."[57]

This second period of US intervention in Zaire's domestic politics once again underscored the importance of crisis situations in significantly altering US Africa policies. With the Kennedy administration faced with the prospects of unilateral Soviet intervention in Zaire almost immediately upon taking office, US policy significantly departed from the more hardline policies of the Eisenhower administration as the worldview of the New Frontier emerged preeminent. As a result, reliance on the covert option was tempered by a willingness to seek a civilian-based coalition government that included the radical political forces led by Gizenga. Once the nationalist coalition government led by Adoula and Kasavubu was successfully in place, however, the White House was confronted with the more delicate issue of the secessionist activities of the anti-communist Tshombe who enjoyed growing support in US and Belgian conservative circles. Despite the White House's willingness to support a military option when initially confronted in 1961 with the possible downfall of the Adoula–Kasavubu alliance and its replacement with a Soviet-supported radical regime, the objections of US allies in Europe and the domestic outcry orchestrated by the Katanga Lobby led Kennedy to back-pedal to the more politically safe option of diplomatic negotiations. This policy only changed in 1962 when, confronted a second time with the possible fall of the Adoula–Kasavubu government and Soviet intervention, both Belgium and the US national security bureaucracies were unamimous in favoring the military option. Due to the quickness of the military operation which successfully led to Tshombe's capitulation in just under four weeks, the Katanga Lobby was unable to bring its influence to bear on the Kennedy White House.

From counterinsurgency to direct military intervention (June 1963–November 1964)

Initial euphoria over the prospects for stability in Zaire soon gave way to increasing concern as disenfranchised Lumumbist leaders transformed rural discontent into a growing revolution against the Kinshasa government from July 1963 to July 1964.[58] In response to Kasavubu's dissolution of parliament – the last stronghold of Lumumbist influence in the central government – Christophe Gbenye, former Minister of the Interior, founded the revolutionary Committee of National Liberation (CNL) at the beginning of October 1963. This act was followed three months later by the creation of the Popular Liberation Army (PLA), the military arm of the CNL. In addition, Pierre Mulele, another Lumumbist who served as Minister of Education, already had returned to his home province of Kwilu in July 1963 where he began organizing a guerrilla insurgency patterned after Mao Tse-Tung's successful efforts in China. Systematically excluded from all positions of power within the central government since Gizenga's arrest in February 1962, the disparate Lumumba factions believed that they had no other alternative than to seek the overthrow of the Kasavubu–Adoula regime through military means.

Reflecting the rising fortunes of the hardline position of the CIA and the declining influence of the Africanist coalition within the policymaking establishment, the US response to the guerrilla insurgency entailed the incremental growth in a CIA-sponsored paramilitary war carried out in conjunction with the Pentagon.[59] During the fall of 1963, a Miami-based CIA front organization contracted with Cuban exiles who had taken part in the Bay of Pigs invasion of Cuba in 1961 to pilot T-6 planes against the Mulelist insurgency in Kwilu. In the spring of 1964, when the insurgency had spread to the eastern provinces of Zaire, the CIA hired additional Cuban paramilitary fighters to pilot six T-28 fighters recently delivered by the Defense Department. Maintenance for the fighters was carried out by European mechanics associated with the Western International Ground Maintenance Operation (WIGMO), a CIA front organization based in Liechtenstein. Although the CIA was strictly prohibited from employing US pilots to fly combat missions, this rule frequently was broken until successfuly contested by the State Department in the aftermath of leaks to the press.[60] CIA efforts were buttressed by the Pentagon's establishment of a US military mission in Zaire in fall 1963, as well as the arrival in spring 1964 of three mobile training teams (MTTs) and approximately seventy technicians to offer guidance in counterinsurgency tactics against the guerrillas.

The Kennedy White House's decision to move away from the Africanist coalition's ideal of fostering a moderate coalition regime in favor of the hardliners' preference for a military strongman capable of maintaining stability constituted an important aspect of growing US involvement in the paramilitary war. The obvious recipient of increasing US attention was the Zairian military under the leadership of the CIA-cultivated and pro-Western Mobutu. Apparently uneasy with the central government's ability to stem the guerrilla insurgency, the US in October 1963 accepted a "military promoted government reorganization" that effectively deprived Adoula of "all but formal power" and eventually led to his resignation.[61] Rather than attempting to pressure the ruling committee into seeking the return of the formerly US–supported Adoula, however, Washington instead gave its official support to the designation of Tshombe as the new Prime Minister of Zaire.

The addition of Tshombe to the central government created a bureaucratic rift within the US policymaking establishment which further revealed the declining fortunes of the Africanist coalition in favor of the more hardline views advanced by the CIA and the Pentagon. The Africanist coalition firmly opposed Tshombe's appointment. The concern of this group was that Tshombe's highly unpopular image within Africa would further delegitimize the Mobutu regime and cast a shadow over the Kennedy administration's policy of cultivating African nationalists. From the paramilitary perspectives of both the CIA and the Pentagon, the addition of Tshombe to the central government was a masterstroke – not only did he control battle-tested mercenary forces which could be brought to bear on the guerrilla insurgency, he carried anti-communist credentials that were crucial for generating support among conservatives in the US and Belgium. It was these two latter arguments which curried favor with a White House wearied with continuous instability in Zaire and desirous of a solution that, once and for all, would prevent any possibility of a radical central government aligned with the Soviet Union.[62]

The rising preeminence of those who were calling for a more hardline approach was solidified by Kennedy's assassination in November 1963 and replacement by his more conservative Vice President, Lyndon B. Johnson. Johnson's assumption of the presidency heralded a realignment of bureaucratic forces in which the Africanists were either replaced or bypassed within the decisionmaking chain of command. Ambassador Gullion was replaced in February 1964 by G. McMurtrie Godley, a career FSO who was more sensitive to Belgian wishes and less enamored of the importance of African nationalism.

69

Back in Washington, Under Secretary of State for Political Affairs W. Averell Harriman, who also downplayed the importance of African nationalism, became the lead person in the State Department for US Zairian policy. This appointment underscored the *de facto* demotion of Williams and other members of the Africanist coalition at the State Department who continued to advocate greater alignment of US policy with the aims of African nationalism.

Despite the significant escalation of the US paramilitary effort during the previous fourteen months, the US–Zairian relationship did not receive sustained high-level attention until the guerrilla insurgency reached regime-threatening proportions. The turning point in the perception of crisis at the level of the White House occurred on August 4, 1964, when the provincial capital of Kisangani fell to the insurgents. At this point in time, disparate groups of guerrilla armies successfully had eliminated central government control over as much as 50 percent of Zairian territory. To make matters worse, the fall of Kisangani also led to the imprisonment of a five-person US consular staff – four of whom reportedly constituted a CIA team.[63] The growing sense of crisis in Washington over the deterioration of the military situation clearly was portrayed in a cable sent by Secretary of State Dean Rusk to the Belgian government two days after Kisangani's fall: "It is our judgement that events in the Congo have reached so critical a point that you and we and all our European friends must move immediately and vigorously to prevent total collapse." Rusk further noted that deterioration of the situation was "so rapid" that the central government could be gone in the "next several weeks."[64]

Despite a significant degree of White House concern over the deterioration of the military situation, two political issues – growing US military involvement in Indochina and the 1964 presidential elections – tempered the willingness of the Johnson administration to take military action consistent with its worldview. On the same day that Kisangani fell, Johnson ordered carrier-based air strikes against North Vietnam in retaliation for a confrontation that had taken place between the USS *Maddox* and North Vietnamese torpedo boats. Several days later, Johnson used this and other North Vietnamese "provocations" as the pretext for seeking congressional approval of the Gulf of Tonkin Resolution – an act which, in the absence of a formal declaration of war, was used by the White House to commit combat troops to the defense of South Vietnam. With 16,000 US military personnel already stationed in South Vietnam, the White House was becoming preoccupied with expanding US military involvement in Indochina.

Of equal or even greater importance to White House strategists were the potentially disastrous political effects that another US military engagement – only this time in Central Africa – could have on Johnson's chances of winning the presidential elections in three months. Hoping to avoid the political fall-out that could accompany either doing nothing or taking drastic action, Johnson opted for a politically safe middle-of-the-road policy designed to upset the fewest people in an election year and keep US involvement off the front pages of national newspapers. The essential thrusts of this policy were the escalation of the US-backed paramilitary war while at the same time pressuring Belgium to take the lead in committing its military forces to the counterinsurgency effort.[65]

The CIA and the Pentagon once again were directed by the White House to coordinate the escalation of the paramilitary war. During the month of August, the Defense Department shipped a variety of arms, jeeps, light tanks, and, most important, five B-26 bombers which were flown by CIA-commissioned Cuban exiles. The growing role of the Defense Department especially was signaled by the arrival of four C-130 transport planes. These planes were flown by fifty US crew members and guarded by an elite unit of fifty-six paratroopers from Fort Bragg, North Carolina.[66]

The second cornerstone of the Johnson administration's paramilitary strategy was to pressure Belgium into assuming a more direct military role. This stance reflected the traditional White House proclivity to put the former colonial power "out front" when confronted with a crisis situation. To the chagrin of US policymakers, this strategy was rebuffed by Belgian Foreign Minister Spaak, who explained that the Belgians did not completely share Washington's ideological concerns.[67] The Belgian government was willing, however, to support the US fall-back position: white mercenary forces, organized by Belgian Colonel Frédéric Vandewalle and a limited number of Belgian staff officers, would be recruited to lead selected divisions of Zairian troops in the counterinsurgency campaign.

The decision to rely on white mercenaries, particularly those from South Africa and Southern Rhodesia, stirred quite a debate within the Johnson administration and further reflected the declining fortunes of the Africanist coalition. For example, Williams preferred to avoid the use of mercenaries altogether by relying on the creation of an expeditionary force composed from the armed forces of moderate African regimes. Even Godley, who voiced no objection to the use of mercenaries, preferred to avoid reliance on those of South African or Southern Rhodesian nationalities. These preferences reflected the

Africa Bureau's desire to avoid any action that ran counter to African opinion and risked tarnishing the US image in Africa. In stark contrast to these political concerns, the CIA and the Pentagon perceived the white mercenaries as battle-tested forces who could be relied upon to get the job done quickly.[68] As long as the insurgency could be contained through a low-key paramilitary campaign, the White House deferred to CIA and Pentagon arguments for the gradual enhancement of US involvement.

Events once again intervened to push the issue of direct US military intervention in Zaire before the President and his closest foreign policy advisers. On September 4, 1964, PLA military leader Nicolas Olenga announced that his forces were holding 500 expatriate whites hostage as insurance against any further government air strikes against PLA positions. Fearful of the fate awaiting the approximately twenty-five US citizens (five Embassy personnel and roughly twenty missionaries) who were being held hostage, Harriman that same day requested Under Secretary of Defense Cyrus Vance to oversee the development of a military rescue plan. The result was Operation Golden Hawk, a covert military plan which received the strong approval of the Joint Chiefs of Staff.[69]

Like others that had been or would be proposed, the rescue operation was put on hold. Although the reasons for White House hesitation remain unclear, one obvious concern had to be the political consequences that a failed operation would exert on the upcoming presidential elections that were less than two months away. White House officials were also concerned with the growing criticism of administration policies by members of Johnson's own party in Congress, such as Senator John Stennis (D-Mississippi), who questioned whether Zaire might become another Vietnam.[70] To make matters worse, Olenga ordered his troops on October 7 to execute one foreigner for each Zairian who was killed due to air attacks against PLA-controlled territory. Over the objections of Harriman and Godley, as well as officials at the CIA and the Pentagon, Rusk on October 15 ordered the grounding of the US-supplied T-28s and B-26s until agreement was reached with Tshombe that no further air attacks would be made against guerrilla-held cities.[71] The last thing Johnson desired less than three weeks before the elections was the execution of US citizens in which the White House, fully aware of Belgian unwillingness to become more greatly involved, would be faced with the delicate question of direct military intervention.

The unwillingness of the White House to consider the option of direct military intervention significantly changed once it became clear in October 1964 that Belgium was willing to take the military lead if supported by Washington. The reason for Belgium's newfound interest in direct military intervention was an altered political situation in Zaire which clearly threatened Belgian nationals and economic interests. As the Belgian-led mercenary forces were making steady headway against the disorganized and isolated PLA guerrilla forces, an increasingly desperate Gbenye warned in a cable to Belgian King Badouin that he could "no longer guarantee the security of Belgian subjects and their properties." The following day, the Belgian Consul in Kisangani cabled home under obvious duress that nearly 300 Belgians in the city were under "house arrest" and that their safety depended on the cessation of Belgian involvement with the mercenary effort. These words took on concrete meaning on November 2 when PLA guerrillas executed three Belgians just before mercenary forces entered the Zairian town of Kibombo. The following day, these same mercenary forces were able to rescue approximately 100 white captives, including twenty-four Belgian men who had been stripped in preparation for execution.[72]

With mercenary columns converging on the PLA stronghold of Kisangani, Spaak arrived in Washington on November 8 to discuss a joint US–Belgian military operation if negotiations failed to win the release of the hostages. The key outlines of the proposed plan, which fostered a lively bureaucratic debate within the US policymaking establishment, were that US-piloted transport planes would drop Belgian paratroopers on Kisangani at the same time that ground-based mercenary columns entered the city. Foreseeing the violent eruption of anti-US protests that ultimately did follow execution of the operation, the Africa Bureau opposed direct military intervention. The Bureau of International Organization Affairs, whose most outspoken member was Stevenson, voiced similar concerns over the inevitable "charges of imperialism" at the UN. Dissenting voices were drowned out by the pro-interventionist stances of the CIA, the Pentagon, and Johnson's two closest advisers at the State Department, Harriman and Rusk.[73]

With the November presidential elections securely behind the victorious Johnson and the Belgians now willing to take the military lead, Operation Red Dragon was authorized by the White House and launched on November 24, 1964. The operation consisted of twelve US-piloted C-130s dropping 545 Belgian paratroopers on the Kisangani airport where, along with their equipment, they fanned out to rescue the hostages being held throughout the city. On November 26, in a secondary military attack entitled Operation Black Dragon, four

US-piloted C-130s dropped 255 paratroopers over the airfield at Paulis (a town currently named Isiro that is northeast of Kisangani) where they again fanned out with their equipment to rescue hostages being held in town.[74] Although the US–Belgian military operation was successful in rescuing over 2,000 hostages and was credited with breaking the psychological back of the guerrilla insurgency, the negative side of the operation was the execution of at least 185 white hostages and thousands of Zairians, as well as violent demonstrations against the US and Belgium throughout the world.[75]

This third period of US intervention in Zairian domestic politics nicely demonstrated the incremental growth of US involvement once a policy path had been set by the White House. In the aftermath of Mobutu's visit to the White House in May 1963 which implicitly revealed his centrality to the future of US–Zairian relations, US policy moved away from support for a civilian-based coalition to one based on a strong military leader able to maintain stability. As a result, when the Zairian government was faced with a rapidly growing guerrilla insurgency, the White House deferred to CIA and Pentagon arguments to expand paramilitary efforts designed to bolster the Mobutu–Tshombe government. When the conflict reached crisis proportions, however, the White House rejected CIA and Pentagon pressures for direct military involvement due to political considerations connected with the 1964 presidential election and the Vietnam War, as well as Belgium's strong opposition to direct military involvement. In this regard, the White House reaction demonstrated that political motivations, as opposed to an administration's worldview, could serve as the crucial ingredient in presidential decisionmaking even during crisis periods. Yet once one political ingredient – the 1964 elections – was resolved and, most important, the Belgians agreed to take the military lead, the White House supported direct US military involvement in Zaire.

The continuing search for stability (December 1964–December 1967)

Once the immediate crisis of rescuing Western hostages and preventing the defeat of the Zairian central government had been resolved by the joint US–Belgian military operation in 1964, the White House diverted its attention to areas of more pressing concern – most notably growing US military involvement in Indochina – and directed the national security bureaucracies to resolve the ongoing problem of defeating disparate groups of insurgents who still controlled portions of the Zairian countryside. The CIA's growing central role in promoting the stability of the Zairian central government ensured that this bureaucracy, and particularly its Africa Division, emerged as the primary bureaucratic player in determining US policy toward Zaire. In a report written in the immediate aftermath of Operation Red Dragon, CIA analysts offered numerous rationales as to why the paramilitary war needed to be expanded, such as the absence of "competent" Zairian military forces and administrative officials, as well as the continuation of Soviet-bloc arms shipments to scattered elements of guerrilla armies.[76] Among the key elements of what became an expanded, and very successful, paramilitary war were the continued loan of eight US-piloted C-130s which had arrived in August 1964, and the delivery of two additional T-28 fighters and at least three additional B-26 bombers.

An irony of the success of the CIA-sponsored paramilitary war in contributing to political stability in Zaire is that it paved the way for a growing power struggle between Kasavubu and Tshombe, both of whom aspired to the presidency. The struggle between the two leaders began to intensify when, in the aftermath of Tshombe's formation in February 1965 of his own national political party – the National Confederation of the Congo (CONACO) – he began posing a threat to Kasavubu's reelection bid by achieving majority victories in national and provincial legislative elections held during March and April. In response, Kasavubu illegally sought to stymie Tshombe's use of his legislative victories as a stepping-stone to the presidency by annulling election results in four provinces and refusing to convene parliament.[77]

The political paralysis caused by the power struggle at the highest reaches of the Zairian government contributed to a bureaucratic rift between the State Department and the CIA. According to the State Department, the best hope for achieving long-term stability in Zaire was maintenance of the Kasavubu–Tshombe alliance, while at the same time strengthening Mobutu's role as a behind-the-scenes player. "Unless they [Kasavubu and Tshombe] stick together," explained National Security Adviser McGeorge Bundy in an internal memorandum to Johnson which summarized the position of the State Department, "the Congo will split as it did when Tshombe went it alone in Katanga."[78] The CIA instead favored a "strongman" approach to the situation. According to this policy approach, the best way of handling the unending squabbling among the politicians was to replace the civilian regime with one central figure who commanded the respect of the military. Of greatest concern to the CIA was that several thousand guerrillas still operating on Zaire's northeastern border along Lake Tanganyika could provide the basis for renewed rebellion throughout the country. "Unless the political leaders turn their attention from infighting to solving the problems which caused the rebellion in the first place," warned a CIA intelligence report focusing on the Kasavubu–Tshombe rift, "the now relatively dormant insurrection may eventually reawaken."[79]

Rather than heeding the strong recommendations of both the State Department and the CIA to work for national unity, Kasavubu succeeded in dismissing Tshombe and replacing him with Evariste Kimba, a former representative of Shaba province to the UN and a perceived sympathizer of radical political forces in Zaire.[80] In a chain of events reminiscent of when Kasavubu dismissed Lumumba in 1960, Tshombe, like his predecessor, rallied his legislative supporters and created a political deadlock in the Zairian political system by arranging a vote of no confidence against the Kasavubu–Kimbe government.[81] This deadlock ended on November 24 when Mobutu – allegedly with the blessing and support of the CIA – dismissed all politicians in his second major military intervention against the Zairian civilian leadership since 1960.[82] In the culmination of a trend, beginning with his recruitment by the CIA in 1959 and significantly aided by a meeting with Kennedy in May 1963, Mobutu announced his intention to retain control of the government for a period of five years, at which time elections were to be held.

According to his supporters within the national security bureaucracies, Mobutu's actions during the next year-and-a-half constituted exactly the kind of rule that was necessary to bring stability to Zaire and ensure against communist inroads in Central Africa. Suspending all political activity and harshly dealing with continued pockets of resistance throughout the country, Mobutu also cultivated neighboring states which had aided anti-government guerrilla insurgencies. One measure of this strategy's success from the perspective of the CIA was a significant decline in the need for CIA-sponsored counter-insurgency activities by the middle of 1967.[83] As summarized in a CIA intelligence report written in June 1967: "Although the Congo still faces hard times, its future looks brighter at present than at any time since independence." The report concluded that "a great deal of the credit" for this progress was due to Mobutu who, "with careful and skillful exercise of power, plus an unusual amount of luck, has brought the Congo to its present pacified position."[84]

The CIA's highly favorable perception of Mobutu's handling of his new position as head of state was shared throughout the national security bureaucracies. However, State Department officials were naturally more conscious than their CIA counterparts of Mobutu's and, by association, Washington's image in Africa as a result of his politico-military policies. Although pleased by Mobutu's decision to phase out the employment of South African and Southern Rhodesian mercenaries originally hired by Tshombe (a source of contention with many African states), the State Department exerted intense pressure (to no avail) to halt the execution of Kimba and three ex-ministers for their alleged role in the so-called "Pentacost Plot" to overthrow Mobutu. In fact, the State Department often sought to restrain what it considered to be Mobutu's ill-conceived domestic and foreign policy initiatives.[85] One result of these continued pressures was Mobutu's angry demand for Ambassador Godley's recall. The State Department quietly acquiesced by bringing Godley back to Washington for indefinite consultations in October 1966, replacing him eight months later with Robert H. McBride, a career FSO more sensitive to Mobutu's new status as head of state.

A low-level crisis event in 1967 once again pushed the issue of US–Zairian relations to the level of the White House and confronted Johnson with the delicate subject of direct US military intervention. On July 5, approximately 160 white mercenaries and over 1,500 Shaban troops loyal to Tshombe mutinied and seized several eastern cities, including Kisangani and Bukavu. Although obviously due to a variety of factors, not least of which was Mobutu's failure to provide timely payment of salaries, the trigger of the uprising was the kidnapping of Tshombe to Algiers, Algeria, where he awaited extradition to Zaire and almost certain death.[86] (Tshombe three months earlier had been sentenced to death in absentia in Zaire under the orders of Mobutu.) Unable to trust the pro-Tshombe mercenary pilots who flew Zairian planes and fearful that the rebellion, unless quickly contained, could spread and threaten his rule, Mobutu made an "urgent" request to Washington for three C-130 aircraft and accompanying pilots to transport Zairian forces and matériel into the interior.[87]

In a notable departure from the bureaucratic infighting that surrounded the 1964 decision to intervene in Zaire, the national security bureaucracies unanimously agreed on July 6 to recommend that Johnson accede to Mobutu's request.[88] In contrast to its negative vote in 1964, the primary bureaucratic proponent of this interventionist course was the State Department's Africa Bureau. Always mindful of African opinion and harboring a deep distrust for Tshombe's mercenary forces, the Africa Bureau argued that quick support for an African government besieged by foreign-supported, white mercenaries would bolster the US image among African countries. This argument was bolstered by the State Department's Bureau of International Organization Affairs which claimed that expeditious action would preempt Third World claims of "Western imperialism" in the UN Security Council. Mindful of Belgium's tacit support of US actions despite domestic constraints limiting its own involvement, the European Bureau noted that US action could prevent the spread of anti-white propaganda in Zaire which inevitably would be injurious to both Europe and the United States. Even those bureaucracies less concerned with African opinion also supported US intervention, although for slightly different reasons. For example, the CIA was concerned with reassuring Mobutu that his CIA link was secure. The Joint Chiefs of Staff, who raised no objection, perceived the operation as a limited military action consistent with past US air support for the Zairian regime.

What bureaucratic deliberations failed to contemplate (or at least miscalculated) was the congressional uproar that accompanied the limited military action. On July 10, the day after Johnson announced the departure of three C-130 transport planes and a contingent of 150 US soldiers, Senator Richard Russell (D-Georgia), chairperson of the Senate Armed Forces Committee, attacked the administration's policy as an "immoral" and "unjustified" intervention in a "local disturbance." Russell's concerns were echoed that very day by other ranking members of the Democratic Party, including J. William Fulbright (D-Arizona), chairperson of the Senate Foreign Relations Committee, and Senate Majority Leader Mike Mansfield (D-Montana), as well as by thirteen Republican Senators, including Strom Thurmond (R-South Carolina) and Howard H. Baker, Jr. (R-Tennessee), who cosponsored a letter to Johnson expressing "strong disapproval" of administration actions and urging an immediate withdrawal of US aircraft and personnel.[89]

The primary motivation behind congressional disapproval of administration policy was the fear that military involvement in an area of little or no vital interest to the US could lead to another Vietnam, a conflict which by July 1967 was costing the lives of nearly 1,000 US soldiers a month. "We do not want another war in Africa," explained Representative Robert L. F. Sikes (D-Florida) in a speech before the House. "It was a token intervention, much like the one in the Congo, which led to full-scale involvement in Vietnam."[90] Still other members of Congress, especially conservative Senators, felt that the mercenary uprising was a self-inflicted wound caused by Mobutu's irresponsible attempts at physically eliminating Tshombe. "It is only natural that

Mobutu's drive to get custody of Tshombe and execute him should arouse resentment and rebellion among his supporters in that land," noted Senator Thurmond in a strong attack on administration policy, "Indeed, it should arouse indignation in the United States, for Tshombe has proved himself to be an ardent friend of America."[91]

Although Johnson reportedly was "furious" at being unfairly "blindsided" by Congress and later sought to soothe congressional disapproval by issuing an order renouncing any similar military adventures in other African countries,[92] the congressional uproar in reality had little impact on the administration's handling of the mercenary uprising. Rather, the US response demonstrated how, even during short-term crises when an issue attracted the attention of a significant number of congresspersons, control of the policymaking process naturally flowed to the President and the bureaucracies of the executive branch. For example, the State Department ordered the withdrawal of two of the three C-130s (one each on July 26 and August 3) only after it became clear that Mobutu was securely in control of the situation and that the mercenaries were merely seeking a way out of Zaire.[93] Although it is probable that, in the absence of congressional pressure, the administration would have kept these two planes in Zaire for a longer period of time, their usefulness had been superceded by events. The administration's dominance of the foreign policy agenda in this case was further underscored by the fact that the final C-130 was not withdrawn until early December 1967. The State Department authorized the departure of this last plane only after all rebellious troops had retreated to the neighboring country of Rwanda and were under the custody of an OAU-organized commission of African magistrates.[94]

The conclusion of this five-month military operation was significant in three major respects for the evolution of the US–Zairian special relationship. First, it marked the end of approximately seven years of post-independence instability which had made Zaire a superpower flashpoint in the emerging Cold War competition for ideological supremacy in Africa. Second, the military operation marked the strengthening of a consensus throughout the national security bureaucracies that Mobutu was "our man" in Kinshasa and that each bureaucracy should focus on enhancing his ability to maintain stability in Zaire.[95] This feeling was reciprocated by Mobutu who came to view the US as the only external power he "historically" could count upon to come to Zaire's aid during times of crisis.[96] "There is a saying in my country," noted Mobutu during one of his many trips to the US, "that it is in times of need that you know your friends and, indeed, the United States has stood by us and we shall never forget."[97] Finally, the military operation demonstrated that the US would act unilaterally if Belgium was unwilling or unable to fulfill what Washington perceived as that country's historic responsibility for maintaining stability in the region. Whereas in the 1960 crisis it was Belgium which took the lead in militarily intervening in Zaire, and in 1964 the US played a supporting role in which Belgian troops once again assumed a preeminent position, by 1967 it was the US which had assumed primary responsibility for organizing a military response to the mercenary uprising. Despite the larger number of Belgians who continued to live and work in Zaire, the US by the end of 1967 had assumed the position of midwife and preeminent external ally of the Mobutu regime.

Stability and bureaucratic incrementalism (January 1968–March 1974)

The drift of White House attention away from the US–Zairian special relationship and toward other, more pressing, issues was the inevitable result of Zaire's final achievement of post-independence stability in 1968. In contrast to the 1960–67 period in which Eisenhower, Kennedy, and Johnson interjected themselves into the policymaking process as a result of intermittent crises, the lack of crisis in the post-1967 period reinforced the traditional White House proclivity to defer African issues to the Africa specialists within the State Department, the Pentagon, and the CIA. As a result, the next seven years were marked by the process of bureaucratic incrementalism in which a consensus shared within the national security bureaucracies underscored the necessity of maintaining or enhancing US–Zairian ties in accordance with established policies. A critical element of this consensus was the firm belief that "chaos" – meaning territorial disintegration, regional instability, and ultimately communist expansion into Central Africa – was the only alternative to Mobutu's continued hold over power.[98]

Preoccupied with the growing war in Vietnam during the late 1960s and early 1970s, the Defense Department constituted that portion of the national security bureaucracies which was the least supportive of significantly enhancing US ties with the Mobutu regime. Already providing Zaire with one of the largest US Military Assistance Advisory Group (MAAG) Missions in Africa, as well as two in-country military attachés (Army and Air Force), the basic position of the Defense Department was to meet what it perceived as Zaire's minimum security needs by maintaining small, but effective, military programs. For example, an annual $3–4 million was budgeted for the training of

Zairian military personnel through the International Military Education and Training (IMET) program. One notable exception to the Defense Department's conservative position on the issue of military assistance was strong support for Zaire's purchase of six C-130s (three each in 1970 and 1973), the maintenance of which would be handled as part of the US military aid program.[99]

The CIA served as a more enthusiastic bureaucratic proponent for enhancing the US–Zairian special relationship. Among the many responsibilities shouldered by the CIA during the early 1970s were the training of Mobutu's personal bodyguard and providing him with intelligence related to political developments internal and external to Zaire. Mobutu not only constituted a valued anti-communist ally in the eyes of the CIA, but also served as an important conduit to the FNLA – the Angolan guerrilla faction headed by Holden Roberto with which the CIA had maintained links from its Kinshasa station since as early as 1961.[100] The CIA perceived Zaire as a growing regional power which increasingly would play an influential independent role in maintaining stability in Central Africa. Already strong CIA links with Mobutu were further enhanced by the return to Zaire of Devlin, former CIA Chief of Station in Kinshasa. An old and trusted friend of Mobutu, Devlin took up duty as the local representative of Maurice Templesman, a powerful US businessperson with significant economic investments in Zaire.[101]

The most vigorous proponent of greater links between the US and Zaire was the State Department's Africa Bureau, especially its representative in Kinshasa, Ambassador Sheldon B. Vance. A career FSO who had served in Belgium and was the former director of the Africa Bureau's Office of Central African Affairs, Vance was responsible for the expansion of US activities in Zaire from 1969 to 1974. Vance notes in his memoirs, for example, that his primary task upon arriving in Zaire in June 1969 was to change the outmoded perception within the US policymaking establishment that Zaire was "synonymous with chaos."[102] Among Vance's numerous and varied accomplishments toward this end were the creation of a Peace Corps program that eventually would become one of the largest in Africa; the promotion of a public relations bonanza in which the crew of Apollo 11 visited Zaire shortly after returning to earth; and the fashioning of a White House visit built around the theme of foreign investment which resulted in several prominent US companies establishing facilities in Zaire.

Vance's strong advocacy of enhancing the US–Zairian special relationship was indicative of Zaire's image within the State Department's Africa Bureau as a country which would serve as a "showcase" for US efforts in Africa.[103] Several economic and political trends clearly seemed to indicate that Zaire was entering a "golden age" of prosperity unlike many of its less fortunate or mismanaged neighbors. In the economic realm, revenues from copper exports were at an all time high, a 1967 International Monetary Fund (IMF) economic reform package succeeded in bringing inflation under control, foreign exchange accounts were in balance, and the country enjoyed a favorable balance of trade. Economic growth and development were further enhanced by growing numbers of Zairian students who were returning home from overseas university training to staff ministry positions in ever-expanding administrative bureaucracies. Finally, in the equally important political realm, presidential and legislative elections in 1970 (as promised in 1965) led to impressive political victories which seemed to underscore genuine popular support for Mobutu's leadership among the Zairian people.[104]

However, the incrementally growing US–Zairian special relationship was not without conflict. Eager to assert Zaire's potential as one of the leading powers on the African continent, while at the same time mollifying domestic and regional critics who denounced him as a puppet of the US, Mobutu adopted a more independent stance that often conflicted with advice from Washington. The best example of Mobutu's desire to demonstrate his independence from Washington – which earned him both the attention and disdain of Secretary of State Kissinger – was a UN speech in which he publicly ruptured Zairian diplomatic relations with Israel and pledged Zairian identification with Arab causes.[105] The anti-Israeli tone of Mobutu's speech disturbed Kissinger not only because it represented a public denunciation of US policy in a region of special White House concern, but also because no warning had been given that he was planning on making such a bold announcement. Aware that the State Department was seeking to guide a Zairian aid package through an intransigent Congress which surely would not look favorably upon Mobutu's hostile act toward Israel, Kissinger, in a private meeting with Mobutu, is said to have sarcastically made clear his distaste for the Zairian President's actions: "Well, Mr. President, you certainly know how to reach the American people."[106]

A revealing aspect of the UN incident was that it in no way jeopardized Mobutu's relationship with Washington, or even a scheduled White House meeting with Nixon. The rationale provided by the State Department's Africa Bureau, that bureaucratic entity which was the most involved with issues concerning Zaire on a day-to-day basis, was that Mobutu's growing independence was an inevitable, and perhaps necessary, outgrowth of Zaire's increasing status in Africa. Sympathetic to Mobutu's desire to be accepted as a legitimate African nationalist and to disclaim the more objectionable aspects of his close relationship with Washington, the Africa Bureau and other portions of the policymaking establishment were willing to tolerate actions which in the past may have been considered to be more objectionable. "Despite some reservations concerning the nature of Mobutu's rule, as well as minor disagreement over what form a future US–Zairian relationship should take," noted Assistant Secretary of State for African Affairs David Newsom, "a consensus existed within the policymaking establishment that there simply was no acceptable alternative to Mobutu and that we, as the United States, needed to support him."[107] As a result, US policy from 1968 to 1974 was marked by the process of bureaucratic incrementalism in which parochial bureaucratic interpretations of US interests contributed to upward pressures for the strengthening of US–Zairian ties in accordance with established policies.

Tension and cooperation in the face of growing regional crisis (April 1974–January 1977)

The US–Zairian special relationship underwent a period of both growing tension and cooperation during 1974 and 1975. Rising tension partially resulted from the State Department's negative assessment of Mobutu's handling of the Zairian economy. Already under stress due to an ill-managed "Zairianization" campaign of 1973 in which several thousand small businesses owned by Greeks, Portuguese, Arabs, and Indians were nationalized and turned over to Zairian citizens, the economy was subjected to further pressures in November 1974 when Mobutu ordered the nationalization of numerous large firms throughout the country, most notably in the transportation and construction industries. The dislocations caused by these economic decisions were compounded in 1974 and 1975 by a more than 50 percent decline in the price of copper (the country's main export and primary source of foreign currency), the rapid growth in oil prices, and the growing levels of corruption within the Zairian government.[108] Faced with the potential collapse of the Zairian economy, Mobutu turned to Washington for greater levels of economic aid. Much to his chagrin, the State Department responded contrary to Mobutu's expectations by noting that a significant portion of Zaire's economic problems stemmed from wrong-headed economic policies that required reform rather than US dollars. Although the State Department was willing to facilitate Zaire's access to loan relief, Mobutu was informed by Deane R. Hinton, the new US Ambassador to Zaire as of August 1974, that he could not expect the US to "bail him out" of his economic difficulties.[109]

The tension evident in Mobutu's relationship with the State Department was in direct contrast to his growing cooperation with the CIA. The basis of this cooperation was a shared desire to dictate the political make-up of the soon-to-be-independent Angolan government. As discussed in Chapter 2, a successful *coup d'état* on April 24, 1974, overthrew the Portuguese regime of Marcello Caetano and signaled the beginning of the end of Portuguese colonialism in Africa, including Zaire's southwestern neighbor, Angola. The dilemma posed by Angolan independence, according to the perspectives of both Mobutu and the CIA, was that the Soviet-backed MPLA guerrilla group headed by Agostinho Neto, already in control of the major urban areas (including the capital city of Luanda), would politically dominate an independent Angola at the expense of the Zairian and Chinese-backed FNLA forces of Roberto and the South African and Chinese-backed UNITA group headed by Jonas Savimbi. Both the CIA and Mobutu perceived an MPLA-dominated Angolan government as a willing Soviet tool for destabilizing southern and central Africa, most notably Zaire.

Five months prior to receiving official authorization from the 40 Committee, the CIA during July 1974 began delivering small amounts of covert aid to Roberto's FNLA guerrilla forces through its Kinshasa station in Zaire. According to John Stockwell, the CIA chief of the Angola Task Force who managed the US covert operation to assist the FNLA, this initial act was designed to get the "word out" that the CIA was "dealing itself into the race" for Angolan independence.[110] The bureaucratic routines of the CIA and the nature of the US–Zairian special relationship were critical in influencing the outlines of a covert operation that eventually would cost more than $30 million in transfered weapons and other matériel, and entail the dispatch of eighty-three CIA officers to CIA posts in Lusaka (Zambia), Kinshasa, Pretoria (South Africa), and Luanda. For example, due to bureaucratic routines which emphasized cooperation with European security services on the African continent, the Portuguese *coup d'état* caught the CIA completely by surprise and almost entirely out of touch with the various guerrilla groups in Angola. (In deference to Portuguese demands for non-interference in its African colonies, the question of opening a Luanda station had been vetoed every time the topic arose within the CIA.)[111] The lack of CIA operatives within Angola forced the CIA to rely upon the often self-serving intelligence gathered by the Zairian security services and their favored client, Roberto, who maintained his headquarters in Kinshasa. According to Brenda MacElhinney, the CIA's Angola Desk Officer in 1974, it was only this historic relationship with Roberto via Mobutu that led the CIA to support the FNLA – despite convincing arguments by some portions of the State Department that the MPLA not only was the best qualified to run Angola, but that their leaders wanted a peaceful relationship with the United States.[112]

The contradictory nature of growing tension and cooperation in the US–Zairian relationship frustrated Mobutu who correctly perceived one portion of the national security bureaucracies as eagerly seeking Zaire's cooperation to stem Soviet advances in Africa, while another seemingly was unwilling to do little more than "deliver a lecture" concerning Zaire's growing economic problems.[113] This, from Mobutu's perspective, stemmed from the lack of high-level attention and coordination of the US–Zairian relationship. In an effort to shock the White House into reassessing the value of US–Zairian ties and making policy more consistent throughout the executive branch, Mobutu on June 19, 1975, accused Washington of plotting his overthrow, declared Ambassador Hinton persona non grata, and arrested the majority of the CIA's contract Zairian agents.[114]

Mobutu's sense of timing in this incident was excellent. In light of the intensification of hostilities between Angola's three guerrilla groups since March 1975 and a Soviet decision to resupply the MPLA with large deliveries of military weaponry, White House attention was focused squarely on preventing an MPLA victory in Angola. Rather than privately expressing displeasure with Mobutu's actions and then moving on to issues of greater concern (as was the case in October 1973 and January 1975), Ford and Kissinger quickly sought to repair the breach with Mobutu. Former Ambassador Vance and the new Ambassador-Designate, Walter Cutler, immediately were ordered to fly to Kinshasa. In the case of Vance, "immediately" meant that he missed his son's wedding on June 21.[115] Arriving in Kinshasa on June 21, just hours after Hinton had departed, their primary mission was to reassure Mobutu of the strength of US–Zairian ties and that the US was not plotting his overthrow. According to Cutler, it was the Angolan situation which was determining White House directives related to Zaire: "It wouldn't have been such a critical situation," explained Cutler, "had the Angolan situation not been evolving so quickly."[116]

Although the Angolan operation ultimately resulted in failure for the Zairian and US-backed guerrilla forces, Mobutu had been successful in forcing a favorable reassessment of US–Zairian ties at the level of the White House. As of 1975, Kissinger actively pressed the national security bureaucracies to pay greater attention to Zaire and began to underscore that country's strategic importance within the regional framework of US Africa policies. Among the evidence of this growing recognition of Mobutu's importance were Kissinger's directive in 1975 to grant Zaire $60 million in Security Supporting Assistance for 1976 (none had been allocated since 1969); a significant rise in military aid from $3.8 million in 1975 to $30.4 million in 1977; and a White House decision to equip Zaire with much more sophisticated weaponry (including 150 armored cars and tanks) to counter a possible Soviet threat from Angola. This increase in military aid, making Zaire the largest recipient of US security assistance in sub-Saharan Africa in 1976, was capped by two visits by Kissinger in April and October 1976.[117]

This analysis of the 1974–77 period nicely demonstrated how a crisis situation not only prompted the White House to critically examine and review the nature and goals of US foreign policy toward a particular African country, but also how such an event served as a natural opportunity for the White House to make the parochial policies of individual bureaucracies more consistent with each other, as well as that administration's worldview. Underscoring the theme that Presidents and their closest advisers traditionally have ignored Africa relative to other regions of perceived greater strategic importance, Newsom confirmed that Kissinger prior to 1975 saw little strategic importance in that portion of Africa lying between the Zambezi River and the southern border of Morocco, Algeria, Libya, and Ethiopia.[118] As a result, Zaire was ignored as a corrupt African country of little consequence to the overall balance of East–West relations. It is for this reason that Mobutu correctly observed the fragmentation of US foreign policy toward Zaire as each of the national security bureaucracies differently interpreted the proper course of US–Zairian relations, leading to conflict with the State Department at the same time that the CIA was seeking closer cooperation with Zaire. Yet once Kissinger perceived the unfolding of an East–West crisis in Angola that threatened to lead to the establishment of a communist, pro-Soviet regime in Central Africa and upset the global balance of power between the US and the Soviet Union, Zaire suddenly was recognized as a regional pillar of US Africa policies. As one analyst noted, "It was as if a map of that part of the world had come alive."[119] As a result, the conflictual side of the US–Zairian relationship was downplayed as Kissinger specifically ordered each of the national security bureaucracies to pursue policies designed to strengthen Mobutu's role as a regional bulwark for US policies in Central Africa. The most obvious impacts of this directive were an end to State Department criticism of Mobutu's handling of the economy, as well as the strengthening of the historic US–Zairian special relationship throughout the remaining months of the Ford administration.

Crisis and reassessment of the special relationship (January 1977–April 1978)

On March 7, 1977, less than seven weeks after President Carter's inauguration, approximately 1,500 Zairian exiles under the banner of the Front for the National Liberation of the Congo (FLNC) invaded Zaire's Shaba province from neighboring Angola.[120] With the publicly stated goal of overthrowing the Mobutu regime, the FLNC advanced virtually unopposed and threatened to capture the mining center of Kolwezi, the source of nearly 75 percent of Zaire's foreign export earnings. The so-called "Shaba I crisis" quickly became the focus of the highest reaches of the Carter administration due to its regime threatening nature, origins in Marxist-ruled Angola, and the possibility that the insurgents were being accompanied by Cuban advisers and troops.[121]

As the first foreign policy crisis faced by the Carter White House, the Shaba I invasion demonstrated the importance of an administration's worldview in significantly altering an entrenched US relationship with an African country. As discussed in Chapter 2, the Carter administration entered office speaking of the need to transcend traditional preoccupations with anti-communism and containment of the Soviet Union, in favor of more positive goals, such as promoting human rights and basic human needs. Reminiscent of the vision advanced by the New Frontiersmen during the Kennedy administration, this so-called "regionalist" worldview recognized the potent force of African nationalism and the need to focus on the internal, as opposed to the external, causes of conflict in the African continent. Unlike the New Frontiersmen, however, the regionalists downplayed the importance of communism as a threat to US interests in Africa, calling into question the need to support authoritarian dictators simply because of their anti-communist beliefs. Among those within the administration who are said to have shared this regionalist orientation were Secretary of State Cyrus Vance, UN Ambassador Andrew Young, and Assistant Secretary of State for African Affairs Richard Moose.

The response of the White House to the Shaba I crisis clearly reflected the preeminence of the regionalist worldview. Resisting

Mobutu's efforts to paint the insurgents as Soviet tools led by Cuban troops, Vance and Carter emphasized the internal roots of the conflict and limited US involvement to the provision of merely $15 million worth of already promised non-lethal assistance.[122] As a result, Mobutu was forced to appeal to other sources – most notably the leaders of France and Morocco – who provided the military transport planes and troops that were necessary to defeat the FLNC. Although cynics can note that the White House was able to turn down Mobutu's requests for massive military aid due to confidence that US allies would fill the gap, the importance of Washington's limited response clearly was not lost in Kinshasa. "I confess we are bitterly disappointed by America's attitude," noted Mobutu in an interview with *Newsweek* magazine, "Neto [the now deceased leader of Angola] is a pawn of the Cubans and Russians, but you won't face up to the threat. It is your weakness versus their willpower and strength."[123] Despite the efforts of Umba Di Lutete, Zaire's Ambassador to the UN, to downplay Mobutu's public criticism of the US,[124] the Carter administration's response to the Zairian crisis clearly indicated that the US–Zairian special relationship was being called into question. As one member of the administration explained, "Mobutu must realize that times have changed. No longer can raising the banner of an East–West confrontation send Washington into dithers, nor can US support for an unsteady Mobutu be assumed."[125]

Almost unanimous criticism of White House policy by members of the national security bureaucracies demonstrated the importance of the Carter administration's worldview in setting a new direction for the US–Zairian special relationship. For example, although these officials agreed with the administration's goal of keeping the US response as low-key as possible, they sharply criticized the White House's decision only to provide Zaire with "non-lethal" aid. In a statement characteristic of sentiments held by members of the State Department, the Pentagon, and the CIA, Ambassador Cutler explained that, although he "understood the rationales" for the prohibition – helping Zaire without provoking something worse – he felt that the non-lethal prohibition was "too stringent." This criticism especially was prevalent among field officers at the US Embassy in Kinshasa who believed that the aid restriction prohibited them from effectively carrying out their respective bureaucratic missions. "Simply put," explained Cutler, "if the United States was going to support the Mobutu regime – the consensus opinion within both the national security bureaucracies and the White House – to draw a line between a gun and a truck was unnecessary."[126]

The most significant outcome of the Shaba I crisis was that it placed a critical spotlight on the political and economic shortcomings of the Mobutu regime, as well as Washington's support for what appeared to be a corrupt, authoritarian ruler.[127] Despite Washington's provision of over $850 million in economic and military aid from 1960 to 1976, the Mobutu regime still was incapable of stemming the advance of only 1,500 insurgents. The leader of a small but growing voice within both houses of Congress seeking to cut off aid to Mobutu, Representative Solarz questioned even the decision of the Carter administration to provide the Zairian government with non-lethal aid. "Why is it in our interest that Mobutu should triumph over the insurgency rather than to have either the insurgents triumph or Mobutu deposed and replaced by someone else who will in turn be able to contain the insurgency," noted Solarz before the House Subcommittee on Africa while the invasion was in progress, "particularly when the American taxpayer is being asked to spend a substantial amount of money in Zaire, essentially designed to enable Mobutu to survive?"[128]

Despite their willingness to call into question Washington's Cold War inspired imperative of supporting authoritarian dictators simply because of their anti-communist beliefs, the mainstream regionalists within the Carter administration believed that cutting off aid to Mobutu constituted too radical a policy option. As Vance frankly noted in his memoirs, "None of us wished to face the uncertain consequences that might flow from the collapse of his [Mobutu's] regime and the disintegration of Zaire into unstable segments open to radical penetration."[129] Rather, the guiding theme of the regionalist approach was to condition the future of the US–Zairian special relationship on Mobutu's willingness to implement reforms in the political, economic, and military spheres. Whereas some of these were acceptable to Mobutu, as well as to the national security bureaucracies, others were considered ill-conceived and opposed.

The issue of human rights reforms was a characteristic starting point for the Carter administration and figured prominently in State Department instructions to the US Embassy in Kinshasa.[130] Although willing to recognize that human rights "problems" existed in Zaire, the State Department believed that it was improper to designate the country as a "gross and consistent violator" of those rights.[131] More problematic was that several Africa specialists within the State Department's Africa Bureau had serious misgivings about the human rights approach (which were shared by their counterparts at the CIA and the Pentagon). According to these officials, especially those who had served in Zaire, not only was Mobutu an "unavoidable evil" who had to be dealt with, there was, in actuality, "very little" that Washington could do to make Mobutu meet the human rights demands of the Carter White House.[132] In short, for a bureaucracy which perceived its mission as the maintenance of untroubled relations with African regimes, the sensitive issue of human rights threatened that mission.

Concern with human rights constituted but one part of a broader interest among the administration's regionalists to pressure Mobutu to enact political reforms. Intended to enhance Mobutu's domestic legitimacy and political stability, the central themes of political reform were the partial decentralization of power and the institutionalization of a process ensuring popular input into the policy arena. In this regard, Mobutu himself had recognized the need to ensure greater political competition within Zaire's one-party system, although his rule would remain unquestioned. For example, whereas previous to the Shaba I crisis the 270 Representatives of the Legislative Council had been appointed by the party's thirty-member Political Bureau (which, in turn, had been appointed by Mobutu), the Zairian President opened up both bodies to popular elections.[133] Yet although supportive of the concept of political decentralization, career professionals within the State Department's Africa Bureau, including Cutler, as well as officers at the Pentagon and the CIA, argued that Washington should be "extremely cautious" in telling the Zairian government how to reform itself politically. These officers believed that US pressures for political reforms inevitably could prove destabilizing and unintentionally weaken the Mobutu regime – the exact opposite of what Washington was attempting to accomplish.

Economic reform constituted a third area of concern among the regionalists. Unlike the topics of human rights and political reforms, pressure for economic reforms – particularly those dealing with high levels of corruption within the upper reaches of the Mobutu regime – was considered a traditional part of the US–Zairian dialogue and was supported widely by the State Department, including the Africa Bureau. In a landmark speech delivered on November 25, 1979, Mobutu responded to these concerns by noting that Zairian society was pervaded by a "Zairian sickness" (le "mal Zairois") strikingly reminiscent of, and perhaps purposely patterned after, Carter's description of an "American malaise." The "cure" for this sickness, according to Mobutu, was one in a long line of so-called "Mobutu plans" built around the twin themes of economic reorganization and development.

Reform of the Zairian military constituted the final area of interest among the regionalists within the Carter administration. In its final year in office, the Ford administration had laid the groundwork for the transfer of sophisticated military weaponry to Zaire to counter a possible threat from Angola. As demonstrated by Zaire's inability to single-handedly stem the advance of a relatively small number of insurgents, however, the primary failing of the Zairian Armed Forces was not its lack of equipment, but rather the lack of training and discipline, the pervasiveness of corruption, and the lack of a trained officer corps.[134] In this regard, the State Department and the Pentagon coordinated with the French and the Belgians to put together a reform package for the Zairian Armed Forces. Whereas the Belgians focused primarily on in-country officer training and the formation of three infantry batallions, and the French assumed the training of a paracommando battallion and the expansion of an existing Mirage fighter program, the Pentagon concentrated its efforts in the areas of ground and air transportation, such as maintenance of US-supplied C-130s and logistics coordination.[135]

The Carter administration's handling of the Shaba I invasion once again demonstrated the importance of a crisis situation in significantly altering US Africa policies. In the absence of this invasion and the interest it generated at the highest levels of the policymaking establishment, it is unlikely that reform of the Mobutu regime would have acquired such a position of prominence within the Carter administration. Yet rather than serving as the basis for downgrading or severing US ties with Mobutu, the issue of reform became the central rationale within the national security bureaucracies, as well as the Carter White House and among prominent regionalists within the administration, to maintain or enhance the US–Zairian special relationship during 1977 and the early part of 1978. Whereas proponents of the Mobutu regime could point to his apparent willingness to reform, skeptics within Congress, particularly the House Subcommittee on Africa, were forced to recognize that Mobutu was incorporating several reforms, even if their sincerity or long-term impact was in doubt.

Crisis and resurgence of Cold War rhetoric (May 1978-August 1978)

Rather than fade into the bureaucratic landscape – typically the case in the aftermath of a crisis situation – a second Shaba crisis once again made the US–Zairian special relationship the central focus of the highest levels of the Carter administration. On May 13, 1978, Assistant Secretary of State for African Affairs Richard Moose awoke to a phone call informing him that, on the night before, the FLNC had mounted its second invasion of Zaire in little over a year.[136] Unlike the first Shaba invasion, the FLNC invaded from Zambia and in just four days was able to capture Kolwezi, the economic heart of Shaba province. The swiftness of the attack placed over 2,500 Europeans and 88 US citizens under FLNC control. With the safety of US and European citizens potentially in jeopardy and Mobutu facing a serious threat to his rule, the situation room at the NSC dealt with requests first, from the Belgians (on May 17), and second, from the French and the Zairians (on May 18), to take part in a rescue operation that would include military engagements with the FLNC.

In a sharp departure from his low-key response to Shaba I, Carter on May 18 adopted the consensus opinion within the national security bureaucracies to take part in the European operation. Reminiscent of the Johnson administration's involvement in Operation Red Dragon, the US role included the provision of transport and logistical support for Belgian and French paratroopers. In a total of thirty-eight flight missions, US C-141s transported approximately 2,500 Belgian and French troops and accompanying munitions and transport vehicles to the staging area of Kamina for an airdrop of roughly 400 French paratroopers over the primary objective of Kolwezi. Although the French forces were successful in establishing control over Kolwezi and routing the remainder of FLNC forces in Shaba, over 100 Europeans lost their lives.[137]

Apart from the administration's willingness to become militarily involved on the African continent, the most important distinction between the responses to Shaba I and Shaba II was the level of Cold War rhetoric related to Soviet–Cuban involvement. In an opening statement at a press conference on May 25, 1978, less than two weeks after the beginning of the Shaba II invasion, Carter sternly remarked that Fidel Castro bore a "heavy responsibility" for the "deadly attack" that was launched from Angolan territory.[138] This statement was made despite private assurances from Castro on May 19 that, not only was Cuba uninvolved in the invasion, but he personally had attempted to stop it from occurring.[139] When pressed on this point by members of the press, Carter questioned Castro's truthfulness. "The fact is," explained Carter, "that Castro could have done much more had he genuinely wanted to stop the invasion."[140] This tough talk was backed up by even stronger Cold War rhetoric by National Security Adviser Brzezinski. In a May 28 television appearance on "Meet the Press," Brzezinski implied that the invasion had been launched with Moscow's blessing and charged the Soviets with a "shortsighted attempt to exploit global difficulties."[141]

Presidential politics played an important role in the shift in policy associated with the White House's response to Shaba II. Although public opinion polls in the immediate aftermath of the Shaba I invasion demonstrated strong public support for Carter's handling of the crisis by a margin of 42 to 25 percent, by Shaba II the administration was beginning to appear weak and confused in the face of Soviet–Cuban advances in Africa.[142] Not only were more than 20,000 Cuban troops in Angola, but the Soviets and the Cubans massively and decisively had intervened on the side of Ethiopia in that country's 1977–78 war with Somalia – leaving behind nearly 15,000 Cuban troops and Soviet advisers (see Chapter 4). Already under fire from conservative congressional critics for advancing a Strategic Arms Limitations Talks (SALT) treaty with the Soviet Union, a low-key response to Shaba II also would have left Carter open to charges of being "soft" on communism, potentially damaging the chances for ratification of the treaty in the Senate. According to Moose, the primary objective of Carter's White House advisers during Shaba II was to show how "tough" and "decisive" he could be when it came to communism. Even when it became clear that there was no substance to initial intelligence reports of Cuban involvement in Shaba II, and that the anti-communist rhetoric was misguided, Carter's White House advisers dismissed that crucial point as "inconvenient."[143]

Although it would be mistaken to discount the importance of presidential politics in the change in US policy, of greater significance was an actual shift in the Carter administration's worldview. Similar to the nature of the Kennedy administration, the Carter administration was split between two competing foreign policy visions as manifested by disagreements between Carter's two closest foreign policy advisers, Vance and Brzezinski. In the early days of the adminstration, and especially during the Shaba I invasion, it was the regionalist vision as promoted by Vance which held sway. Those within the administration who emphasized the traditional US proclivity to view African issues – and conflict there – through an East–West lens generally deferred to the preeminence of Vance and the State Department. Among this group were Brzezinski and, to a lesser degree, Secretary of Defense Harold Brown. Yet in the aftermath of massive Soviet–Cuban intervention in the Horn of Africa during 1977–78 and the crisis that entailed for US foreign policy, the so-called "globalists" became increasingly attentive to Africa and challenged the preeminence of the State Department's regionalist approach. It was during this period that Brzezinski began talking of an "arc of crisis" from Asia to southern Africa in which the Soviet Union was said to be exploiting instability according to a well-defined grand strategy. Although promoting détente was desirable according to this vision, the inherently expansionistic nature of the Soviet Union made US–Soviet cooperation highly unlikely; containment therefore was revived.[144] In short, the increased attention of the globalists led to a shift in the Carter administration's worldview as underscored by the rising preeminence of Brzezinski at the expense of Vance.

An equally important factor contributing to the shift in the Carter administration's worldview was the wavering belief of Carter himself as concerned the threats posed to US interests in the Third World by the Soviet Union and Cuba. According to Moose, although Carter did not completely share Brzezinski's deep distrust of the Soviet Union, he did hold a deep mistrust of the Cubans. In this regard, Carter perceived the Cuban role in Africa, especially after their involvement in the 1977–78 Ogaden War, as a much more serious threat than did either Vance, Moose, or Young.[145] As a result, he was more prone to accept the interpretation of Brzezinski when confronted with the second invasion of Zaire's Shaba province in less than two years.

A notable aspect of the Shaba II episode was the impact of crisis in altering an administration's worldview. Until this point, crises were focused on as the triggering mechanism of presidential attention and, subsequently, the formulation of a policy more reflective of a particular administration's worldview. In this case, the twin Shaba crises, as well as the related crisis in the Horn of Africa, served as important factors in contributing to a *change* in the Carter administration's worldview. Already in evidence in 1978, this increasingly globalist-oriented worldview was solidified further by the 444-day Iranian hostage crisis in which US diplomats were held captive by the Islamic fundamentalist regime of Ayatollah Khomeini, as well as by the Soviet invasion of Afghanistan in December 1979.

Bureaucratic incrementalism versus congressional activism (September 1978–January 1981)

The issue of reforming the Mobutu regime intensified in the aftermath of Shaba II. "After all," noted one FSO formerly stationed in Zaire, "Mobutu had been the target of two invasions in less than fourteen months and neither the Carter administration nor its European allies wished to consider the necessity of having to bail him out a third time."[146] As expected, the primary push for reforms did not come from the national security bureaucracies, which were generally opposed to placing undue pressure on Mobutu, but rather from the senior-level regionalists within the Carter administration who wished to avoid the occurrence of "Shaba III," or yet another military invasion of Zaire in less than three years. As one of the most prominent members of the regionalist coalition, Vance made a speech in Atlantic City on June 20, 1978, in which he outlined how the future of the US–Zairian special relationship was to be conditioned on Mobutu's adoption of both economic and political reforms.[147]

Despite the best intentions of Vance and other senior-level regionalists, the reformist approach suffered two major shortcomings. First, policymakers lacked the cooperation of key US allies in Europe, particularly France and Belgium, who were the leading sources of military aid to the Mobutu regime, as well as significant avenues of trade and investment. According to Robert Remole, former head (1978–80) of the political section of the US Embassy in Kinshasa and an outspoken critic of US–Zairian policies, although France and Belgium welcomed reform efforts in the economic sphere, they vigorously opposed Washington's efforts to seek political, administrative, and human rights reforms. "Unless we can get the Belgians and French to agree with us, we lack leverage," explained Remole. "All we can do, all we can expect are cosmetic changes, and that is exactly what we have had – cosmetic changes."[148] Remole's recommended policy stance, which earned him the disdain of numerous colleagues at the State Department, was for Washington to "brusquely, brutally terminate aid." Remole argued that such an act would serve as a "sign to the Mobutu regime and to the Zairian man in the street that the United States is serious about reform and really believes in human rights for Africa."[149]

The second shortcoming of the Carter administration's reform efforts revolved around the willingness of senior-level policymakers to remain active on the issue of Zaire. In order to achieve optimal effectiveness, pressure for reforms ideally required ongoing, high-level attention capable of overcoming bureaucratic intransigence by career officers who firmly believed that certain reformist policies would lead to chaos and instability. In the case of Zaire, the Shaba crises initially focused the attention of Carter and Vance who offered such high level guidance – at least in the immediate aftermath of Shaba I and Shaba II. Once these crises subsided, however, Zaire was relegated to a relatively "benign" bureaucratic landscape in which efforts to monitor and enforce reforms after 1978 usually did not go beyond the much less influential level of the State Department's Africa Bureau (most often in the person of the Ambassador and only rarely at the level of the Assistant Secretary of State for African Affairs).[150] Moreover, the Africa Bureau's reluctance to pressure for political reforms undoubtedly meant a less than enthusiastic pursuit of this duty. The net result was a growing business-as-usual attitude beginning in late 1978 (and carried over into the Reagan administration) that would support ongoing pressure for economic reforms but tread increasingly softly in the realms of political and human rights reforms. For example, when thirteen prominent members of the Zairian Legislative Council were arrested in 1980 for printing an open letter questioning Mobutu's honesty, the situation was treated within the Africa Bureau as a routine matter that did not impinge upon the US–Zairian special relationship.[151] "It pains me to accept that it became business as usual with Mobutu," noted Moose as he reflected on the record of the Carter administration in Zaire, "but it probably did."[152]

However, unlike the 1968–74 period of bureaucratic incrementalism in which established programs were either maintained or enhanced, the growing business-as-usual attitude did not result in the strengthening of the US–Zairian special relationship as a more activist Congress entered the policy equation. Specifically, the two Shaba crises placed a glaring spotlight on the shortcomings of the Zairian regime and attracted the attention of critical groupings within Congress, most notably the House Subcommittee on Africa. The next seven years were marked by a growing clash between the national security bureaucracies and congressional subcommittees on Africa as each pursued their own foreign policy agendas. Of particular importance was an ongoing conflict between the State Department's Africa Bureau and the House Subcommittee on Africa.

As that portion of the executive branch dealing most extensively with Zaire on a day-to-day basis, it fell to the Africa Bureau to go before Congress and justify why that country deserved economic and military aid. Characteristic of statements made before the House Subcommittee on Africa regardless of administration, Deputy Assistant Secretary of State for African Affairs Lannon Walker argued in 1980 that Zaire warranted support due to its historic friendship with Washington. The reasons that Walker stressed clearly reflected the Africa Bureau's primary focus on the political benefits accruing to Washington as a result of the US–Zairian special relationship. Among these were the country's pro-Western, moderate foreign policy and Mobutu's consistent "voice of reason" in regional and international organizations, including the OAU, the Non-Aligned Movement, and the UN.[153]

Fully aware that such platitudes were not enough to overcome the subcommittee's growing disenchantment with Mobutu's rule, Walker was careful to qualify his testimony by noting that the administration's policy was not one of "blind or massive support."[154] Walker instead emphasized that US support was conditioned on Mobutu's willingness to carry through on promised political, economic, and military reforms, the progress of which were the subject of the remainder of his testimony. In an effort to preempt congressional focus on Mobutu's continuing faults, as opposed to the apparent progress he was making, Walker concluded his testimony thus: "Though we continue to be encouraged by progress across the board toward achieving basic reforms in Zaire, it is obvious that there remains much to be done by way of implementing the program outlined by President Mobutu in 1977 and 1978."[155]

In sharp contrast to executive branch testimony, the House Subcommittee on Africa consistently questioned both Mobutu's sincerity to reform and the validity of the need to maintain a special relationship with his regime. Of special concern was the wipespread corruption within the Zairian ruling elite. "The bureaucracy seems more interested in extracting the wealth of the country from the Zairian people than in utilizing that wealth for national development," noted Solarz during congressional hearings in March 1979. "The Army, which consists of what can only be called a rapacious rabble, seems more interested in plundering the people than protecting them." Of even greater concern was the increasingly clear conclusion that a significant portion of US foreign assistance had "gone into the pockets of the political and military elite instead of being used for its intended purposes on behalf of the economic and military security of the people."[156] These claims were substantiated not only by the congressional testimony of several academic experts on Zaire, but also that of Nguza Karl-I-Bond, the former Prime Minister of Zaire who resigned in April 1981 and fled to Europe.[157]

The issue of greatest concern to the House Subcommittee on Africa was the inherent danger of supporting a regime lacking domestic political legitimacy. An especially relevant example for policymakers at the end of the 1970s was Washington's support for Shah Mohammad Reza Pahlavi of Iran and the intense anti-US hatred that emerged in that country once he was overthrown in 1978. Drawing parallels between US support for the Shah and Mobutu, Solarz warned in a 1979 congressional hearing that the US potentially had "another Iran" on its hands. "For what seemed good reasons at the time," Solarz began, "we became identified with a government which now appears to have lost the support of its own people, and which may not survive no matter what we are likely to do for it."[158] According to this perspective, US economic and military aid does not contribute to reform, but serves as the basis for internal suppression of dissent. The inherent danger for US foreign policy is that, when the often violent end to the unpopular regime does occur, its successors often vent an accompanying anti-US rage.[159] In direct opposition to the Africa Bureau's desire to protect and enhance the US–Zairian special relationship, one of the primary objectives of the House Subcommittee on Africa therefore became the termination of US security assistance to the Mobutu regime.

The widely diverging foreign policy objectives of the State Department's Africa Bureau and the House Subcommittee on Africa were most notably demonstrated by a battle over 1980 budget allocations for military aid to Zaire. Similar to previous years, the Africa Bureau presented a request for a 25 percent increase in aid over the roughly $10 million allocated in 1979. In sharp contrast, the House Subcommittee on Africa for the first time sought the termination of all military assistance to the Mobutu regime. Although this proposal met "no resistance" in the Foreign Affairs Committee and only "mild resistance" on the floor of the full House, the Senate, reacting to what several of its members saw as a "snub" of an "old and strategically important friend," approved the entire administration request. It was only in a House–Senate conference committee that this request was reduced by 25 percent, with $6.9 million eventually being disbursed in 1980. This budget dispute marked the first of several such encounters in which the House Subcommittee on Africa successfully sought incremental reductions in State Department requests for military assistance to Zaire.[160]

This third period of the Carter administration's involvement in Zaire nicely demonstrated how, in the aftermath of a crisis situation, reformist policies became less than enthusiastically enforced once the White House turned its attention to other matters, and management of the US–Zairian special relationship once again fell to the national security bureaucracies. Although willing to accept the necessity to press for economic reforms, bureaucrats within the national security bureaucracies felt that an overemphasis on political reforms ran the risks of destabilizing "our man" in Kinshasa, leading to instability and civil war similar to the 1960–67 period. The decline of White House attention was matched by the growth of congressional criticism of the US–Zairian special relationship as led by the House Subcommittee on Africa. The primary reason for congressional attention was the combination of two military crises in Zaire that served to highlight the severe human rights shortcomings of the Mobutu regime. Although able minimally to restrict the amounts of military aid available to Zaire, the House Subcommittee on Africa was unable to achieve the more far-reaching goal of completely severing US links with the Mobutu regime. In the absence of an extended crisis situation, the innumerable partisan and ideological splits both within and between the two houses of Congress continued to limit the ability of these bodies to pass legislation counter to the established policies of the executive branch.

Regional conflict and the bureaucratic-congressional split (January 1981–September 1991)

Clearly unhappy with the state of US–Zairian relations under the Carter administration, Mobutu's expectations supposedly "soared" when Reagan was elected in November 1980.[161] Entering office with a highly ideological worldview that emphasized the need to offer greater support to anti-communist, strategic allies, such as Zaire, the Reagan White House was expected to reaffirm and strengthen the US–Zairian special relationship. Yet in sharp contrast to the dramatic changes in US foreign policy toward other regions of the world, such as Central America, which were visible almost immediately after Reagan was inaugurated, initial policies toward Zaire demonstrated significant continuity with the final two years of the Carter administration. "It was clear when I left for Zaire," noted Peter Dalton Constable, US Ambassador to Zaire from 1982 to 1984, "that the only thing Washington was going to do was profess its friendship for Mobutu and try to push him into an agreement with the International Monetary Fund."[162] As a result, the aid levels that Mobutu felt would and "should" be forthcoming from the Reagan administration never materialized. As another US Ambassador to Zaire, Brandon Hambright Grove, Jr., commented, Mobutu was "very disappointed" in economic and military aid levels under the Reagan administration. "He never could understand or believe that President Reagan couldn't pick up the phone, call the speaker of the House, and get aid doubled."[163]

Mobutu's fortunes within the policymaking establishment only began to shift in 1985 when, as the result of bureaucratic and congressional politics, Zaire once again became an important regional component of US intervention in Angola. Culminating a five-year struggle principally waged by CIA Director William Casey and conservative forces in Congress (most notably Senator Jesse Helms), the House of Representatives in July 1985 followed the Senate's lead and repealed the Clark Amendment, thereby allowing for renewed US aid to anti-communist insurgents in Angola.[164] Despite the vigorous opposition of Secretary of State George Shultz and Assistant Secretary of State for

African Affairs Chester Crocker, as well as the House Subcommittee on Africa and the Congressional Black Caucus, conservative elements within Congress successfully sought to make Jonas Savimbi's UNITA guerrilla forces the recipients of US paramilitary aid under the rubric of the so-called Reagan Doctrine: an ideologically based program for arming insurgencies intent on overthrowing self-proclaimed Marxist regimes in the Third World.

The CIA assumed the primary responsibility for implementing the specifics of the Reagan Doctrine in southern Africa. Similar to the covert action program designed to defeat the MPLA in the mid-1970s, Mobutu's cooperation was perceived as crucial to the CIA's anti-communist bureaucratic mission; he not only hosted one of the largest CIA contingents on the African continent, but his country's well-established links with Savimbi and strategic southwestern border with Angola made it one of two logical conduits (the other being South Africa) of covert paramilitary aid to the UNITA forces. The corner-stones of this paramilitary program were the alleged creation of at least six training camps for UNITA insurgents along Zaire's southwestern border and the establishment of the St. Lucia air network to facilitate the direct transfer of US weapons to Savimbi's forces.[165] Zaire's import-ance especially grew in the aftermath of the US-brokered Angola Accords in 1988 in which both South Africa and Angola agreed to "non-interference" in each other's domestic affairs, effectively cutting the land-based link of US covert aid to Savimbi through South Africa and Namibia.

Pressures for strengthening US–Zairian ties also emerged during the 1980s from Pentagon strategists who demonstrated a growing interest in Africa. In the case of Zaire, the Pentagon in 1985 began focusing on Kamina airbase, which one military official described as an "irresistible attraction."[166] The strategic importance of this airbase – described as a natural transshipment gateway to Central and southern Africa – derived primarily from growing Defense Department involvement in military contingencies in Chad, the Sudan, and elsewhere in Africa. Other bureaucratically inspired reasons for rising Pentagon interest in Kamina were the need to maintain a base for future contingency operations in the region and the acquisition of "training space" for exercises of the US European Command (EURCOM). Toward these ends, Air Force General Richard Lawson inspected Kamina in Novem-ber 1985 presumably to assess its potential benefits to overall US defense needs. Prior to this visit, a group of engineers had determined that the cost of refurbishing and upgrading the airbase to suit US military needs would range between $60–100 million.[167]

Fully aware of the potential lucrative payoff to Zaire due to evolving US interests in the region, Mobutu visited Washington in late November 1985 to make a pitch for, among other things, a major Pentagon presence at Kamina. Although supported at the lower levels of the Defense Department, the upper levels, most notably the Joint Chiefs of Staff, vetoed the project as both unnecessary and overly risky.[168] Ironically, even if the Joint Chiefs of Staff had sought such a presence at Kamina, this would have been opposed fiercely by the CIA which reportedly was "horrified" that Pentagon officials were even considering such a commitment. According to one official, the CIA wanted "absolutely no part" of the Defense Department "stumbling in on top" of, and attracting a lot of attention to, what was an important CIA asset.[169]

The rejection of Mobutu's offer set in motion a scramble among various Pentagon officials who, among other reasons, had sought the commitment to Kamina as a means for rewarding the Zairian President. For example, several members of the Office of the Deputy Assistant Secretary of Defense, International Security Affairs, argued that Washington owed Mobutu a favor for supporting US military efforts in Chad, as well as facilitating the application of the Reagan Doctrine to Angola.[170] Still determined to reward the Mobutu regime, a new proposal focused on the initiation of US–Zairian joint military training exercises combined with the limited upgrading of facilities at Kamina. Even this limited proposal caused bureaucratic tension with the State Department when, at the recommendation of Air Force lawyers, the Defense Department announced it was seeking a formal access agreement with the Mobutu regime.[171] According to the Air Force, a formal access agreement not only was necessary to authorize the expenditure of military construction monies, but would better ensure access whenever needed.[172] Yet it was the opinion of the State Department that an access agreement would make US involvement in Angola too visible and would create unnecessary problems with a Congress unwilling to appropriate the necessary funds.[173] Backing away from any further talk of an access agreement, Pentagon officials finally succeeded in rewarding the Mobutu regime by establishing a small program which, beginning in 1987, included annual outlays of between $1–2 million for joint US–Zairian military maneuvers and selected military construction projects at Kamina.[174]

Whereas the CIA and the Pentagon sought to reward Zaire's willingness to get involved in the paramilitary side of US foreign policy toward Angola, the State Department's Africa Bureau since June 1989 began hailing Mobutu as a distinguished "peace-broker" for his medi-

101

ation efforts in the Angolan civil war. In efforts that grew out of the 1988 US-brokered Angolan Accords between Angola, Cuba, and South Africa, Mobutu presided over an African diplomatic effort which resulted in an historic cease-fire between the MPLA and UNITA on June 22, 1989. Although the cease-fire began unraveling two months later, the State Department described Mobutu's efforts as a "watershed" in African diplomacy and a "decisive step" in the path to regional peace.[175] Indeed, Zaire's critical role as a regional ally in US foreign policy toward Angola resulted in Mobutu being honored as the first African leader to be invited by the Bush administration for an official White House visit. Engineered by the State Department's Africa Bureau as the best way to reward Mobutu in a time of constrained financial resources, the meeting clearly underscored Mobutu's strengthened image at the highest levels of the policymaking establishment.[176] "Just last week, he brought together, for the first time, in the presence of 18 African Chiefs of State, the leadership of Angola's warring factions, setting the stage for national reconciliation in that country," noted an appreciative Bush on June 29, 1989, "And thanks to President Mobutu, we are nearer the goal long sought, yet long elusive – peace and opportunity in southwestern Africa."[177]

Despite the accolades offered by Bush and other members of the executive branch, two important factors constrained any major strengthening of the foreign aid dimension of the US–Zairian special relationship. First, the passage of the Gramm-Rudman-Hollings Deficit Reduction Act in 1986 served as an important brake on any major increases in foreign aid, especially in Africa. As Assistant Secretary of State for African Affairs Herman J. Cohen explained in 1989, overall allocations to Africa declined because of greater US priorities in Egypt, Israel, and base-rights countries, such as the Philippines, Turkey, and Greece. "So after you give money to all of those," noted Cohen, "there's very little left."[178] This trend intensified at the beginning of the 1990s as the Bush administration sought to reward the transition to democracy in Eastern Europe and the former Soviet Union, as well as pay for the enormous costs associated with the US war against Iraq in 1991 known as Operation Desert Storm.

Apart from very real budget difficulties, an activist Congress, particularly the House Subcommittee on Africa, served as the most important constraints on the strengthening of the US–Zairian special relationship. As Mobutu was made painfully aware during his June 1989 Washington visit, the issues of human rights and corruption in Zaire increasingly were becoming the focus of activists both within and outside the halls of Congress.[179] As even noted in the 1989 edition of the annual State Department human rights report to Congress, freedom of speech and other civil rights in Zaire were "substantially circumscribed," with numerous human rights abuses stemming from "endemic corruption" among Zairian officials.[180] Adopting a much harsher tone, the House Foreign Affairs Committee labeled the Mobutu regime as a "gross violator" of human rights.[181] Of particular concern to budget-conscious critics within Congress was the allegation that Mobutu had amassed a personal fortune of over $5 billion – a sum roughly equal to Zaire's entire national debt – by treating the Zairian economy as if it were his private estate.[182]

According to congressional critics, the combination of human rights abuses and endemic levels of corruption – largely verified by specialists of Zaire regardless of their partisan beliefs – confirmed the utter uselessless of any further aid to the Mobutu regime. Although successful in incrementally reducing the amount of military aid from a cap of $6 million in 1982 to $3 million in 1990, these activists, such as Representative Dellums, the sponsor of several anti-Mobutu bills, sought even further restrictions. As a result, several influential members of Congress responded to a request by the Bush administration to provide approximately $56 million in aid (including $4 million in military aid) to Zaire in 1991 by calling for the complete termination of all security assistance, as well as the channeling of all humanitarian assistance through non-governmental organizations. In testimony before the House Appropriations Subcommittee on Foreign Operations on April 5, 1990, for example, Solarz supported a cut-off in aid by comparing the future of Mobutu to the fates that befell other dictators, such as Nicolae Ceausescu of Romania, Eric Honecker of (the former) East Germany, Ferdinand Marcos of the Philippines, and Anastasio Somoza Debayle of Nicaragua. "Sooner or later, Mobutu will go," explained Solarz. "When that time comes, it will not be in our interest to have been perceived as propping up this discredited dictator."[183]

Although partisan differences of opinion in both the House and the Senate forestalled attempts at radically altering the US–Zairian special relationship, events in 1990 further underscored the human rights shortcomings of the Mobutu regime and provided ample ammunition for congressional activists. In response to growing popular demands for some sort of multiparty political system, Mobutu made a major address on April 24, 1990, in which he announced significant political reforms, most notably the legalization of opposition parties. An important aspect of the reform process was the establishment of a "national conference on democracy" – a political body composed of prominent government and opposition political figures which assumed the task of refashioning Zaire's political system, particularly the constitution, in preparation for national, multiparty elections. Similar to past pronouncements of reform, rhetoric severely clashed with reality when opposition figures took Mobutu at his word and parties, such as the Union for Democracy and Social Progress (UDPS), actively began campaigning for a true alternative to the Mobutu regime. In one of the most publicized examples of government repression designed to intimidate opposition figures, at least 12 (some figures go as high as 150) students at Lubumbashi University were killed during the night of May 11, 1990, when members of Mobutu's elite presidential guard attacked a group of student protestors.[184]

In the culmination of a trend that began in the late 1970s, congressional activists in October 1990 seized upon the Lubumbashi massacre as the basis for terminating already reduced levels of military aid, as well as ensuring that the majority of economic aid scheduled to be dispersed in 1992 and beyond would be channeled through non-governmental organizations. In sharp contrast to traditional State Department arguments that cutting off aid only served to undercut the process of reform, congressional critics expressed doubts that changes would ever occur in the Zairian political system as long as Mobutu remained in power. "Every six months we are told Mobutu has seen the light," explained Representative Wolpe, former chairperson of the House Subcommittee on Africa, "Invariably, those announcements are followed by a new wave of arrests, repression and corruption."[185] In an event which substantiated this viewpoint, at least three people were killed on September 3, 1991, when Zairian government troops opened fire on thousands of demonstrators who had taken to the streets within the capital and other cities to protest Mobutu's apparent rigging of the national conference on democracy.

At the center of an ongoing and escalating debate within the US policymaking establishment was whether a Zaire without Mobutu – the end result of those seeking a true alternative to his single-party regime – would lead to political chaos, ethnic separatism, and, ultimately, regional instability reminiscent of the 1960s when the country was faced with territorial disintegration.[186] The consensus opinion within the national security bureaucracies was that, despite his shortcomings, Mobutu had contributed to domestic and regional stability and, most important, had served as a faithful US ally in Africa. "The point is we need him," explained Irvin Hicks, Deputy Assistant Secretary of State for African Affairs, who lauded Mobutu's "important role" in US initiatives in Chad, Mozambique, and "particularly Angola."[187]

"If we push Mobutu too hard," explained another State Department official, "we will only have ourselves to blame for the political chaos and instability that surely will ensue."[188] This type of reasoning was firmly rejected by congressional critics. "What jeopardizes the prospects of regional stability," explained Solarz, "is the existence of a kleptocracy in Zaire that has driven the standard of living lower than it was at the time of independence three decades ago."[189] Pointing to the civil instability spreading throughout Liberia and Somalia – countries in which authoritarian dictators once supported by the US had been overthrown in brutal civil wars – one congressional critic warned in August 1991 that time was quickly running out for US foreign policy. "If we wish to avoid the bloodshed currently raging in both Liberia and Somalia – countries in which the deaths of innocent victims are at least partially due to shortsighted policies – we must adopt a proactive policy that firmly supports the departure of Mobutu and the creation of a truly democratic political system."[190]

The evolution of the US–Zairian special relationship during the 1980s and the beginning of the 1990s clearly demonstrated the importance of bureaucratic incrementalism during non-crisis periods as first the Reagan and, subsequently, the Bush White House largely left policy in the hands of the Africa specialists within the national security bureacracies. As a result, US–Zairian ties were enhanced incrementally, especially in the aftermath of congressional repeal of the Clark Amendment in 1985, as bureaucratic missions associated with renewed US support for Savimbi's guerrilla forces led to upward pressures for seeking ways of rewarding the Mobutu regime. Due to congressional concerns over the continuing human rights abuses of the Zairian government, however, the national security bureaucracies were forced to find non-military aid-related means of demonstrating US appreciation for what was perceived as Mobutu's crucial role in southwestern Africa. Although unable to completely rupture the US–Zairian special relationship, congressional activists nonetheless were successful in limiting the amounts of foreign assistance provided to the Mobutu regime.

Growing domestic turmoil amidst an altered Cold War environment (September 1991–January 1993)

In one of the most serious challenges to Mobutu's twenty-six years of authoritarian rule, nearly 3,000 mutinous troops protesting the lack of pay touched off two days of violent riots in Kinshasa during September 1991 that quickly spread to regional capitals and cities, most notably in Shaba province, and left at least 30 dead and more than 1,250 injured. Fearful that the mobs were going to turn on Western nationals living within the country, approximately 1,750 French and Belgian troops intervened on September 24 with the blessing of Mobutu to ensure the evacuation of nearly 8,000 foreigners, including over 700 US citizens. Although the US did not directly take part in the rescue operation, several C-141 military transport planes were "loaned" to France to facilitate the evacuation of foreigners living within the country.[191]

Despite the regime-threatening nature of the September 1991 riots, two factors contributed to the lack of a perception of crisis at the highest levels of the policymaking establishment and, as a result, White House inattention, as policy was largely left to the Africa specialists within the national seurity bureaucracies. First, the willingness of Belgium, aided by France, to take the lead in its former colony effectively precluded the necessity of deciding on the issue of direct military intervention by US forces. As indicated by Pentagon statements concerning the limited US role in the evacuation operation, US policy reflected French and Belgian desires to remain neutral in the growing conflict between Mobutu and opposition forces. "The sole purpose of this activity is to assist in the protection and evacuation of Americans and other foreigners," explained a spokesperson for the Defense Department, "It does not constitute an involvement in the internal affairs of Zaire."[192]

The decline of the Cold War was of even greater importance in contributing to the lack of a crisis atmosphere at the highest levels of the policymaking establishment. In sharp contrast to earlier conflicts, such as the 1978 Shaba crisis, in which a perceived communist threat posed by the Soviet Union and its allies served as the primary justification for intervention, the September 1991 riots and the possibility of Mobutu's removal from power were not perceived through the ideological context of Cold War competition. The obvious reasons for the lack of high-level concern were the fragmentation of the former Soviet Union into several independent and non-communist countries, as well as the resolution of regional conflicts which had become East–West flashpoints. In the case of Angola, for example, the MPLA's willingness to submit to internationally monitored multiparty elections that took place in December 1992 meant that the US no longer needed a regional ally capable of funneling US paramilitary aid to anti-communist insurgents.[193]

However, the decline of Zaire's strategic importance to US interests in the aftermath of the end of the Cold War did not mean that either the White House or the Africa specialists of the national security bureaucracies were willing to accept the critical arguments of certain portions of Congress and seek the removal of the Mobutu regime. Less than three weeks after Belgium and France intervened during the September 1991 riots, for example, a career FSO in the State Department's Africa Bureau cautioned that any transition from the Mobutu regime to some sort of multiparty system had to proceed "peacefully and, above all, slowly." "Regardless of the fact that we are no longer faced with a communist threat," explained this officer, "the destabilization of Zaire – which borders nine other African countries – could have a tremendously negative impact on regional stability." Although this FSO supported US involvement in gently pressuring Mobutu to "recognize the inevitable" and "accept the growing involvement of opposition politicians," such as Etienne Tshisekedi, the UDPS leader who was elected Prime Minister by delegates of the national conference on democracy in September 1992, the approach was tempered by the strongly engrained belief that a "Zaire without Mobutu could entail a Zaire engulfed by chaos."[194] "It is not in our interest that Mobutu suddenly disappear," explained another diplomat with extensive experience within the region. "What may replace him is unclear, and meanwhile, the situation could prove chaotic."[195]

It was the continued importance of the "Mobutu or chaos" argument which led US officials to cautiously respond to Mobutu's efforts at maintaining himself in power, including his appointment (over the vociferous opposition of opposition parties) of Nguza Karl-I-Bond as Prime Minister in November 1991, his suspension of the national conference on democracy from January to April 1992, and his refusal to relinquish control over the Zairian military and intelligence services prior to the holding of national, multiparty elections. "We're not asking him to leave," explained Cohen in testimony before the Senate Subcommittee on Africa. "We feel he should remain as president so he can control the military force until there is an election at which point the people will decide."[196] In short, Mobutu is perceived throughout the national security bureaucracies as both "part of the problem" and "part of the solution" to what may become an increasingly violent political situation in Zaire. "If Mobutu, with his control of the security apparatus, including people who engage in covert operations ... does not support a transition process," concluded Cohen, "then it cannot succeed."[197]

As Mobutu continues to seek some sort of solution that enables him to remain in power, the Africa Bureau most likely will continue to argue for a policy stance favoring slow, incremental change. Other portions of the policymaking establishment, of course, will demonstrate different levels of interest and activism in what potentially may become a growing debate over how to respond to changes in Zaire – especially if the political condition in the country continues to deteriorate. Whereas members of the CIA and the Pentagon have argued more strongly than their State Department counterparts for greater caution as concerns any type of political pressure designed to remove Mobutu from power, congressional critics have noted a desire to see Mobutu removed from power as quickly as possible. "He has established a kleptocracy to end all kleptocracies, and has set a new standard by which all future international thieves will have to be measured," explained Solarz, "He makes Marcos look like a piker by comparison."[198] In the absence of any major crisis event capable of reordering US priorities, however, the most likely result of an ongoing congressional-executive deadlock will be an incrementalist approach to changes within the bureaucratic and congressional confines of the established status quo.

Conclusion

The importance of the relationship between the nature of events within Africa and the operation of the US policymaking process is vividly portrayed by the evolution of US interventionist practices in Zaire during the post-World War II period. Born out of crisis and nurtured along by the varying and sometimes opposing bureaucratic missions of the State Department, the Pentagon, and the CIA, the US–Zairian special relationship evolved with each new crisis and subsequent period of routine and relative calm.

During the initial post-independence period from 1960 to 1967, a series of crises ensured the periodic attention of Eisenhower, Kennedy, and Johnson. In each case, presidential attention usually meant the reorientation of US interventionist practices in Zaire consistent with that administration's worldview. During the Eisenhower administration, this involvement led to a covert policy that sought to permanently remove the threat posed by Lumumba and other so-called "radicals" within the Zairian government. This approach was tempered by Kennedy's desire to seek a civilian-based coalition government that included the radical political forces led by Gizenga. Finally, the assassination of Kennedy and his replacement by Johnson favored a return to a more hardline policy approach as demonstrated by White House approval of US military involvement in Operation Red Dragon.

However, an administration's worldview was not the sole determinant of US responses to crises during the 1960–67 period. In at least two cases, the White House adopted an approach inconsistent with its worldview. For example, Kennedy's initial willingness to seek a military solution to the Shaba secession in 1961 quickly was replaced by the more politically safe option of pursuing diplomatic negotiations. Of primary importance in this shift in policy was the drawn-out nature of the Shaba crisis which gave congressional critics and the Katanga Lobby ample time to orchestrate a popular, pro-Tshombe campaign. The Johnson administration's unwillingness to approve direct US military involvement in Zaire until after the presidential elections of 1964 also clearly demonstrated the importance of domestic political considerations in influencing White House decisions. In contrast to Kennedy's political back-pedaling, however, direct US military intervention was merely delayed until the political obstacle of presidential elections had been removed.

The most important aspect of the 1960–67 period is that it led to the rise of Mobutu as the undisputed leader of Zaire. In this regard, the successful resolution of the 1967 mercenary uprising marked the strengthening of a consensus within the diverse national security bureaucracies that Mobutu was "our man" in Kinshasa and that each bureaucracy should focus its energies on maintaining him in power. From this point forward, US policies were oriented toward the "man" rather than the country or the government of Zaire. As a result, approximately seven years of stability (1967–74) were marked by the process of bureaucratic incrementalism in which each of the national security bureaucracies sought to maintain or enhance the US–Zairian special relationship in accordance with established policies. This pattern was enhanced when, as a result of the Angolan civil war, the *realpolitik* worldview of the Nixon–Ford administrations ensured the designation of Zaire as a regional pillar of US Africa policies.

The US–Zairian special relationship was called into question for the first time when the Shaba I crisis of 1977 coincided with the inauguration of the Carter administration. Rather than come to Zaire's aid as was the case under earlier Democratic and Republican administrations, the preeminence of a regionalist worldview led to a very limited response that clearly indicated a general reassessment of the US–Zairian special relationship. Indeed, the desire of senior-level policymakers to press for economic, political, and military reforms in Zaire – despite the varied opposition of the national security bureaucracies – was an important outcome of the Shaba I crisis. Yet a growing shift away from the regionalist worldview was clearly evident in the Carter administration's more militaristic response to the Shaba II crisis in early 1978. Although the issue of reform, once again, initially was promoted by senior-level policymakers in the immediate aftermath of this second crisis, the post-1978 period was marked by the less than enthusiastic pursuit of this goal as the White House turned its attention to other matters, and management of the US–Zairian special relationship once again fell to the national security bureaucracies. As a result, US–Zairian ties were enhanced in accordance with established policies, especially in the aftermath of congressional repeal of the Clark Amendment in 1985 and the subsequent renewal of US paramilitary support for Savimbi's UNITA guerrilla forces in Angola.

Unlike the 1967–74 period, the process of bureaucratic incrementalism in the post-1978 period was matched by the growth of congressional criticism of the US–Zairian special relationship as led by the House Subcommittee on Africa. The primary reasons for congressional attention were the successive Shaba I and Shaba II crises which highlighted the severe human rights shortcomings of the Mobutu regime. Although able to incrementally reduce, and ultimately terminate, military assistance, as well as place restrictions on how economic aid should be dispersed, congressional critics, led by the House Subcommittee on Africa, were unable to achieve the more radical goal of completely severing US links with the Mobutu regime. In the absence of an extended crisis situation able to generate widespread popular and congressional attention and involvement, the innumerable partisan and ideological splits both within and between the two houses of Congress continued to limit the ability of these bodies to radically alter US relations with the Mobutu regime.

As a potentially explosive political situation continued to unfold in Kinshasa at the beginning of 1993, the US–Zairian special relationship found itself being pulled in two different directions. Whereas Mobutu's congressional and domestic opponents sought Washington's principled disassociation from what they perceived as a corrupt and illegitimate regime, the national security bureaucracies underscored the need for caution in order to avoid the chaos and instability which gripped Zaire during the 1960s. The most notable aspect of Mobutu's apparently slipping hold on power was that it did not create a crisis atmosphere in Washington, as perhaps would have been the case even two years earlier. The relatively low-key US response to spreading riots throughout Zaire during September 1991 suggested that, in the emerging post-Cold War era, Mobutu's almost unquestioned status within the executive branch as "our man" in Kinshasa was beginning to fade – or at least be questioned more openly. In short, the termination of a host of Cold War-driven bureaucratic missions – inclusive of Zaire's role in facilitating the provision of US paramilitary aid to Savimbi's UNITA forces – no longer required policies that once led Washington to disregard the internal nature of the Mobutu regime in favor of its role within the global East–West conflict. Although the national security bureaucracies continued to advance the "Mobutu or chaos" syndrome which had guided US foreign policy toward Zaire for over a quarter of a century, there nonetheless appeared to be a growing commitment to fashion a democratic alternative that could slowly lead to Mobutu's peaceful departure from office. However, in the absence of a significant crisis event capable of attracting the extended attention of the White House, the US–Zairian special relationship seemed destined to evolve slowly within the bureaucratic and congressional confines of the established status quo.

Table 3.1. *US economic and military aid to Zaire, 1959–1992 (bilateral loans and grants, millions of dollars)*

Program	1959	1960	1961	1962	1963	1964	1965	1966	1967	1968	1969	1970	1971	1972	1973
I. Economic aid–total	*	0.1	11.0	20.3	38.3	19.3	10.5	16.3	23.2	11.7	5.4	13.1	29.1	5.9	51.6
A. Aid & predecessors	–	*	2.4	3.8	3.0	1.2	1.5	.9	3.1	.8	1.3	9.3	13.4	2.0	3.6
B. Food for peace	*	0.1	8.2	16.5	35.3	18.1	9.0	15.4	20.1	10.9	4.1	3.8	1.4	2.3	3.2
Title I-total	–	–	–	10.9	27.2	15.3	7.6	12.5	17.4	7.6	3.8	3.7	–	2.0	2.7
Repay in $-loans	–	–	–	–	–	–	–	–	17.4	7.6	3.8	3.7	–	2.0	2.7
Pay. in for. curr.	–	–	–	10.9	27.2	15.3	7.6	12.5	–	–	–	–	–	–	–
Title II-total	*	0.1	8.2	5.6	8.1	2.8	1.4	2.9	2.7	3.3	0.3	0.1	1.4	0.3	0.5
Economic relief	–	–	7.6	4.0	4.7	–	–	*	–	–	–	0.1	0.5	–	0.1
Vol. relief agency	*	0.1	0.6	1.6	3.4	2.8	1.4	2.9	2.7	3.3	0.3	–	0.9	0.3	0.4
C. Other econ. grants	–	–	–	–	–	–	–	–	–	–	*	*	0.6	1.2	2.4
Peace Corps	–	–	–	–	–	–	–	–	–	–	*	*	0.6	1.2	2.4
Other	–	–	–	–	–	–	–	–	–	–	–	–	–	–	–
D. Other econ. loans	–	–	–	–	–	–	–	–	–	–	–	–	13.7	0.4	42.4
Export–Import bank	–	–	–	–	–	–	–	–	–	–	–	–	13.7	0.4	42.4
All other	–	–	–	–	–	–	–	–	–	–	–	–	–	–	5.4
II. Military aid–total	–	–	–	*	2.2	8.5	6.2	3.7	3.4	2.1	1.9	13.6	2.3	6.5	
A. MAP grants	–	–	–	–	2.1	4.7	5.6	2.5	3.2	1.7	2.0	1.3	*	–	–
B. Credit financing	–	–	–	–	–	–	–	–	–	–	–	–	13.2	2.0	6.2
C. IMET	–	–	–	–	0.1	0.2	0.3	0.3	0.1	0.3	0.4	0.4	0.3	0.3	0.3
D. Tran-Excess stock	–	–	–	*	*	3.6	0.3	0.8	*	*	0.3	0.2	–	–	–
E. Other grants	–	–	–	–	–	–	–	–	–	–	–	–	–	–	–
III. ESF	–	–	64.9	63.4	35.0	20.0	15.0	19.0	17.2	15.3	3.0	–	–	–	–
IV. Total	*	0.1	75.5	83.7	75.5	47.8	31.7	39.0	43.8	29.1	11.1	15.0	42.7	8.2	58.1
Loans	–	–	–	0.3	0.7	15.3	18.7	31.5	36.9	22.6	6.8	11.7	38.9	8.2	53.3
Grants	*	0.1	75.5	83.4	74.8	32.5	13.0	7.5	6.9	6.5	4.3	3.3	3.8	3.8	4.8

Figures for 1959–90 are derived from US Agency for International Development (USAID), *U.S. Overseas Loans and Grants. Series of Yearly Data (Volume IV. Africa). Obligations and Loan Authorizations. FY 1946-FY 1990.* Washington, DC: USAID, 1990.
Figures for 1991–92 were provided by USIA.
(–) no aid provided during the fiscal year
(*) less than $50,000 provided in aid during the fiscal year
(?) data unavailable
(TQ) transition quarter

1974	1975	1976	TQ	1977	1978	1979	1980	1981	1982	1983	1984	1985	1986	1987	1988	1989	1990	1991	1992
127.7	61.6	67.3	11.1	45.2	39.8	87.8	26.4	28.6	13.1	25.9	45.8	50.7	47.4	52.2	63.8	64.3	52.3	31.2	0.6
1.1	1.6	.6	7.0	–	–	11.9	6.9	10.6	10.3	9.5	15.6	25.1	23.6	22.7	31.4	36.4	30.8	21.5	–
0.5	0.4	12.6	*	22.8	18.5	21.4	16.3	13.5	10.0	10.9	15.8	20.6	20.2	26.1	23.2	24.6	16.4	6.1	–
–	–	12.4	–	22.7	18.0	17.0	15.7	10.0	10.0	10.0	15.0	20.0	20.0	19.7	23.0	24.0	16.0	6.1	–
–	–	12.4	–	22.7	18.0	17.0	15.7	10.0	10.0	10.0	15.0	20.0	20.0	19.7	23.0	24.0	16.0	–	–
–	–	–	–	–	–	–	–	–	–	–	–	–	–	–	–	–	–	–	–
0.5	0.4	0.2	*	0.1	0.5	4.4	0.6	3.5	–	0.9	0.8	0.6	0.2	6.4	0.2	0.6	0.4	–	–
0.2	0.2	0.2	*	0.1	0.5	1.9	*	–	–	–	–	*	–	6.2	–	–	–	–	–
0.3	0.2	–	–	–	–	2.5	0.6	3.5	–	0.9	0.8	0.6	0.2	0.2	0.2	0.6	0.4	–	–
2.9	3.2	3.5	0.9	2.9	3.2	3.9	3.2	4.5	3.7	4.5	4.6	5.0	4.0	3.3	–	–	3.0	3.6	0.6
2.9	3.2	2.5	0.9	2.9	3.2	3.9	3.2	4.5	3.7	4.5	4.6	5.0	4.0	3.3	–	–	3.0	3.6	0.6
118.7	56.4	50.6	3.2	19.6	18.1	50.5	–	–	10.9	1.0	9.9	–	–	–	5.5	–	2.1	–	–
113.3	56.4	44.3	–	19.6	16.7	46.5	–	–	–	–	–	–	–	–	–	–	–	–	–
–	6.3	3.2	–	1.3	4.0	4.0	–	–	10.9	1.0	9.9	–	–	–	5.5	–	2.1	–	–
3.9	3.8	19.4	10.2	30.4	19.5	9.8	6.9	6.8	10.7	10.1	7.8	8.3	8.0	5.3	4.1	4.0	4.0	*	–
–	–	–	0.2	–	–	–	–	–	3.0	7.5	7.0	7.0	6.7	4.0	3.0	3.0	–	–	–
3.5	3.5	19.0	10.0	28.0	17.5	8.0	6.1	6.0	7.5	2.0	–	–	–	–	–	–	–	–	–
0.4	0.3	0.4	–	2.4	2.0	1.8	0.8	0.8	0.2	0.6	0.8	1.3	1.3	1.3	1.1	1.0	1.0	*	–
–	–	–	–	–	–	–	–	–	–	–	–	–	–	–	–	–	–	–	–
–	–	–	–	–	–	–	–	–	–	–	–	–	–	–	–	–	3.0	–	–
–	–	12.0	–	20.0	10.0	–	–	–	–	5.0	10.0	10.4	24.6	10.0	–	–	–	–	–
127.1	65.4	98.7	21.3	95.7	69.3	97.6	33.3	35.4	45.7	41.1	63.6	69.5	80.3	67.4	67.9	68.3	54.2	31.2	0.6
122.2	60.6	92.0	16.7	86.9	99.9	81.8	21.8	18.0	30.4	13.0	24.9	20.4	20.0	19.7	28.5	24.0	16.0	6.1	–
4.9	4.8	6.7	4.6	8.8	10.3	15.8	11.5	17.4	15.3	28.1	38.7	49.1	60.3	47.5	39.4	44.3	38.2	25.1	0.6

4 US FOREIGN POLICY TOWARD ETHIOPIA AND SOMALIA

Our objective should be to exclude military bases or related facilities
for foreign powers from the Horn of Africa. The military forces of
both Somalia and Ethiopia are all out of proportion to their true
national security requirements and should be scaled down.

Raymond L. Thurston, US Ambassador to Somalia (1965–68).[1]

The Horn of Africa ... has considerable strategic importance for the
United States as it is relevant to both the security of the Middle East
and to Africa ... .We seek access to airfields and harbors for our
military forces should they, in times of crisis, be required to defend
against Soviet expansionism in the Persian Gulf or the Indian Ocean.

Chester Crocker, Assistant Secretary of State for African Affairs
(1981–89), November 13, 1985.[2]

Either be a mountain, or have a mountain to lean on.

Somali proverb

Introduction

The Horn of Africa is the site of a centuries-old competition between a
multi-ethnic Ethiopian state and Somali nationalists who historically
have sought to unify their traditionally divided peoples within one
political system.[3] As early as the sixteenth century, this competition
erupted in conflict as the Christian-ruled Ethiopian empire of Emperor
Lebna Dengel was beset militarily by Muslim sultanates led by Ahmed
Gurey, a famed Islamic conquerer in Somali folklore and political
history. Nearly four centuries later, the names had changed but the
conflict continued as Ethiopia and Somalia went to war in 1977–78
over the Ogaden region, a border territory largely inhabited by
Somalis and claimed by both countries. A crucial aspect of this historical rivalry remains the determination of both Ethiopians and
Somalis to pursue their regional agendas by seeking the support of the
major international powers of their time. During the sixteenth century,
this quest led Dengel to seek the military support of the Portuguese

empire, whereas the Somali forces led by Gurey received support from the Ottoman empire. Four centuries later the external patrons of preference would be either the Soviet Union or the United States. This approach to regional politics – eagerly accepted by both superpowers during the Cold War era – is aptly summarized by the Somali proverb, "Either be a mountain, or have a mountain to lean on."[4]

The origins of US involvement in the Horn of Africa (prior to August 1948)

Strategic necessities associated with expanding involvement in World War II laid the foundations of US foreign policy toward the Horn of Africa.[5] In an effort to oppose the military expansionism of Nazi Germany and Fascist Italy, and to bolster the beleagered military forces of Great Britain, the Roosevelt administration declared Ethiopia eligible for inclusion in a military aid program known as "lend-lease" in March 1941. In Northern Africa, aid was designed to strengthen Britain's defenses in Libya and Egypt against Germany's famed Afrika Corps. The Horn of Africa entered into this equation as a War Department-designated assembly point and distribution center for US aid. The focal point of these lend-lease efforts was Eritrea – a former Italian-ruled colony commanding a strategic location bordering the Red Sea that had been liberated by British forces in 1941.

The War Department's efforts in Eritrea were twofold. First, in the aftermath of a secret meeting held in Washington on November 19, 1941, a Royal Air Force (RAF) support base was established at the Eritrean town of Gura. Codenamed "Project 19," the purpose of the base was to repair and return damaged RAF aircraft to the North African battle zone with "minimal delay."[6] The War Department also refurbished the Eritrean port of Massawa to provide direct support for the British Mediterranean fleet, as well as to maintain a naval salvage operation to raise over forty ships scuttled by the Italian Navy.[7] By August 1942, less than one year after the War Department's decision to establish a presence in Eritrea, 336 US military personnel were directing projects that employed nearly 16,000 workers, including 2,819 US civilians, 5,611 Italians, and 7,384 Eritreans.[8]

The most important aspect of US military involvement in British-ruled Eritrea during World War II revolved around the War Department's establishment in May 1943 of a radio communications center at a former Italian installation known as Radio Marina located on the outskirts of the Eritrean town of Asmara. The military benefits associated with this base, initially named Asmara Barracks, rested on a unique convergence of altitude and geographical location that allowed its operators to achieve long-distance radio transmissions without the need for numerous frequency changes. By March 1948, an initial seven-person detachment of the US Army Signal Corps had grown to over 100 military personnel, inclusive of a five-person detachment associated with a naval communications program.[9]

The Asmara Barracks quickly became an integral link in a global telecommunications network that ranged from its headquarters in Arlington, Virginia, to a variety of other regional client states, such as the Philippines and Morocco. According to a report published by the Joint Chiefs of Staff in August 1948, the strategic benefits offered by Asmara Barracks could be obtained from "no other location in the entire Middle East-Mediterranean area," and were of such "high military importance," that all efforts were to be undertaken to avoid any compromise of the US military position in Eritrea.[10] Specifically, the War Department – reorganized as the Department of Defense under the National Security Act of 1947 – was concerned with the Cold War necessities of establishing a worldwide telecommunications network directed against the Soviet Union in preparation for responding to East–West military conflicts in Europe and the Middle East.

This initial period of US involvement in the Horn of Africa demonstrated the importance of a bureaucracy's organizational mission in contributing to the establishment of a US presence on the African continent. Originally seeking to fulfill its wartime mission of supporting a beleaguered European ally, the War Department by August 1942 was seeking long-term access to facilities in British-controlled Eritrea – most notably Asmara Barracks – to carry out global missions associated with the Cold War. This presence did not derive from an assessment of the needs or interests of the local African peoples, but instead stemmed from the military necessity of using African territory as a means for responding to non-African problems and contingencies.

Establishment of a US–Ethiopian security relationship and pan-Somalism (August 1948–November 1960)

Several political developments called into question the Pentagon's goal of ensuring access to military facilities in Eritrea. First, a newly constituted democratic government in Italy was demanding the return of its former colonies in Africa, including Libya, Eritrea, and Italian Somaliland, which had been relinquished in 1947 by the Treaty of Paris. The Italians argued that they should not have been stripped of their colonies in light of their willingness to participate in the Allied

116

war effort after overthrowing Italian dictator Benito Mussolini in 1943.[11] This demand was matched by a strong appeal on the part of Ethiopian Emperor Haile Selassie, saying that Eritrea historically fell under the jurisdiction of the Ethiopian empire, and therefore should be restored to Ethiopian sovereignty. As a leader whose country had been occupied by the Italian Fascists during World War II, Haile Selassie was adamant in opposing the return of even a "democratic" Italy to the Horn of Africa. Of greatest concern to the Defense Department was Great Britain's determination in 1948 to terminate its colonial presence in the region, including its administration of Eritrea.[12] Pentagon officials feared that an independent Eritrea might not be as favorably disposed as were the British to a continued US military presence.

The Defense Department was not alone in its concern over political developments in the Horn of Africa. As early as July 1947, the Central Intelligence Group (the precursor to the CIA) warned that "Soviet objectives in the Near and Middle East and in the Mediterranean area have been and can again be advanced by using the Italian colonies issue ... to extend Soviet influence into the Mediterranean and African areas."[13] The State Department's Bureau of Near Eastern and African Affairs concurred in this assessment, noting that independence for the colonies "would result in the creation of weak states which would be exposed to Soviet aggression or infiltration."[14] According to the consensus opinion within the national security bureaucracies, the favored solution to the Eritrean question was British trusteeship over northern Eritrea, or that portion of the territory containing Asmara Barracks, with the southern and eastern portions being ceded to Ethiopia to placate Haile Selassie's demands.[15] Despite the logic of this plan from Washington's point of view, it failed to recognize Great Britain's complete opposition to trusteeship responsibilities over any part of Eritrea. The British also refused to entertain the US fallback position – postponement of negotiations concerning northern Eritrea – because they did not wish to remain responsible for the financial and military costs associated with continued administration. Instead, striking a bargain that surely delighted the Emperor, the British acknowledged in August 1948 that they were predisposed to grant Ethiopia control over the entire territory of Eritrea.[16]

The diplomatic dilemma associated with Britain's refusal to maintain a presence within the region was complicated by Soviet and French support for placing Eritrea under some form of Italian trusteeship, as well as the diplomatic positions of several Third World countries which favored independence for the territory. Faced with essentially three options – Ethiopian sovereignty, Italian trusteeship, and independence – a new consensus within the national security bureaucracies favored granting Ethiopia control over the entire territory. Independence was ruled out by policymakers who believed that an economically unviable Eritrea would be subject to communist aggression. Italian trusteeship was ruled out because it was feared that a victory for the Italian Communist Party in the 1948 Italian national elections would also pave the way for a communist Eritrea. Even if this worst-case scenario did not take place, policymakers argued that a UN trusteeship council would not approve of a US military base on Eritrean soil.[17]

The primary driving force behind these conclusions was the firm belief that "every effort" had to be made "to assure the maintenance of essential US military rights" in Eritrea, "particularly in the Asmara-Massawa area" (the site of Asmara Barracks).[18] In short, once it became clear that the British were unwilling to maintain their presence in the region, the search for a "friendly and cooperative" administering power became the primary goal of middle-range bureaucrats concerned with protecting US strategic interests.[19] Since neither Italian trusteeship nor independence would serve this objective, the process of elimination resulted in the establishment of a US–Ethiopian understanding in November 1948 that traded US support for Ethiopian sovereignty over Eritrea in return for "unhampered use" of Asmara Barracks and other military facilities in the Asmara–Massawa region.[20]

Haile Selassie's assiduous wooing of the US policymaking establishment was an important factor in Washington's growing involvement in the region. Ever since the defeat of the Italian Fascists in 1941 and Britain's establishment of a highly resented military administration over Ethiopian territory, the Emperor had sought US support in reasserting Ethiopia's national sovereignty and making his country the premier regional power in the Horn of Africa.[21] Of greatest importance to Haile Selassie was the creation of a US–Ethiopian security relationship in which the US was to serve as the primary benefactor for the expansion and modernization of the Ethiopian Armed Forces.[22]

Despite the Pentagon's desire to ensure unhampered access to military facilities in Ethiopia, Haile Selassie's requests for a military assistance program initially were rejected by US policymakers. Indicative of Africa's low standing within the global hierarchy of Pentagon missions, a US Army mission led by Lt. General Charles L. Bolte concluded in June 1951 that the creation of a military training program was both politically unadvisable and militarily of little strategic benefit to the United States. According to Bolte's final report, not only was

Ethiopia unthreatened by its regional neighbors, but the initiation of a military assistance relationship would lead to undesirable requests for even greater amounts of aid. This report reinforced an earlier assessment of the Joint Chiefs of Staff that, due to rising US military commitments in Korea, Europe, and elsewhere, scarce military resources had to be targeted to those countries truly threatened by "direct or subversive communist aggression."[23]

The negative response of the Defense Department surely must have surprised Haile Selassie, especially in light of his willingness to grant the US access to facilities throughout Ethiopia. In an effort to force the military assistance issue, negotiations were demanded in the aftermath of Ethiopia's acquisition of Eritrea in 1952 to determine the official status of the US presence at Asmara Barracks – renamed "Kagnew Station" in honor of an Ethiopian brigade which had distinguished itself in the Korean War. After the negotiations reached an impasse over the levels of military aid suggested by the Defense Department, as well as the length of the projected lease (twenty-five years), the talks were moved to the US and reopened in December 1952. In the end, the Ethiopian government dropped its objection to an extended lease and the Defense Department agreed to support the creation of a limited military assistance program.

The resolution of all outstanding bargaining issues resulted in the signing of two US–Ethiopian military agreements on May 22, 1953.[24] The first consisted of a twenty-five year access agreement which assured the US complete freedom of access to facilities on Ethiopian soil by surface, land, and sea, as well as freedom of flight throughout the country. The Ethiopian government also agreed to provide lands for the future expansion of US facilities, although the terms of their provision were to be negotiated in each case. The second military agreement required the US to establish a Military Assistance Advisory Group (MAAG) Mission in Addis Ababa to oversee a $5 million military assistance program that entailed the equipping and training of three Ethiopian divisions, each of which numbered approximately 6,000 soldiers.[25] These two accords represented but the beginning of what Haile Selassie undoubtedly hoped would constitute a long-term US–Ethiopian security relationship. Having secured a grant of $5 million in US military aid, the next logical step was to make that initial commitment the basis of a more permanent military aid relationship. In order to achieve this goal, the Emperor made his first official head of state visit to Washington in May 1954, taking advantage of numerous opportunities to reiterate Ethiopia's need for greater amounts of economic and military aid.

Rather than endearing himself to US policymakers, Haile Selassie's requests merely intensified an ongoing debate within the national security bureaucracies over Ethiopia's importance to the United States. Although underscoring the importance of maintaining access to Kagnew, the Pentagon argued that, relative to other countries and regions of greater concern, Ethiopia was of "no strategic importance" to the global security needs of the United States, subsequently opposing Ethiopian pressures for an extended military aid program.[26] The State Department's Bureau of Near Eastern and African Affairs countered by citing the political benefits that Washington derived from close ties with the Ethiopian regime. In addition to being described as someone who had achieved a respected leadership role among African nationalists due to his valiant efforts in the Italo-Ethiopian War of 1935–36, Haile Selassie was praised as an anti-communist and pro-US leader who had not hesitated to support Washington on numerous international issues, most notably the Korean War. Most important, Ethiopia was perceived as occupying a strategic location at the crossroads of the Middle East and Africa, both of which prior to 1958 fell under the area of political responsibility claimed by the Bureau of Near Eastern and African Affairs.[27]

Although political arguments ultimately prevailed in earning an additional, one-year, $5 million extension in military aid in 1955, apparent foot-dragging on the part of the Defense Department led to Ethiopian expressions of dissatisfaction in early 1956 over the inadequacy of US military assistance – both in terms of the levels of aid and the slow delivery dates of promised matériel. In response to these growing criticisms, Ambassador Joseph Simonson and the Bureau of Near Eastern and African Affairs stridently argued for the establishment of a multi-year military assistance program, and were supported by a new bureaucratic ally – the recently created US MAAG Mission in Addis Ababa – which had become the focal point of numerous Ethiopian requests for greater amounts of military aid.[28] Nonetheless, Pentagon officials in Washington remained steadfastly opposed to any further military commitments.

The rising bureaucratic debate was only resolved in October 1956 after the Bureau of Near Eastern and African Affairs succeeded in seeking an NSC review of US–Ethiopian relations.[29] The NSC had acquired an interest in the Horn of Africa due to the rise to power and growing Soviet ties of Gamal Abdul Nasser, the militantly nationalist leader of Egypt. In recognition of the timely arguments advanced by the Bureau of Near Eastern and African Affairs, the NSC acknowledged Ethiopia's overriding political importance to the US as a regional bulwark against the spread of Egyptian and communist radicalism in the Middle East and the Horn of Africa, and directed the Defense Department to "provide the Ethiopian Armed Forces with limited military equipment and training of a kind suitable for maintaining internal security and offering resistance to local aggression."[30] Toward this end, approximately $20.9 million in military aid was allotted for the 1957–60 period to fund the equipping and training of 28,000 soldiers of the Ethiopian Army (including 4,000 support troops), the purchase of ten coastal patrol vessels for the Ethiopian Navy, and a survey to determine the needs of the Ethiopian Air Force. In an effort to reassure Pentagon strategists who opposed further US involvement in the Horn of Africa, the NSC underscored that the State Department was to undertake "every effort to avoid a military build-up which would seriously strain the Ethiopian economy or lead to commitments for indefinite US support."[31]

However, a more formal and expanded military commitment was exactly what Haile Selassie was seeking from the United States. Since the end of World War II, the driving force behind the Emperor's foreign policy was to ensure that neither the Red Sea nor the Indian Ocean coastal regions became sources for future attacks against the Ethiopian empire. Having successfully neutralized such a threat in the Red Sea region through his acquisition of Eritrea in 1952, Haile Selassie's main concern – some would say "obsession" – during the remainder of the 1950s was the threat posed to Ethiopia's territorial integrity by the Somali peoples inhabiting the Horn of Africa.[32]

Haile Selassie's foreign policy concerns derived from the simple reality that Somali nationalists during the 1950s were calling for a redrawing of inherited colonial boundaries in order to create a pan-Somali state.[33] As symbolized by the five-pointed star emblazoned on the Somali flag, this irredentist quest envisioned the unification of the Somali nation which arbitrarily had been divided among four European and African powers into five separate territories: the British Somaliland Protectorate, Italian Somaliland, the French Territory of the Afars and the Issas (as of 1977 the Republic of Djibouti), the Northern Frontier District (the Northern Province of Britain's former colony of Kenya), and Ethiopia's Ogaden region. Once it became clear that the former British and Italian Somaliland territories were going to merge and acquire independence as the Republic of Somalia in July 1960, Haile Selassie became increasingly concerned that such an event would only strengthen Somali desires to create a pan-Somali state, inclusive of the Ogaden. According to the Emperor, the loss of the Ogaden not only would result in a significant loss of Ethiopian territory (roughly 26 percent of the country's total landmass), but set in motion separatist desires in Eritrea and other ethnically diverse regions of the Amhara-ruled Ethiopian empire. Just as Washington's support was crucial to Ethiopia's acquisition of Eritrea in 1952, so too would Haile Selassie seek to enlist US support for his regional designs related to the Somaliland territories under British and Italian rule.

The growing US–Ethiopian security relationship ensured that Haile Selassie's concerns over the Somali issue received a sympathetic hearing in Washington. As early as 1956, policy memoranda of the national security bureaucracies were drawing attention to the growing Somali "problem," or the threat posed by an independent Somalia for the future stability and territorial integrity of Ethiopia."[34] The fact that the word "problem," as opposed to a more objective term, such as the Somali "issue," dominates the written record underscores that Ethiopia's opposition to pan-Somalism was supported by the national security bureaucracies, especially the Bureau of Near Eastern and African Affairs. This position was formalized in February 1959 when the NSC explicitly rejected the notion of a pan-Somali state that included Ethiopia's Ogaden region.[35]

Despite opposition to any initiatives that threatened the territorial integrity of Ethiopia, Washington informed Haile Selassie on January 12, 1959, that it intended to support the unification of the British and Italian Somaliland territories in accordance with the wishes of the former European colonial powers.[36] Especially unhappy with this decision, the Emperor sought to jolt Washington into reassessing the entire US–Ethiopian relationship by a careful "playing of the Soviet card." In a much publicized trip to the Soviet Union and Eastern Europe in June 1959, Haile Selassie broached the possibility of Ethiopia's realignment within the international system by accepting long-term Soviet bloc economic credits in excess of $110 million. The initial US response reflected the impact that such a ploy could have during the charged Cold War atmosphere of the late 1950s. Ambassador Don Bliss is reported to have been "stunned" by the Emperor's opening to the socialist bloc. Echoing arguments that became the hallmark of the State Department's newly created Bureau of African Affairs, Bliss argued throughout the latter half of 1959 for providing even greater amounts of economic and military aid to Ethiopia, as well as more clearly underscoring Washington's intention to support that country in any future conflict with Somalia.[37] These arguments were echoed by a July 1960 NSC report which asserted that "the existence of large-scale Soviet bloc credits" had "given a new complexion to US–Ethiopian relations." The report further noted that "continued success in curtail-

ing serious Soviet penetration and preserving Ethiopia's friendly attitude" would depend on the ability of the US and its allies to "demonstrate their interest in Ethiopia and its problems," most notably that
country's territorial dispute with Somalia.[38]

A rising consensus within the national security bureaucracies that
Washington needed to reaffirm US interest in Ethiopia led to two very
important tangible results for the future of the US–Ethiopian security
relationship. First, Washington agreed in 1959 to provide the Ethiopian
Air Force with a squadron of F-86 fighter aircraft that originally had
been proposed by a US Air Force survey team in 1957, only to be
rejected that same year by the Joint Chiefs of Staff. Similar to the
majority of military aid provided to Ethiopia during the 1950s, the
fighter aircraft were sought by the State Department and justified on
political grounds. The State Department was particularly adamant in
underscoring the "psychological importance" that Haile Selassie had
attached to refurbishing the Ethiopian Air Force with the most techno-
logically advanced fighter aircraft in the US arsenal.[39] The signing of a
secret military agreement in August 1960, just two months after the
independence and unification of the British and Italian Somaliland
territories, constituted a second important tangible result of bureaucratic pressures to reaffirm the US–Ethiopian security relationship.[40]
The agreement committed the US to train and equip a fourth division
of the Ethiopian Army (which would then total approximately 40,000
troops) in exchange for the expansion of US activities at Kagnew, and
underscored Washington's "interest in the security of Ethiopia and its
opposition to any activities threatening the territorial integrity of
Ethiopia."[41] Although US officials would later state that this wording
did not constitute a military commitment to defend Ethiopia if threatened with territorial dismemberment, it nonetheless placed the US
squarely on the side of Ethiopia in any future conflict with Somalia.

This second period of US involvement in the Horn of Africa nicely
demonstrated the relationship between routine situations and bureaucratic dominance of the policymaking process in contributing to an
outcome marked by bureaucratic incrementalism. In the absence of
direct policy guidance from either the President or his closest advisers,
a variety of Cold War inspired bureaucratic missions associated with
ensuring unhampered access to Kagnew and other military facilities
led to US support for Ethiopian control over Eritrea, as well as a
rejection of the pan-Somali quest to unite all the Somali peoples of the
Horn of Africa under one government. Most important, parochial
bureaucratic interpretations of US interests in Ethiopia contributed to
upward pressures for the strengthening of US–Ethiopian ties which, in

turn, led to the signing of two US–Ethiopian military agreements in 1953. These accords symbolized the beginning of a US–Ethiopian security relationship which, from 1953 forward, prompted the national security bureaucracies to seek the maintenance and enhancement of this tie at the expense of pursuing a similar relationship with Somalia. In short, the bureaucratic basis was laid for favoring Ethiopia in that country's historical competition with Somalia.

The national security bureaucracies and low-level crises (December 1960–May 1964)

The US–Ethiopian security relationship was tested by two potential crisis situations during the early 1960s. The first test began on December 13, 1960, when Haile Selassie's Imperial Bodyguard arrested members of the royal family, as well as prominent leaders of the Ethiopian Armed Forces, in an attempted military *coup d'état* against the government. Moving against the government while the Emperor was touring South America, the Imperial Bodyguard, supported by the Ethiopian Police Force, quickly established control over the airport and radio station in Addis Ababa, and secured all roads leading to the Imperial Palace. The following day Ambassador Arthur L. Richards was summoned to the Ethiopian Foreign Office and was asked to transmit a cable to Washington requesting formal recognition of the new regime, which by nightfall had proclaimed itself the People's Republic of Ethiopia.[42]

Faced with a rapidly unfolding situation, the initial response of the US Embassy was to remain "nominally" neutral until it could be determined whether the forces loyal to Haile Selassie were capable of reestablishing control over the capital. For example, although US telecommunications facilities in both Addis Ababa and Asmara were allowed to transmit messages of the loyalist forces to the Emperor, Richards made it clear to the Embassy staff on the morning of December 14 that they were "neutrals" in the unfolding conflict.[43] This policy stance was supported by General Chester de Gavre, Chief of the US MAAG Mission, who ordered his personnel to remain at home and avoid contact with their Ethiopian counterparts. Only Lt. Colonels Willis Gary and W. H. Crosson, US Air Force and Army attachés, respectively, were ordered to maintain contact with both sides of the conflict so as to provide the Embassy with "up-to-the minute information."[44]

This wait-and-see attitude changed the following morning (December 15) after it became apparent to US military officers that the combined loyalist forces of the Ethiopian Army and Air Force had amassed superior firepower capable of overwhelming the Imperial Bodyguard. Confident that the loyalists would prevail, de Gavre, with the support of Richards, announced at a morning meeting of the principal Embassy officers that "the time had come" for the US MAAG Mission to meet its advisory obligations to the Ethiopian government as provided for in the US–Ethiopian military agreements. "This was particularly apropos," noted Crosson, "since all estimates indicated that the loyalist forces were now in – or were rapidly approaching – a position of such superiority as to leave little doubt as to the final outcome in a military sense."[45] During the subsequent three days of military operations in which the Imperial Bodyguard was defeated, US military support ranged from tactical advice to soldiers in the field, the airlift of urgently needed medical supplies, to attempts at frightening rebels in control of the Imperial Palace by overflights that broke the sound barrier and created sonic booms.[46] These efforts were warmly appreciated by Haile Selassie who, upon his return to Addis Ababa on December 17, summoned Richards to the airport to express his "sincere gratitude" for US military support.[47]

Despite the potentially devastating impact that Haile Selassie's over-throw could have exerted on the US–Ethiopian security relationship, the coup attempt never was perceived as a crisis situation which required the ongoing attention of either President Eisenhower or his closest advisers, and therefore was handled largely at the level of the national security bureaucracies, especially the US Embassy in Addis Ababa. The lack of an East–West dimension explains why the coup attempt never was perceived as a crisis situation at the highest levels of the policymaking establishment. Dismissing any possibility of Soviet involvement, middle-range bureaucrats instead focused on rising homegrown dissatisfaction with the Emperor's military and edu-cational policies as the primary cause of the coup attempt.[48] The coup plotters also preempted the emergence of a perceived crisis in Wash-ington by assuring Richards and other Embassy officers that US citi-zens and property would be completely protected by the new regime, and that its leaders desired continued close security links with the US on a "most friendly basis."[49] In a sense, whether the loyalist forces prevailed or not, the US stood little chance of losing its special access rights to military facilities in Ethiopia. It is for this reason that both Richards and de Gavre counselled caution once it became clear that a coup was underway, replacing sympathetic neutrality with full support only after it became clear that Haile Selassie's forces would emerge victorious.

The second test of the US–Ethiopian security relationship grew out of Ethiopia's intensifying conflict with the newly independent Republic of Somalia over the Ogaden region.[50] Never having established effective control over this portion of the country, the Ethiopian Army found itself confronted with growing ethnic unrest that, at the very least, received moral support from the Somali government headed by President Adan Abdullah Osman. In late July 1960, fierce clashes between Somali fighters and the Ethiopian Army northeast of the Ogadeni city of Dire Dawa resulted in over 800 Somali and 1,000 Ethiopian casualties. In early August, some 300 Somalis attacked and derailed a train traveling on the Djibouti–Addis Ababa railroad, Ethiopia's primary economic lifeline to the outside world. As someone who warned that Somali independence would only inflame pan-Somali designs to detach the Ogaden from Ethiopia, Haile Selassie must have perceived these initial acts of violence as the beginning of a major threat from his neighbor to the east. Most important, the Emperor underscored that Washington's support for the Ethiopian position on the Ogaden was central to the continued strength of the US–Ethiopian security relationship. As recognized by the NSC in a December 1960 review of US foreign policy toward the Horn of Africa, the US position on the Ogaden became, and remained, "an obsession" of Haile Selassie which affected his "attitude on all other matters."[51]

The primary obstacle to the enhancement of US–Somali relations was a firmly entrenched bureaucratic mindset that regarded the pan-Somali ideal as both illegitimate and counterproductive to US interests,[52] and which was reinforced in May 1963 when the newly established OAU enshrined the concept of "territorial integrity" as one of the fundamental principles of its charter; in essence accepting the permanence of existing boundaries inherited from the colonial era. The impact of this mindset was portrayed by Washington's responses to Somali requests for military assistance in 1960 and 1962. In deference to Ethiopian sensibilities, the State Department's Africa Bureau rejected both requests, preferring instead that Italy and Britain take the lead on this issue as the former colonial powers.[53] In order to maintain a moderating influence with the Somali regime, however, it was deemed useful by the Africa Bureau – over the protests of Haile Selassie and the new Ambassador to Addis Ababa, Edward Korry – to maintain a limited economic aid program that included funds for training and equipping the Somali Police Force.

An important concern of the national security bureaucracies was to prevent a massive build-up of the Somali Army which could lead to a regional arms race and ultimately threaten the political stability of

Ethiopia. Despite some success in gaining initial Somali acceptance of an $8.4 million British–Italian military aid package, the plan quickly fell through in the face of Somalia's growing conflict with Britain over the future disposition of ethnic Somalis in Kenya's Northern Frontier District, as well as growing Soviet overtures that they could better supply Somalia with its military needs.[54] In response to Soviet initiatives, the Africa Bureau cooperated with Italy and West Germany in putting together a $10 million military aid package that was conditioned on Somalia's willingness to refrain from seeking military aid from any other source, most notably the Soviet Union. Originally conceived by Horace G. Torbert, Ambassador to Somalia from 1963 to 1965, this ill-disguised attempt at controlling the size of the Somali Army offended the Somali leadership who, in any case, received a much better offer from the Soviet Union in October 1963.[55] The Soviet offer constituted $30 million of unrestricted aid designed to equip a Somali Army of 20,000 troops, including a squadron of MIG fighter aircraft. Since matching this offer would have created a tremendous strain in US–Ethiopian relations, Washington yielded the military field of maneuver to the Soviet bloc, but continued to fund and train the Somali Police Force. "Since there was no question that our primary interests lay in Ethiopia," noted Torbert, "it wasn't that important to us to start a program that was going to give us trouble forever."[56]

The difficulty of maintaining even a limited diplomatic relationship with Somalia was portrayed by the US response during the latter half of 1963 to the intensification of the Somali insurgency in the Ogaden – a conflict that ultimately led to a series of border clashes between Ethiopia and Somalia during early 1964. On June 16, 1963, a full-scale rebellion intent on making the Ogaden ungovernable was launched after a meeting of 300 Somali notables at Hodayo, a watering place north of the Ogadeni town of Warder. Numbering over 3,000 guerrilla fighters, the Ogadeni insurgency became adept at ambushing military convoys and forcing the Ethiopian Army to restrict itself to administrative centers in the region. In response, the Haile Selassie regime decided to place direct military pressure on Somalia, the perceived instigator and source of the insurgency. During mid-January 1964, the Third Division of the Ethiopian Army headed by General Aman Adom launched air and ground attacks against Somali territory at numerous points along the Ethiopian–Somali boundary, including a bombing raid against the northeastern city of Hargeisa, Somalia's second largest urban area and the former capital of British Somaliland.[57]

The initial US response to the insurgency – unequivocal support for Ethiopia's military operations in the Ogaden – reflected the organizational missions of those bureaucracies most involved with Ethiopia on a day-to-day basis. Whereas the US MAAG Mission in Addis Ababa offered advice on the deployment of Ethiopian forces and the employment of counterinsurgency tactics, the State Department's Africa Bureau underscored the illegitimacy of the guerrilla campaign and placed pressure on Mogadishu to end its support for the Ogadeni insurgents. This policy stance obviously did not endear the US to the Somali leadership in Mogadishu who, in both private and public statements, accused the US of aiding Ethiopia in carrying out a program of "repression" against ethnic Somalis in the Ogaden, as well as "aggression" against the sovereign state of Somalia.[58] This harsh rhetoric did not win Somalia any favor in Washington, but rather served to reinforce the prevailing image of that country within the national security bureaucracies as an expansionistic threat to the territorial integrity of Ethiopia.

The transformation of the conflict from a guerrilla insurgency in the Ogaden to direct military clashes along the Ethiopian–Somali frontier raised concern within the State Department's Africa Bureau that Ethiopia might attempt a full-scale invasion of Somalia. As it increasingly became apparent that Haile Selassie was contemplating the absorption of the newly independent Republic of Somalia in line with Ethiopia's historical claims to all territories inhabited by Somalis, restraint of Ethiopia and a negotiated Ethiopian–Somali settlement became the primary objectives of the State Department's Africa Bureau. It has been noted, for example, that the US Embassy in Addis Ababa forced the Ethiopian Army to withdraw to its bases in the Ogaden by threatening to cut off all US foreign assistance.[59] In personal meetings with the Somali and Ethiopian Ambassadors stationed in Washington, as well as in cabled instructions to US Embassies in Mogadishu and Addis Ababa, Assistant Secretary of State for African Affairs G. Mennen Williams followed up this threat by pressing for a peaceful resolution of the border conflict.[60] Toward this end, the Africa Bureau fully supported OAU mediation efforts that ultimately resulted in the establishment of a cease-fire agreement on March 30, 1964.

It is important to note that the Africa Bureau's willingness to pressure its most valued client on the African continent extended only to cross-border operations in the Republic of Somalia, and not to the counterinsurgency efforts of the Ethiopian military in the Ogaden region. At the request of the US Embassy in Addis Ababa, the Africa Bureau authorized the dispatch of four, twelve-person Mobile Training Teams (MTTs) to the Ogaden to train the Ethiopian military in counterinsurgency warfare tactics. The arrival of these teams in May

1964 reflected the desire of the Africa Bureau to reassure Haile Selassie that the US appreciated the "seriousness" of the "internal security problem" posed by the Ogadeni Somalis."[61]

A significant aspect of this second test of the US–Ethiopian security relationship was that operational control over policy, once again, remained in the hands of the national security bureaucracies, most notably the State Department's Africa Bureau. Apart from the overwhelming military superiority of the Ethiopian Armed Forces which outnumbered the poorly equipped Somalis by almost four to one, the absence of a significant East–West dimension served as the primary reason for the lack of high-level attention to the Ethiopian–Somali conflict.[62] Although the Soviet Union had signed a military aid agreement with Somalia in December 1963, Moscow firmly supported the concept of territorial integrity, and rejected any attempt to attain the pan-Somali ideal by force. Moreover, the substantial Italian presence in Somalia was perceived in Washington as a moderating influence that offset the impact of Mogadishu's growing ties with the Soviet Union. In short, the Ethiopian–Somali dispute simply became "one of a hundred pressure points in the world" that, at least according to senior-level policymakers, was best left to the specialists in the Africa Bureau.[63] As a result, the US response to the Ogadeni conflict reflected the established policy of favoring Ethiopia's territorial integrity at the expense of Somalia's irredentist claims.

Bureaucratic incrementalism amidst the rise of an African détente (May 1964–September 1969)

An expanding number of Cold War oriented bureaucratic missions associated with Kagnew and related facilities in Ethiopia led to a tremendous growth in the official US presence to over 7,000 civilian and military personnel (including over 3,500 at Kagnew) by May 1964. Whereas Pentagon officials increasingly viewed Ethiopia as "strategically vital" to preparing for a potential global conflict with the Soviet Union,[64] CIA officials similarly underscored Kagnew's growing importance as an "irreplaceable listening post" capable of intercepting a vast array of transmissions to and from the Soviet bloc countries.[65] These traditional arguments were reinforced by a series of new bureaucratic missions associated with the establishment of a top secret telecommunications installation – the Stonehouse Project – that required close cooperation between the Pentagon and the National Aeronautics and Space Administration (NASA). Although "officially" devoted to space research, the interception of Soviet space telemetry was the most important mission of the facility.[66] Even Congress got into the act. Representative Frances P. Bolton (R-Ohio), chairperson of the House Subcommittee on the Near East and Africa, characterized Kagnew as the "most important radio facility in the entire world."[67]

The importance attached to maintaining unhampered access to Kagnew provided a powerful rationale for the incremental enhancement of the US–Ethiopian security relationship.[68] Even the Pentagon, which in the past had opposed increasing US military assistance to Ethiopia, ultimately yielded to rationales of Kagnew's importance.[69] As a result, military assistance increased from $8.5 million in 1964 to $18.2 million in 1967, with a similar increase in economic assistance during the same period from $9.2 to $19.0 million. In the clearest indication of this upward trend, Ambassador Korry was authorized on June 18, 1964, to inform Haile Selassie of Washington's willingness to provide the Ethiopian Air Force with a squadron of 12 F-5 Freedom Fighter aircraft.[70] This decision was significant in that it followed nearly two years of efforts on the part of the State Department, particularly the US Embassy in Addis Ababa, to discourage the Emperor from seeking the sophisticated aircraft. An important reason for the reversal was Ethiopia's willingness to host the Stonehouse Project – the first major parts of which began arriving just weeks prior to the date on which the US had agreed to supply the fighter aircraft.

A desire to maintain military access also led the Pentagon to support the Ethiopian government in counterinsurgency efforts against Eritrean guerrillas who began seeking independence through military means in September 1961. Fully aware that a guerrilla victory meant the possible end of US access, the Defense Department supported the sale of sophisticated weaponry to the Haile Selassie regime, as well as the periodic deployment of US military teams to enhance the capabilities of the Ethiopian Army. Beginning in 1966, approximately 164 US Army officers were assigned to Ethiopia for a period of two to three years to train the Ethiopian Army in the art of counterinsurgency warfare and instill a sense of professionalism within its officer corps. Two years later, a counterinsurgency civic action team was deployed for a period of twenty-six weeks.[71]

The Kagnew rationale, however, was not without limitations. First, the staggering costs of growing US military involvement in the Vietnam War led to congressionally mandated cuts in the overall foreign aid budget, most notably as concerned Africa, that resulted in a ceiling of $12 million in military aid to Ethiopia beginning in 1968. Second, advances in satellite technology ensured that land-based telecommunications systems, such as Kagnew and its related Stonehouse

Project, were becoming obsolete as the Defense Department increasingly looked to outer space.[72] Most important, the Pentagon decided in 1966 to construct a military base at Diego Garcia, a lightly populated British possession in the middle of the Indian Ocean. The long-term implication of base construction at Diego Garcia was that the US military presence in the Horn of Africa could become obsolete if the Defense Department sought to transfer its installations to a less threatening and less demanding spot within the region.[73]

The combination of these three trends contributed to a more cautious policy stance within the State Department's Africa Bureau, especially as concerned Haile Selassie's repeated requests for increased military aid. For example, the US Embassy in Addis Ababa was notified that assistance would continue as long as US interests required, but that Washington did not have a "legal commitment for indefinite support." Most important, the US Embassy was cautioned to avoid any use of the term "support commitment" as neither the State Department nor the Pentagon were willing to guarantee the replacement of worn out military equipment over an indefinite period of time.[74]

The same bureaucratic imperatives that led to the incremental enhancement of the US–Ethiopian security relationship ultimately served as constraints on any similar expansion of US–Somali ties from 1964 to 1967. The single most important obstacle to enhanced US–Somali ties continued to be Mogadishu's support for irredentist movements in Ethiopia, Kenya, and, to a lesser degree, the French colony of Djibouti. Even the State Department's Africa Bureau, which sought to maintain some semblance of balance between US relations with Ethiopia and Somalia, recognized the overriding importance of US–Ethiopian ties and the necessity of avoiding "any action which would appear to support Somali irredentism."[75] "The most the US realistically could hope for," according to one member of the Africa Bureau, "was the maintenance of a friendly relationship that kept Somalia from abandoning its neutralist foreign policy and strengthening its links with the Soviet Union."[76] In keeping with this posture, the Africa Bureau administered a small foreign assistance program that supported roughly 100 Peace Corps volunteers, the building of a port at Kismayu, and the ongoing training for the Somali Police Force.

Proponents of closer US–Somali ties, most notably the US Embassy in Mogadishu, received a significant boost when, in the aftermath of Abdirashid Ali Shermarke's accession to the Somali presidency on June 10, 1967, he appointed Mohammed Ibrahim Egal as Prime Minister.[77]

In addition to being a moderate, pro-Western, English-speaking politician who, in the words of a former US diplomat stationed in Mogadishu, was "our man" in Somalia,[78] Egal became very popular within the State Department's Africa Bureau, and the West in general, due to his pursuit of a regional détente that renounced the use of force in the pursuit of pan-Somalism. Egal instead committed his government to peaceful diplomatic initiatives that led to a substantial decline in regional conflict and, ultimately, political accords with Ethiopia and Kenya.[79]

Egal's détente policies led to a warming of US–Somali relations, as demonstrated by Vice President Hubert Humphrey's visit to Mogadishu in January 1968, followed by an official visit to Washington by Egal during March of that same year. Both visits were promoted by the Africa Bureau to underscore US support for Egal's diplomatic initiatives and create opportunities for strengthening US–Somali ties.[80] However, whereas an increase in economic aid was conceivable, military aid remained out of the question. "Not only would Haile Selassie object to military aid," noted a former US diplomat stationed in Mogadishu, "but it was difficult enough getting Defense Department support for military aid to Ethiopia even in light of the extensive US military facilities in that country."[81] Other factors for policymakers to consider were the continuation of Ethiopian–Somali border tensions, albeit at a lower level than prior to the Shermarke–Egal government, and the expanding presence of the Soviet Union in Somalia. Despite these potential problems, the US and Somalia at the end of 1969 appeared poised to enhance their limited economic and diplomatic cooperation.

The evolution of US foreign policy toward the Horn of Africa during the 1964–69 period clearly demonstrated the importance of the national security bureaucracies in determining US Africa policies during routine periods. Rather than being determined by a centralized decision-making process at the highest levels of the policymaking establishment, the incremental enhancement of the US–Ethiopian special relationship instead was due to a variety of bureaucratic missions associated with Kagnew and related facilities in Ethiopia. An important aspect of this process was Haile Selassie's ability to successfully bargain for greater commitments of US military aid, inclusive of growing US military involvement in counterinsurgency efforts against Eritrean guerrillas. However, the same rationales which led to the enhancement of the US–Ethiopian security relationship served as constraints on any meaningful expansion of US–Somali ties.

Bureaucratic reassessments amidst an altered regional environment (October 1969–December 1973)

The proponents of closer US–Somali ties suffered an important setback on October 21, 1969, when, in the aftermath of Shermarke's assassination by a disgruntled member of his own clan, Major-General Mohammed Siad Barre dismissed the civilian leadership and assumed power in a bloodless military *coup d'état*. Determined to overcome what he perceived as the corrupt excesses of civilian rule, Siad announced the creation of a military government under the stewardship of the newly created Somali Revolutionary Council.[82]

The military coup was especially disconcerting for Somalia's proponents within the State Department's Africa Bureau. Not only had a pro-Western leader been overthrown by a military general favoring closer links with the Soviet Union, but the coup was perceived as eliminating one of the remaining multiparty democracies in Africa.[83] The Africa Bureau nonetheless sought to preserve the advances achieved by Egal's détente policies by underscoring its willingness to work with the Siad regime. According to Fred L. Hadsel, the Ambassador to Somalia from 1969 to 1971, these overtures were met with assurances of continued, positive ties by the new Somali leadership. "Siad noted right away that he was going to maintain his international obligations," explained Hadsel, "This was key to us."[84]

Initial hopes for maintaining a constructive relationship were soon dampened by a series of low-level conflicts between Washington and Mogadishu. First, the US Peace Corps contingent was expelled in December 1969 on the charge that some among their ranks were working as intelligence agents for the CIA. Second, amid charges that the CIA-trained Somali Police Force was involved in an unsuccessful plot against the government, Siad ordered the expulsion of all CIA officers who were known to be working in Somalia. In both cases, the Africa Bureau cited the "understandably" suspicious and defensive nature of the new revolutionary regime in an attempt to downplay the impact of Siad's actions on the US–Somali relationship.[85]

The most damaging diplomatic dispute between Washington and Mogadishu grew out of Somalia's willingness to allow North Vietnamese merchant ships to trade under Somali flags of convenience. The dispute arose due to congressional legislation which prohibited the US from providing any foreign assistance to a country trading with North Vietnam. Ironically, the Somali practice of reflagging North Vietnamese ships – which "technically" counted as trading with North Vietnam – did not begin with the Siad regime, but was problematical for US–Somali relations even under Egal.[86] Apparently it was Egal's pro-Western foreign policy which had enabled the US Embassy in Mogadishu to plead for patience and keep the law from being invoked.[87] Once Siad was in power, such a rationale no longer sufficed and foreign assistance was terminated after 1971. Despite the best efforts of the Africa Bureau to avoid disruption in the US–Somali relationship, the arrival of the Siad regime seemingly only served to reinforce the engrained distrust of Somali intentions within the national security bureaucracies.

The downturn in US–Somali ties is noteworthy in that neither the October 1969 coup nor the low level diplomatic disputes "raised many eyebrows in Washington."[88] The primary client in the Horn of Africa always had been Ethiopia and, as such, developments within Somalia were perceived as best left to the Africa specialists in the State Department's Africa Bureau. Even Somalia's relationship with the Soviet Union was downplayed by the relevant bureaucracies. Reasoning that the Soviets ultimately were seeking the greater "prize" of Ethiopia, both the State Department and the Joint Chiefs of Staff predicted during the 1960s that the Soviets "would not go forward with the heavy armament of Somalia."[89] Even when it became clear in early 1972 that the Soviet Union had decided to seek a closer military relationship with Somalia, as witnessed by the signing of a Soviet– Somali Treaty of Friendship and Cooperation on July 11, 1974, the Somali military was dismissed by both the State Department and the Pentagon as no match for the superior Ethiopian Armed Forces.

The pro-Ethiopian bias within the US government did not mean that the US–Ethiopian security relationship was beyond reproach. As part of a general reassessment of US security relationships throughout the world, Senator Stuart Symington (D-Missouri) conducted hearings in 1970 as chairperson of the Senate Subcommittee on US Security Agreements and Commitments Abroad, to determine whether the foundations had been laid for any "future" Vietnams.[90] In the case of Ethiopia, the so-called Symington hearings focused on the relationship between the extensive US presence at Kagnew and the potential for greater US involvement in a counterinsurgency war against Eritrean guerrillas. Of particular concern to the committee was the "civic action" component of US military aid in light of Washington's 1960 military commitment to "oppose any activities threatening the territorial integrity of Ethiopia." Although Assistant Secretary of State for African Affairs David Newsom sought to allay the committee's fears by noting that it had been "our policy for many years to seek to avoid direct involvement in the internal security problems of Ethiopia," the delicacy of the US position certainly was clear to all those present. "We have ... a very difficult question here," admitted Newsom. "We have commited ourselves to equip and train the Ethiopians for forces to be used for internal security."[91]

Despite probing questions by the Symington committee, the lack of concern among the vast majority of congresspersons for what was perceived as a "minor insurgency" ensured the continuation of US military policy in accordance with established bureaucratic routines. From 1969 to 1973, US military aid continued to average roughly $12 million a year. In addition to providing the Ethiopian Air Force with three additional F-5 fighter aircraft, the Defense Department authorized a five-year, across-the-board modernization program that included equipping the entire Ethiopian Army with M-16 rifles. Comprising roughly 80 percent of all US security assistance to the African continent, this military aid program was managed with the help of the largest US MAAG Mission in Africa. Averaging over 100 military personnel during the 1969–73 period, US military attachés were stationed in the Ethiopian cities of Addis Ababa, Massawa, Asmara, and Harar.[92]

Even though the levels of US military aid to the Haile Selassie regime remained at a constant level during the early 1970s, the primary bureaucratic rationale – unhampered access to Kagnew – which had led to the dramatic expansion of the US–Ethiopian security relationship at the beginning of the 1960s was becoming irrelevant. The combination of advances in satellite technology and the establishment of a telecommunications center on Diego Garcia in March 1973 had rendered obsolete almost all similar operations at Kagnew. Whereas Army communications and CIA intelligence gathering operations were shifted to the Defense Satellite Communications System, the Navy's ship-to-shore communications operations were transferred to Diego Garcia. Even the Pentagon's highly sensitive Stonehouse Project was closed down in July 1973.[93] In light of Kagnew's decreased importance to the bureaucratic missions of the Defense Department, Secretary of Defense James R. Schlesinger received White House approval in August 1973 to completely phase out US military operations at the station and related facilities.

The impact of Kagnew's declining importance was demonstrated by Haile Selassie's visit to the US in May 1973. Apparently alarmed by the Soviet military build-up of Somalia and seeking to allay "mounting concern" among his ministers and the Ethiopian Armed Forces, the Emperor sought approximately $450 million in military aid that included M-60 tanks, Phantom jets, and surface-to-air and air-to-ground missiles.[94] Although supported by the US Embassy in Addis Ababa, the request was rejected by the Pentagon and the State Department. An important consideration of both bureaucracies was growing congressional opposition to military aid in general as a result of US military involvement in Vietnam. Faced with definite budget cuts and difficult questions of allocation, requests for greater aid to an African country confronted with a threat of dubious distinction was out of the question, and Haile Selassie returned to Addis Ababa bearing only the "promise" of the White House to "study" Ethiopia's military requests.[95]

This fifth period of US foreign policy toward the Horn of Africa demonstrated that the process of bureaucratic incrementalism is not irreversible. Once the Cold War inspired bureaucratic missions previously handled by Kagnew were satisfied by other, more self-sufficient means, such as satellite technology and the US base at Diego Garcia, the Pentagon's presence in Ethiopia gradually declined. This turn of events did not signify, however, the abandonment of either Ethiopia or Haile Selassie. As it became clear that the military imperative of maintaining unhampered access to Kagnew no longer could be employed as a bureaucratic weapon to force a reluctant Pentagon into accepting higher levels of US military involvement in Ethiopia, the State Department's Africa Bureau began to place greater emphasis on political rationales to ensure continued close ties with one of its most favored clients on the African continent. This continuation of a bureaucratically inspired relationship that, until the Ethiopian revolution of 1974, spanned nearly twenty-six years, underscored how the day-to-day management of US Africa policies in the absence of crisis fostered support for the status quo. Even if one bureaucracy or a portion thereof loses interest in a particular African country, the institutional ties which have developed over the years form a bureaucratic web heavily resistant to change.

Revolution and gradual US–Ethiopian estrangement (January 1974–April 1977)

Initiated in the 1940s and gradually strengthened amidst a variety of bureaucratic missions over a period of more than a quarter of a century, the US–Ethiopian security relationship did not receive the extended scrutiny of the highest levels of the US policymaking establishment until that relationship was threatened, and ultimately shattered, by the unfolding of a revolutionary situation in Ethiopia from 1974 to 1977. The first salvo of the Ethiopian revolution was a series of mutinies within the Ethiopian Armed Forces during the first two months of 1974 over demands for higher pay and better living conditions. By September of that same year, Haile Selassie had been removed from power and replaced by the Provisional Military Administrative Council (PMAC), a group of approximately 120 junior grade and non-commissioned officers of the Ethiopian military who came to be known as the "Dergue." The nominal head of the PMAC was Defense Minister Aman Adom, a popular, pro-Western Ethiopian general who had distinguished himself in the 1964 Ethiopian–Somali border conflict, and who favored seeking a negotiated settlement to the protracted guerrilla insurgency in Eritrea.

What in reality at first constituted a "creeping coup" against a faithful US ally did not immediately create, as one might expect, a crisis atmosphere in Washington that attracted the attention of the President and his closest advisers in the policymaking process. As early as 1961, Ethiopia specialists within the national security bureaucracies had been issuing reports citing Haile Selassie's tenuous hold on power, particularly due to his unwillingness to undertake much-needed economic and political reforms, as well as the expectation that the US–trained Ethiopian Armed Forces would play an important role in any change in government, serving as the guarantor of US–Ethiopian ties. Therefore, when the Ethiopian Armed Forces deposed the Emperor in favor of a moderate military government dedicated to political and economic reforms, nearly thirteen years of political and military reporting rang true.[96] Indeed, although the CIA voiced concerns over the presence of "radical" elements within the Dergue, Aman's emergence as the head of this group generally was perceived within the national security bureaucracies as a "blessing" to US interests.[97]

The State Department's Africa Bureau took the lead in fashioning a policy response that underscored the necessity of strengthening pro-US moderate factions within the Dergue, most notably by ensuring the continuation of US military assistance.[98] Especially concerned with maintaining Washington's image as a "reliable partner" in Africa, the Africa Bureau warned that any hesitation on the part of US policymakers "would only strengthen the hands of radical elements among the military and further frustrate the moderates, perhaps leading them to concur in more radical initiatives."[99] Reflecting the consensus opinion within the national security bureaucracies, the Africa Bureau successfully argued for providing Ethiopia with over $100 million in military credits and cash sales during the first half of 1974.

The Africa Bureau's optimistic policy stance was called into question by events in Ethiopia beginning in November 1974. In the aftermath of a dispute over how to deal with the issues of political prisoners and the guerrilla insurgency in Eritrea, the ascendency of a hardline faction within the Dergue led to the death of Aman and his replacement by two proponents of radical change: Brigadier-General Teferi Banti, who assumed the office of chairperson of the Dergue, and Colonel Mengistu Haile Mariam, who acquired the first vice-chairman slot and would ultimately emerge as the leader of Ethiopia. Among the radical steps undertaken by the Dergue in the months that followed were the execution of fifty-seven officials of the deposed imperial regime, the creation of a one-party socialist state, the nationalization of all financial institutions and major companies, and the initiation of a full-scale military offensive in Eritrea to end, once-and-for-all, that province's guerrilla insurgency. In short, the limited objectives of the military *coup d'état* of early 1974 evolved under the leadership of Teferi and Mengistu into a full-scale internal revolution intent on completely transforming Ethiopian society.[100]

The radical initiatives of the Dergue were accompanied by an Ethiopian request on February 12, 1975, for an immediate US airlift of $30 million in small arms and ammunition, touching off a policy debate between the State Department's Africa Bureau and the "Arabist" coalition within the Bureau of Near Eastern and South Asian Affairs, as well as within US society. Whereas the Africa Bureau favored complying with the Ethiopian request to demonstrate that the US would not turn its back on reform-minded, radical regimes, this stance was predictably challenged by the Arabists at the State Department who were sympathetic to growing Arab diplomatic and military support for the Eritrean cause, especially in light of the radical drift of the Ethiopian revolution.[101] Indicative of a growing public debate that went beyond the national security bureaucracies, newspapers began questioning what one columnist described as Washington's involvement with a "bloodthirsty and despotic regime."[102] As a result of this rising public interest, Congress entered the debate by holding a hearing on the issues surrounding the Ethiopian request for US arms.[103]

Rising debates over the proper course of US–Ethiopian relations pushed the issue of Ethiopia's military aid request to the level of the White House, presenting the Ford administration with a foreign policy dilemma. A purely *realpolitik* response to the request, based on the worldview shared by Presidents Nixon and Ford, and largely crafted by Kissinger, required strong support for the Dergue in line with the Africa Bureau's recommendations so as to counter any further Soviet inroads in the Horn of Africa. "Not only was Moscow making overtures to the Dergue," explained Arthur W. Hummel, Jr., the Ambassador to Ethiopia from 1975 to 1976, "but since 1975 it had dramatically increased its military presence in neighboring Somalia, making the Horn of Africa an area of increasing concern in Kissinger's global foreign policy calculations."[104] However, in addition to possibly incurring the wrath of Congress and the US public, both of whom had grown wary of military commitments to Third World countries in light of the Vietnam War, such an approach risked alienating important Arab states (such as Saudi Arabia and Egypt) which backed the Eritreans and whose support was crucial to Kissinger's more highly valued diplomatic initiatives in the Middle East. On March 17, 1975, Kissinger announced a compromise solution designed to please all parties and maintain US influence. In addition to agreeing to provide the Dergue with $7 million of the requested $30 million in aid, the administration noted that it was pursuing a parallel diplomatic track of fostering negotiations between the Ethiopian government and the Eritrean guerrillas.[105]

A decision to provide the Dergue in April 1976 with two squadrons of F-5E aircraft – one of the best US fighter-bombers available in the US arsenal – demonstrated the lengths to which the Ford administration was prepared to go in order to preserve the US–Ethiopian security relationship and counterbalance Soviet influence in the Horn of Africa. Initially proposed several years earlier as part of a US–sponsored modernization of the Ethiopian Air Force, the State Department sought congressional support for delivery of the aircraft when Ethiopia's turn on a Pentagon waiting list came up in October 1975. In a confidential letter addressed to the Speaker of the House and other congressional leaders, the State Department emphasized that provision of the fighters had become a matter of "great importance" to the Dergue and a "touchstone" of US–Ethiopian relations.[106] Kissinger ultimately granted final approval in February 1976, with the first squadron of F-5Es arriving in Addis Ababa roughly two months later on April 15. Describing his willingness to act favorably upon Ethiopian requests as "taking a chance," Kissinger also authorized the sale of a further $100 million in military equipment to the Mengistu regime.[107]

A series of reports underscoring the brutality and human rights violations of the Ethiopian regime during the spring and summer of 1976 called into question the wisdom of the Ford administration's policies and led to increased pressures on the part of the media, human rights organizations, and members of Congress to terminate the US–Ethiopian military relationship. At the beginning of August, the Senate Subcommittee on Africa held three days of hearings devoted to US foreign policy toward Ethiopia, paying particular attention to the July 1976 purge and execution of eighteen of Mengistu's rivals within the Dergue – including the US–educated Major Sisay Habte – who were accused of harboring pro-Western sympathies.[108] In what was recognized at the time as putting the "best possible face on a bad situation," Assistant Secretary of State for African Affairs William Schaufele appeared before the subcommittee to support continued US military aid to Ethiopia.[109] "As long as there remained a possibility that a more moderate government could emerge," explained a FSO who once worked at the US Embassy in Addis Ababa, "the State Department's Africa Bureau resisted abandoning an historical relationship that had lasted nearly twenty-four years."[110] Despite these efforts the US–Ethiopian security relationship continued to deteriorate throughout the last year of the Ford administration. Among the events contributing to the growing chasm between Washington and Addis Ababa were Ethiopia's signing of a $100 million military aid agreement with the Soviet Union in December 1976, the adoption of an increasingly shrill, anti-US tone by the Ethiopian press during the spring of 1977, and, most important, Mengistu's emergence as the undisputed leader of Ethiopia on February 3, 1977, after having eliminated his remaining rivals in the Dergue.[111]

The growing crisis in US–Ethiopian relations presented the newly inaugurated Carter administration with a foreign policy dilemma that highlighted an important contradiction in its basic approach to Africa and other regions of the Third World. In addition to upgrading human rights as an important yardstick of foreign policy, Carter sought to overcome the traditional proclivity of previous administrations to automatically oppose radical African regimes. Although applauded by Africanists tired of the Cold War-oriented policies of previous administrations, these two themes clashed when applied to the Ethiopian revolution. "The basic dilemma," noted Assistant Secretary of State for African Affairs Richard Moose, "was how to reconcile seeking some sort of accommodation with the Mengistu regime when it clearly was one of the greatest violators of human rights throughout all of Africa."[112]

The combination of Mengistu's radical excesses, increasingly strident anti-US rhetoric, and congressional pressures to reassess military aid ultimately ensured that the issue of human rights carried the day. In an act which formalized the *de facto* policy of the Ford administration (no military aid had been included in the 1977 budget), the Carter administration on February 24, 1977, supported human rights legislation that officially designated Ethiopia as a gross violator of human rights, and terminated all grant military aid after 1977.[113] This highly public stance was followed by a 50 percent reduction in the number of US military officers associated with the US MAAG Mission in Addis Ababa, as well as official notification that the few remaining US activities at Kagnew would be completely phased out by September 1977 – roughly eight months prior to the formal termination date of the original twenty-five year lease.[114]

From the perspective of Addis Ababa, notification of the closure of Kagnew, when combined with the Carter administration's publicly announced human rights stance and unwillingness to provide military aid, proved the final straw, and served as the basis for severing the majority of remaining links of the US–Ethiopian security relationship. On April 22, 1977, Mengistu ordered the expulsion of most US government personnel from Ethiopia, most notably those associated with the US MAAG Mission and the United States Information Service (USIS). Several days later, he unilaterally terminated the US–Ethiopian Mutual Defense Assistance Agreements. The response of the Carter administration was swift and acrimonious. On April 28, Carter highlighted the human rights abuses of the Mengistu regime and announced the suspension of all outstanding US military aid programs, including the delivery of nearly $100 million in military *matériel* (portions of which had already been paid for by the Ethiopian government). As underscored by Moose, we "slammed the door on the way out for emphasis."[115]

The evolution of US interventionist practices in Ethiopia during the 1974–77 period nicely demonstrated the importance of crisis situations in leading to a reassessment of US Africa policies at the highest levels of the policymaking establishment. During the initial stages of the Ethiopian revolution when it appeared that the moderate, pro-Western forces of Aman would prevail, responsibility for fashioning the proper policy response largely remained the realm of the national security bureaucracies, particularly the State Department's Africa Bureau. As a result, policy reflected the Africa Bureau's position of strong support for one of Washington's oldest and most trusted allies on the African continent. In the aftermath of the radicalization of the revolution, growing debate within the national security bureaucracies and US society forced the issue of further military aid to the Mengistu regime to the highest levels of the Ford and Carter administrations. In a move consonant with its *realpolitik* beliefs, the Ford administration decided to take a chance and provided the Mengistu regime with limited amounts of military aid and sophisticated weaponry, most notably fighter aircraft. The driving force behind what turned out to be a futile White House policy was a desire to prevent a Soviet victory in Ethiopia that would upset the regional balance of power. It was in this atmosphere that the Carter administration entered office with a somewhat contradictory worldview that favored both restricting and strengthening the US–Ethiopian security relationship. In this regard, growing pressures on the part of Congress and the US media to "do something" made it difficult for Carter to remain passive in the face of the increasingly violent and abusive side of the Ethiopian revolution. As a result, Carter adopted a critical human rights stance consistent with his worldview that significantly altered the US–Ethiopian security relationship.[116]

Crisis and attempts at "playing the Somali card" (April 1977–March 1978)

The expulsion of US personnel from Ethiopia in April 1977 signaled the end of Washington's oldest and most extensive security relationship on the African continent, but not the end of US involvement in the Horn of Africa. Parallel to the gradual deterioration of US–Ethiopian ties, Somali leaders were becoming vocal about their unhappiness with Soviet intentions to establish a military relationship with Ethiopia. Privately warning Moscow that Somali–Soviet ties would suffer if the Soviet Union proceeded with such a plan, Somalia began cultivating the US and other Western countries, as well as the Arab world, as alternative sources of military support. It was in this atmosphere that some within the policymaking establishment raised the possibility of "playing the Somali card" to restore US influence in the Horn of Africa.[117]

The Arabist coalition led by the State Department's Bureau of Near Eastern and South Asian Affairs emerged as the most vocal proponent of establishing closer security ties with Somalia. Seeking to support the diplomatic initiatives of pro-Western client states in the region, such as Egypt, Iran, and Saudi Arabia, which had been attempting to stem Soviet influence by weaning Somalia away from the Soviet bloc, the Arabist coalition favored supplying all of Somalia's military needs with US equipment largely paid for by Saudi Arabia. This approach ran counter to the deeply engrained distrust of Somalia within the national security bureaucracies. In addition to still perceiving Ethiopia as the primary objective of any diplomatic initiatives in the Horn of Africa, the Africa Bureau underscored Somalia's pariah status within the OAU and military support for a mounting guerrilla insurgency in the Ogaden as potential minefields for US interests in Africa. According to this viewpoint, which was shared by Moose and Secretary of State Cyrus Vance, Siad's overtures to the West did not constitute a genuine shift in Somali foreign policy, but the self-interested calculations of a leader intent on securing external support to militarily change the frontiers of the Horn of Africa. "The risks of getting involved with the Somalis in such an atmosphere," noted a former member of the Africa Bureau, "simply outweighed any potential short-term gains that proponents of closer US–Somali military ties hoped to achieve."[118]

Despite overwhelming opposition throughout the national security bureaucracies, the rising debate was resolved at the level of the White House in favor of pursuing a security relationship with Somalia. The primary reason for this shift in policy was the involvement of Carter who, in response to the dramatic unfolding of events within the Horn of Africa, reportedly was reviewing "voluminous studies" on the region just weeks after taking office. Indeed, after apparently instructing Vance and National Security Adviser Zbigniew Brzezinski "to move in every possible way to get Somalia to be our friend,"[119] Carter agreed "in principle" on July 15, 1977, to help meet Somalia's defense needs in conjunction with other countries, most notably Saudi Arabia.[120] Whereas leaders in Addis Ababa undoubtedly perceived this decision as final proof of Washington's hostility toward the Ethiopian revolution, leaders in Mogadishu must have looked upon this statement as the next best thing to an official declaration of support for Somali objectives in the Ogaden.

Several explanations have been offered as to why Carter so early in his administration ignored the advice of his senior advisers, and pursued a military relationship with Somalia. According to those who focus on the importance of presidential politics, Carter was seeking to overcome the political embarassment of the US expulsion from Ethiopia. Although clearly not responsible for this break, establishing ties with Somalia was one way of demonstrating to Congress that the administration was "doing something" to offset the perceived US loss in the Horn of Africa. Another explanation that also derived from presidential politics focused on Carter's desire to appear "tough" in the face of perceived Soviet advances in the Horn of Africa. The overriding objective in this scenario was to placate conservative members of Congress who were opposed to negotiating a SALT treaty with the Soviet Union.[121]

Although it would be incorrect to downplay the importance of presidential politics, Carter's beliefs played a greater role in his decision to seek a military relationship with Somalia. In keeping with his regionalist worldview, Carter sought to demonstrate early in his administration that even radical Third World leaders who broke with the Soviet Union could count on Washington for diplomatic, economic, and even military support. When confronted with the combination of Siad's overtures to the West and the willingness of several US regional allies to take the lead in fostering the growing Somali–Soviet split, Carter perceived the situation as an irresistible opportunity to "make his mark" in the realm of foreign policy. Undaunted by the objections of his foreign policy advisers, Carter reportedly assumed that his personal involvement would serve as a check upon the expansionist aims of the Somalis. "He loved to be in direct touch with foreign leaders," explained an NSC staff member who strongly opposed the decision to seek a security relationship with Somalia. "He was tempted to play with the Somalis" due to a "naive but at that point essentially boundless faith in his own ability to convince any leader of his and his country's good and peaceful intentions everywhere in the world."[122]

Carter's willingness to "play the Somali card" quickly evaporated as the worst-case scenario predicted by the Africa Bureau became a reality. On July 17, just two days after Carter approved providing Mogadishu with military aid, the Somali Army invaded the Ogaden region of Ethiopia with a force of roughly 250 tanks, 12 mechanized brigades, and 30 fighter aircraft and bombers.[123] By mid-November the Somali Army had conquered the majority of the Ogaden and was laying seige to the strategically located city of Harar. When the Somali Army failed to achieve final victory in Harar and the Ogaden War became a set battle of attrition, Siad made a series of diplomatic moves at least partially designed to win US and Western recognition of Somali sovereignty over the captured regions of the Ogaden. On November 13, he announced the abrogation of the Somali–Soviet Friendship Treaty of 1974, expelled nearly 1,700 Soviet civilian and military advisers and their dependents, and broke diplomatic relations with Cuba.[124]

The initial US response to the crisis generated by the Ogaden War reflected the preeminence of the "regionalist" worldview within the Carter administration. Branding the Somali invasion as an illegal transgression of international law and the concept of territorial integrity as enshrined in the OAU Charter, Moose informed the Somali Ambassador to Washington on August 4, 1977, that the US could not provide arms as long as Somali forces were active in the Ogaden. Two weeks later on August 14, the Somalis were informed that this ban extended to the transfer of US-manufactured arms in the possession of "friendly" third countries, most notably Saudi Arabia and Iran.[125] This policy stance was facilitated by the simple reality that the Somalis were the clear aggressors in the conflict, a factor which also contributed to broad congressional support for Carter's handling of the crisis.[126] At the urgings of Vance and Moose, Carter downplayed the external dimension of the war in favor of its African roots, and emphasized his administration's support for an arms embargo against both Ethiopia and Somalia, as well as diplomatic initiatives sponsored by the OAU.[127]

Any possibility of a negotiated settlement rapidly dissipated at the end of 1977 when Soviet–Cuban intervention in the conflict raised the regional ante and threatened to turn an African conflict into a major East–West confrontation. On December 22, the Soviet Union began a massive airlift of Cuban combat troops from bases in Cuba, Angola, and the People's Republic of the Congo in a move designed to break the military stalemate. Accompanied by Soviet tactical commanders and nearly $2 billion in Soviet military weaponry, the number of Cubans airlifted into Ethiopia by mid-January exceeded 2,500 troops, and grew to 15,000 within less than two months. These troops spearheaded an Ethiopian counteroffensive in late January 1978 that quickly overwhelmed the outnumbered and internationally isolated Somali troops within a matter of weeks, forcing them to flee across the border on March 9.

This massive and decisive intervention on the part of the Soviet Union and Cuba intensified a growing policy debate. Vance continued to voice the State Department view that there was little the US could do to help the Somalis as long as they continued their illegal invasion of the Ogaden. "The Somalis brought this on themselves," he explained, "They are no great friends of ours, and they are reaping the fruits of their actions."[128] Brzezinski countered by arguing that the massive levels of Soviet and Cuban involvement had turned the Ogaden conflict into an East–West test of US resolve and credibility. "I believed that if Soviet-sponsored Cubans determined the outcome of an Ethiopian–Somali conflict," noted Brzezinski, "there would be wider regional and international consequences, such as greater regional uncertainty and less confidence in the United States."[129] It was in this context that Brzezinski sought and received authorization from Carter to heat up the war of words with the Soviets.[130] As early as December 1977, for example, Brzezinski began referring to the Ogaden War as part of a Soviet "grand strategy" designed to exploit instability in Africa and elsewhere on the Soviet periphery – the so-called "arc of crisis."[131] Even Carter adopted anti-Soviet rhetoric, signaling the beginning of a significant shift in policy.[132] "There is a danger," he noted in his State of the Union Address of January 19, 1978, "that the Soviet Union and Cuba will commit their own soldiers in this conflict, transforming it from a local war to a confrontation with a broader strategic implication."[133]

Whether the rising globalist rhetoric of the administration would turn into concrete foreign policy acts and replace the restraint favored by the regionalists became clear in mid-February 1978. As joint Ethiopian–Cuban columns advanced toward the Somali border, the Carter administration debated whether a Soviet-backed invasion force seeking retribution would cross over into Somalia and attempt to overthrow the Siad regime. Even though Deputy National Security Adviser David Aaron had just returned from Addis Ababa with an "unequivocal" pledge from Mengistu that Ethiopian and Cuban troops would not violate the Ethiopian–Somali border,[134] Brzezinski argued in an NSC meeting on February 23 for a US "show-of-force," preferably the deployment of a US carrier task force in the waters off the Horn of Africa, to ensure that the Soviets and Cubans would "think twice" before embarking on such an invasion.[135] Of crucial importance to Brzezinski was not Somalia, per se, but rather a globalist-inspired desire to avoid any appearance that the US had remained passive in the face of Soviet and Cuban intervention.

The military thrust of Brzezinski's proposal was opposed by senior officials in the State Department and the Pentagon. Both Vance and Moose predictably favored a diplomatic approach to ensure Ethiopian restraint, and were concerned with avoiding any actions, such as military support of Somalia, that would further damage any chance of a US–Ethiopian rapprochement. "If Moscow would hold back the Ethiopians and Cubans while we pressured the Somalis to get out of the Ogaden before their army was completely destroyed," explained Vance, "we might rescue Somalia from its obsession with the Ogaden and improve our own position in the Horn as well."[136] These arguments were reinforced by Secretary of Defense Harold Brown and General David Jones of the Joint Chiefs of Staff, both of whom made their assessments in light of the bureaucratic missions of the Pentagon. Since Africa, particularly Somalia, was of little strategic interest to the Defense Department, neither Brown nor Jones wanted to run the risk of damaging the credibility of their bureaucracy if the bluff was called and the regime was overthrown by an invading military force. Not only would such a "failure" inevitably be blamed on the inability of the task force to accomplish its assigned mission, explained Brown, it would "impair the credibility" of similar task forces in future, more important crises in other regions of the world.[137] In the end, the combination of State Department and Pentagon opposition to any sort of military option ensured the temporary isolation of Brzezinski and the continuation of a policy of restraint favored by the regionalists.

Despite the regionalist victory in opposing the use of force, a subsequent debate over the issue of "linkage" between the broader realm of US–Soviet relations and Soviet actions in the Horn of Africa suggested a rising tendency within the Carter administration to view African issues from an East–West perspective. Despite Vance's public statements to the contrary, Brzezinski led a linkage campaign that seemingly was supported by Carter. For example, when asked by the media on March 1 whether the administration would link Soviet actions in Ethiopia with negotiations over a US–Soviet SALT treaty, Brzezinski replied that, although the US was not in the business of imposing linkages, they "may be imposed by unwarranted exploitation of local conflict for larger international purposes." When asked to clarify the inherent contradiction in the positions of his two most trusted foreign policy advisers, Carter leaned toward the interpretation of Brzezinski.[138] This growing shift in the Carter administration's worldview was bitterly denounced by Vance. "We were shooting ourselves in the foot," he explained, "By casting the complex Horn situation in East–West terms, and by setting impossible objectives for US policy – elimination of Soviet and Cuban influence in Ethiopia – we were creating the impression that we were defeated when, in fact, we were achieving a successful outcome."[139]

The 1977–78 period of US intervention in the Horn of Africa clearly underscored the importance of a crisis situation in significantly altering US Africa policies. The dramatic rupturing of the US–Ethiopian security relationship squarely focused the attention of Carter who, in sharp contrast to the cautionary warnings of senior advisers and an anti-Somali bias within the national security bureaucracies, sought a military opening to the Siad regime. When that opening was followed by a Somali invasion of Ethiopia, the preeminence of the regionalist worldview ensured a low-key response that emphasized the illegality of Somalia's actions. Even when the Somali invasion was repulsed by the massive introduction of Cuban troops and Soviet advisers, the dominance of the regionalist worldview ensured continuation of a policy of restraint. However, the rising Cold War rhetoric that accompanied rejection of a more forceful military option suggested the beginning of a shift in the Carter administration's worldview. As discussed in Chapter 3, this shift became readily apparent in the Carter administration's Cold War response to the Shaba II invasion of Zaire in May 1978.

Bureaucratic incrementalism and the strengthening of US–Somali ties (March 1978–January 1981)

A decline in White House attention in favor of bureaucratic management of US foreign policy toward the Horn of Africa was the inevitable outcome of Somalia's withdrawal from the Ogaden. In the case of Ethiopia, the State Department's Africa Bureau led the way in seeking the reestablishment of formerly close US–Ethiopian ties, as witnessed by the June 1978 appointment of Frederic L. Chapin as the first Ambassador to Ethiopia since Hummel's departure in July 1976. Advancing the argument that if the US "wanted to stay in the ballgame, we had to give some type of aid," Chapin requested $20 million in economic assistance upon arriving at his post to demonstrate a willingness to seek better ties with the Mengistu regime.[140] As explained by Moose in testimony before the House Subcommittee on Africa, the Africa Bureau was setting its sights on the future of US–Ethiopian relations. "As the Ethiopians begin to take a longer term view of their broader relationships, we would like to encourage them ... to have a relationship with us, not withstanding the difficulties that we have had."[141]

The Africa Bureau's initiative failed largely due to US–Ethiopian disagreements over several issues that led to the imposition of congressionally mandated sanctions against Ethiopia. At the center of continuing US–Ethiopian tensions was the unresolved issue of compensation for over twenty US–owned businesses that had been nationalized in the immediate aftermath of the Ethiopian revolution, the largest of which was the Ethiopian subsidiary of the Michigan-based Kalamazoo Spice Extraction Company (valued at roughly $11 million).[142] Whereas the Africa Bureau characterized the issue of compensation as a "test" of Ethiopia's willingness to pursue better ties,[143] the Mengistu regime could not understand why Washington was raising this embarrassing topic at such a delicate point in US–Ethiopian relations, especially over what one Ethiopian diplomat described as a "paltry sum of money" for a country as "rich" as the United States.[144] Nonetheless, according to legislation known as the Hickenlooper Amendment and the Gonzolez Amendment, the lack of good faith steps on the part of Ethiopia to promptly compensate US citizens or corporations for expropriated properties required the State Department to suspend all bilateral aid, as well as use its position on the boards of regional and international development banks to vote against any multilateral aid extended by those agencies.[145] To make matters worse, Ethiopia had not made any payments since mid-1976 on military weaponry purchased through Foreign Military Sales (FMS) credits. In accordance with another piece of legislation known as the Brooke–Alexander Amendment, aid is supposed to be suspended for any country in default on a US–sponsored loan for longer than a calendar year.

Despite the efforts of the Africa Bureau to prevent the formal suspension of aid that US laws required, one by one they were applied as a result of a normal review process in Congress. In January 1979, the Brooke–Alexander Amendment was invoked, preventing any further military assistance to the Mengistu regime. Two months later, the Gonzolez Amendment was applied. As a result, the State Department in March 1979 voted for the first time to oppose an African Development Bank loan to Ethiopia. Finally, two months after the Senate Foreign Relations Committee voted in May 1979 to terminate development assistance to the Mengistu regime, passage of the Hickenlooper Amendment signaled the termination of all US assistance to Ethiopia save for humanitarian aid.[146] In a far cry from the optimism surrounding the July 1978 opening to the Mengistu regime, US–Ethiopian relations hit an all-time low on July 5, 1980, when the Ethiopian Foreign Ministry officially demanded Chapin's recall.

Initiatives designed to strengthen US relations with Somalia similarly met with defeat. Despite its strenuous objections, the State Department's Africa Bureau was instructed by the White House to seek a US–Somali military relationship as witnessed by Moose's arrival in Mogadishu on March 18, 1978.[147] In return for providing Somalia with "defensive" weapons, the Africa Bureau sought a formal pledge from Siad that his country would refrain from any further military involvement in the Ogaden region. Although this pledge apparently was given on April 23, approximately two weeks after Siad successfully defeated a coup attempt, intelligence reports of Somalia's continued military involvement in the region as of July 1978 resulted in the suspension of negotiations.[148]

The deeply engrained distrust of Somalia within the national security bureaucracies, exacerbated by Siad's apparent unwillingness to stick to the spirit, let alone the letter, of his pledge to the Carter administration, served as a significant brake on any further military openings to the Somalis. As explained by Donald K. Petterson, the Ambassador to Somalia from 1978 to 1982, US–Somali discussions during 1978–79 played like a broken record: Siad would repeatedly raise the existence of a communist threat from neighboring Ethiopia as the primary rationale for a US–Somali military agreement, and the State Department's Africa Bureau would emphasize the impossibility of any aid as long as Somalia remained militarily involved in the Ogaden. Impassioned Somali denials of any such involvement in the Ogaden inevitably would be followed by equally strident US claims that Washington knew, beyond a shadow of a doubt, of such illegal Somali activities.[149] In short, as long as the Somalis continued their military involvement in the Ogaden and the Africa Bureau maintained responsibility for US foreign policy in the Horn of Africa, the prospects of a US–Somali military relationship remained very slim.

Two crisis events in 1979 dramatically altered Washington's perceptions of the Indian Ocean region and Somalia's place therein, contributing to a realignment of bureaucratic forces that worked against those who had been successful in resisting a US–Somali military relationship. On November 4, 1979, Islamic fundamentalist forces loyal to the Ayatollah Khomeini seized all US diplomatic personnel stationed at the US Embassy in Tehran, marking the beginning of a 444-day hostage crisis that eventually consumed the foreign policy agenda of the Carter administration. Less than two months later, the Soviet Union invaded Afghanistan with a force of over 100,000 troops, leading to Washington's concern over a potential Soviet threat to the Western oil lifeline of the Persian Gulf.

The White House response to these twin crises represented the rising supremacy of the globalist view among senior policymakers that had begun emerging as a result of the 1977–78 Ogaden War. On December 4, 1979, the NSC directed both the State Department and the Pentagon to seek military access agreements with friendly countries in the region, including Kenya, Oman, and Somalia. Access was perceived as necessary should the White House seek a military solution to the Iranian hostage crisis or to any other radical or Marxist threats to US strategic interests in the Persian Gulf region.[150] This rising globalist trend became especially prominent in the aftermath of the Soviet invasion of Afghanistan. "Let our position be absolutely clear," emphasized Carter in his 1980 State of the Union Address, "An attempt by any outside force to gain control of the Persian Gulf region will be regarded as an assault on the vital interests of the United States of America, and such an assault will be repelled by any means necessary, including military force."[151]

The immediate impact of the globalist-inspired need for military access in southwestern Asia was a debate within the national security bureaucracies over seeking such a relationship with Somalia. Opposition forces led by the State Department's Africa Bureau predictably noted that Siad had demonstrated that he could not be trusted to keep Somali forces out of the disputed Ogaden region, and that military aid ran the risk of entangling the US on the wrong side of an African conflict.[152] "Even if one agrees with the need for military access in the region," explained one opponent of seeking a military relationship with Somalia, "access to other countries in the region, such as Oman, Kenya, and Egypt, were more than sufficient when compared to the redundant facilities available in Somalia."[153] Sharply disagreeing with what they perceived as "irrelevant" political arguments, Pentagon officials sought to overcome what they considered a "technical problem" of enhancing US military flexibility in the Persian Gulf region.[154] Political arguments citing Somalia's unwillingness to abide by the established frontiers of the Horn of Africa, for example, simply did not carry weight with a bureaucracy whose organizational mission demanded the rapid creation of an operational capability for potential US military intervention in the region. In short, access to Somali facilities was looked upon as a technical solution to a non-African problem.

The Carter administration's growing concern with perceived Soviet expansionism and radical threats in the Persian Gulf region ultimately worked in favor of proponents of negotiating an access agreement with Somalia. After initial negotiations had broken down over the levels and kinds of aid, the US and Somalia, over the continued protests of the Africa Bureau, signed a formal access agreement on August 22, 1980. In exchange for roughly $65 million in military aid to be dispersed over a period of three years, the Defense Department was granted access to air and port facilities throughout the country, most notably at the Soviet-built port and airfield at Berbera. Despite the signing of this agreement, however, the anti-Somali bias within the national security bureaucracies continued to act as a constraint upon an open-ended US military commitment to Somalia. In order to avoid providing Somalia with an offensive capability that could lead to a repeat of the 1977-78 Ogaden War, US aid was restricted largely to "defensive" weapons, most notably a radar defense system and "non-lethal" items, such as trucks and anti-aircraft guns.[155] Most important, opponents of the accord, including the House Subcommittee on Africa, demanded oral and written assurances from the Siad regime that the Somali Armed Forces would refrain from military involvement in the Ogaden.[156]

Before the terms of the agreement could be carried out, the warnings of the Africa Bureau and House Subcommittee on Africa were once again borne out by intelligence reports in August 1980 confirming that regular Somali Army units were still operating in the Ogaden. Once appraised of this situation, the House Subcommittee on Africa led an effort to suspend the US access agreement with Somalia. In a letter signed by seven of its members, the Africa Subcommittee warned the administration that the access agreement "could very well exacerbate the ongoing military conflict between Ethiopia and Somalia over the Ogaden, increase the dangers of US involvement in the conflict, and estrange the US from important African states who overwhelmingly oppose Somalia's efforts in the Ogaden."[157] Yet due to the absence of crisis, the concerns of this small but vocal group within Congress carried little weight with the majority of congresspersons who knew and cared little about Somalia. Indeed, frustrated over the decline of US prestige as a result of the ongoing Iranian hostage crisis, most members favored the overall thrust of the administration's Persian Gulf policy. In the end, the first installment of US military assistance to Somalia ($20 million) was simply conditioned upon the "verified assurance" that no regular Somali armed forces remained in the Ogaden region.[158] (A condition which allowed the Siad regime to continue providing support to guerrilla fighters.) The State Department provided these assurances to the necessary congressional committees in January 1981, removing the final obstacle to the implementation of the US–Somali access agreement.[159] The newly inaugurated Reagan administration therefore found itself responsible at the beginning of 1981 for implementing a new US security commitment in the Horn of Africa.

US foreign policy in the Horn of Africa during the 1978–81 period once again underscored the importance of bureaucratic incrementalism as the primary determinant of US Africa policies during routine periods. In the case of Ethiopia, the Africa Bureau predictably sought to enhance ties with what once constituted the closest US ally in the region, only to be stymied by a combination of Ethiopian intransigence and a variety of congressionally mandated restrictions. In the case of Somalia, the engrained anti-Somali bias within the national security bureaucracies continued to serve as an important constraint on the pursuit of a military opening to the Siad regime. In the aftermath of the twin crises of the Iranian hostages and the Soviet invasion of Afghanistan, however, proponents of closer US–Somali ties profited from the Pentagon's newfound bureaucratic mission of ensuring the widest possible US access to military facilities in the region. In short, military arguments emphasizing Somalia's strategic location took precedence over the cautionary political arguments still advanced by the State Department's Africa Bureau.

Incrementalism, crisis, and growing constraints
(January 1981–April 1988)

Entering office with a highly ideological worldview that harkened back to the militant Cold War internationalism of the Eisenhower administration, most notably the "roll-back" policies advocated by Dulles, one would have expected the Reagan White House to significantly alter US foreign policy toward the Horn of Africa. Yet in sharp contrast to the dramatic changes that occurred in the substance of US policies directed toward other regions of the world, such as Central America, which were immediately visible after the Reagan administration entered office, initial policies toward Ethiopia and Somalia demonstrated remarkable continuity with the policies of restraint associated with the Carter administration.[160] In the case of Ethiopia, despite the fact that Mengistu was a symbol of everything to which the Reagan administration was opposed – a self-proclaimed Marxist leader willing to host Cuban combat forces and to serve as Moscow's closest ally in Africa – his country did not become a target of the so-called Reagan Doctrine and its support for guerrilla insurgencies intent on overthrowing Marxist regimes in the Third World. Similarly, although Siad seemingly was a perfect candidate for lavish attention as a staunchly pro-US leader who had ruptured ties with the Soviet Union and whose country occupied a strategic corner of the world, administration rhetoric underscoring the importance of US access to Somali military facilities was not matched by the levels of attention expected by the Somali government. Indeed, not only did military aid remain at the $20 million level negotiated by the Carter administration, but no attempt was made by the Pentagon during either 1981 or 1982 to act upon the promised refurbishment and expansion of the airfield and harbor facilities at Berbera, and no deliveries of promised weaponry had taken place by June 1982, nearly eighteen months after the military access agreement had been implemented.

In a classic example of why it is rare that one sees a significant change in policy even when an administration with seemingly different beliefs than its predecessor takes power, the lack of crisis, coupled with the traditionally low level of attention paid to African issues by the President, favored the delegation of policy to the Africa specialists who, in turn, predictably approached the Horn of Africa according to the status quo oriented organizational missions of their respective bureaucracies. As a senior member of the Africa Bureau explained, "Africa wasn't even on the map for the top policymakers in the Reagan administration."[161] This disinterest was best noted, perhaps, by the fact that the administration's policy review of the Horn of Africa was not completed until July 1982 – nearly seventeen months after Reagan's inauguration in February 1981.[162] Even Assistant Secretary of State for African Affairs Chester Crocker, the most likely individual to press for a change in policy during the initial months of the administration, had his sights, as well as those of the Africa Bureau, firmly focused on southern Africa (see Chapter 5).

White House neglect of Somalia sharply changed in the aftermath of military clashes between Ethiopia and Somalia during July 1982. In retaliation for a Somali raid on an Ethiopian army unit outside Shilabo, a town roughly 100 kilometers from the Ethiopian–Somali frontier, the Ethiopian Army invaded Somalia with 5,000–7,000 troops at several points along the common border. Whereas the Somali raid was conducted in cooperation with the Western Somali Liberation Front (WSLF), the Ogadeni guerrilla organization seeking independence for the region, the Ethiopian invasion was carried out in conjunction with the Democratic Front for the Salvation of Somalia (DFSS), a Somali guerrilla movement supported by Addis Ababa and seeking the overthrow of the Siad regime. The conflict became especially tense when, in the aftermath of Ethiopia's occupation of the Somali border towns of Balenbale and Goldogob during July and August, respectively, it appeared that Somalia would be cut in two by the eastward-driving Ethiopian Army. In response to "frantic" Somali appeals for US military support, the White House ordered two emergency airlifts of military weaponry, consisting of $5.5 million in rifles, small arms, and ammunition, as well as twenty-four armored personnel carriers (APCs) that were "married up" with TOW anti-tank weapons.[163] The White House also encouraged Italy, Egypt, and Saudi Arabia to transfer various types of military equipment.[164]

The 1982 Ethiopian–Somali border conflict was significant in that it demonstrated how a crisis with a significant East–West component attracted high-level attention to a previously neglected region of the world, and brought policy in line with the dominant beliefs of a particular administration. Rather than focusing on Somalia's illegitimate historical claims to the Ogaden as constituting the key issue in the conflict, Reagan administration policymakers instead perceived a pro-US ally that was threatened by a Marxist neighbor supported by the Soviet Union, Cuba, and Libya. As explained by David Korn, the US Chargé d'Affaires accredited to Ethiopia at the time of the crisis, this was "just the kind of test" welcomed by Reagan officials who firmly believed that Carter had failed to stand up for its friends and

make the US respected by its adversaries.[165] Of greatest significance
from the Somali point of view was the final recognition in Washington
of the need to cut through the bureaucratic red tape and provide
Somalia with greater levels of military assistance. Although still not
reaching the levels ideally preferred by Somali leaders, US security
assistance rose from $20.4 million in 1981 to $45.4 million in 1982 and
$51.6 million in 1983.

The Reagan administration's growing attention to Somalia was complemented by an important generational change taking place in the
Africa Bureau. Since 1980, newly hired FSOs were socialized into the
bureaucratic mindset that Somalia, not Ethiopia, was the US ally in the
Horn of Africa, and therefore was more deserving of support. In words
highly reminiscent of Africa Bureau praise for the US–Ethiopian
relationship during the 1960s, a career FSO of the Africa Bureau
explained in 1989 that Somalia's "unswerving support" for US interests
in the Horn of Africa demanded equally firm US support for the Siad
regime. "We've had more support and cooperation from that country,
that government, than any other in the region in terms of access and
facilities."[166]

The growing advocacy of the Africa Bureau during the mid-1980s for
strengthened US–Somali ties was complemented by similar arguments
from Pentagon officials who sought to carry out their organizational
mission of creating a capability to project US military force into the
Middle East region. In addition to expanding and refurbishing air and
port facilities at Berbera beginning in 1983, the Defense Department
conducted joint military maneuvers with the Somali military as part of
its Bright Star exercises in the region, and managed an IMET program
that had grown to $1.1 million in 1985. Although other countries in the
region were considered more important as forward staging areas for
US troops, Somalia's special significance derived from its willingness to
allow the US Navy to stage P-3 anti-submarine flights out of Berbera to
track the movement of Soviet submarines. Geographical location made
Somalia an ideal part of this monitoring network because Soviet
submarines were forced to travel through the narrow Straits of Bab
el-Mandeb where they could be easily sighted and tracked.[167]

The House Subcommittee on Africa emerged during the mid-1980s
as the harshest critic of growing US–Somali ties, most notably due to
Somalia's continued support for WSLF guerrillas in the Ogaden, the
rising human rights abuses of the Siad regime, and concern that US
military aid was serving as one of the cornerstones of a counterinsurgency campaign directed against dissident groups in northern
Somalia. In March 1987, for example, hearings conducted by the Africa

Subcommittee cited widespread ill-treatment and torture of political prisoners, as well as political killings associated with the guerrilla insurgency in the north, as evidence that the State Department was underestimating the human rights abuses of the Siad regime.[168] In the absence of widespread congressional interest, however, the combination of growing advocacy on the part of both the State Department and the Pentagon contributed to the incremental growth in US economic and military aid to Somalia during the mid-1980s. By 1985, security assistance to Somalia had risen to $64.1 million ($34.1 million of which was military aid), while development assistance remained at the fairly constant rate of $52.6 million. Although the concerns of the House Subcommittee on Africa undoubtedly served to limit the rate of growth in US security assistance, the upward incrementalist trend was only reversed in 1986 as a result of the passage of the Gramm-Rudman-Hollings Deficit Reduction Act. Faced with a shrinking foreign aid budget in which Africa fell near the bottom of the geographical pecking order, security assistance to Somalia dropped to $42.2 million in 1986 and $25.3 million in 1987.

Despite the best efforts of the Africa Bureau to foster enhanced ties with Ethiopia in the aftermath of the Somali–Ethiopian border conflict in 1982, inclusive of sending an unsuccessful diplomatic mission led by Deputy Assistant Secretary of State for African Affairs Princeton Lyman to Addis Ababa in April 1983, the strained nature of the US–Ethiopian relationship showed little improvement during either 1983 or 1984, and in fact deteriorated. Even in the area of humanitarian assistance, budget cuts led to a reduction in the level of Public Law 480 (PL 480 – "Food for Peace") aid provided to Ethiopia from $5.0 million in 1981 to $2.8 million in 1983, culminating in an administration request that none be sent during 1984.[169] These cuts were notable in that they occurred at the same time that the Ethiopian government was requesting increased food relief to combat a spreading nation-wide famine.

Although critics charged the Reagan administration with maliciously seeking to overthrow the Mengistu regime by fostering the famine-induced events that led to the downfall of Emperor Haile Selassie, such a scenario assumed a significant degree of White House attention and coordination which simply did not exist. A more probable scenario was that Addis Ababa's requests were ignored at the highest levels of the policymaking establishment because Ethiopia was perceived as the client, and therefore the responsibility, of the Soviet bloc. Had the famine remained limited in both scope and intensity, such a policy stance most likely would have withstood the test of time. However, the unfolding of what at the time was described as the "worst human disaster in the history of the continent" led to demands on the part of both Congress and the public for a reassessment of policy at the highest levels of the Reagan administration.[170]

Private relief organizations attempting to deal with the growing famine "on the ground" in Ethiopia were the first to criticize White House inattention. As one of the largest relief organizations in Africa responsible for distributing PL 480 food aid, the Catholic Relief Services (CRS) expressed frustration as early as August 1983 over the slowness and inadequacy of the Reagan administration's response. Four months later, a group of relief organizations publicly chastised the administration for failing to move fast enough.[171] By the spring of 1983, a growing portion of Congress (over 150 members) traditionally responsive to such humanitarian concerns was actively pressuring the administration to increase the levels of famine aid, culminating in the visit of a congressional study mission to Ethiopia in August 1983.[172]

The combined effect of relief agency and congressional prodding resulted in the provision of approximately $10 million in US humanitarian aid to Ethiopia during 1984. Although surely welcomed by relief proponents, this aid was inadequate if disaster was going to be averted. As of March 1984, it was estimated that 6.4 million Ethiopians were affected by drought and that 900,000 metric tons of foodstuffs were required immediately.[173] To make matters worse, initial legislative proposals targeted toward famine relief fell prey to narrow political interests. Whereas one series of legislation was defeated due to a White House supported amendment calling for paramilitary aid to anti-Sandinista contras, another series of amendments requiring emergency food credits to US farmers were simply unacceptable to the administration.[174]

The turning point in US relief efforts occurred due to dramatic media coverage of the Ethiopian famine beginning in September 1984. For months thereafter, images of starving Ethiopian children fostered popular relief efforts, ranging from individual donations and letter writing campaigns to live media extravaganzas, such as "Live-Aid" and the hit single "We are the World." In one of the greatest ironies of US Africa policies during the Reagan administration, popular pressures to "do something" clearly forced the staunchest anti-communist administration during the post-World War II period to became the largest official donor to the most doctrinaire Marxist country on the African continent. In sharp contrast to the 41,343 metric tons of relief assistance provided in 1984, for example, early 450,000 metric tons were delivered in 1985 at a cost of $87.5 million – the highest level of US aid ever allocated to the Ethiopian government prior to 1985, inclusive of the Haile Selassie years.[175]

In addition to sparking an outpouring of popular support for famine relief, the 1983–85 famine also highlighted the human rights short-comings of the Mengistu regime. Although famine had been part of Ethiopia's socio-political landscape for centuries, the Mengistu regime adopted one particularly draconian measure – the forceful resettle-ment and collectivization of peasants from the drought stricken north-central highlands to the more fertile southwest – in an attempt to halt the vicious cycle of drought, famine, and death. This issue was seized upon by conservative members of Congress who, beginning in 1985, sought the imposition of comprehensive sanctions against Ethiopia not unlike those favored against South Africa by the anti-apartheid movement (see Chapter 5).

The sanctions effort initially was spearheaded by a small group of conservatives led by Representative Toby Roth (R-Wisconsin), a member of the House Subcommittee on Africa. This small group represented a core of congresspersons willing to oppose even humani-tarian aid to Ethiopia on the grounds that it amounted to subsidization of a communist dictatorship.[176] Building upon this ideological core, Roth introduced a joint resolution (HJ-RES-324) in the House of Repre-sentatives on June 25, 1985, that called for the suspension of all US aid to Ethiopia, as well as a complete ban on trade. After languishing in the Africa Subcommittee as a result of opposition by Subcommittee Chair-person Wolpe, a watered-down version calling for the suspension of foreign assistance (except humanitarian aid) was passed as Section 812D of the International Security Cooperation Act of 1985. In sharp contrast to the majority of such Africa-related bills initially advanced by a small group within Congress, the combination of the politicization of the famine issue (which contributed to an unusually attentive Congress as concerned Ethiopia), Mengistu's human rights abuses, and Ethiopia's low standing within the adminstration made the watered-down bill relatively easy to pass.[177]

Seeking to impose even stricter sanctions in light of ongoing human rights abuses within Ethiopia, Roth introduced legislation (HR-588) during the first week of 1987. Unlike its 1985 predecessor, the 1987 bill carried special weight in that it was cosponsored by Representative Gray, an influential member of the Congressional Black Caucus. De-scribing the Mengistu regime as a "brutal dictatorship" which had forcibly resettled over 600,000 Ethiopians under "grossly inhumane conditions," HR-588 called for the imposition of comprehensive economic sanctions, including a ban on the importation of Ethiopian coffee, a prohibition on loans and new investments, the revocation of most-favored-nation trading status, and opposition to economic assistance from international financial institutions.[178] Once again languishing in committee, a watered-down version "urged" but did not legally bind the executive branch to impose sanctions against Ethiopia.

Despite the added influence of Gray, the bill was opposed by influential members of the House Subcommittee on Africa, most notably Wolpe, who sought to avoid contentious legislation that would detract from ongoing efforts to strengthen sanctions against South Africa. The primary reason for the bill's defeat, however, stemmed from the lack of concern among members of Congress, as Ethiopia and the issue of famine gradually faded into the political background. Whereas the Ethiopian famine remained an important political issue in 1986, and generated approximately $78 million in US relief aid, by 1987 the tremendous outpouring of public support seemed only a distant memory, as marked by the small sum of $6.1 million in food aid allocated to Ethiopia during that year.[179]

The evolution of US interventionist practices in the Horn of Africa during the 1981–88 period once again demonstrated the importance of the relationship between events within Africa and the operation of the US policymaking process. During the first two years of the Reagan administration, the lack of crisis in the Horn of Africa fostered the continuation of policies established under the Carter administration and maintained in accordance with the established missions of the national security bureaucracies. In the case of Somalia, the status quo was only altered in the aftermath of a crisis situation – the 1982 Ethiopian–Somali border conflict – which attracted the attention of senior policymakers in the Reagan administration, resulting in a policy more consonant with that administration's worldview. In the case of Ethiopia, the status quo was only altered in the aftermath of an extended crisis situation – the 1983–85 Ethiopian famine – in which Congress, responding to popular pressures, forced the Reagan White House to dramatically increase the levels of humanitarian aid to the Mengistu regime.

Civil conflict and the bureaucratic-congressional split (April 1988–October 1990)

In a move cautiously supported by the State Department's Africa Bureau as an important first step on the path to regional peace, Mengistu and Siad signed an accord on April 3, 1988, in which both leaders agreed to reestablish diplomatic relations and withdraw their forces from the disputed Ogaden frontier. The overriding concern of both leaders was not the resolution of the Ogaden conflict, but a shared desire to defuse conflictual external relations in order to free military resources for effectively dealing with internal, regime-threatening guerrilla insurgencies. In Somalia, the stability of the government was threatened since 1981 by the military successes of the Somali National Movement (SNM), a northern-based guerrilla insurgency deriving the majority of its support from the Isaak clan, as well as by smaller insurgent groups, such as the Hawiye-dominated United Somali Congress (USC) and the Ogadeni-dominated Somali Patriotic Movement (SPM).[180] In Ethiopia, the Mengistu regime found itself threatened by what became known as the Ethiopian People's Revolutionary Democratic Front (EPRDF), a movement dominated by the Tigrean People's Liberation Front (TPLF), and the Oromo Liberation Front (OLF) and the Eritrean People's Liberation Front (EPLF).[181]

The April 1988 Ethiopian–Somali accord would have generated little, if any, change in US foreign policy toward the Horn of Africa had it not been for the unforeseen developments that accompanied implementation of the agreement. Faced with the loss of their base of operations in Ethiopia, SNM guerrillas entered the Somali city of Burao on the evening of May 27, 1988, and assassinated all senior government officials. The first stage of a "final offensive" designed to ensure the collapse of the Siad regime, the guerrillas initially scored stunning successes against the Somali Armed Forces; most notable among these victories was the capture of large portions of Hargeisa, the second largest urban area within the country. When faced with trading hit-and-run tactics for the need to defend fortified positions, the SNM was devastated by Somali counterattacks in July and August that virtually destroyed Burao and damaged three-quarters of all the buildings in Hargeisa. In a wave of terror that followed the initial military assault, the Somali Armed Forces reportedly engaged in a "systematic pattern" of attacks against unarmed, Isaak villages, as well as summarily arresting and executing an unknown number of suspected SNM supporters.[182]

Rather than engaging the attention of the highest levels of the policymaking establishment, the formulation of the proper US response to the intensification of Somalia's civil war was handled at the level of the national security bureaucracies. At a critical stage in the conflict, the Pentagon on June 28, 1988, delivered $1.4 million in lethal aid to the Somali Armed Forces, including 1,200 M-16 rifles and 2.8 million rounds of ammunition. Although originally authorized in November 1986, delivery of the aid had been delayed because of the unwillingness of traditional carriers to ship such a small amount of cargo.[183] When the Somali government requested air shipment on June 4, 1988, and paid the extravagant price that such transport required, the matter was handled routinely at the lowest levels of the bureaucracy.[184] As far as the Pentagon was concerned, Somalia's status as an important regional client state left little, if any, doubt that Washington should quickly respond to Mogadishu in its hour of need.

Congressional critics of the US–Somali relationship, most notably the House Subcommittee on Africa, did not accept the military rationale of coming to the aid of a strategic ally, and complained of US weaponry being used by the Somali Armed Forces to bomb urban areas indiscriminately and to execute civilians whose only crime was belonging to the northern Isaak clan. In a hearing of the House Subcommittee on Africa hastily convened during the civil conflict, Wolpe noted that the uprising in the north was the outcome of "years of political repression."[185] Having never fully accepted the idea of a US–Somali security relationship, critics such as Wolpe seized upon the intensification of Somalia's extended civil war as a vehicle for terminating all US assistance to the Siad regime.

The State Department responded to growing pressures on the part of the House Subcommittee on Africa, and touched off a bureaucratic conflict with the Defense Department, by voluntarily placing a hold on any further lethal military aid to the Siad regime in July 1988. Unwilling to do battle with Congress against the backdrop of widespread abuses on the part of the Somali Armed Forces, the State Department rationalized the hold by underscoring the need to protect the far more substantial levels of economic assistance. "It simply did not make good bureaucratic sense," explained a State Department official involved in the decision, "to take a chance on losing all the economic assistance for a small amount of military assistance."[186] The Defense Department responded by accusing the State Department of caving in too quickly to the demands of the House Subcommittee on Africa, and argued for the need to stand behind Washington's promises to Mogadishu, especially during a crisis period in which US credibility was on the line. "Either we're allies or we're not," explained one proponent of continued military aid. "What is the sense of having this program if we're not going to give them the military support when it counts the most?"[187]

The combination of congressional pressure and State Department acquiescence led the Bush administration to reprogram $2.5 million in military aid originally targeted for Somalia in 1989. In addition, Economic Support Fund (ESF) assistance as of 1988 became subject to the "notification" demands of Congress. In short, the State Department was legally required to give a fifteen-day notification of any intent to disburse funds to Somalia, during which period any congressperson could request a "hold" on the funds pending further discussion. Although the State Department legally can disburse funds in the absence of binding legislation, congressional holds are generally honored as concerns those countries in Africa, such as Somalia, which are subject to notification requirements.[188] As a result of this policy, $21 million in suspended 1988 ESF funds ultimately were reprogrammed in September 1989 to other African countries to avoid their deletion from the Bush administration's cash-starved foreign assistance budget for 1990.

The escalating civil war contributed to an ongoing debate within the national security bureaucracies over the future of the US–Somali security relationship. Officials within the State Department and the Pentagon who favored continuation of the relationship pointed to several political reforms as goodwill intentions, including the creation of a constitutional committee to investigate the ongoing war in the north, the release of roughly 300 political prisoners identified by the State Department's Africa Bureau, and Siad's announced intention to establish a multiparty political system complete with parliamentary elections. Despite these actions, even FSOs within the Africa Bureau admitted that, aside from the initial release of several hundred political prisoners and some economic reforms, there was a significant gap between what the Siad regime said it would do and what actually occurred. These same officers nonetheless noted that, despite continued human rights abuses, even gradual movement toward reform, when combined with strong Defense Department pressures for ensuring continued US access to Berbera, demanded continued US support. "We're stuck with the relationship," explained one FSO, "and we'll stick with it and see it through."[189]

Proponents of disengagement pointed to no less than four major reports – including one commissioned by the State Department – that underscored the severe human rights problem in Somalia.[190] In July 1989, for example, approximately 450 civilians allegedly were killed when, in the aftermath of the arrest of four prominent Muslim leaders, Somali Armed Forces fired on demonstrators emerging from the principal mosques in Mogadishu. This event occurred just prior to the Bush administration's request for approximately $20 million in ESF aid to Somalia for 1990. Not surprisingly, congressional critics seized upon this event and blocked the administration's aid request. Perhaps the most vocal and influential opponents of continued US aid to Somalia, members of the House Subcommittee on Africa described Siad's reform package as "meaningless" in the absence of sincere efforts to meet the legitimate demands of the SNM and other guerrilla insurgencies seeking the overthrow of the government.[191]

In the words of a member of the State Department's Africa Bureau, the net result of the congressional-executive deadlock over the US–Somali security relationship was a "muddle-through" policy. While opponents were unable to completely sever the relationship, proponents were also constrained in what they could do. In short, the US continued to occupy an uneasy middle ground that neither completely supported nor opposed the Somali regime, while hoping that political conditions in Somalia would improve. "Its fine to say let's cut off aid, even if that's what the American people want," explained one member of the Africa Bureau in attempting to justify having the US remain politically engaged with the Siad regime. "But then what are the consequences?" Reflecting the bureaucratic mindset which usually favors the maintenance of established ties, this official explained that the inevitable result of cutting aid would be a loss of US influence.[192]

The controversy surrounding the US–Somali security relationship coincided with an ongoing debate over the future of US–Ethiopian relations. As demonstrated by Assistant Secretary of State for African Affairs Herman J. Cohen's visit to Addis Ababa in August 1989 in an effort to find a diplomatic settlement to Ethiopia's ongoing civil war, an issue that also engaged the mediation efforts of former President Carter in the late 1980s, the State Department's Africa Bureau led the way in seeking to enhance the extremely cool, but correct nature of US–Ethiopian ties. These efforts inevitably were challenged by a conservative-based coalition within Congress seeking to place the spotlight on the human rights violations of the Mengistu regime. Led by Representatives Roth and Gerald B. H. Soloman (R-New York), this coalition expressed great frustration with the House Subcommittee on Africa's unwillingness to pass economic sanctions against the Marxist regime of Ethiopia, while at the same time seeking additional sanctions against the apartheid regime of South Africa, especially when both grossly violated the human rights of their respective populations. In an April 28, 1988, hearing on proposed sanctions against South Africa, Roth reminded the House Committee on Foreign Affairs of the "double standard" which existed concerning the issue of human rights as applied to Africa.[193] This same theme had been broached one week earlier by Representative Dan Burton (R-Indiana) in a special Africa Subcommittee hearing devoted to the unfolding 1988 famine in Ethiopia. Accusing the Mengistu regime of pursuing policies that had resulted in the deaths of thousands and "possibly millions" of its own people, Burton claimed that it was "inconceivable" that Congress would consider additional sanctions against South Africa while taking "virtually no action" against the Mengistu regime.[194]

Despite their failure to push a comprehensive sanctions bill against Ethiopia through a largely disinterested Congress, congressional activists continued efforts to place the Mengistu regime in a negative light. For example, a watered-down version of HR-588 finally was passed in September 1988 as Section 1310 of the National Defense Authorization Act for 1989. Indicative of the difficulties of passing a bill in the absence of an extended crisis situation drawing substantial public, and subsequently congressional, support, the amendment only required the State Department to provide quarterly reports over a period of two years on the human rights abuses of the Mengistu regime. This relatively non-controversial legislation received a boost as a result of an unsuccessful military *coup d'état* against the Mengistu regime in May 1989. Responding to the widespread repression and killings of political dissidents and university students that followed the coup attempt, several congresspersons known for their activism on the issue of South Africa joined with the TransAfrica lobby to denounce publicly the Mengistu regime. In sharp contrast to the conservative coalition's opposition to Mengistu's brand of Marxism, this same group one month later indicated a willingness to consider a renewal of US assistance if Ethiopia demonstrated an improvement in human rights conditions and some progress in seeking a negotiated settlement of the country's civil war.

Rather than seeking a negotiated settlement to what Cohen in April 1990 described as the "most destructive conflict in the world," the Mengistu regime continued to seek a military solution, most notably with the support of Israeli advisers and weaponry.[195] Israel supported the Ethiopian central government as part of a more than two-decades long strategy of preventing the creation of an independent Eritrea. The reason for this support stemmed from a belief shared by many Israeli policymakers that an independent Eritrea would become another Arab-oriented (and anti-Israeli) state effectively turning the Red Sea into a hostile "Arab lake." In short, the Eritrean conflict became a southern extension of the Arab–Israeli conflict.[196]

The critical element of an Israeli–Ethiopian *rapprochement* in 1990 grew out of Israeli humanitarian and political concerns over the evacuation and resettlement of Ethiopia's minority Jewish population, the Falashas. A notable episode in this process was a secret airlift – dubbed Operation Moses – of more than 7,000 Falashas in 1984 who had fled to the Sudan as a result of the 1983–85 Ethiopian famine; a smaller airlift, Operation Joshua, evacuated some 800 more in March 1985.[197] At the beginning of the 1990s, more than 14,000 remaining Falashas, particularly those who had fled to Addis Ababa to escape growing civil conflict in the north, were at the center of an "arms-for-visas" exchange designed by the Mengistu regime to obtain greater levels of much-needed military weaponry from Israel. This renewal of traditional Israeli–Ethiopian relations underscored Mengistu's growing problems with his primary patrons within the rapidly changing Eastern bloc. In addition to the withdrawal from Ethiopia of Cuban troops and East German advisers, the Soviet Union informed Mengistu that the Soviet–Ethiopian military agreement would not be renewed after 1990. As a result, the Ethiopian government began looking, once again, to forge closer ties with the United States. "We realize a superpower is a superpower," explained Foreign Minister Tesfaye Dinka, "and there is no conflict of interest with the US."[198]

As far as Washington was concerned, several factors restrained the extension of a warm reception to Ethiopian diplomatic overtures at the end of October 1990, resulting in a "wait-and-see" attitude that strengthened the continuation of the established bureaucratic status quo. First, several conservative members of Congress continued to oppose any opening to Ethiopia because of the Marxist orientation of the Mengistu regime. Then, after Mengistu's March 5, 1990, announcement that his regime was abandoning its commitment to Marxism, congressional critics discounted the move as the superficial ploy of a threatened leader. "Once a Marxist, always a Marxist," explained one congressional critic who cited Mengistu's May 22, 1990, execution of twelve senior military officers as "proof positive that a leopard cannot change its spots."[199] Even if it were possible to overcome this ideological opposition, such as was the case of the Reagan administration's willingness to work with the self-proclaimed Marxist regime of Mozambique, the issue of Ethiopia's internal civil wars – most notably in Eritrea – remained an important stumbling block. Although willing to make minor concessions, such as accepting Eritrea's longstanding demand that UN observers be present at the negotiating table, the Mengistu regime was unwilling to budge on the matter of Eritrean independence. As a result, negotiations with the Eritreans, especially in the aftermath of renewed military cooperation with Israel, broke down in favor of both sides continuing to seek a military solution. As long as Mengistu refused to seek a negotiated settlement designed to bring a just peace to Ethiopia, even proponents of responding to Ethiopia's diplomatic initiatives, such as the House Subcommittee on Africa, continued to underscore the necessity for restraint.

A final concern of critics centered on what was perceived as Mengistu's blatant manipulation of Falasha desires to emigrate in order to obtain greater levels of financial assistance and military weaponry from Israel. In July 1990, the House Subcommittee on Africa expressed concern that Israel illegally had transfered 100 US-supplied cluster bombs to Ethiopia as part of a secret deal to ensure the continued flow of Jewish refugees.[200] More important, members of Congress sympathetic to the repatriation effort denounced the sporadic halting of an already tenuous process which was handling about 500 refugees a month. As underscored by Wolpe, it was obvious that Mengistu was using the Falashas as "pawns" to replace stocks of weaponry that the Soviet Union would no longer supply.[201]

The evolution of US foreign policy toward Ethiopia and Somalia from 1988 to 1990 demonstrated the type of bureaucratic-congressional stand-off that can result from low-level African conflicts that are severe enough to cause internal debate within the policymaking establishment, but not attract the involvement of the White House. In the case of the intensification of the Somali civil war in 1988, the fashioning of a proper policy response was left to the national security bureaucracies, particularly the Defense Department, which resupplied the Somali military in accordance with established bureaucratic routines. However, the civil war also attracted the attention of a small, but highly vocal group within Congress that, although unable to completely sever US ties with the Siad regime, was successful in forcing the State Department to declare a voluntary hold on US military aid. In the case of Ethiopia, the policy process was also marked by a congressional-executive deadlock that essentially resulted in the continuation of status quo policies. Despite small, albeit growing pressures within the national security bureaucracies to seek a renewal of links, such openings were thwarted by a small group of congresspersons concerned with Ethiopia's intensifying civil war and gross human rights abuses. An irony of this congressional attention was that it was sparked by the periodic famines in Ethiopia, particularly the 1983–85 disaster that resulted in one of the greatest outpourings of popular support for a humanitarian relief program. In the absence of some sort of crisis situation capable of attracting the extended attention of the White House, US foreign policy toward Ethiopia continued to evolve slowly within the bureaucratic and congressional confines of the established status quo.

Low-level crises amidst an altered Cold War environment (November 1990–July 1992)

A new chapter in the international relations of the Horn of Africa began unfolding at the beginning of 1991 as first the Siad and, subsequently, the Mengistu regimes were overthrown by guerrilla insurgencies, followed by the secession of northern Somalia and the creation of a provisional government in Eritrea pending a national referendum on independence to be held in 1993. These tumultuous events began on January 26, 1991, when Siad fled to his birthplace of Garba Harre as victorious elements of the USC guerrilla army captured the capital. The entry of the USC followed nearly four weeks of brutal urban warfare in Mogadishu, in which a total breakdown of law and order had resulted in the deaths of thousands of people.[202]

The departure of the Siad regime did not mean the end of conflict in the country. Rather than abide by an October 2, 1990, accord in which the major guerrilla groups agreed to decide the shape of a post-Siad political system, the USC, by virtue of its control of the capital, unilaterally named a Hawiye, Ali Mahdi Mohammed, president of the country. This move heightened the already tense relations between the Isaak-dominated SNM, the Hawiye-dominated USC, and the Ogadeni-dominated SPM, as well as among scores of other, less organized, clan groupings. In a move based on a strongly held Isaak belief that the north would continue to be victimized by a southern-dominated government, the SNM announced on May 17, 1991, that the former British Somaliland territory was seceding from the 1960 union and henceforth would be known as the Somaliland Republic. This announcement was followed by the intensification of clan conflict in the southern portion of the country between the USC and the SPM, which, in turn, was exacerbated by a regrouping of Siad's Darod clan groupings under the military banner of the Somali National Front (SNF). In short, once the common political enemy no longer existed, traditional clan differences, exacerbated by the dictatorial divide-and-rule practices of the Siad years, made any hope of national reconciliation highly unlikely.

The intensifying civil war prior to the departure of the Siad regime from power had the potential of becoming a crisis situation at the highest levels of the US policymaking establishment, especially after Ambassador James K. Bishop sent an urgent cable on January 3, 1991, warning that the lives of Embassy personnel were being threatened by armed looters surrounding the 40-acre compound. Hastily moving up an evacuation planned for January 5, two rescue helicopters and seventy Marines were dispatched from the *USS Trenton*, a warship stationed in the Indian Ocean as part of the US war against Iraq in 1991 known as Operation Desert Storm. In a 460-mile flight that twice required mid-air refueling in the middle of the night, the Marine detachment took up positions at the US Embassy and airlifted over sixty people out of the country on January 4. The following day, nearly 200 more people were evacuated by five helicopters launched from the *USS Guam*. At the end of the operation, nearly 260 people from 30 countries had been airlifted.[203]

Despite the fact that Bush had to authorize the rescue mission, the decline of Cold War tensions ensured that the escalating civil war never constituted a crisis situation with the potential of attracting the ongoing attention of the White House.[204] Unlike the 1970s and the 1980s, when the region had become an East–West flashpoint, the Soviet Union was pursuing a policy of disengagement that underscored the importance of superpower cooperation in settling local conflicts. In addition to ongoing discussions, primarily at the level of the Assistant Secretary of State for African Affairs and a counterpart in Moscow, a significant example of how superpower cooperation was replacing superpower conflict in a rapidly developing post-Cold War era was the evacuation of the Soviet Ambassador and thirty-five members of his staff by the aforementioned US rescue mission. As aptly summarized by one US official, superpower competition had become a "thing of the past" in the Horn of Africa.[205]

The net result of White House inattention was the delegation of policy to the national security bureaucracies, particularly the State Department's Africa Bureau. Severely constrained by congressional disfavor with the human rights abuses of the Siad regime, the Africa Bureau presided over a reactive policy that emphasized the internal roots of the conflict and the need for national reconciliation through peaceful means. This stance was reinforced by the simple reality that the guerrilla groups opposed to the Siad regime professed strong desires to maintain, and in fact enhance, Somalia's relationship with the US should they emerge victorious. "In short," explained a former member of the State Department's Africa Bureau, "a kind of 'win-win' situation prevailed in which risk-averse bureaucrats could count on maintaining US influence regardless of whether the Somali government or the guerrilla opposition emerged victorious."[206]

A decline in the perceived need for military access to Somalia in the wake of decreased Cold War tensions constituted another important reason for the less than enthusiastic bureaucratic arguments for shoring up the Siad regime. In an interesting conclusion to a long-simmering policy debate over Somalia's strategic importance to the US, the naval facility at Berbera turned out to be completely unnecessary for the massive deployment of US troops and *matériel* associated with Operation Desert Storm. Although at first Somalia's strategic location – the cornerstone of globalist-inspired arguments seeking close US–Somali security ties – made it a potentially important player in what in 1991 constituted the largest US military operation abroad in the post-Vietnam era, the Berbera base was simply stripped of its fuel stocks and left dormant by military planners. This turn of events seemed to validate the position of critics who had asserted throughout the 1980s that, even if one accepted globalist rationales for ensuring US military access, the Somali bases were unnecessary in light of other, more extensive, facilities readily available in the region.[207]

The changing fortunes of the Siad regime within the national security bureaucracies was best demonstrated by growing criticism within the Defense Department, one of the staunchest proponents during the 1988 SNM guerrilla offensive of sending a strong signal of support to the Somali government. For example, Colonel Alfred F. Girardi, a retired military attaché who served at the US Embassy in Mogadishu from 1987 to 1989, argued in congressional hearings against any further aid on the basis that the Somali Armed Forces were "poorly motivated" and "poorly led by inept officers."[208] This testimony was matched by a growing respect in some quarters for the military successes and the pro-Western leanings of some guerrilla leaders, such as Omar Jess, the renegade military leader of SPM. Such arguments notwithstanding, few, if any, career officers within the Pentagon foresaw an end to the internal fighting in Somalia that could lead to a beneficial US relationship with any future government. As Colonel Girardi presciently warned in 1989, the most likely outcome of a post-Siad Somalia was continued "turmoil and instability" as opposing clan factions vied for control.[209]

A third round of fighting broke out in the southern part of the country in September 1991, and less than two months later turned into an all-out struggle for control of Mogadishu. Unlike the first round (to overthrow Siad) and the second round (inter-clan fighting) of the Somali civil war, this round was between factions of the Hawiye-based USC guerrilla army. Specifically, a brutal intra-clan power struggle erupted between forces loyal to interim President Mahdi, a member of the Abgal subclan of the Hawiye, and those led by General Mohammed Farah Aidid, a member of the Habar Gedir subclan of the Hawiye. Despite the efforts of outside mediators to establish a series of cease-fires, the fighting as of February 1992 had resulted in more than 30,000 (mostly civilian) casualties in the Mogadishu region. Even after a UN-sponsored truce was finally achieved on March 3, 1992, and remained partially implemented as of July of that same year, the total collapse of the Somali state led to the division of the former Republic of Somalia into dozens of fiefdoms controlled by clan-based politico-military movements.[210]

In the absence of any bureaucratic missions which could have prompted a more proactive response, the State Department's Africa Bureau oversaw a two-track policy that sought to limit US involvement in what one FSO described as a "clan-based quagmire destined to last years, if not decades."[211] First, the Africa Bureau argued that the US should support the efforts of Secretary-General Boutros Boutros-Ghali to place the United Nations in the forefront of a multilateral effort designed to meet the *humanitarian* needs of the Somali peoples. However, a desire to avoid direct involvement in the *politics* of resolving ongoing clan warfare was clearly demonstrated by a US vote on March 17, 1992, for a Security Council resolution related to Somalia only after language calling for a UN-sponsored peace-keeping mission had been removed. Although a State Department official claimed that congressional concerns over "dramatically rising costs" associated with peace-keeping operations throughout the world was a major factor, Africans pointed to decisive US support for a UN peace-keeping mission in war-torn Yugoslavia, and accused the US of adopting a double standard concerning Africa.[212]

The second element of the Africa Bureau's two-track policy, already evident in the immediate aftermath of Siad's departure from office, was that Britain, and especially Italy, should take the lead in their former colonial territories. This policy stance not only was applied to the resolution of intra-clan fighting, but also to the diplomatic controversy involving the secessionist Somaliland Republic. As demonstrated by its involvement in the "national reconciliation" talks held in Djibouti during 1991, for example, the Africa Bureau carefully avoided statements that went beyond the desires of either Italy or Great Britain, and therefore favored the preservation of the Republic of Somalia as originally constituted in 1960. "We'll deal with a legally constituted government in Mogadishu first because that is what the Europeans and especially Italy wants," explained an FSO in the Africa Bureau. "The most likely scenario in which we would recognize northern independence is if both the north and the south extend mutual recognition of the internal legitimacy of both governments, and this decision is diplomatically recognized by both Italy and Great Britain."[213]

In sharp contrast to the largely reactive response to events in

Somalia, US policymakers adopted a more proactive approach to resolving Ethiopia's civil war.[214] When guerrilla advances during the first four months of 1991 made it clear that Mengistu's days were numbered, the US intensified its involvement in negotiations between the Ethiopian government and the guerrilla opposition by sending a high-level delegation to Addis Ababa that included Deputy Assistant Secretary of State for African Affairs Irvin Hicks, Robert C. Frasure (a member of the NSC), and former Senator Rudy Boschwitz (R-Minnesota) who acted as Bush's personal envoy. In addition to meeting with Mengistu, both Hicks and Frasure traveled to Khartoum to meet with Isaias Afwerki, leader of the EPLF, and Meles Zenawi, the head of the TPLF. The level of US involvement in these negotiations intensified when, in the aftermath of Mengistu's departure from power on May 21, 1991, Cohen flew to London to mediate personally between the guerrilla factions and a collapsing Ethiopian government.

The net result of US involvement was a significant contribution to a transfer of power which largely avoided the bloodshed and clan conflict still evident in Somalia more than a year after Siad's departure from power. As part of an agreement that was publicly endorsed by Cohen on May 28, 1991, the TPLF took control of Addis Ababa and began putting together a broad coalition government that was expected to include representatives from all of the country's major ethnic groups and political organizations. A criticial element of the May agreement – which led to rioting in Addis Ababa – was US support for a UN-supervised referendum in Eritrea within a period of roughly two years to determine if the people of the territory desired independence. This decision to support regional self-determination through the ballot box – fully cognizant of the fact that the outcome would be an independent Eritrea – represented a significant change in foreign policy. Rather than giving unswerving support for the territorial integrity of the Ethiopian empire as had been the case from the 1950s to the 1980s, the US endorsed a policy that questioned the hallowed OAU concept of territorial integrity. Regardless of the referendum's outcome, the Africa Bureau made it clear that foreign assistance beyond humanitarian relief depended on the establishment of some type of legitimate democracy in Ethiopia. As succinctly summarized by Cohen: "No democracy, no cooperation."[215]

Several factors accounted for the proactive US response to events in Ethiopia. First, both the Mengistu government and the guerrilla opposition sought a greater role for Washington as a mediator between their conflicting claims.[216] These positive signals coincided with rising pressures within the national security bureaucracies, particularly the

State Department's Africa Bureau, to avoid the policy disasters that had occurred in Liberia and Somalia.[217] In both cases, US–supported leaders were driven from power by coalitions of guerrilla forces which, after achieving initial victories, presided over the escalation of ethnically or clan-based violence. Having "learned" that policies of inaction potentially entail far greater costs than initially may have been apparent, the Africa Bureau sought immediate action in order to avoid another disaster in Africa. "We want to see law and order," explained a diplomat who was stationed at the US Embassy in Addis Ababa during 1991. "What we want to do is facilitate a soft landing and prevent the kind of bloodshed that has affected Liberia and Somalia."[218]

The decline of Cold War competition in the Horn of Africa was an important element in the calculations of Ethiopian and US officials. As far as several segments of the policymaking establishment were concerned, the hardline Marxist positions of both the Mengistu regime and the guerrilla opposition made support for either side highly unlikely during the 1980s. The decisions of both sides to modify their attachment to Marxism in the face of Soviet retrenchment at the end of the 1980s removed a major obstacle to the reestablishment of closer ties with Washington. "If this had happened five years ago, we wouldn't have been involved because in the Cold War, it would have been hard to work with the Marxists," explained Cohen. "Even two years ago," he continued, "it was hard for me to work with SWAPO [South West African People's Organization]," a reference to the difficulties of dealing with a guerrilla organization that maintained a strong attachment to Marxism prior to taking power in Namibia. "The big difference now," he concluded, "is that people talk about Marxism and people laugh."[219]

The end of the Cold War was also an important reason for the new US position concerning the territorial integrity of Ethiopia. During the Cold War era, when unimpeded access to Kagnew Station and other facilities in Eritrea guided US foreign policy toward Ethiopia, support within the national security bureaucracies for the territorial status quo remained virtually unquestioned. It was greatly feared that an independent Eritrea would terminate access to what at the time was considered to be one of the most valuable US telecommunications centers in Africa, Asia, and the Middle East. With the decline of the Cold War, the bureaucratic justifications for Ethiopia's territorial integrity no longer rang true. Although portions of the national security bureaucracies, such as the CIA and, to a lesser extent, the Pentagon questioned whether an independent Eritrea would be financially insolvent and potentially susceptible to "radical" foreign powers (such as Libya), the Africa Bureau successfully argued for a policy that supported the pursuit of self-determination through legal means. This position was based on the simple facts that the EPLF, which had been fighting for Eritrean independence for over thirty years, militarily controlled the entire region, and that the TPLF, although in favor of maintaining the territorial integrity of the country, was willing to recognize Eritrean independence if a majority of the population in the territory truly desired that.

An equally important aspect of the proactive US response was the episodic involvement of the highest levels of the US policymaking establishment, including Bush, despite the fact that the White House never perceived the unfolding events in Ethiopia as constituting a crisis in the Cold War mold. For example, the need to create an orderly transfer of power in Ethiopia captured the attention of the White House when it became clear that a humanitarian disaster on a par with the 1983–85 famine was in the making. Already faced with a domestic uproar over the plight of Iraq's Kurdish population – a group for whom no domestic constituency existed – the White House sought to avoid the public criticism that resulted from the Reagan administration's slow response to the conditions contributing to the 1983–85 famine. An integral aspect of this approach was a political calculation that domestic demands for higher levels of humanitarian aid to Ethiopia, already annually topping $150 million since 1984, would multiply dramatically in the event of ongoing civil war and bloodshed in a post-Mengistu era similar to what was occurring in Liberia and Somalia.[220]

The delicate process associated with the emigration of Ethiopia's Falashas, approximately 14,000 of whom found themselves stranded in Addis Ababa while awaiting departure for Israel, served as an even more important reason for White House involvement in the policymaking process. The White House began paying greater attention to this issue not only because of ongoing congressional concerns with the Mengistu regime's practice of trading visas for arms, but also due to a private appeal to Bush from Israeli Prime Minister Yitzak Shamir. Desirous of avoiding the political fallout that could have accompanied any deterioration of the personal safety of the Falashas stranded in Addis Ababa, Bush dispatched Boschwitz as his personal envoy and, in the aftermath of Mengistu's departure from power, sent a letter to Acting President Tesfaye Gebre-Kidan, requesting that the group be allowed to emigrate. The highly publicized outcome of this and other appeals was a two-day airlift on May 24–25, 1991, dubbed Operation Solomon, in which more than 14,000 Falashas were flown to Israel in exchange for $35 million in "exit" fees.[221]

A new era in Ethiopian domestic politics tentatively began in July 1991 with the appointment of an 87-member Council of Representatives that, among other duties, was to draft a new constitution and oversee a two-year transitional period to democracy. As one stage in this process, Ethiopia held its first-ever democratic elections at both the district and regional levels on June 21, 1992, and began preparing for national elections scheduled for 1993.[222] Despite the fact that the elections were judged by international observers to be neither completely free nor fair, the State Department's Africa Bureau nonetheless announced that they represented an "historic" and "useful" exercise, and could provide the basis for a more democratic process in the future.[223]

The US response to the ongoing democratization process is instructive in that it underscores the nascent beginnings of a renewed US–Ethiopian special relationship. Indeed, despite growing reports of a "low-intensity" guerrilla war between the ruling EPRDF and the Oromo-based guerrilla forces of the OLF, the Africa Bureau has downplayed the differences between the two sides, and has sought to maintain its role as a mediator in resolving ethnic conflict in Ethiopia.[224] As underscored by a country desk officer associated with the Africa Bureau, this policy should come as no surprise in that Ethiopia is still considered to be the "most attractive" of all of the countries of the region. Among the reasons cited were Ethiopia's large population and economic potential, the historic nature of US–Ethiopian ties, the ability of the Ethiopian bureaucracy (unlike "others" in Africa) to "get the job done," a strategic location bordering the Red Sea, a Christian heritage that could serve as a bulwark against Islamic fundamentalist movements, and Ethiopia's role as host to the headquarters of the OAU.[225]

This period of analysis clearly demonstrated that the decline of the Cold War has important implications for the relationship between the nature of events on the African continent and the operation of the US policymaking process. In sharp contrast to the crisis atmospheres that most likely would have accompanied the downfall of the Siad and, to a lesser degree, the Mengistu regimes had they occurred during the early 1980s, these events at best constituted low-level crisis events largely handled by the national security bureaucracies. In the absence of a perceived communist threat, involvement by the White House only became a factor when, as in the case of Ethiopia's Falasha Jews, domestic political concerns entered policy calculations. Otherwise, policy was largely left to the Africa specialists within the national security bureaucracies. In the case of Somalia, this entailed the downgrading of a troubled security relationship in favor of following the leads of the former European colonial powers. In the case of Ethiopia, the downfall of the Mengistu regime facilitated the renewal of an historical relationship, as well as the promotion of an Eritrean policy that recognized local African realities. In both cases, the decline of the Cold War set the stage for a reordering of bureaucratic priorities that ensured the growing importance of the State Department's Africa Bureau as the lead agency for US foreign policy in the Horn of Africa.

Extended crisis and humanitarian military intervention (August 1992–January 1993)

The Africa Bureau's strategy of limiting US involvement in Somalia's intensifying clan conflicts was slightly altered on August 14, 1992, when the White House announced that the Pentagon would coordinate a UN-sponsored, short-term humanitarian airlift of food aid designed to alleviate spreading famine in central and southern Somalia.[226] Two weeks later on August 28, a contingent of 500 US soldiers oversaw the first flight of four C-140 transport planes from their bases in Mombasa, Kenya, to a variety of drop-off points in Somalia. White House authorization of the operation followed in the aftermath of a UN agreement with General Aidid, the USC militia leader who controlled access to the port, which in turn permitted the deployment during September of a UN force of 500 Pakistani soldiers to protect food supplies and relief workers in Mogadishu. These forces were deployed with the support of four US warships carrying 2,100 Marines. The White House also supported a Security Council resolution authorizing the deployment of an additional 3,000 UN troops into other parts of Somalia. This deployment was hampered, however, by the inability of the UN to reach any further accords with either Aidid or the multitude of other clan and militia leaders within central or southern Somalia.

As it became increasingly clear that the UN Security Council was incapable of generating the leadership necessary to stem intensifying levels of clan conflict and famine, President Bush announced in a live television address to the US public on December 4, 1992, that US troops would be deployed in Somalia to "create a secure environment" for the distribution of famine-relief aid. "In taking this action, I want to emphasize that I understand the United States alone cannot right the world's wrongs," explained Bush, "but we also know that some crises in the world cannot be resolved without American involvement, that American action is often necessary as a catalyst for broader involvement of the community of nations."[227] Five days later on December 9, the first contingent of US troops led by three teams of Navy SEALs (Sea-Air-Land Commandos) landed on the beaches of Mogadisu and secured the airport and the port.

The US military landing, designated Operation Restore Hope, was carried out under the auspices of a UN Security Council resolution sanctioning foreign intervention.[228] In the weeks that followed, over 36,000 foreign troops from over twenty countries (including approximately 24,000 US military personnel) occupied various cities and towns throughout central and southern Somalia, and began the task of opening food supply routes as well as creating distribution networks where none existed before. In order to demonstrate his commitment to the humanitarian relief operation, as well as to underscore to the international community the high-minded principles which he felt were guiding US policy, President Bush visited US troops in Somalia at the end of December while *en route* to a summit meeting with Boris Yeltsin in Russia, designating him as only the second US President to make an official visit to Sub-Saharan Africa during the post-World War II era. (President Carter spent three days in Nigeria in 1978.)[229]

The White House decision to deploy US combat troops in Somalia – initially agreed upon as the proper course of action during a meeting of the National Security Council on November 25 – was significant in that it previously was opposed by the national security bureaucracies.[230] For example, several FSOs within the State Department's Africa Bureau strongly opposed direct US military intervention, and instead favored a more proactive diplomatic approach that centered on resolving clan differences, as well as pressuring the UN Security Council to take a much more active role in military operations if deemed necessary. The CIA and the Pentagon also initially opposed the introduction of US combat troops into Somalia. In a view characteristic of that adhered to by CIA analysts of the Horn of Africa, Robert M. Gates, Director of Central Intelligence, warned that "anarchy" was "so sweeping" and "the warring factions so firmly entrenched" that the US was potentially setting itself up for the unintended long-term responsibility of maintaining stability in Somalia.[231]

One of the harshest critics of Operation Restore Hope within the US policymaking establishment was Smith Hempstone Jr., the US ambassador to Kenya, who argued that Somalia could become a quagmire for US foreign policy. "Somalis, as the Italians and British discovered to their discomfiture are natural born guerrillas," explained Hempstone in a strongly worded cable to Washington that reportedly was "circulated widely" within the national security bureaucracies. "They will mine the roads. They will lay ambushes. They will launch hit and run attacks. They will not be able to stop the convoys from getting through. But they will inflict – and take – casualties."[232] Taking such a risk, according to Hempstone, was ill-advised for the simple reason that Somalia did not constitute a country of vital interest to the United States. "Aside from the humanitarian issue – which admittedly is compelling (but so it is in the Sudan) – I fail to see where any vital interest is involved."[233]

The primary reason for the shift in US policy was growing public and congressional pressures on the White House to "do something" to resolve what James R. Kunder, the head of the US Office of Foreign Disaster Assistance, labeled the "world's worst humanitarian disaster."[234] By August 1992, nearly nine months after fighting had broken out between rival factions of the USC, as many as 1.5 million of an estimated Somali population of 6 million were threatened with starvation, with approximately 300,000 Somalis already having died, including roughly 25 percent of all children under the age of five.

As media reports of this extended humanitarian crisis increased in quantity beginning in July 1992, particularly in terms of live satellite broadcasts that portrayed images of starving Somali children on morning talk shows and nightly newscasts,[235] criticism of executive branch inaction from a variety of quarters increasingly was taken more seriously by the White House. In addition to being "bombarded with appeals" from private relief organizations, the White House found itself being criticized by prominent newspaper columnists calling for a "shoot-to-feed" policy.[236] In the case of Congress, this criticism reached its height on August 3, 1992, when a bipartisan resolution co-sponsored by Senators Simon and Kassebaum, and calling for a more activist response on the part of the White House, overwhelmingly passed the Senate, followed by passage of this same bill in the House of Representatives on August 10.[237] Indeed, according to a *New York Times*/CBS public opinion poll conducted just prior to the beginning of Operation Restore Hope, 81 percent of the US public believed that President Bush was "doing the right thing in sending troops to Somalia to make sure food gets to the people there," with 70 percent believing that sending troops was even "worth the possible loss of American lives, financial costs and other risks."[238]

Critics of the Bush administration have suggested that presidential politics in an election year also played an important role in the White House's handling of the Somali crisis.[239] According to this viewpoint, the White House only began playing attention when rising congressional and public concerns threatened to make Somalia a campaign issue in the 1992 presidential election, and therefore it should have come as no surprise that the President decided to announce the beginning of the humanitarian airlift of food on the eve of the beginning of the Republican Party national convention in August 1992. However, the upcoming election also potentially served as an important political constraint on the White House's preferred course of action. Although senior administration officials strongly denied that political concerns associated with the upcoming presidential elections influenced the pace of policy, they nonetheless admitted that White House campaign advisers were "fearful of accusations that all the President cared about was foreign policy," and therefore "strongly urged him to take a lower public profile on all foreign issues" inclusive of Somalia "until after the election."[240] Ironically, defeat in the election removed any such constraints, allowing President Bush to initiate a major military operation that clearly was going to carry over into the newly elected Clinton administration. Yet critics still argued that President Bush was less interested in Somalia than in ensuring that the history books remember him as ending his term of office as a "decisive leader" as opposed to a "vanquished politician."[241]

Regardless of whether domestic pressures, more narrow political concerns, or high-minded principles were of greatest importance in prompting the Bush administration to militarily intervene in Somalia – indeed, it is arguable that all three were operative, with the former exerting the most influence – Operation Restore Hope nonetheless signaled a significant departure in US foreign policy in the Horn of Africa, as well as in Africa generally. As succinctly stated by one observer of the Bush administration, "for the first time American troops are entering a country uninvited, not to shore up an anti-communist regime, protect American wealth or stifle a strategic threat, but simply to feed starving people."[242] In this regard, the operation clearly reflected the globalist worldview of President Bush and his two closest foreign policy advisers – Secretary of State James A. Baker III and National Security Adviser Brendt Scowcroft – specifically in terms of their collective desire to fashion a "new world order" based on active US involvement within the international system as the sole remaining superpower. "Only the United States," explained President Bush on December 4, 1992, "has the global reach to place a large security force on the ground in such a distant place quickly and efficiently and thus save thousands of innocents from death."[243]

The formulation and implementation of Operation Restore Hope also reflected a classic element of White House involvement in US Africa policies: a desire to relegate responsibility to other powers that presumably are better able to resolve Africa's political and economic problems. Specifically, the Bush administration originally envisioned a short-term US led military operation that, once having achieved the immediate humanitarian objective of preventing mass starvation, was to be quickly replaced by UN peace-keeping forces directly responsible to the UN Security Council. Toward this end, the Bush administration authorized a token but highly symbolic withdrawal of approximately 550 US troops from Somalia on January 19, 1993, just one day prior to the inauguration of President Clinton.[244] Most important, the Bush administration stated from the beginning of Operation Restore Hope that it wanted to stay out of Somali politics, and therefore relegated to the UN Security Council the responsibility of creating a new political system in Somalia. "Our mission has a limited objective, to open the supply routes, to get the food moving, and to prepare the way for a UN peace-keeping force to keep it moving," explained President Bush on December 4, 1992, "This operation is not open-ended. We will not stay one day longer than is abolutely necessary."[245]

The Bush administration's desires to quickly withdraw US troops and to limit US involvement in political reconstruction led to a growing rift between the White House and UN Secretary-General Boutros Boutros-Ghali, who strongly favored a much more expanded politico-military role for the United States.[246] Indeed according to Boutros-Ghali and other critics, the US was involved – whether it wanted to be or not – in the internal politics of the country as soon as US troops landed on the beaches in Mogadishu. Most important, the military objective of ensuring famine relief only addressed the "symptom" of the more critical underlying problem of clan competition and warfare. If the political conflict is not resolved, and US troops are withdrawn from the country prematurely, argue the critics, one may witness the reemergence of a similar (or worse) crisis in the years to come. It is for this reason that Boutros-Ghali was sharply critical of the initial redeployment of US troops back to the US, leading to countercharges by some within Washington that the UN was dragging its feet in assuming its rightful primary responsibility for the political reconstruction of Somalia.[247]

Far from being resolved as the Bush administration left office on January 20, 1993, the Somali crisis presented the newly inaugurated Clinton administration with the difficult task of reviewing Operation Restore Hope and determining when and how the US should disengage from Somalia. According to Robert B. Oakley, former Ambassador to Somalia who returned to the country to aid in the coordination of Operation Restore Hope, disengagement will be neither as easy nor as quickly attained as originally envisioned by the Bush White House.

Oakley projected the necessity of maintaining a long-term presence of 20,000 UN troops, including approximately 2,000 US combat troops who could be held in reserve in case they were needed. Oakley also recommended the long-term stationing of between 5,000 to 8,000 US logistical troops. Although Oakley has cautioned that the US is not likely to play a central role in non-military matters, he nonetheless acknowledged that the US "cannot stand aloof" from aiding in the restoration of governance in Somalia.[248]

This final period of analysis clearly demonstrated the importance of domestic politics in contributing to a significant change in US foreign policy toward Africa. Similar to events in the mid-1980s in which public perceptions of a mounting humanitarian crisis in Ethiopia prompted the Reagan administration to act, the Bush administration's initial disregard for the unfolding famine in Somalia was clearly altered by growing public awareness of the issue. However, unlike the US response to famine relief in Ethiopia, the nature of the Bush administration's response – sending in over 20,000 US combat troops – surprised many within the administration, especially in light of the fact that, due to his defeat in the 1992 presidential elections, President Bush would be leaving office in little over a month after the beginning of the military operation. It is for this reason that critics have argued that domestic political considerations, most notably a desire to be remembered as a decisive President in the realm of foreign policy, rather than President Bush's foreign policy beliefs, contributed to what may be considered to be the most significant departure in US foreign policy toward Africa during the post-World War II period.

Conclusion

The importance of the relationship between the nature of events within Africa and the operation of the US policymaking process is nicely portrayed by the evolution of US interventionist practices in Ethiopia and Somalia during the post-World War II period. Born out of the strategic necessities of US involvement in World War II and nurtured along by the varying and sometimes opposing bureaucratic missions of the State Department, the Pentagon, and the CIA, US security relationships in the Horn of Africa evolved with each new crisis and subsequent period of routine and relative calm.

The evolution of US intervention in Ethiopia and Somalia from 1948 to 1974 clearly demonstrated the importance of the process of bureaucratic incrementalism during routine periods. With little if any input from the White House, the national security bureaucracies oversaw the establishment and expansion of a US–Ethiopian security relationship at the expense of closer ties with Somalia. The primary factor driving US involvement in Ethiopia – which would ultimately yield Haile Selassie over $600 million in US foreign assistance – was a host of bureaucratic missions that relied upon maintaining unhampered access to Kagnew, one of the most important US bases on the African continent during the 1950s and 1960s. Ironically, it was the State Department's Africa Bureau which, during this period, assumed the advocacy role of convincing a reluctant Defense Department to support increases in US military aid to the Haile Selassie regime.

An important outgrowth of the expanding US presence in Ethiopia from 1948 to 1974 was the lack of high-level consideration over the implications of US involvement in the territorial disputes of the region. Rather than unduly concerning themselves with the domestic politics or the regional relations of Ethiopia and Somalia, US policymakers perceived these countries in terms of their places within a larger strategic policy that generally treated Africa as a solution to non-African problems. In Ethiopia, Washington's involvement in Kagnew derived from the Cold War necessities of establishing a worldwide telecommunications and eavesdropping network directed against the Soviet Union, and ultimately led to Washington's support for Haile Selassie's claim to Eritrea, as well as to support for Ethiopia in its historical conflict with Somalia. As a result, Washington's policies partially contributed to nearly thirty years of civil war in Ethiopia between the central government and the guerrilla forces in Eritrea, as well as the intermittent border conflicts between Ethiopia and Somalia. Indeed, support for the territorial integrity of Ethiopia led to the strengthening of a consensus within the national security bureaucracies that the pan-Somali quest to unite all the Somali peoples of the Horn of Africa under one government was both illegitimate and undesirable.

The preeminence of the process of bureaucratic incrementalism during the 1948–74 period does not imply, however, that there were no changes in US policies in the Horn of Africa. Despite the opposition of Haile Selassie and his staunch proponents within the national security bureaucracies, the State Department's Africa Bureau was successful in expanding a limited US economic relationship with Somalia in the aftermath of the 1964 election victory of Egal. In Ethiopia, once the military missions formerly handled by Kagnew were satisfied by other, more self-sufficient means, such as satellites and the growing US base at Diego Garcia, the Pentagon presence in the country accordingly declined. In this regard, the crucial importance of the process of bureaucratic incrementalism is that if one wants to understand the evolution of US Africa policies during routine periods, one must focus on the level of the national security bureaucracies and the nature of evolving bureaucratic missions. Even during the low-level crises of the 1960 attempted *coup d'état* in Ethiopia and the 1964 Ethiopian–Somali border conflict, the formulation of policy responses was handled by the national security bureaucracies, and therefore reflected the established bureaucratic status quo. In both of these cases, the lack of high-level attention was due to the absence of an East–West dimension which traditionally has triggered White House involvement within the policymaking process as concerns US Africa policies.

It was only in the aftermath of the 1974–77 Ethiopian revolution that US policies in the Horn of Africa were altered significantly due to White House involvement within the policymaking process. During the initial stages of the revolution, expectations of a moderate, pro-Western government ensured that the White House would defer to the Africa specialists within the national security bureaucracies. In the aftermath of the radicalization of the revolution, however, both the Ford and Carter White Houses were confronted with the dilemma of how to respond to a pro-Soviet regime headed by Mengistu. The Ford administration's response – continuation of a military aid relationship best noted by the delivery of sophisticated military aircraft – clearly demonstrated the importance of the *realpolitik* worldview as shared by Kissinger and Ford. Similarly, the Carter administration's response – the upgrading of human rights as the yardstick by which to judge US relationships with African countries – reflected the dominance of that administration's regionalist worldview as shared by Carter and Vance. In both cases, the perception of a crisis within the Horn of Africa led to policies more consistent with each administration's worldview.

The most significant aspect of the 1974–77 Ethiopian revolution was that it led to a break in the US–Ethiopian security relationship in favor of growing US military ties with Somalia. Despite strong opposition within the national security bureaucracies, Carter sought a military opening to the Siad regime that resulted in a US commitment to meet Somalia's defense needs. Although temporarily put on hold due to the 1977–78 Ogaden War and the preeminence of regionalist arguments against arming an expansionistic Somalia, a formal US–Somali access agreement was implemented due to the strengthening of a globalist worldview within the Carter administration in the aftermath of the Iranian hostage crisis and the Soviet invasion of Afghanistan. In this regard, the 1977–78 Ogaden crisis served as an important element in the evolution of the Carter administration's worldview, away from the regionalist focus favored by Vance, to the more globally inspired arguments promoted by Brzezinski.

The evolution of US interventionist practices in both Somalia and Ethiopia during the 1980s and the beginning of the 1990s further demonstrated the importance of the relationship between the nature of events in Africa and the operation of the US policymaking process. In Somalia, the absence of crisis in the aftermath of the 1977–78 Ogaden War ensured that policy, once again, fell to the Africa specialists within the national security bureacracies. As a result, the engrained historical distrust of Somali intentions served as an important constraint on the rapid expansion of US–Somali ties. Indeed, in a sharp departure from the State Department's advocacy role during the 1950s and 1960s for closer US attention to the US–Ethiopian relationship, the Pentagon emerged during the 1980s as the primary advocate for closer US ties with Somalia. The primary focus of the Defense Department – which yielded Siad nearly $800 million in US bilateral economic and military aid from 1980 to 1991 – was military access to Somalia's northern port city of Berbera, although it was only in the aftermath of the 1982 Ethiopian–Somali border conflict that US military aid to Somalia significantly increased. The East–West dimension of this conflict was the crucial element that attracted the attention of the Reagan White House, contributing to a new policy more consonant with that administration's worldview. Six years later, the intensification of the civil war – which had nothing to do with East–West relations – largely was ignored by the White House, and instead attracted the attention of a small but highly vocal group within Congress that was successful in forcing the State Department to declare a voluntary hold on all military aid to Somalia.

In the case of US–Ethiopian relations, the absence of crisis in the aftermath of the 1977–78 Ogaden War ensured that policy remained the realm of the Africa specialists within the national security bureaucracies, leading the State Department's Africa Bureau to seek a renewal of US ties with what was once Washington's most important client on the African continent. However, the Mengistu regime's unwillingness to budge on the issue of nationalized US properties led to the routine application of restrictive legislation by Congress, effectively prohibiting any major expansion of US–Ethiopian ties, as well as the provision of all types of aid save for humanitarian. It was only in the aftermath of an extended crisis situation – the 1983–85 Ethiopian famine – that pressures on the part of the public and Congress forced the White House to focus its attention on Ethiopia and alter its policy of neglect.

Table 4.1. *US economic and military aid to Ethiopia, 1950–1992 (bilateral loans and grants, millions of dollars)*

Program	1950	1951	1952	1953	1954	1955	1956	1957	1958	1959	1960	1961	1962	1963	1964	1965	1966	1967	1968	1969
I. Economic Aid–Total	–	0.1	1.2	1.5	2.6	4.1	12.3	9.6	4.9	9.3	7.9	41.6	9.2	14.7	9.2	18.3	51.4	19.0	9.0	20.8
A. Aid & predecessors	–	–	1.2	1.5	2.6	4.1	2.9	9.6	4.9	6.6	4.8	38.7	6.7	10.0	5.2	6.2	35.3	13.6	6.5	17.2
B. Food for peace	–	–	*	–	–	–	*	*	*	2.7	3.1	2.9	2.0	2.4	0.6	0.3	6.4	2.7	0.1	1.0
Title I-total	–	–	–	–	–	–	–	–	–	–	–	–	–	1.5	–	–	2.7	1.9	–	–
Repay. in $-loans	–	–	–	–	–	–	–	–	–	–	–	–	–	1.0	–	–	2.7	1.9	–	–
Pay. in for. curr.	–	–	–	–	–	–	–	–	–	–	–	–	–	0.5	–	–	–	–	–	–
Title II-total	–	–	*	–	–	–	*	*	*	2.7	3.1	2.9	2.0	0.9	0.6	0.3	3.7	0.8	0.1	1.0
Economic relief	–	–	–	–	–	–	–	–	–	2.5	2.9	2.7	1.5	–	0.4	–	3.4	0.4	–	0.8
Vol. relief agency	–	–	*	–	–	–	*	*	*	0.2	0.2	0.2	0.5	0.9	0.2	0.3	0.3	0.4	0.1	0.2
C. Other econ. grants	–	0.1	–	–	–	–	–	–	–	–	–	–	0.5	2.3	3.4	3.9	4.5	2.7	2.4	2.6
Peace Corps	–	–	–	–	–	–	–	–	–	–	–	–	0.5	2.3	3.4	3.9	4.5	2.7	2.4	2.6
Other-	0.1	–	–	–	–	–	–	–	–	–	–	–	–	–	–	–	–	–	–	–
D. Other econ. loans	–	–	–	–	–	–	9.4	–	–	–	–	–	–	–	–	7.9	5.2	–	–	–
Export-Import bank	–	–	–	–	–	–	9.4	–	–	–	–	–	–	–	–	7.9	5.2	–	–	–
All other	–	–	–	–	–	–	–	–	–	–	–	–	–	–	–	–	–	–	–	–
II. Military Aid–Total	–	–	–	–	5.1	1.1	5.1	11.2	7.6	8.9	6.2	17.8	18.2	8.4	8.5	10.1	15.9	18.2	12.0	12.4
A. MAP grants	–	–	–	–	5.0	0.9	4.6	10.5	6.3	6.6	3.8	12.7	7.7	5.3	6.0	7.2	12.3	14.4	9.9	10.3
B. Credit financing	–	–	–	–	–	–	–	–	–	–	–	–	–	–	–	–	–	–	–	–
C. IMET	–	–	–	–	0.1	0.2	0.5	0.4	0.4	1.9	1.3	0.6	1.1	0.4	1.2	1.5	1.9	1.7	1.5	1.2
D. Tran-Excess stock	–	–	–	–	*	–	*	0.3	0.9	0.3	1.2	4.5	3.9	2.7	1.4	1.4	1.7	2.2	0.7	0.8
E. Other grants	–	–	–	–	–	–	–	–	–	–	–	–	5.5	–	–	–	–	–	–	–
III.ESF	–	–	–	–	–	–	–	–	–	–	–	–	–	–	3.0	–	–	0.3	–	
IV. Total	–	0.1	1.2	1.5	7.7	5.2	17.4	20.8	12.5	18.2	14.1	59.4	27.4	23.1	17.7	32.4	67.3	37.2	21.3	33.2
Loans	–	–	–	–	–	–	9.4	–	–	0.5	–	29.1	–	5.5	0.7	11.9	37.8	7.7	1.0	13.0
Grants	–	0.1	1.2	1.5	7.7	5.2	8.0	20.8	12.5	17.7	14.1	30.3	29.4	17.6	17.0	20.5	29.5	29.5	20.3	20.2

Figures for 1950–90 are derived from US Agency for International Development (USAID), *US Overseas Loans and Grants Series of Yearly Data (Volume IV, Africa), Obligations and Loan Authorizations, FY 1946–FY 1990*, Washington DC: USAID 1988.
Figures for 1991–92 were provided by USIA.
(–) – no aid provided during the fiscal year
(*) – less than $50,000 provided in aid during the fiscal year
(?) – data unavailable
(TQ) – transition quarter

1970	1971	1972	1973	1974	1975	1976	TQ	1977	1978	1979	1980	1981	1982	1983	1984	1985	1986	1987	1988	1989	1990	1991	1992
18.9	23.4	33.0	12.0	36.4	23.8	13.5	0.5	5.6	10.3	31.8	15.0	5.0	2.5	2.8	13.1	87.4	78.3	6.1	51.4	33.1	72.3	52.2	185.4
15.6	20.4	31.1	8.8	20.7	17.2	5.6	*	0.9	5.2	3.3	–	–	–	–	–	0.5	–	–	0.7	0.6	0.4	0.8	41.2
1.3	0.9	0.8	1.0	13.9	5.2	7.2	0.4	4.6	5.0	12.6	15.0	5.0	2.5	2.8	9.8	86.9	78.3	6.1	50.6	32.4	71.9	51.4	–
–	–	–	–	–	–	3.4	–	–	–	–	–	–	–	–	–	–	–	–	–	–	–	–	–
–	–	–	–	–	–	3.4	–	–	–	–	–	–	–	–	–	–	–	–	–	–	–	–	–
–	–	–	–	–	–	–	–	–	–	–	–	–	–	–	–	–	–	–	–	–	–	–	–
1.3	0.9	0.8	1.0	13.9	5.2	3.8	0.4	4.6	5.0	12.6	15.0	5.0	2.5	2.8	9.8	86.9	78.3	6.1	50.6	32.4	71.9	51.4	144.2
1.1	0.8	0.7	0.9	13.9	5.2	3.2	0.4	2.2	4.6	11.4	13.5	1.6	–	0.2	1.9	14.4	–	–	–	4.7	4.5	21.8	?
0.2	0.1	0.1	0.1	*	–	0.6	–	2.4	0.4	1.2	1.5	3.4	2.5	2.6	7.9	72.5	78.3	6.1	50.6	27.7	67.4	29.6	?
2.0	2.1	1.1	2.2	1.8	1.4	0.7	0.1	0.1	–	–	–	–	–	–	–	–	–	–	–	•	–	•	–
2.0	2.1	1.1	2.2	1.8	1.4	0.7	0.1	0.1	–	–	–	–	–	–	–	–	–	–	–	•	–	•	–
–	–	–	–	–	–	–	–	–	–	–	–	–	–	–	–	–	–	–	–	•	–	•	–
–	–	–	–	–	–	–	–	–	–	16.0	–	–	–	–	3.3	–	–	–	–	–	–	–	–
–	–	–	–	–	–	–	–	–	–	16.0	–	–	–	–	3.3	–	–	–	–	–	–	–	–
–	–	–	–	–	–	–	–	–	–	–	–	–	–	–	–	–	–	–	–	–	–	–	–
11.9	13.2	12.1	12.2	23.4	38.0	6.2	0.8	2.7	–	–	–	–	–	–	–	–	–	–	–	–	–	–	–
9.3	10.5	9.4	8.8	10.8	12.1	5.2	0.8	2.5	–	–	–	–	–	–	–	–	–	–	–	–	–	–	–
–	–	–	–	11.0	25.0	–	–	–	–	–	–	–	–	–	–	–	–	–	–	–	–	–	–
1.2	1.3	1.2	0.7	0.8	0.8	1.0	–	0.3	–	–	–	–	–	–	–	–	–	–	–	–	–	–	–
1.4	1.4	1.5	2.7	0.8	0.1	–	–	–	–	–	–	–	–	–	–	–	–	–	–	–	–	–	–
–	–	–	–	–	–	–	–	–	–	–	–	–	–	–	–	–	–	–	–	–	–	–	–
–	–	–	–	–	–	–	–	–	–	–	–	–	–	–	–	–	–	–	–	–	–	–	3.0
30.8	36.6	45.1	24.2	59.8	61.8	19.7	1.3	8.4	10.3	31.8	15.0	5.0	2.5	2.8	13.1	87.4	78.3	6.1	51.4	33.1	72.3	52.2	188.4
10.6	14.9	26.7	4.8	26.0	32.2	3.4	–	–	–	16.0	–	–	–	–	3.3	–	–	–	–	–	–	–	?
20.2	21.7	18.4	19.4	33.8	29.6	16.3	1.3	8.4	10.3	15.8	15.0	5.0	2.5	2.8	9.8	87.4	78.3	6.1	51.4	33.1	72.3	52.2	?

Table 4.2. *US economic and military aid to Somalia, 1954–1992*
(bilateral loans and grants, millions of dollars)

Program	1954	1955	1956	1957	1958	1959	1960	1961	1962	1963	1964	1965	1966	1967	1968	1969	1970	1971	1972
I. Economic Aid–Total	0.7	0.3	0.1	1.4	0.6	3.1	3.0	4.2	15.1	8.8	4.4	7.9	5.4	16.4	5.3	3.5	3.0	0.3	–
A. Aid & predecessors	0.7	0.3	0.1	1.4	0.6	3.1	2.7	4.2	11.8	7.6	3.7	4.9	4.4	15.5	3.7	2.6	2.2	0.3	–
B. Food for peace	–	–	–	–	–	–	0.3	*	2.9	1.0	*	2.5	0.2	0.1	0.8	*	0.5	–	–
Title I–total	–	–	–	–	–	–	–	–	–	–	–	–	–	–	0.6	–	–	–	–
Repay. in $–loans	–	–	–	–	–	–	–	–	–	–	–	–	–	–	0.6	–	–	–	–
Pay. in for. curr.	–	–	–	–	–	–	–	–	–	–	–	–	–	–	–	–	–	–	–
Title II–total	–	–	–	–	–	–	0.3	*	2.9	1.0	*	2.5	0.2	0.1	0.2	*	0.5	–	–
Economic relief	–	–	–	–	–	–	0.3	–	2.8	1.0	–	2.3	–	–	0.2	–	0.5	–	–
Vol. relief agency	–	–	–	–	–	–	*	*	0.1	*	*	0.2	0.2	0.1	*	*	–	–	–
C. Other econ. grants	–	–	–	–	–	–	–	–	0.4	0.2	0.7	0.5	0.8	0.8	0.8	0.9	0.3	*	–
Peace corps	–	–	–	–	–	–	–	–	0.4	0.2	0.7	0.5	0.8	0.8	0.8	0.9	0.3	*	–
Other	–	–	–	–	–	–	–	–	–	–	–	–	–	–	–	–	–	–	–
D. Other econ. loans	–	–	–	–	–	–	–	–	–	–	–	–	–	–	–	–	–	–	–
Export–Import bank	–	–	–	–	–	–	–	–	–	–	–	–	–	–	–	–	–	–	–
All other	–	–	–	–	–	–	–	–	–	–	–	–	–	–	–	–	–	–	–
II. Military aid–Total	–	–	–	–	–	–	–	–	–	–	–	–	–	–	–	–	–	–	–
A. MAP grants	–	–	–	–	–	–	–	–	–	–	–	–	–	–	–	–	–	–	–
B. Credit financing	–	–	–	–	–	–	–	–	–	–	–	–	–	–	–	–	–	–	–
C. IMET	–	–	–	–	–	–	–	–	–	–	–	–	–	–	–	–	–	–	–
D.Tran–excess stock	–	–	–	–	–	–	–	–	–	–	–	–	–	–	–	–	–	–	–
E. Other grants	–	–	–	–	–	–	–	–	–	–	–	–	–	–	–	–	–	–	–
III. ESF	–	–	–	–	–	–	–	–	–	–	–	–	–	–	–	–	–	–	–
IV. Total	0.7	0.3	0.1	1.4	0.6	3.1	3.0	4.2	15.1	8.8	4.4	7.9	5.4	16.4	5.3	3.5	3.0	0.3	–
Loans	–	–	–	–	–	2.0	–	–	–	3.6	–	0.6	–	13.2	0.6	–	–	–	–
Grants	0.7	0.3	0.1	1.4	0.6	1.1	3.0	4.2	15.1	5.2	4.4	7.3	5.4	3.2	4.7	3.5	3.0	0.3	–

Figures for 1954–90 are derived from US Agency for International Development (USAID), *US Overseas Loans and Grants, Series of Yearly Data (Volume IV, Africa), Obligations and Loan Authorizations, FY 1946–FY 1990*, Washington, DC: USAID, 1990.
Figures for 1991–92 were provided by USIA.
(–) – no aid provided during the fiscal year
(*) – less than $50,000 provided in aid during the fiscal year
(?) – data unavailable
(TQ) – transition quarter

1973	1974	1975	1976	TQ	1977	1978	1979	1980	1981	1982	1983	1984	1985	1986	1987	1988	1989	1990	1991	1992
–	–	5.2	1.6	0.7	0.8	19.0	28.8	62.3	57.0	35.8	48.7	46.7	52.6	46.9	37.5	18.2	12.6	5.8	3.7	38.5
–	–	0.6	–	–	–	3.3	10.9	12.3	12.1	14.4	26.9	15.6	21.0	22.5	18.5	6.1	5.2	0.8	0.6	–
–	–	4.6	1.6	0.7	0.8	15.8	18.0	50.0	44.9	21.4	21.8	31.1	31.7	24.4	19.0	12.1	7.4	4.8	3.1	38.5
–	–	–	–	–	–	7.0	10.7	17.7	15.0	14.5	15.0	16.0	20.0	16.5	1.1	–	–	–	–	–
–	–	–	–	–	–	7.0	10.7	17.7	15.0	14.5	15.0	16.0	20.0	16.5	1.1	–	–	–	–	–
–	–	–	–	–	–	–	–	–	–	–	–	–	–	–	–	–	–	–	–	–
–	–	–	–	–	0.8	8.8	7.3	32.3	29.9	6.9	6.8	15.1	11.7	7.9	17.8	12.1	7.4	4.8	3.1	38.5
–	–	4.6	1.6	0.7	0.8	8.8	7.3	32.3	29.9	6.9	6.8	15.1	11.7	7.9	17.8	12.1	7.2	4.0	3.1	?
–	–	4.6	1.6	0.7	–	–	–	–	–	–	–	–	–	–	–	–	0.2	0.8	–	?
–	–	–	–	–	–	–	–	–	–	–	–	–	–	–	–	–	*	0.2	–	–
–	–	–	–	–	–	–	–	–	–	–	–	–	–	–	–	–	–	–	–	–
–	–	–	–	–	–	–	–	–	–	–	–	–	–	–	–	–	*	0.2	–	–
–	–	–	–	–	–	–	–	–	–	–	–	–	–	–	–	–	–	–	–	–
–	–	–	–	–	–	–	–	–	–	–	–	–	–	–	–	–	–	–	–	–
–	–	–	–	–	–	–	–	–	–	–	–	–	–	–	–	–	–	–	–	–
–	–	–	–	–	–	–	–	20.0	20.4	25.4	30.6	33.0	34.1	20.2	8.2	6.5	0.9	0.8	–	–
–	–	–	–	–	–	–	–	–	–	15.0	20.0	32.0	33.0	19.1	7.5	5.5	–	–	–	–
–	–	–	–	–	–	–	–	20.0	20.0	10.0	10.0	–	–	–	–	–	–	–	–	–
–	–	–	–	–	–	–	–	–	0.4	0.4	0.6	1.0	1.1	1.1	0.7	1.0	0.9	0.8	–	–
–	–	–	–	–	–	–	–	–	–	–	–	–	–	–	–	–	–	–	–	–
–	–	–	–	–	–	–	–	–	–	–	–	–	–	–	–	–	–	–	–	–
–	–	–	–	–	–	–	–	5.0	–	20.0	21.0	35.0	30.0	22.0	17.1	4.0	8.0	–	–	–
–	–	5.2	1.6	0.7	0.8	19.0	28.8	87.3	77.4	81.2	100.3	114.6	116.8	89.1	62.7	28.7	21.5	6.6	3.7	38.5
–	–	–	–	–	–	7.0	10.7	37.7	35.0	24.5	25.0	16.0	20.0	16.5	1.1	–	–	–	–	?
–	–	5.2	1.6	0.7	0.8	12.0	18.1	49.6	42.4	56.7	75.3	98.6	96.8	72.6	61.6	28.7	21.5	6.6	3.7	?

As it became increasingly clear during 1991 and 1992 that the Cold War for all practical purposes was coming to an end, events within the Horn of Africa provided the backdrop for a significant change in policy equivalent to the dramatic shift in alliances that occurred from 1974 to 1977. In less than a six-month period, pressures within the national security bureaucracies and Congress for a closer relationship with Ethiopia were realized due to the overthrow of the Mengistu regime. Similarly, growing pressures to downgrade security ties with Somalia reached their apogée with the overthrow of the Siad regime. In both cases, the termination of a host of Cold War driven bureaucratic missions no longer required policies that once led Washington to disregard the internal nature of either regine in favor of its role within the global East–West framework. The most notable aspect of these events is that they did not create a crisis atmosphere at the highest levels of the policymaking establishment as would have been the case ten, or even five, years earlier. Rather, the end of the Cold War had relegated policy to the Africa specialists within the national security bureaucracies unless events touched upon a politically sensitive domestic nerve, such as was the case when the White House concerned itself with the fate of Ethiopia's Falasha Jews.

However, the Bush administration's military response to the intensification of clan warfare and famine in Somalia demonstrated the continued importance of the relationship between extended crisis situations and domestic politics in contributing to a significant shift in US Africa policies even in the aftermath of the end of the Cold War. Moreover, although the Bush administration's initial decision to intervene was supported overwhelmingly within Congress and among the US public, it nevertheless left a potentially problematical foreign policy legacy to the Clinton administration. Specifically, as the media increasingly ignores the US military operation in favor of other, more pressing topics, such as the US budget deficit and the escalating conflict in former Yugoslavia, the Clinton administration may find itself hard pressed to maintain popular interest in, and support for, a continued US military presence in Somalia. Most important, if past events are to serve as a guidepost to the future, one can expect that the inevitable decline in popular interest for Operation Restore Hope almost guarantees that Somalia increasingly will be ignored by President Clinton, and that policy – including the proper means for resolving the conflict – increasingly will be left to the Africa specialists within the national security bureaucracies.

5 US FOREIGN POLICY TOWARD SOUTH AFRICA

> The good relations which so happily exist between our two countries are a source of the greatest satisfaction and encouragement to me, and I assure you that the traditional ties of friendship and understanding between us shall be strengthened to our mutual benefit.
>
> President Dwight D. Eisenhower in a statement to the South African Ambassador, November 15, 1954.[1]

> I knew that I could never again raise my voice against the violence of the oppressed in the ghettos without having first spoken clearly to the greatest purveyor of vnce in the world today – my own government . . . Five years ago [the late John F. Kennedy] said, "Those who make peaceful revolution impossible will make violent revolution inevitable." Increasingly, this is the role our nation has taken.
>
> Martin Luther King, Jr., April 1967.[2]

> The struggle is my life. I will continue fighting for freedom until the end of my days.
>
> Nelson Mandela, June 26, 1961.[3]

Introduction

No other country within the broad framework of US foreign policy toward Africa has generated as much popular discussion and emotional debate among the public as South Africa.[4] Embracing a political system known as "apartheid" in which minority white ethnic groups comprising roughly 15 percent of the population have denied political franchise to a largely black majority comprising 73 percent of the population (Asians and people of mixed race comprise the remainder), South Africa became the target of a growing anti-apartheid movement increasingly prone to draw parallels between the legitimacy of the struggle by South African blacks and the US civil rights movement of the 1960s. The efforts of this movement culminated in congressional passage of the Comprehensive Anti-Apartheid Act of 1986 which mandated a variety of sanctions designed to force the dismantling of apartheid. Although various sanctions measures were repealed five years later in an effort to reward and facilitate ongoing negotiations in South Africa which are expected to lead to the creation of a non-racial, democratic government, the 1986 legislation represented a watershed in US–South African relations, and underscored the importance that domestic politics can play in the formulation and implementation of US Africa policies.

The creation of South Africa and the origins of US–South African ties (prior to May 1948)

The first white settlers arrived at the Cape of Good Hope in southern Africa in 1652 to establish a "refreshment station" for the Dutch East India Company. As time went by, this settler population began to speak a unique language – Afrikaans – and think of itself as a unique people – Afrikaners – with permanent roots in the coastal areas of southern Africa. Yet when faced with the imposition of British colonial rule at the beginning of the nineteenth century, approximately 20 percent of the Afrikaner population undertook the so-called "Great Trek" into the hinterland, subsequently establishing independent Afrikaner states known as the Transvaal and the Orange Free State. Under pressure from both the migrating Afrikaners and the imperial conquests of the British colonial army, the indigenous black populations of the region were not as fortunate. In a series of bloody colonial wars that to a considerable degree were beneficial to the Afrikaner population, British military operations led to the subjugation of the region's numerous black African nations, such as the Zulu, the Xhosa, and the Swazi.

The Afrikaner desire to avoid what they perceived as the "foreign" encroachment of the British was soon dashed by the discoveries of diamonds in Kimberley in 1867 and of gold in Johannesburg in 1886. Intent on adding these resources to an expanding imperial colonial order, Great Britain annexed the Transvaal in 1877, and contributed to rising British–Afrikaner tensions that culminated in the Boer War of 1899–1902. The defeat of the Afrikaners in this war not only resulted in the supremacy of British colonial rule over the region, but to the unification of Afrikaner territories within a self-governing, and British-controlled, dominion known as South Africa on May 31, 1910, followed by Britain's recognition of that country's legal sovereignty within the British Commonwealth in 1931. Although the Afrikaners were granted full political franchise within the South African political system, they nonetheless were dominated by an English-speaking elite. As for the indigenous African nations which comprised the majority of the region's population, they were largely stripped of their lands and political rights.

As demonstrated by President Theodore Roosevelt's assertion in 1896 that it was in the "interests of civilization" that the English-speaking whites of British origin "should be dominant in South Africa," early official US attitudes toward the British colony of South Africa were shaped by a Europe-centric bias that placed the interests of the British–American alliance above those of any non-British peoples in Africa, including the Afrikaners.[5] This pro-British sentiment was demonstrated most clearly by US neutrality in the Boer War, an act which clearly favored, and helped secure, British colonial rule over the Afrikaners. In addition to becoming the largest supplier of military equipment to the British Army, Washington opposed attempts by European powers to seek a negotiated settlement of the conflict, denied all Afrikaner requests for economic and military assistance, and only mildly protested British violations of US neutrality, such as the seizures of US ships bound for the neutral South African port of Delagoa Bay. This pro-British attitude on the part of the executive branch was notable in that it ran counter to rising pro-Afrikaner sentiment among the US public and within Congress.[6]

Positive attitudes concerning South Africa's place within the international system were reinforced by the influential roles played by South African diplomats in the creation of the Covenant of the League of Nations and the Charter of the UN. Of particular preeminence was Jan Christian Smuts, a decorated hero of the Boer War who was credited with playing a "major role" in the peace conference following World War I, and who ruled South Africa from 1939 to 1948 as the head of the relatively moderate United Party.[7] South Africa also achieved recognition in Washington as a result of its active military participation on the side of the Western allies during World War I and World War II. In the case of World War II, South Africa was provided with over $100 million in US lend-lease aid that was promptly repaid by the South African government in 1947. In exchange for this aid, the US War Department was granted the right to establish several air bases on South African soil as part of the Allied war effort.[8] In short, by the beginning of 1948, South Africa's diplomatic and military initiatives had cultivated strong proponents within the State Department and the War Department.

Despite enjoying a generally positive image in Washington, three aspects of South Africa's political system foreshadowed potential problems for US–South African relations. First, a fragile political monopoly of the English-speaking political elite was threatened by the rising power of a splinter Afrikaner Party whose leaders firmly believed that the country's political leadership had "betrayed" Afrikaner culture, most notably by placing South Africa on a path that eventually would lead to "destructive" black rule.[9] In World War II, for example, several National Party leaders openly admired Adolf Hitler's brand of National Socialism, and opposed entry into the conflict on the side of Great Britain in favor of giving support to Nazi Germany.[10] As the April 1948 parliamentary elections approached, Daniel Malan – dubbed the "Boer Moses" by both critics and supporters – campaigned on a National Party platform of white supremacy and stricter segregation of the races, including a proposal for the "separate development" of the races – "apartheid" in the Afrikaner language – in which it was clear that non-whites would be stripped of any remaining legal, political, or economic rights. These developments, however, were dismissed by the US Mission in Pretoria as the minority view of "narrow racialists" who were "parochial in outlook."[11]

A second potential problem revolved around discriminatory practices directed against the Indian ethnic groups of South Africa. Despite conclusion of an agreement with India in 1927 that guaranteed Indian minority rights, parliament dominated by the United Party in 1946 passed legislation which restricted Indian property rights and provided for separate political representation.[12] The ensuing conflict between India and South Africa led to India bringing the issue before the UN General Assembly. In what constituted the first of many future debates over the issue of non-white groups in South Africa, the State Department followed the lead of its European allies, most notably Great Britain, in arguing that the internal affairs of member states did not fall under the jurisdiction of the UN. Instead an argument was made for adjudication by the International Court of Justice (ICJ) and, failing that, direct negotiations primarily between India and South Africa.[13]

The final potential problem revolved around South Africa's occupation during World War I of the German colony of South West Africa (Namibia). Rather than acceding to UN demands to place the territory under "trusteeship" status in preparation for eventual independence, the South African government announced in 1946 its intention to seek the formal incorporation of Namibia as an integral part of South Africa. Once again following the lead of its European allies, most notably Great Britain, the State Department opposed the South African plan. Unlike the more nebulous "internal" issue of ethnic rights, the Namibia question seemed to challenge the "international" mission of the UN system and its primary goal of promoting collective security. In a statement seemingly reflecting US beliefs that South Africa eventually would see the light, UN Representative John Foster Dulles (who later became Secretary of State under the Eisenhower administration) expressed "satisfaction" in September 1947 that the South African government had not yet made a final decision concerning the matter.[14]

Despite these potential problems, policymakers in Washington perceived Jan Smuts and his United Party as moving South Africa along a reformist path that eventually would include political franchise for all groups within the country, and therefore they were opposed to US intervention in the internal affairs of a sovereign nation. "After all," explained William Edmondson, a young FSO stationed in Africa during the 1950s and future Ambassador to South Africa during the 1980s, "the issues of national independence and black majority rule on the African continent had only begun to emerge as topics of debate."[15] Furthermore, with its own emerging civil rights dilemmas, the US was "diplomatically sensitive" to forcing the issue lest it backfire by drawing international attention to US domestic political problems. Most important, the relatively few US policymakers who were following events in South Africa held the optimistic belief that South African leaders eventually would "see the light" and adopt a more equitable political system.[16] In short, South Africa was perceived within the national security bureaucracies as a stable ally that, like any country in the world, had domestic problems with which it had to deal.

Cold War imperatives of anti-Communism versus racial concerns (May 1948–February 1957)

The relatively unquestioned nature of US–South African ties was altered when the Afrikaner National Party achieved an upset victory in the May 1948 parliamentary elections. Receiving only a minority of the popular vote, the National Party nonetheless was able to obtain a working majority within the parliament by allying itself with the splinter Afrikaner Party. In a series of legislative actions, the National Party consolidated its power and carried out an electoral promise to institutionalize a political system based on apartheid. Among the most significant pieces of apartheid legislation were three laws passed in 1950: the Population Registration Act which initiated the classification and registration of all South Africans according to race; the Group Areas Act which divided the country into racially segregated living areas; and the Suppression of Communism Act which banned the South African Communist Party (SACP) and enabled the government to suppress any criticism of the National Party or its official apartheid policies. The ideology of apartheid was further strengthened in 1951 when, in the aftermath of the extension of parliamentary representation that accompanied Namibia's formal annexation by the Afrikaner-dominated government, the National Party achieved an absolute majority within parliament.

The victory and entrenchment of the more radical racial vision of the Afrikaner Party resulted in the emergence of a dilemma for US policymakers that intensified in the decades following the late 1940s and the 1950s. As summarized by a January 1949 CIA assessment of the political situation in South Africa, the dilemma revolved around the relative merits of anti-communism and anti-racism as the guiding themes of US–South African relations. According to the CIA, the greatest asset of US–South African ties was the Afrikaner government's fervent anti-communism and strong support for the US in its ideological competition with the Soviet Union. However, an equally important drawback of these ties was the "propaganda" liability of Washington's association with apartheid. As the inevitable process of African independence continued to gather strength, warned the CIA, support for South Africa not only risked the alienation of future black governments on the African continent, but also would offer the Soviet Union an opportunity to brand the US as an opponent of decolonization.[17] Yet in the charged Cold War atmosphere of the late 1940s and early 1950s, the imperatives of anti-communism and containment of the Soviet Union clearly outweighed any misgivings over the racial policies of the Afrikaner government. The net result was pressure within the national security bureaucracies to strengthen US–South African ties from 1948 to 1957.

The State Department led the way in seeking closer ties, responding favorably at the end of 1948 to a South African request to upgrade each country's respective diplomatic missions to Embassy status and exchange Ambassadors rather than Ministers. On March 23, 1949, North Winship became the first US Ambassador accredited to Pretoria. The State Department was primarily interested in South Africa's unswerving support for US containment policies in both Europe and Asia. For example, not only was South Africa one of the first countries to send an aircrew for the US-led Berlin airlift in 1949, but its leaders also provided support for the US-led military effort in the Korean War.[18] Actions such as these were strongly rewarded, as evidenced by the State Department's handling of anti-apartheid resolutions at the UN. Although the State Department supported the right of the UN General Assembly to "discuss" the issue of apartheid, US representatives were instructed to refuse to vote for specific resolutions. In a classic diplomatic balancing act, the State Department's primary objectives were to win the favor of anti-apartheid critics while at the same time avoiding any actions that would strain US–South African ties.[19]

The Pentagon also lobbied for stronger US–South African relations. In keeping with its primary bureaucratic mission of preparing for a global military conflict with the Soviet Union, the Defense Department argued that strategic location, excellent port facilities, and experienced military forces ensured both "offensive and defensive roles" for South Africa in a major East–West military confrontation.[20] As a result, military cooperation between the two countries took on many forms. In addition to routine exchange visits by ranking officers of both militaries, a 1951 military agreement authorized reimbursable US military assistance under the Mutual Defense Assistance Act. Of even greater importance was maintaining access to South African ports, such as the former British naval base at Simonstown. In exchange for this access, the Defense Department coordinated joint military maneuvers with the South African Navy. Finally, the Defense Department encouraged the sale of arms, particularly fighter aircraft, to the South African Armed Forces. In 1952, for example, the US agreed to sell over $112 million in arms to the South African military. The Joint Chiefs of Staff envisaged the fighters as being "immediately available for use in collective defense in the event of Communist aggression."[21]

The CIA constituted the third major proponent of closer US ties with South Africa. Having begun under the Truman administration what one CIA officer described as a "long and cordial relationship" with the South African intelligence community, the CIA looked upon its South African counterpart as a natural ally in the global struggle against communist expansionism led by the Soviet Union.[22] The primary reason for this outlook was the zealous anti-communist beliefs of the Afrikaner elite that equaled, if not surpassed, those of the most doctrinaire anti-communists within the US government. For example, it is striking to note that the South African government adopted its Suppression of Communism Act at the same time as Senator Joseph McCarthy (D-Wisconsin) was leading a domestic witch-hunt against suspected US communists and "fellow travelers." In the specific case of southern Africa, the CIA especially was interested in building up the counterintelligence capabilities of the South African security apparatus as a counterweight to potential revolutionary upheaval within the region. As early as January 1949, the CIA was warning US policymakers about the possibility for Soviet manipulation of African nationalism and the decolonization process to the detriment of US interests on the African continent.[23]

Nuclear cooperation under the auspices of the US Atomic Energy Commission constituted a final element of the growing US–South African security relationship. Because domestic reserves of uranium oxide (a crucial element in the development of nuclear devices) were insufficient to fuel the massive development of the US nuclear arsenal during the 1950s, an agreement was signed with South Africa in November 1950. In return for US scientific and technical collaboration, as well as guarantees of any capital required to develop and expand production, the South African government agreed to provide the US with its entire output of uranium oxide. The strategic importance of this link was underscored by US purchases of over $1 billion worth of South African uranium production from 1952 to 1966.[24] As a result of this agreement, the national security bureaucracies began citing South Africa's willingness to accommodate the US with respect to a vital strategic component of US–Soviet nuclear rivalry as another rationale for strengthening US–South African relations.

It is important to note that, despite the common denominator of downplaying anti-apartheid concerns in pursuit of anti-communist objectives, the growth in US–South African relations from 1948 to 1957 did not constitute the unfolding of a coordinated strategy devised by the White House. Even a staunchly anti-communist South Africa was of little if any concern to White House strategists who ignored Africa as largely inconsequential to overriding preoccupations with containment of the Soviet Union in Europe and Asia.[25] Rather, this period demonstrated how, in the absence of crisis, the process of bureaucratic incrementalism led to the strengthening of US–South African ties as the State Department, the Pentagon, and the CIA carried out their respective bureaucratic missions associated with the Cold War.

The beginnings of pressures for change (March 1957–January 1961)

Two important developments contributed to pressures for change in US foreign policy toward South Africa during the late 1950s. First, a growing US civil rights movement striving for the political equality of African Americans ensured greater official attention to the issue of race in both US domestic and international policies. In efforts that presaged the victories of the anti-apartheid movement during the 1980s, Reverend Martin Luther King led a demonstration on December 10, 1957, to denounce apartheid and call attention to South Africa's refusal to sign the UN Declaration on Human Rights. During that same month, US civil rights activists failed in an attempt in Johannesburg, South Africa, to duplicate the successful Montgomery, Alabama, bus boycott.[26] An important aspect of such actions was that they constituted part of a movement that politically conscious policymakers began to consider when examining US foreign policy toward the minority white-ruled governments on the African continent.

The dramatic growth in the number of African countries achieving independence from colonial rule during the late 1950s constituted the second dimension of growing pressures for change in US foreign policy toward South Africa. In the aftermath of Ghana's independence on March 6, 1957, seventeen African countries followed suit from 1957 to 1960, with ten more becoming independent from 1961 to 1964. As each country assumed its rightful place in the UN General Assembly, their common bond of nationalist struggle against various forms of white colonial rule made the apartheid government of South Africa a special target of concern. In this regard, it is notable that representatives of the State Department's Bureau of International Organization Affairs – that portion of the national security bureaucracies which had the most to gain by cultivating the favor of a growing and potentially decisive African voting bloc within the UN – led the way in seeking changes in US–South African relations. In a report entitled, "Estimate of the Next Five Years in Africa," Mason Sears, one of the US representatives on the UN Trusteeship Council, argued that the US risked alienating the majority of black African states if it maintained close ties with the Afrikaner government.[27]

An important outgrowth of political changes in both the US domestic and international arenas was the creation in 1958 of a separate Bureau of African Affairs within the State Department. Although the top echelons of the Africa Bureau in its initial years were dominated by European specialists who continued to approach the continent from a Europe-centric point of view, an important bureaucratic mission of the office became the maintenance of smooth and stable relationships with all African countries. Most important, young FSOs within the newly created bureau became the most sensitive of any members of the executive branch to the importance that African countries attached to opposition to the apartheid system of South Africa. In short, the creation of the Africa Bureau marked the emergence of a bureaucracy whose organizational missions eventually fostered a greater questioning of US–South African relations.

An immediate result of growing pressures for change in US foreign policy toward South Africa was reflected in State Department voting patterns in the UN General Assembly. At the urging of US representatives to the UN, the State Department for the first time authorized support for a General Assembly resolution expressing "regret and concern" over the apartheid policies of South Africa. A similar UN resolution was supported in 1959. Those seeking more substantive action against the apartheid government, however, correctly perceived little change in US foreign policy. Indeed, indicative of the State Department's desire to placate both anti-apartheid critics and the South African government, approval of the 1958 resolution was only granted when sponsors agreed to remove stronger language "condemning" apartheid. Yet despite a disinclination to move beyond rhetoric or even adopt more forceful language, the positive US vote reflected the beginning of a willingness to officially question previously unqualified support for South Africa.

The emerging international debate over the issue of apartheid was brought into focus as a result of what has become known as the "Sharpeville incident."[28] On March 21, 1960, a large crowd of Africans gathered at the police station in the town of Sharpeville, South Africa, to peacefully demonstrate against the "pass laws" – legislation which controlled the movement of Africans throughout the country. Although South African police had attacked black demonstrators in the past, their response to the Sharpeville demonstration stunned international observers. Apparently without provocation, the South African police opened fire on the demonstrators, killing 69 and wounding over 180. As demonstrations began to break out in other parts of the country, the South African government declared a state of emergency and outlawed all African political organizations.

The immediate reaction of the State Department touched off a mild debate within the policymaking establishment that reflected growing divisions over the issue of apartheid.[29] In a statement that apparently was not cleared by the upper levels of the bureaucracy, an official State Department press briefing declared that the US "deplored" the violence in South Africa and expressed hope that the African peoples of that country would be able to "obtain redress for their legitimate grievances by peaceful means."[30] That the statement went beyond established, acceptable bounds of official criticism of South Africa was noted by sharp attacks on the authors by senior members of both the Defense Department and the State Department, most notably Secretary of State Christian Herter.[31] Nonetheless, the domestic and international uproars that accompanied the Sharpeville massacre were influential in prompting another minor shift in US policy at the UN.

Less than two weeks after the killings took place, the State Department for the first time authorized support for a UN Security Council resolution that "deplored the policies and actions" of the South African government and called upon it to "abandon its policy of apartheid and racial discrimination."[32]

Despite the harsh language of the 1960 Security Council resolution which seemed to herald a dramatic reassessment of US–South African relations, the continuation of a variety of bureaucratic missions associated with the Cold War ensured continued cooperation with the apartheid government. For example, the growing voices of concern within the State Department's fledgling Africa Bureau, as well as among members of the US delegation to the UN, were softened by career FSOs within the State Department who sought to maintain a diplomatic balancing act between critics of apartheid and what was perceived as a faithful ally in southern Africa. In the case of the Defense Department, ties were actually enhanced, as witnessed by the initiation of Operation Cape, a joint military exercise that brought together ships from the US, Great Britain, South Africa, and other Western countries for anti-submarine maneuvers off South Africa's coast in October 1959.[33] Finally, the CIA continued to emphasize that the "radical" nationalist tendencies of several independence movements in southern Africa made them susceptible to Soviet influence and manipulation, and therefore called for strengthening US–South African cooperation.

The importance of established bureaucratic missions in maintaining and strengthening US–South African ties – even in the aftermath of the Sharpeville incident – was best demonstrated by South Africa's role in the burgeoning US space program. In 1957, the establishment of a Minitrack and Data Acquisition Station near Johannesburg for tracking unmanned scientific satellites made NASA the latest bureaucratic arrival of the US diplomatic family in South Africa. The following year, NASA oversaw the construction at Olifontsfontein of an Optical Tracking Station also designed to support the space program. Most significant, however, was a September 1960 agreement that not only covered the first two NASA facilities, but included the establishment of a Deep Space Instrumentation Facility near Johannesburg.[34] Signed less than six months after the Sharpeville incident, this latter agreement was indicative of a general consensus within the US national security bureaucracies that politico-strategic concerns outweighed any potential drawbacks of association with the apartheid government of South Africa.[35]

Rhetoric versus reality in the "New Frontier" (January 1961–January 1969)

The inauguration of President Kennedy in January 1961 generated high expectations among newly independent African countries and domestic activists that the "New Frontier" administration would take a stronger stand than its predecessors against the apartheid government of South Africa. The primary reason for these expectations was the administration's appointment of strong proponents of racial equality at home and majority rule in Africa to positions of authority within the State Department, such as Chester Bowles as Under Secretary of State, G. Mennen Williams as Assistant Secretary of State for African Affairs, and Adlai E. Stevenson as US Ambassador to the UN. Most important, the willingness of these new political appointees to go beyond the quiet disapproval of previous administrations and publicly denounce apartheid was immediately evident in official speeches and policy pronouncements. Promising that the US would "stand up and be counted" when it came to issues of racial inequality, Williams noted in speeches that apartheid was a "wrongheaded policy, fraught with dangers not alone to the peoples of South Africa, but to international peace."[36] Similarly, Stevenson directed the anti-apartheid war of words at the UN. In perhaps the sharpest language ever heard in the UN General Assembly from a US representative prior to 1961, UN Representative Francis T. P. Plimpton declared that the US was "squarely, utterly and irreversibly opposed to the policy of racial discrimination epitomized in the word apartheid."[37]

Despite the dramatic rise in anti-apartheid rhetoric, the New Frontiersmen found themselves isolated within a bureaucratic network strongly opposed to significant change in US–South African relations. In the case of the State Department, Williams' initial efforts to mobilize the Africa Bureau in pursuit of punitive measures against South Africa were stymied by officials, such as Secretary of State Dean Rusk, who favored a more cautious, traditional approach, and therefore sought to balance criticism of apartheid with the recognition that strategic interests required continued US–South African cooperation. This approach was supported by Joseph Satterthwaite, the Ambassador to South Africa and the first Assistant Secretary of State for African Affairs under the Eisenhower administration. Satterthwaite represented that generation of FSOs who believed that, since changes in apartheid – at least in the short-term – were unlikely, the US should avoid undue interference in the domestic affairs of South Africa.[38] Even the younger FSOs in the Africa Bureau who welcomed the verbal assault on South Africa were opposed to the punitive measures proposed by political appointees such as Williams. "Whereas the traditionalists such as Ambassador Satterthwaite erred on the side of too little criticism," explained one FSO who joined the Africa Bureau in 1963, "the more activist political appointees such as Williams erred on the side of seeking too much change, too quickly."[39] Any question over which group held sway over policy was settled by an internal State Department document that, building from the assumption that US leverage over South Africa was "limited," emphasized US–South African cooperation in all fields except those associated with the maintenance of apartheid.[40] In short, there existed a growing chasm between the anti-apartheid "rhetoric" of the New Frontier and the "reality" of ongoing US–South African cooperation.

The growing chasm between rhetoric and reality was demonstrated by a rising Defense Department presence in South Africa. Against the objections of the State Department's Africa Bureau, a bilateral military agreement was signed in December 1961 that established a Missile Range Tracking Station at Grootfontein. Constituting the endpoint of the Pentagon's Atlantic Missile Range Telemetry Network, the station not only contributed to missile development and space programs, but also served as an important intelligence collection site for tracking Soviet missiles and satellites.[41] Of greatest concern to opponents of the agreement were the benefits derived by the South African government. In exchange for Defense Department access to the facilities, the US agreed to sell arms to support a build-up of the South African Armed Forces. Although officials sought to emphasize that the US was providing arms that were to be used for "external defense," as opposed to weapons that could be used "internally" against opponents of apartheid, the reality for African diplomats seeking to isolate South Africa was one of growing US–South African military cooperation.[42]

The activities of the CIA constituted an especially vivid example of how established bureaucratic missions associated with the Cold War confounded the anti-apartheid rhetoric of the New Frontier. In the aftermath of South Africa's withdrawal from the British Commonwealth on May 31, 1961, the CIA assumed greater responsibility for cooperative arrangements with the South African government that previously had been handled by British intelligence agencies.[43] Perceiving the South African government as a natural ally in the global struggle against communism, the CIA during 1961 and 1962 became concerned over the willingness of "subversive groups" in South Africa to use sabotage and terrorism in their quest for black majority rule.[44] According to the CIA, the various organizations associated with the

Congress Alliance Movement – an umbrella group whose most prominent member was the African National Congress (ANC) – were all heavily "infiltrated" or completely "dominated" by South African communists.[45] As a result, the primary aims of the CIA during the early 1960s were the infiltration and incapacitation of these organizations, as well as the training of the South African security services in counter-intelligence penetration techniques. In what CIA officers at the time considered to be one of their "greatest coups," a CIA tip from a "deep cover" agent in the inner circle of the ANC branch in Durban led to the August 5, 1962, arrest of Nelson Mandela, an underground leader who was perceived as responsible for the sabotage movement.[46]

The CIA's involvement in the arrest of Mandela – a man who remained in jail for nearly twenty-eight years and came to personify the international struggle against apartheid – underscores how US policy was driven by bureaucratic missions associated with the Cold War. Most assuredly unknown at the highest levels of the policy-making establishment, the name of Mandela was confined to lower-level bureaucrats of the national security bureaucracies. In the case of the CIA, perceptions of his threat to a "friendly" South Africa naturally required his removal from the political scene. Although the US Embassy undoubtedly would have concurred in this assessment had they been informed, the CIA apparently acted independently in providing the tip to the South African security services. In short, in the absence of crisis, policy reflected the *ad hoc* response of an individual bureaucracy in the pursuit of its perceived organizational mission. As a result of this incident, the CIA was ordered to first seek State Department approval prior to turning African nationalists over to the South African government.[47]

The continuation of status quo policies was only slightly altered in 1963 when African efforts against white minority regimes in southern Africa intensified an ongoing debate within the national security bureaucracies that required Kennedy's personal attention. In May 1963, the newly created OAU began pressuring the US to adopt a variety of sanctions designed to end white minority rule in Portuguese Africa and South Africa.[48] Capturing the feelings of the newly independent African countries, Tanzanian President Julius Nyerere supported the creation of an OAU "liberation" committee and warned Washington that mere verbal condemnation of white minority rule no longer was acceptable.[49] Parallel to these efforts, momentum was also building in the UN General Assembly to adopt a similar sanctions package. As explained in a letter from Stevenson to Kennedy, the administration was approaching a "decisive situation" in which the US would be forced to make a highly public, and potentially politically embarrassing, choice. "In oversimplified terms," explained Stevenson, "they [Africans] want to know whether, if it comes to that, we will stand for self-determination and human rights and, therefore, for the mind of Africa, or whether we will give our Azores base [in Portuguese Africa] and the tracking stations in South Africa priority."[50]

The ensuing bureaucratic debate and its resolution at the level of the White House reflected the growing chasm between rhetoric and reality in the Kennedy administration. Proponents of sanctions, such as Williams and Stevenson, correctly noted that failure to support African initiatives over the emotionally charged issue of white minority rule would make the promises of the New Frontier look like a sham and severely damage US credibility with the emerging countries of Africa. Opponents of sanctions, such as the Pentagon and the CIA, as well as the State Department's Bureau of European Affairs, predictably countered, however, that such a policy risked compromising access to important strategic assets in Africa. "Not only had the US just signed a bilateral military agreement with South Africa that traded weapons for tracking stations," explained one State Department FSO, "but access to the Portuguese-controlled Azores islands was considered indispensable to US security concerns in Europe and the Middle East."[51] Domestic political considerations also entered the presidential equation. As explained in Chapter 2, the White House feared that any further rifts in the NATO alliance (that potentially would have followed the imposition of sanctions against Portugal) would have opened the administration to Republican attack during the 1964 presidential elections for alleged neglect of vital national interests.[52]

Kennedy's decision constituted a classic political compromise that, in reality, did very little to change the established bureaucratic status quo. First, despite his strong anti-colonial beliefs, Kennedy on July 31, 1963, ordered Stevenson to abstain on a UN resolution calling for economic sanctions against Portugal which the US delegation successfully had sought to treat separately from the issue of South Africa. This decision flowed from domestic political considerations and a pragmatic acceptance of Defense Department arguments that continued US access to the Azores base was indispensable. In the case of South Africa, it was decided that some type of action was necessary to "make up for restraint in the case of Portugal."[53] This approach was facilitated by a letter from Secretary of Defense Robert McNamara to Rusk which suggested that, if necessary, the limited US military facilities in South Africa were expendable.[54] In an effort to preempt African criticism of continued US support for Portugal and head off a determined sanctions movement within the UN, it was announced on August 2, 1963, that the US was adopting a unilateral arms embargo against South Africa to take effect at the end of the year.

Although this announcement on the surface appeared to constitute a significant change in US policy, officials emphasized the "voluntary" nature of the ban and explained that all "existing contracts" with South Africa would be honored.[55] Determined to maintain the difference between providing arms for external, as opposed to internal, defense, officials further noted that the voluntary ban was not intended to cover the sale of weaponry (such as submarines) designed to counter external threats to international peace. Most important, the US ban incorporated a convenient escape clause that allowed for modifications in the face of changing international circumstances. Since the US was a nation "with many responsibilities in many parts of the world," explained Stevenson, the US "naturally reserves the right in the future to interpret this policy in the light of requirements for assuring the maintenance of international peace and security."[56]

Adopted as a tactical political shift that, in reality, had little to do with Kennedy's personal beliefs concerning apartheid, the limited arms embargo became a source of ongoing bureaucratic conflict that outlived the President's death and replacement by Vice President Lyndon B. Johnson in November 1963. Proponents of continued US–South African military cooperation favored a loose interpretation of the "strategic exception" clause, especially as concerned South Africa's efforts during 1963–64 to buy three attack submarines and sixteen Lockheed P3-A anti-submarine aircraft. Candidly affirming his bureaucracy's "parochial viewpoint" in supporting both sales, Deputy Assistant Secretary of Defense Frank K. Sloan invoked a variety of organizational missions requiring "continuing friendly relations" between the US and South Africa.[57] Opponents of the sale, led by Stevenson, countered that the "strategic exception" clause was only meant to be invoked in the event of changed world circumstances. "To enter now into new contracts for such strategic materials as submarines," argued Stevenson, "would in the eyes of the world directly controvert our announced policy as publicly understood."[58]

Since the Johnson White House essentially deferred to the policy guidelines established under the Kennedy administration, the voluntary arms embargo constituted an important barrier to those favoring further military sales to South Africa – even under the strategic exception clause. "In order to succeed in invoking the clause," explained a member of the State Department dealing with South Africa under the Johnson administration, "it was necessary to demonstrate that the strategic importance of the sale outweighed the potential domestic and international fall-out that surely would result." "In essence," continued this FSO, "for an administration sensitive to maintaining the image of the New Frontier, the burden of proof was on the proponents of invoking the strategic exception clause."[59] Even those seeking a middle-of-the-road policy recognized the potential pitfalls of entering into new arms agreements with South Africa. "While the 'strategic exception' clause provides us legal justification," noted a NSC memorandum recommending a delay in consideration until after the November 1964 presidential elections, "there would be a considerable emotional reaction against the US in Africa and Asia, a lot of propaganda, as well as criticism by American liberal and negro groups and many newspapers."[60]

In the aftermath of Johnson's successful victory in the 1964 presidential elections, pressures once again began building among proponents of invoking the strategic exception clause. Yet any hope of altering the established US position was erased by a brief, two-sentence memorandum from Secretary of Defense McNamara to the White House in which he noted that sales of strategic weapons were not essential to US defense, and therefore were to be considered on their "political" merits.[61] As a result, the sale of items under the strategic exception clause were rejected in favor of established Africa Bureau guidelines concerning such issues. The same "burden of proof" was also applied throughout the remainder of the Johnson administration to the sale of so-called "grey area" items that had a dual application within both the civilian and military realms.[62]

The only significant change in the bureaucratic status quo during the Johnson admininistration revolved around the port visits of US ships in South Africa. In the aftermath of an incident in 1965 in which the South African government announced that all visiting sailors would be subject to apartheid segregation laws, the US Navy began an unofficial, voluntary boycott of South African ports. However, military requirements associated with growing US involvement in the Vietnam War resulted in the ordering in February 1967 of a port visit for the USS Franklin D. Roosevelt, an aircraft carrier which had been at sea off the coast of Vietnam for eight months. Although interracial activities had been worked out in advance, the South African government provoked an incident by announcing that all sailors on shore leave were subject to apartheid segregation laws, and shore leave was cancelled and the ship left port earlier than planned. Several days later, the USS Sword Knot, which was also scheduled for a port visit, was ordered instead to set course for the Kenyan port of Mombasa, reflecting the Pentagon's decision to avoid docking any US ships at South African ports.[63]

The incident is significant in that it constitutes one of the earliest examples of pressure by anti-apartheid groups in contributing to a minor change in US foreign policy toward South Africa. Lending truth to the old cliché of "being in the right place at the right time," the American Negro Leadership Conference was being held in Washington, DC, and several of its members coordinated a protest of the visit with sympathetic members of the national security bureaucracies, such as Deputy Assistant Secretary of State for African Affairs J. Wayne Fredericks. These protests were joined by a petition signed by thirty-two members of Congress. Faced with the impracticality of working out future shore leaves in which US sailors would not be subject to officially sanctioned racism, as well as the prospects of growing domestic criticism of even attempting to seek such alternatives, the logical outcome was the suspension of any further ship visits until further review.[64] As explained in a cable from Fredericks to the US Consulate General in Cape Town, South Africa, this decision was deemed "most prudent" in light of the "present intensity" of "anti-apartheid sentiment" that had been generated by the USS Franklin D. Roosevelt incident.[65]

Despite the modifications in policy represented by the voluntary arms embargo and the cancellation of ship visits to South African ports, the absence of crisis in South Africa reinforced the historic neglect of US–South African relations at the highest levels of the US policymaking establishment. As a result, established policies served as important constraints on the activist tendencies of the New Frontiersmen, and in fact contributed to the strengthening of US–South African relations in several spheres, most notably in terms of intelligence and military activities. In essence, the New Frontier publicly excoriated the evils of apartheid while quietly continuing to work with the white South African leadership. "Apart from the growing activist voices of the State Department's Bureaus of African Affairs and International Organization Affairs," summed up one diplomatic observer of US–South African relations, "the fragmented national security bureaucracies continued to look upon South Africa as a stable US ally whose racial system of apartheid was relatively impervious to international pressures for change."[66]

Bureaucratic missions and the "tar baby" option (January 1969–March 1974)

The Nixon administration entered office unconcerned with regions such as southern Africa that were perceived as "peripheral" to the larger strategic issue of East–West relations, and therefore focused little if any attention on South Africa. However, the new administration's desire to undertake a comprehensive review of US foreign policy toward all the regions of the world resulted in the drafting of over sixty-one policy review papers – formally known as National Security Study Memoranda (NSSMs) – the thirty-ninth of which (NSSM 39) was devoted to US relations with the white minority governments of Southern Rhodesia (currently Zimbabwe), the Portuguese colonies (and currently independent countries) of Angola and Mozambique, and South Africa. Southern Africa's lack of importance within the global hierarchy was clearly demonstrated by submission of NSSM 39 to the NSC Review Group nearly seven months after it was commissioned in April 1969, with a final decision on policy not being made until February 1970 – one year after the administration had entered office.

Despite the central role of the NSC staff in drafting NSSM 39 for final approval by Kissinger and Nixon, the tentative policy options which emerged in November 1969 were significant in that they clearly demonstrated the ongoing importance of bureaucratic missions in attempting to frame US foreign policy toward South Africa.[67] The first of five options called for the complete normalization of ties in which the national security bureaucracies would be permitted to undertake "unlimited dealings" with their South African counterparts. Constituting the ideal choice from the perspectives of both the Pentagon and the CIA, the underlying premise of this approach was Washington's inability to change the domestic policies of the Afrikaner government. Such an approach justified close collaboration between the intelligence services of both countries, the relaxation of the 1963 arms embargo, the routine authorization of naval visits, and continued access to tracking stations in the country.[68]

The second option, which constituted the fall-back position of the Pentagon and the CIA, and ultimately became the basis of US policy, was the selective relaxation of existing constraints on US–South African relations. Based on the premises that "the whites are here to stay" and that "the only way that constructive change can come about is through them," this approach assumed that the selective relaxation of punitive measures would "encourage some modification" of the apartheid policies of South Africa. Although dropping the first option's call for "unlimited dealings" with the Afrikaner government, option two found favor in the Pentagon and the CIA because it allowed the same types of US–South African cooperation spelled out in option one.[69]

According to the State Department, particularly the Africa Bureau, option two – dubbed "tar baby" in reference to the Uncle Remus fable of Brer Rabbit and Brer Fox – constituted nothing but trouble for US foreign policy. In the Uncle Remus fable, Brer Rabbit fell prey to the designs of Brer Fox after having embraced a "tarred baby" from which extrication was impossible. Adapting this lesson to US–South African relations, Africa Bureau critics of "tar baby" argued that a closer embrace of South Africa would serve as a quagmire for US foreign policy that would surely damage US ties with the remainder of sub-Saharan Africa.[70] These critics instead favored a third option that entailed the codification of existing policy, including maintaining the voluntary arms embargo and ensuring access to tracking facilities in South Africa. Simply put, the State Department sought to balance the need to retain a variety of strategic interests in South Africa with the diplomatic necessity of avoiding any actions that would further strain US ties with the remainder of sub-Saharan Africa.[71]

The fourth policy option, which was favored by some members of the State Department's Africa Bureau, called for further distancing of the US from the Afrikaner government. Reflecting the bureaucratic missions of the Africa Bureau to maintain smooth and stable relations with sub-Saharan Africa, proponents of option four argued that minimizing US relations with South Africa was the best means for protecting Washington's international standing, particularly in Africa, on the issue of race. Working from the assumption that the variety of perceived strategic interests in South Africa were not vital to US security, proponents of option four argued that Washington had more to gain by completely removing US tracking stations from South Africa, reducing the US diplomatic presence in the country, and enforcing a strict interpretation of the voluntary arms embargo.[72] "No people throughout history has relinquished power without being required to do so," explained Deputy Assistant Secretary of State for African Affairs Clyde Fergusson in a summary of the position advanced by some within the Africa Bureau. "Only a combination of serious international and domestic pressure will bring home to the white South Africans the necessity of moving now rather than waiting until it is too late for any form of peaceful settlement."[73]

Finally, option five called for the complete disengagement of the US from an active role in southern Africa. Proceeding from the assumption that racial confrontation in southern Africa was "unmanageable" and "potentially dangerous" despite any efforts that the US might undertake, this option called for maintaining correct but minimal relations with all countries in the region. Lacking supporters within the national security bureaucracies, such an approach was indicative of the US isolationist heritage in evidence prior to World War II and currently embodied in somewhat altered form by the Cato Institute, a libertarian think-tank located in Washington, DC.[74]

Although Nixon ultimately accepted the recommendation of Kissinger and chose option two – which formally became known as a policy of "communication" – the actual changes in policy that occurred represented more of a "tilt" than the substantial changes envisioned by its framers. Even if such a policy was desirable, explained Anthony Lake, an NSC staff member of the Nixon administration who opposed the basic thrust of communication, its success depended on a "series of delicate judgements" at the highest levels of the administration about how specific US actions affected the political situation in South Africa.[75] In the case of the Nixon administration, such high-level attention was lacking as policy implementation was left to the individual national security bureaucracies. As explained by Roger Morris, the Africa specialist of the NSC who was one of the principal drafters of NSSM 39, one policy (communication) was decided, and another, deriving from parochial bureaucratic interpretations of the national interest, was conducted in its name.[76] Despite embodying some minor changes in policy, option two by default became the basis for a "business-as-usual" approach to South Africa that largely dropped the rhetorical condemnations of apartheid associated with the Kennedy–Johnson years.

The limited impact of the long-debated policy of communication on the established bureaucratic status quo was demonstrated by the actions of the national security bureaucracies during the 1969–74 period. First, the CIA continued to strengthen its ties with the South African intelligence services. These links became especially close after the creation in 1969 of the Bureau of State Security (BOSS), the powerful South African security service currently known as the Department of National Security (DONS).[77] In the case of the State Department, the most noticeable change in policy was simply a negative vote (as opposed to the traditional abstention) against what had become an annual anti-apartheid resolution within the UN General Assembly. In keeping with past policy, however, the US, along with Great Britain and France, continued to abstain on General Assembly resolutions seeking a tightening of the voluntary arms embargo against South Africa. Third, although the Pentagon was forced to abide by the established policy of prohibiting visits by US ships to South African ports, it disregarded the often vehement protests of the Africa Bureau and successfully sought a gradual relaxation on the sale of "gray-area" items to the South African military.[78] Finally, NASA decided in July

1973 to close its disputed tracking stations in South Africa. Although Representative Diggs, chairperson of the House Subcommittee on Africa, claimed that persistent congressional pressure on NASA was the deciding factor, a more plausible explanation derived from the redundancy of the facilities due to technical advances and changes in tracking requirements.[79] In the words of one noted observer of US–South African relations, the net result of communication was merely "to nibble away at the marginal steps of disengagement" that had been initiated by the Kennedy and Johnson administrations.[80]

Despite the general continuity in US–South African relations from the Johnson to the Nixon administrations, two important developments during this period marked the beginning of a more critical role for Congress as concerned the issue of apartheid. First, the appointment of Diggs as chairperson of the House Subcommittee on Africa in 1969 marked the beginning of that body's ongoing role as a critic of executive branch policies in South Africa. With the assistance of Staff Director Goler T. Butcher, an African-American lawyer who had specialized on African issues within the State Department's Legal Adviser's Office, Diggs for the first time made the Africa Subcommittee a forum for illuminating the vast institutional ties that linked the US and South Africa.[81] Second, the creation of the Congressional Black Caucus in 1971 by thirteen African-American members of the House of Representatives signified the beginning of an African-American coalition interested in making US foreign policy toward South Africa an issue of greater concern within Congress as a whole. The first chairperson of the Congressional Black Caucus was none other than Diggs.[82]

The growing activism of the House Subcommittee on Africa and the Congressional Black Caucus was not enough, however, to overcome the limited seniority, and therefore power, of African Americans within Congress, as well as the benign neglect of South African issues by the vast majority of congresspersons. Early attempts at revoking South Africa's sugar quota within the US market, for example, met with defeat in both 1969 and 1971. The 1971 attempt was especially significant as it represented the first time that both houses of Congress had voted to alter some aspect of US–South African relations.[83] (Prior to 1969, Congress had voted on South Africa's sugar quota three times, in 1963, 1965, and 1967, without any questioning of its implications for US support for apartheid.) Moreover, the 1971 vote was heartening to some anti-apartheid activists due to the significant numbers of congresspersons who voted for repeal of South Africa's quota.[84] Whereas the legislation in the Senate was defeated by a narrow margin of 47 to 45, similar House legislation failed by a margin of 213 to 166.[85]

The most important lesson of the 1971 vote was its demonstration of the relationship between events within Africa and the impact of a relatively uninterested Congress as concerns US foreign policy toward Africa. In the absence of some sort of crisis situation, the innumerable partisan and ideological splits both within and between the two houses of Congress historically has limited the ability of these bodies to pass legislation counter to the established Africa policies of the executive branch. In the case of South Africa, this meant that a relatively uninterested Congress would not support the efforts of a small group within that body to significantly alter an established aspect of US–South African relations – namely, South Africa's sugar quota within the US market. Rather, official perceptions of political stability in southern Africa made it difficult, if not impossible, for activist portions of Congress, and particularly the House Subcommittee on Africa, to do little more than highlight the growing contradictions of US foreign policy toward the region. As a result, the lack of congressional activism reinforced the White House's proclivity to delegate US Africa policies to the national security bureaucracies, and therefore resulted in the incremental strengthening of US–South African ties.

Crisis and the strengthening of US–South African cooperation (April 1974–April 1976)

US perceptions of political stability in southern Africa were altered dramatically on April 24, 1974, when a *coup d'état* led by reformist officers overthrew the Portuguese government of Marcello Caetano and signaled the beginning of the end of Portuguese colonialism in Africa. As explained in Chapters 2–3, this event constituted a major crisis for the White House that eventually led President Ford and Secretary of State Kissinger to disregard the majority opinion of their senior Africa specialists and embark upon a major covert action program in Angola. In a classic example of how crisis attracted the attention of senior policymakers and provoked a reevaluation of US Africa policies, the White House felt compelled to act due to its perception of a withdrawing colonial power unwilling to prevent the possible military victory of guerrilla insurgencies sponsored by the Soviet Union and its allies. Having discussed in Chapters 2–3 the unfolding of the US covert action program, as well as its termination by Congress in late 1975, this section explores how this crisis affected US foreign policy toward South Africa.

Kissinger's initial response to the civil war in Angola was to seek regional allies willing to take part in a covert paramilitary operation to

211

be administered by the CIA. Even before December 1974 when covert involvement was fully sanctioned at the highest levels of the Ford administration, the CIA, which looked upon South Africa as the "ideal solution" to preventing the victory of the pro-Soviet MPLA, routinely had begun arming Roberto's FNLA forces. "In July 1974," explains John Stockwell, the chief of the CIA's Angola Task Force who managed the US covert operation, "the CIA began funding Roberto without 40 Committee approval, small amounts at first, but enough for word to get around that the CIA was dealing itself into the race."[86] According to Stockwell, CIA officers "admired" the efficiency of their South African counterparts, and strove to make them integral parts of the CIA paramilitary campaign.[87] For example, Stuart E. Methven, CIA chief of station in Kinshasa, received permission from CIA head-quarters to meet regularly with BOSS representatives in Zaire, the major operational center for the US paramilitary effort (see Chapter 3).[88] On at least two occasions, the head of BOSS, General Hendrik van den Bergh, traveled to Washington to meet with Jim Potts, head of the CIA's Africa Division. Most important, in order to ensure that his briefings with the South African security services were "accurate and up to date," the CIA chief of station in Pretoria was ordered to turn over numerous intelligence reports on the Angolan operation to his BOSS counterparts.[89]

The extensive levels of CIA–BOSS cooperation created ongoing tensions with the State Department, particularly the Africa Bureau. In one instance, CIA Africa Division Chief Potts, at the urgings of local CIA stations in Angola, Zaire, Zambia, and South Africa, broached the idea of formal US–South African cooperation at the official policy-making level at one of several meetings of an interagency working group. As explained in Chapter 2, the State Department initially had opposed covert intervention in Angola, with Assistant Secretary of State for African Affairs Donald Easum being fired in late 1974 for claiming that an MPLA-dominated Angola posed little threat to the region, while his successor, Nathaniel Davis, who also favored a diplomatic approach, resigned after the covert war was escalated in July 1975.[90] Forced to accept *de facto* cooperation with the South Africans as a result of Kissinger's approval, Deputy Assistant Secretary of State for African Affairs Ed Mulcahy drew the line at any mention of formal cooperation, hinting he would go "public" if the matter went any further. Unlike the CIA whose bureaucratic mission demanded close cooperation with the South Africans, Mulcahy and other Africa specialists at the State Department were more concerned with the diplomatic repercussions that eventually did accompany public disclosure of US–South African cooperation in Angola. In brief, different bureaucratic clients – the white regimes for the CIA and the African nationalists for the Africa Bureau – fostered different bureaucratic positions. Although Potts never again broached the idea of official cooperation, the bureaucratic battle had been decided by the White House in favor of the CIA. "Thus, without any memos being written at CIA headquarters saying 'Let's coordinate with the South Africans'," explained Stockwell, "coordination was effected at all CIA levels and the South Africans escalated their involvement in step with our own."[91]

A decisive turning point in the paramilitary war was the South African decision on October 25, 1975, to commit nearly 5,000 of its own troops to battle. The South Africans hoped to capture Luanda, the capital of Angola, and install a pro-Western government comprised of UNITA and FNLA guerrilla forces prior to Angola's scheduled date of independence on November 11, 1975. Rather than ensure victory for the FNLA and UNITA, the South African gambit instead led to the type of result predicted by the Africa specialists within the State Department. Not only did the "worst case" scenario occur – Cuba responded by rushing thousands of troops to the defense of Luanda – but influential African states, such as Nigeria and Tanzania, led the way in recognizing the MPLA as the sole legal government of Angola. Any remaining hopes among the South African government that Washington would raise the regional ante were dashed when Congress passed legislation terminating the CIA's paramilitary campaign. In the face of regional and international condemnation, South Africa began withdrawing its forces in January 1976.

The failure of US–South African intervention in Angola served as a powerful catalyst on US foreign policy toward southern Africa. With revolutionary governments assuming power in neighboring Mozambique and Angola, the White House feared that the rapidly escalating guerrilla war in Southern Rhodesia would become the next target for direct Soviet–Cuban intervention. In order to forestall the radicalization of southern African politics, Kissinger adopted the "shuttle diplomacy" that had been the hallmark of mediation efforts in the Middle East between the Arab countries and Israel. The primary purpose of this diplomacy was to prevent a military victory by radical guerrilla forces in Southern Rhodesia by fostering a peaceful transition of power from the white minority government of Ian Smith to moderate, black nationalists. "My plan was to co-opt the program of moderate evolutionary reform," Kissinger later explained. "We never thought we could co-opt the ideological radicals; our goal was to isolate them."[92] This plan was operationalized in Kissinger's landmark "Lusaka speech" delivered in Lusaka, Zambia, on April 27, 1976, in which he outlined ten steps for achieving black majority rule in Southern Rhodesia within a time-frame of two-to-three years.[93] Although critics are correct in noting that anti-communism, rather than a sincere concern for majority rule, constituted the primary motivating factor of Kissinger's new approach, the Lusaka speech nonetheless marked a turning point in US foreign policy in which the White House for the first time adopted a proactive approach to resolving racial conflict in the region.

To the chagrin of the anti-apartheid movement, Kissinger's new approach did not include placing pressure on South Africa to either grant independence to Namibia or begin the dismantling of its apartheid system. Kissinger instead perceived US–South African cooperation as crucial to the success of his new Southern Rhodesian policy. "Whereas a cooperative South Africa was expected to wield its considerable influence over Southern Rhodesia to seek a peaceful, diplomatic outcome," explained a former member of the State Department under the Nixon administration, "the White House calculated that a threatened South Africa would have declared unequivocal support for the Ian Smith government and bunkered down for a protracted guerrilla insurgency."[94] As a result, Kissinger sought to make the Afrikaner government an important partner in the Southern Rhodesian negotiating process.[95]

This period of US–South African relations clearly demonstrated the relationship between a crisis situation and the operation of the US policymaking process in contributing to a significant change in US Africa policies. Due to Kissinger's perception of unfolding crises in southern Africa in the aftermath of the 1974 Portuguese *coup d'état*, the White House became involved in a covert paramilitary campaign in Angola and a diplomatic initiative in Southern Rhodesia. In both cases, Kissinger's *realpolitik* worldview favored intimate cooperation with South Africa. An integral element of this worldview – which rested on the twin themes of détente and the Nixon Doctrine – was the necessity to maintain and regulate the existing balance of power between the US and the Soviet Union so as to avoid superpower conflict in the Third World. When the Angolan civil war threatened to disrupt that regional balance of power, the racial structure of South Africa's apartheid system became insignificant in comparison to its willingness to act as a regional client under the mantle of the Nixon Doctrine. Similar White House fears in Southern Rhodesia favored intimate cooperation once again with the apartheid government. Despite the most obvious lesson of the Portuguese *coup d'état* – that the white minority regimes of southern Africa were *not* "here to stay" – this event ironically contributed to the strengthening of US–South African ties. In short, the ill-defined policy of communication became one of growing cooperation.

Rhetoric versus reality in the shadow of Soweto (May 1976–January 1981)

The regional political turmoil unleashed by the Portuguese *coup d'état* eventually enveloped South Africa in 1976 when the Afrikaner elite was faced with the most violent political uprising to grip their country since the Sharpeville upheavals of 1960. On June 16, 1976, approximately 15,000 South African schoolchildren taking part in a demonstration at a Soweto secondary school were fired upon by South African security forces. When word spread that at least fifty-eight blacks – most notably a thirteen-year-old grade school student – had been killed by the South African police, riots and strikes spread to nearly all of South Africa's major urban areas. In the months that followed, international perceptions of South Africa's political stability were shattered as the often heavy-handed responses of the Afrikaner regime left at least 575 dead and 2,389 wounded.[96]

Entering office in the shadow of the Soweto uprising, the Carter administration, similar to the Kennedy years, generated high expectations among African countries and the growing US anti-apartheid movement that the days of US–South African cooperation were numbered, if not over. The first indication of the Carter administration's intentions was the Democratic Party's adoption prior to the 1976 presidential election of a party platform severely critical of US–South African relations, inclusive of positions calling for a more stringent arms embargo, the denial of tax credits for US corporations operating in Namibia, and the withdrawal of tax credits for South Africa-based US corporations that supported apartheid policies or practices.[97] These promises were backed up by the appointment of strong proponents of racial equality in South Africa to positions of authority within the State Department, such as civil rights activist Andrew Young as US Ambassador to the UN, Cyrus Vance as Secretary of State, Richard Moose as Assistant Secretary of State for African Affairs, and Anthony Lake as Director for Policy Planning. These individuals were also intellectually bound by a common desire to downplay the importance of East–West relations in their approach to understanding African conflicts, favoring instead a "regionalist" approach that emphasized the internal economic, cultural, political, and historical aspects of such upheavals.

The initial rhetoric of the Carter administration promised a significant departure from the anti-apartheid policies of previous administrations. In May 1977, Young attended a UN conference on African liberation held in Maputo, Mozambique, where he equated the legitimacy of the liberation struggle in southern Africa with the US civil rights movement of the 1960s.[98] During that same month, Mondale held a meeting with South African Prime Minister John Vorster in Vienna, Austria, where he announced that US–South African relations would continue to deteriorate until the Afrikaner government allowed for "full political participation" on an "equal basis" – which Mondale clarified in response to a reporter's question as "one man, one vote."[99] The most comprehensive statement on US policy toward southern Africa was made by Vance. In a speech before the annual meeting of the National Association for the Advancement of Colored People (NAACP) in July 1977, Vance announced that the administration had decided to simultaneously pursue the resolution of three major problems in southern Africa: majority rule in Southern Rhodesia, independence for Namibia, and the reform of South Africa's apartheid system. Sharply critiquing the southern African policies of the Nixon–Ford administrations, Vance described as ill-advised the rationale that the US should have ignored the imperfections of the apartheid system in order to ensure South African cooperation in first achieving progress on the issues of Namibia and Southern Rhodesia. "We believe," concluded Vance, "that we can effectively influence South Africa on [Southern] Rhodesia and Namibia while expressing our concerns about apartheid."[100]

The forceful rhetoric of the administration, however, was not initially met by punitive actions designed to pressure the apartheid government. Although the State Department's Africa Bureau favored a decrease in military cooperation to underscore South Africa's removal from the list of countries with which the US enjoyed "normal" relations, opponents were opposed to any form of disengagement.[101] Approaching the debate according to parochial bureaucratic missions, the Pentagon argued that further restrictions on military cooperation would have severe repercussions on the intelligence collection activities of the Defense Intelligence Agency (DIA). The CIA similarly questioned the wisdom of pressuring a valued regional client at the same time that Soviet–Cuban pressures in neighboring countries required access to South Africa's vast intelligence network.[102] The opponents of disengagement clearly carried the day as indicated by the administration's formal review of US foreign policy toward southern Africa. In a presidential directive issued in March 1977, the White House rejected any immediate punitive measures against South Africa, and instead underscored that "visible steps" at downgrading US–South African relations were only to be enacted if South Africa failed to make significant progress toward "power sharing" with the black majority.[103]

The range of debate within the Carter administration over punitive measures against South Africa was hampered severely by opposition among senior policymakers to consider the use of economic sanctions. Building upon the heritage of the US civil rights movement, administration activists – including Carter – perceived US economic investment as a progressive force for change. For example, Young argued that, just as banks in Atlanta, Georgia, had served as important factors in eliminating segregation during the 1960s, so too would an expanding financial market in South Africa eventually force changes in the apartheid system. Carter similarly noted during the election campaign that increased corporate activity – both foreign and domestic – was the "only way" to achieve racial justice in South Africa.[104] As a result, senior policymakers opposed punitive economic sanctions in favor of measures, such as the "Sullivan Principles," a set of guidelines for US corporations doing business in South Africa drawn up by Reverend Leon Sullivan, a member of the General Motors board of directors, which were designed to enhance the progressive impact of US corporations in South Africa.[105]

The unwillingness of the Carter administration to move beyond rhetoric in its denunciations of apartheid led to a growing schism with portions of an increasingly vocal anti-apartheid movement.[106] As early as September 1976, a Black Leadership Conference on Southern Africa organized by the Congressional Black Caucus was calling for the adoption of comprehensive economic sanctions against South Africa, as well as support for armed struggle against the white minority governments of the region. Toward these ends, the conference supported the creation of a foreign policy lobby – which became officially incorporated as TransAfrica in July 1977 – that was to organize and mobilize the African-American electorate in support of more progressive US policies toward Africa, particularly southern Africa (see Chapter 2). In addition, the NAACP created a Task Force on Africa that, among other foreign policy objectives, called for the adoption of comprehensive economic sanctions against South Africa, and the complete withdrawal of US investments from the country. Sharply critical of Carter's belief in the progressive nature of corporate investments, proponents of sanctions argued that US investments supported and encouraged apartheid by strengthening the repressive capabilities of the South African state.[107]

The commitment of the Carter administration to move beyond rhetoric was tested by the intensification of civil violence in South Africa during September 1977. During this month, student leader Steve Biko – the head of the "Black Consciousness Movement" – was beaten to death while in the custody of the South African police.[108] Hoping to preempt civil uprisings expected to accompany the official explanation of "accidental" death, the South African government instituted a wave of repression that included a ban on eighteen African organizations and two newspapers, the arrest of forty black leaders, and the banning of seven white opposition leaders. Seemingly the last straw in a series of similar deaths that had occurred since the initial outbreak of violence in Soweto in June 1976, the country once again was engulfed in riots and uprisings.

The international response to Biko's murder forced the Carter White House to take a stand that clearly demonstrated the growing rift within the US policymaking establishment. In October 1976, no less than three anti-apartheid resolutions, including a ban on foreign investment, an end to nuclear cooperation, and a mandatory embargo on arms sales and licensing agreements, were placed before the UN Security Council, and received the firm support of congressional activists led by the Congressional Black Caucus. Yet apart from Young, who announced that he supported "some form of sanctions," as well as the State Department's Africa Bureau, which favored a more comprehensive arms embargo, the majority of policymakers in the executive branch – despite their strong anti-apartheid rhetoric – were generally opposed in principle to the imposition of mandatory sanctions against South Africa.[109] In a political compromise reminiscent of the Kennedy years, the Carter administration, along with Britain and France, first vetoed all three UN resolutions, and supported instead a resolution that merely made the voluntary arms embargo of 1963 a mandatory requirement of UN member nations. In sharp contrast to the original resolution favored by sanctions proponents, the compromise resolution neither impeded existing international licensing agreements for the manufacture of military weaponry in South Africa nor questioned the use of foreign investment in the development of military technology. Although the US took the additional measure of calling home the US Ambassador to Pretoria, the largely symbolic military sanctions did not significantly alter US foreign policy toward South Africa and clearly demonstrated the limits of the anti-apartheid rhetoric of the Carter administration.

The remainder of Carter's term of office was marked by growing conflict with anti-apartheid forces within Congress who sought to force the executive branch to adopt comprehensive sanctions against South Africa. "Because of the White House's seeming ambivalence toward adopting measures regarding South Africa that go beyond mere verbal condemnation and support for the mandatory United Nations arms embargo against Pretoria," explained Diggs, "it is up to Congress to move decisively to give concrete expression to our policy pronouncements."[110] This viewpoint was shared by Senator Clark who, as chairperson of the Senate Subcommittee on Africa, added his subcommittee's voice to the growing anti-apartheid constituency within Congress.

The growing anti-apartheid activism of certain portions of Congress, however, was not enough to overcome the ambivalence of the majority of congresspersons over the issue of US–South African relations. In the absence of the perception of some sort of extended crisis situation, the innumerable partisan and ideological splits both within and between the two houses of Congress continued to limit the ability of these bodies to pass legislation counter to the established Africa policies of the executive branch. This simple fact was marked by the defeat of numerous anti-apartheid bills in both the House and the Senate during 1977–80.[111] Even at the height of the short-lived Soweto disturbances, the House was only able to pass a resolution calling upon the Carter administration to "take effective measures" against South Africa "in order to register the deep concern of the American people about the continued violation of human rights in that country."[112] Moreover, the one piece of anti-apartheid legislation actually passed by Congress in the aftermath of Soweto was anything but a victory for the anti-apartheid movement. Originally seeking a complete ban on US trade and investment, the anti-apartheid coalition only succeeded in passing a watered-down bill that restricted the US Export–Import Bank from making loans to companies doing business with the South African police or military. The symbolic nature of this bill – similar to the actions of the executive branch as concerned the mandatory arms embargo – was demonstrated by the increase in US exports to South Africa by over 30 percent between 1978 and 1979.[113]

Any possibility that either administration regionalists or congressional activists could go beyond official rhetoric and further restrict US–South African cooperation effectively was precluded by the resurgence of Cold War thinking within the policymaking establishment in 1978 and beyond. As a result of the two Shaba invasions of Zaire from neighboring Angola in 1977–78 (see Chapter 3), as well as the massive levels of Soviet–Cuban involvement in the 1977–78 Ogaden War (see Chapter 4), National Security Adviser Zbigniew Brzezinski's tendency to view South Africa as a regional bulwark against communism gained greater credibility within the administration. Foreshadowing the policy to be followed under the Reagan administration, Brzezinski held the belief that, if the US hoped to achieve any sort of compromise with South Africa, the US first had to deal with the issue of Soviet–Cuban involvement in southern Africa.[114] Even the regionalists within the administration who initially favored pressuring South Africa to change its apartheid system pragmatically downplayed this goal in exchange for South African cooperation in other regional matters. Whereas this pragmatism was successful in enlisting South African support that eventually contributed to the independence of Zimbabwe in April 1980, negotiations over Namibian independence did not fare as well. After a group of Western nations led by the US had succeeded in achieving regional and international acceptance of an independence blueprint embodied in UN Resolution 435, South Africa backed out of the agreement just weeks before the Reagan administration was scheduled to take office. Even if one accepts the ongoing arguments of certain regionalists that the administration did not "prioritize" problems in southern Africa and "consciously go easy" on South Africa in order to achieve settlement on more pressing issues, the record seems to indicate that this was the de facto result in 1978 and beyond.[115]

The bureaucratic imperatives of "constructive engagement" (January 1981–August 1984)

The inauguration of President Reagan in January 1981 was viewed as a blessing by a South African leadership disenchanted with the "duplicity" of the Ford administration and the "overly moralistic rhetoric" of the Carter administration.[116] Reagan had won the admiration of the Afrikaner elite by castigating the lack of US resolve in countering Soviet moves in Africa and promising to renew covert support for an important South African regional ally – Jonas Savimbi's UNITA guerrilla army – in its quest to overthrow the Marxist government of Angola. These expectations were further strengthened by Reagan's response to a question posed by Walter Cronkite on March 3, 1981, concerning the possibility of US support for punitive sanctions against South Africa: "Can we abandon a country that has stood by us in every war we've ever fought, a country that strategically is essential to the free world in its production of minerals we all must have and so forth?"[117]

Reagan's statement on US–South African relations did not mean that either Africa or southern Africa had achieved positions of strategic priority relative to other regions of the world among senior policy-makers within the new administration. Unlike Central America, where senior policymakers almost immmediately began directing a covert paramilitary operation against Nicaragua consistent with the Reagan administration's worldview of "rolling back" self-proclaimed Marxist regimes in the Third World, Africa policies largely were left to the Africa specialists within the State Department. As lamented by a conservative member of the State Department who had hoped for a more activist stance on Africa by the new occupants of the White House, "Africa wasn't even on the map for the vast majority of the Reagan conservatives." "Instead," he continued, "they were seemingly only interested in the Soviet Union, Western Europe, Central America, and Afghanistan." "Even in Angola," he concluded, "where Savimbi's credentials made him a perfect candidate for the roll-back policies of the Reagan worldview, the new administration was not willing to expend valuable political capital on an almost certain bloody congres-sional battle when other regions required priority attention."[118]

The key to understanding US foreign policy toward South Africa during the 1981–84 period was Chester A. Crocker, the State Depart-ment's newly appointed Assistant Secretary of State for African Affairs who was given a "long leash" by both the White House and the senior levels of the State Department in formulating and implementing US Africa policies.[119] Although he shared the administration worldview that characterized the Soviet Union as an aggressive, destabilizing factor in the Third World, including Africa, Crocker opposed the tendency of administration ideologues to counter Soviet inroads through the use of military or paramilitary options, and instead favored regional diplomacy that emphasized the negotiated resolution of conflicts. Crocker not only was influential in defeating the efforts of far right conservatives to provide paramilitary support to the Mozam-bique National Resistance Movement (RENAMO), a right-wing guer-rilla group attempting to overthrow the Marxist government of Mozambique, he also continued the Carter administration policy of offering support to Robert Mugabe, the self-proclaimed Marxist leader of Zimbabwe. Crocker successfully distinguished between pro-Soviet, Marxist countries that maintained a Soviet–Cuban "combat presence" on their territory, such as Angola, and therefore posed a threat to the region, and those countries, such as Mozambique and Zimbabwe, which espoused Marxism for "their own practical purposes."[120] It is for these reasons that far right conservatives, such as Senator Helms, sought to prevent Crocker's appointment as Assistant Secretary of State for African Affairs.

The cornerstone of Crocker's diplomatic strategy was a reconceptualization of US–South African cooperation under the concept of "constructive engagement."[121] Rather than representing a radical departure from established US policy, constructive engagement both reasserted and went beyond the so-called "tilt" of the Nixon administration's policy of communication. Similar to the policy of communication, two underlying components of Crocker's strategy were that South Africa remained the premier politico-military power in the southern African region, and that constructive change was only possible through cooperation with the Afrikaner elite. Unlike the Nixon administration's policy of communication, Crocker sought to foster changes in South Africa's regional relations and domestic system of apartheid through a sophisticated monitoring of regional events and graduated levels of US–South African cooperation. In this regard, US–South African relations were perceived as approaching an historic turning point in which the US could both support and foster the reformist tendencies of the Botha government – a "modernizing autocracy" both willing and capable of enforcing changes in the apartheid system from above.[122] In order to dispel any misgivings that constructive engagement meant a reversion to the complacency of communication, Crocker emphasized in meetings with South African officials that they did not have a "blank check" and that official rhetoric was not to serve as a "smokescreen" for South African "actions and misadventures with their neighbors."[123]

Crocker perceived the issue of Namibian independence as the "crucial first phase" of US–South African cooperation under the framework of constructive engagement.[124] Claiming that ongoing conflict over Namibia had "complicated" US relations with its European allies and the majority of countries in sub-Saharan Africa, Crocker argued that an internationally acceptable solution to this problem would enable Washington not only to "work to end South Africa's polecat status in the world," but restore South Africa's standing as a "legitimate and important regional actor" with whom the US could "cooperate pragmatically."[125] In sharp contrast to the harsh, anti-apartheid rhetoric of the Carter administration which, Crocker believed, only made the isolated South African government more intransigent, this new approach sought to allay Afrikaner fears by demonstrating that the US and South Africa shared the same strategic concerns in southern Africa. Since a major concern of both the Afrikaner government and the Reagan administration was the presence of Cuban combat troops in Angola, a first step in Crocker's diplomatic strategy directly linked the withdrawal of these troops to Washington's support of the independence process for Namibia embodied in UN Resolution 435.

The policy of constructive engagement received strong support within the national security bureaucracies and gave the State Department's Africa Bureau a degree of influence and prestige unparalleled in that organization's history. Despite dissenting with Crocker's opposition to the renewal of US covert intervention in Angola, the CIA supported the overall thrust of constructive engagement because it legitimized already close US–South African cooperation in the intelligence field. Any efforts designed to further bolster US–South African cooperation naturally were supported by a bureaucracy whose organizational missions looked upon the staunchly anti-communist Afrikaner government as a natural ally. Most important, the CIA shared the underlying premise of constructive engagement – the removal and preclusion of any further Soviet–Cuban gains in southern Africa – even if there existed some doubt over the efficacy of diplomacy in achieving such a goal.[126]

The Pentagon constituted a second important proponent of constructive engagement. Sharing the CIA's concern over the growing levels of Soviet involvement in southern Africa, the Defense Department favored any policy approach that rationalized growing levels of US–South African military cooperation. In addition to loosening the mandatory arms embargo by permitting the sale of non-military items to the South African security forces, the policy of constructive engagement favored increased personnel exchanges between both countries, such as was the case in the training of South African military officers by the US Coast Guard in New York.[127] The Pentagon was particularly supportive of the administration's willingness to upgrade military ties by fully staffing unfilled military attaché positions (four US slots in South Africa and two South African slots in the US), most notably due to the fact that these officers served an invaluable intelligence function.[128]

The initial opponents of constructive engagement were a group of career FSOs within the State Department's Africa Bureau. There was a certain degree of irony in this opposition in that the policy as articulated by Crocker clearly placed the Africa Bureau in the forefront of policy formulation and implementation as concerned southern African issues.[129] The simple reason for this opposition was the perception of constructive engagement as running counter to the Africa Bureau's primary mission of maintaining smooth and stable relationships with the countries of sub-Saharan Africa. Critics within the Africa Bureau felt that any tilt toward the minority white regime, especially if accompanied by increased US–South African military cooperation, would further strain the always tenuous US relations with the majority of sub-Saharan African countries. "Although the majority of us within the Africa Bureau viewed comprehensive economic sanctions as too radical of a step in voicing US disfavor with apartheid," explained one FSO who initially questioned the tilt of constructive engagement, "we nonetheless wanted to make clear to the South African government and everyone else that we did not regard the South Africans as close allies or friends or people with whom we should have a perfectly normal relationship."[130] According to this group, constructive engagement, which did lead to closer US–South African military cooperation, was counterproductive to this goal.

Despite these initial misgivings, constructive engagement was strongly supported by the State Department and the majority of FSOs working within the Africa Bureau. The critical reason for this support, regardless of any perceived overemphasis on placating the fears of the Afrikaners, was the policy's emphasis on seeking the diplomatic resolution of conflicts in southern Africa. Specifically, the policy nicely bridged a bureaucratic gap within the State Department between the bureaus, such as Politico-Military Affairs, which tended to focus on issues from an East–West perspective, and those, such as the Africa Bureau, with a greater sensitivity as to how African governments may react to a particular US initiative in Africa. The more strategically minded FSOs, similar to their counterparts in the CIA and the Pentagon, looked upon constructive engagement as a means of precluding any further Soviet encroachment in southern Africa, and strongly favored Crocker's linkage of Namibian independence with the withdrawal of Cuban troops from Angola. As for those FSOs more sympathetic to African sensitivities, the successful implementation of even just the short-term objectives of constructive engagement promised to provide enormous diplomatic benefits for the US in Africa. Not only would Washington receive praise for securing the independence of Namibia, but resolution of this problem could lead to formal diplomatic relations with Angola, as well as facilitate closer links with other African countries, such as Nigeria and Tanzania, previously suspicious of US foreign policy in southern Africa.[131] In short, the intellectual underpinnings and promises of constructive engagement naturally earned the support of a bureaucracy which continues to condition its members to seek the negotiated resolution of conflicts.

The fact that constructive engagement was intellectually consistent with the State Department's organizational culture of favoring the negotiated resolution of conflicts contributed to an interesting socialization process within the Africa Bureau. Although the policy initially was opposed by some FSOs whose frame of reference had been growing official rhetoric against apartheid and the gradual restriction of US–South African relations under the Carter administration, FSOs entering the Africa Bureau after 1981 (especially those with little Africa experience) were socialized into supporting the new bureaucratic status quo. "Speaking for myself," explained one FSO who worked in the Africa Bureau under the direction of Crocker, "I always looked upon sanctions as the self-evident thing to do in relation to South Africa." Despite the fact that he lobbied for the imposition of economic sanctions against South Africa after earning a doctoral degree in the 1960s, this individual, like others who joined the Africa Bureau after 1981, became an adherent of existing policy. "Since I joined the bureau," he explained, "I gained a more sophisticated understanding of the nuances of US–South African relations and have come to reject the utility of sanctions."[132]

Criticized from the beginning by various factions within Congress and the anti-apartheid movement, constructive engagement fell prey to even harsher criticism when it initially failed to live up to official expectations. In addition to being unable to achieve the quick settlement originally envisioned for Namibia, the policy seemed to flounder in the face of South Africa's resort to a regional destabilization policy. In the words of one noted analyst of US–South African relations, there existed an inherent contradiction between Crocker's "stabilizing diplomacy" and Pretoria's "destabilizing militancy."[133] While continuing to drag out negotiations over the issue of Namibia, South Africa launched numerous military raids on the neighboring territories of Angola and Mozambique. In Angola, these raids ranged from a March 1981 bombing of Namibian refugee camps to Operation Askari, a December 1983 invasion that comprised thousands of troops and led to South Africa's long-term occupation of Angolan territory just north of Namibia.[134] Similar military operations against Mozambique ranged from the launching of a commando raid against suspected ANC safe houses in Maputo just weeks after Reagan's inauguration, to paramilitary support for RENAMO. Originally created by the Rhodesian security services to weaken Mozambique's support for anti-Rhodesian guerrillas, RENAMO became a willing client of South Africa's security services when Zimbabwe's independence in April 1980 terminated its only external source of support. As a result of these events, opponents of administration policy argued that constructive engagement actually encouraged South African intransigence and the militarization of regional relations in southern Africa.

Dissatisfaction within Congress over the escalation of military conflict in southern Africa and the failure of constructive engagement to achieve any of its major goals led to renewed attempts at legislating economic sanctions against South Africa. In November 1983, the Democratic controlled House of Representatives included five sets of anti-apartheid provisions in the annual Export Administration Act, including a ban on new corporate investment, the termination of any exports destined for the South African police and military, a ban on commercial loans to the South African government, the termination of the sale of Kruggerands in the US, and the mandatory adoption of the Sullivan Principles by all US corporations doing business in South Africa. The Senate, however, refused to adopt any anti-apartheid provisions and the legislation ultimately died in conference. As in the past, the lack of domestic pressures for congressional action favored continuation of established executive branch policies.

An important reason for Senate rejection of economic sanctions was the firm belief among the relatively few Senators keeping track of US foreign policy toward South Africa that constructive engagement had not been allowed a sufficient amount of time to prove itself as a viable policy. Indeed, proponents of constructive engagement were strengthened when the State Department's Africa Bureau was able to broker non-aggression treaties between South Africa and the bordering countries of Angola and Mozambique. In the case of Angola, a February 1984 agreement known as the Lusaka Accord established a joint South African–Angolan commission to monitor the withdrawal of South African troops from Angolan territory in exchange for a commitment by the Angolan government to prevent any further attacks by SWAPO guerrillas on South African installations in Namibia. In the case of Mozambique, a March 1984 agreement known as the Nkomati Accord required South Africa to discontinue its support for the RENAMO guerrilla insurgency in exchange for Mozambique's commitment to prevent ANC guerrillas from using Mozambique as a springboard for attacks against South Africa.

Although both the Lusaka and Nkomati Accords eventually unraveled and led to the renewal of regional hostilities between South Africa and its neighbors, their initial success seemed to vindicate the underlying assumptions of constructive engagement. Despite the ongoing criticisms of members of Congress, such as Dellums and Gray, numerous congresspersons in both the House and the Senate were willing to give Crocker's policies the benefit of the doubt. As the first term of the Reagan administration drew to a close, therefore, the Africa Bureau under the leadership of Crocker continued to maintain control over the formulation and implementation of US foreign policy toward South Africa. The growing concern of some FSOs within the Africa

Bureau notwithstanding, constructive engagement remained firmly supported by the State Department, the Pentagon, and the CIA.

Extended crisis and passage of the Comprehensive Anti-Apartheid Act of 1986 (September 1984–October 1986)

The underlying assumptions of constructive engagement were called into question by the most severe domestic crisis in South African political history. On September 3, 1984, a series of protests broke out out in several black townships over the South African government's adoption of a tricameral parliament that extended limited political rights to Asians and Coloreds but continued to deny political franchise to the majority black population. Serving as a spark for the release of decades of pent-up hostility that to a lesser degree had surfaced at Sharpeville and in Soweto in earlier years, these protests turned into a popular rebellion that pitted blacks against the South African security and police forces over a period of two years. When the dust had settled, over 2,000 blacks had died and nearly 30,000 others had been detained for political reasons, including nearly 3,000 black children under the age of eighteen.[135]

The brutality of the South African government's response captured the attention of the world media and became a nightly staple of US news broadcasts. Vivid film footage of white police officers attacking black protesters in black townships with whips and dogs offered a strong indictment of the horrors of apartheid and the shallowness of reforms undertaken by the Afrikaner government. Yet in a hearing convened by the Senate Subcommittee on Africa less than three weeks after the outbreak of violence, Crocker stressed that it was still "premature" to dismiss the "new willingness" of the Afrikaner government to "support the concept of reform."[136] Capturing the mood of several congresspersons who had decided in 1981 to "keep quiet" and give Crocker "a chance to show what could be done with constructive engagement," Senator Paul Tsongas (D-Massachusetts) strongly criticized Crocker's continued support for a failed policy.[137]

This clash between Crocker and Tsongas marked a turning point in the domestic debate over the proper course of US foreign policy toward South Africa. As violence in South Africa continued to mount, apartheid became a domestic political issue for US citizens increasingly prone to draw parallels between the legitimacy of the struggle by blacks in South Africa and the US civil rights movement of the 1960s. In the absence of White House concern and given the arguments emanating from the national security bureaucracies that called for continuation of the status quo, rising popular demands for the US to "do something" slowly captured the attention of vote-conscious members of Congress who had ignored the issue of apartheid. In short, the extended violence in South Africa served as a spark for the pro-sanctions viewpoint within the policymaking establishment in which Congress increasingly would assume the initiative in altering the direction of US–South African relations.

The opening salvo of growing domestic concern over the violence in South Africa was launched by TransAfrica and its activist Executive Director, Randall Robinson, who on November 21, 1984, staged a peaceful sit-in at the South African Embassy in Washington, DC, that led to his arrest. Accompanied by other notable African Americans, such as Representative Walter Fauntroy (D-District of Columbia), and Mary Frances Berry, a member of the US Civil Rights Commission, this act captured the imagination of anti-apartheid activists and led to the creation of the Free South Africa Movement, an umbrella organization of anti-apartheid groups seeking to impose sanctions against South Africa. Rather than constituting a one-day media stunt, Robinson's arrest was duplicated by anti-apartheid activists who staged similar sit-ins at the South African Embassy and consulates around the US during the twenty-three months that followed. The significance of these acts was further strengthened by the involvement and arrest of eighteen prominent members of Congress, the most notable being Senator Lowell Weicker (R-Connecticut) and Representative Patricia Schroeder (D-Colorado).

Congress soon responded to growing popular demands for punitive actions against South Africa. On June 4, 1985, the House of Representatives passed a sanctions bill (HR-1460) by a vote of 295 to 127 that called for bans on new US corporate investment in South Africa, US bank loans to the South African government, the importation of Kruggerands, computer sales to the South African government, and US–South African nuclear cooperation.[138] The bill also included a clause that mandated consideration of new sanctions within twelve months.[139] Despite an unsuccessful filibuster attempt by Helms, the Senate passed its version of sanctions legislation (S-995) on July 11 by a margin of 80 to 12.[140] The Senate version, however, was much weaker than its House counterpart, and included a ban on bank loans to the South African government, restrictions on the export of computer and nuclear products, mandatory adherence of US corporations in South Africa to the Sullivan Principles, and consideration of new sanctions after a period of two years. A joint House–Senate conference committee on July 31 adopted the more limited sanctions bill. The only measures included from HR-1460 were a ban on the import of Krug-gerands and consideration of new sanctions legislation within twelve months.

The prospect of congressional passage of economic sanctions ensured the end of the parochial control that the State Department's Africa Bureau wielded over US foreign policy toward South Africa and placed the issue of apartheid squarely in the hands of the Reagan White House. In contemplating whether the administration could veto the legislation and prevent a congressional override – the position favored by the State Department's Africa Bureau, the Pentagon, and the CIA – Reagan and his advisers were faced with the Afrikaner government's "untimely" declaration of a state of emergency on July 25, 1985, and subsequent intensification of civil conflict in South Africa. Moreover, Republican Senators, most notably Foreign Relations Committee chairperson Richard Lugar (R-Indiana), warned Reagan that unless some sanctions were adopted by the administration, there was a strong possibility that a White House veto would be overridden by both the House and the Senate.[141]

Despite Reagan's opposition to any punitive actions against South Africa, political pragmatism required taking the advice of Lugar. In a tactical move which initially prevented Senate passage of the compromise sanctions legislation (the House already had passed the bill), Reagan issued Executive Order 12532 on September 9, 1985, which included bans on US government loans to the South African government and the sale of computers to South African security agencies, placed limited restrictions on US–South African nuclear cooperation, and ordered an investigation into the legality of banning US imports of Kruggerands.[142] The biggest differences with the congressional bill were executive branch discretion as to when sanctions could be lifted, and the omission of any clause requiring the automatic reconsideration of sanctions within a specific time. This attempt at co-opting the legislative process might have been successful in the long run had it been matched by decreasing levels of civil conflict in South Africa. However, growing levels of black rebellion were met by even stronger acts of suppression by the South African government, culminating in a second state of emergency being declared in June 1986 as part of a determination to crush all opposition.[143] To make matters worse, on May 19, 1986, the South African government launched coordinated military strikes against suspected ANC headquarters in Botswana, Zambia, and Zimbabwe. According to proponents of sanctions within Congress, South Africa's internal and external policies completely discredited any arguments on the part of the Reagan administration that the Afrikaner elite was committed to reform.[144]

The intensification of civil conflict in South Africa led to renewed congressional efforts in 1986 to pass anti-apartheid sanctions legislation. A comprehensive sanctions bill (HR–4868) calling for a complete trade embargo and divestment of all economic holdings in South Africa passed by a voice vote in the House on June 12, 1986.[145] After sharp debate over several pieces of legislation and amendments, the Senate on August 14 passed its version of economic sanctions (S-2701) by a vote of 84 to 14.[146] Among the bill's most significant elements were the incorporation of the major provisions of the 1985 Executive Order, a ban on private bank loans to the South African government, and a prohibition on new investment in South Africa. A joint House–Senate conference committee in August 1986 voted to accept without amendment S-2701 as the conference report. As a result, both the Senate and the House passed that same month what has become known as the Comprehensive Anti-Apartheid Act of 1986. In addition to the major provisions already noted, the act included a ban on products produced or marketed by South African parastatals, a ban on imports of South African uranium, steel, and textiles, the withdrawal of landing rights for South African Airways, and the denial of visas for all South Africa officials, except embassy personnel.

Passage of the 1986 Anti-Apartheid Act once again placed the issue of sanctions squarely in the hands of the White House. Hoping to coopt the legislative process as he effectively had done in 1985, Reagan vetoed the sanctions bill, and offered instead a milder version in the form of another Executive Order.[147] Convinced that if he could only take his case to the US electorate, they would understand the logic of what the administration sought to accomplish in southern Africa, Reagan in a July 22, 1986, policy address broadcast live on network television, rejected the imposition of further sanctions as "immoral" and "utterly repugnant."[148] In the eyes of opponents of constructive engagement, as well as of those sympathetic to Reagan's viewpoint, the halfhearted measures included in the speech and codified in the Executive Order were too little, too late. On September 29, 1986, the House voted 317 to 83 to override Reagan's veto. Four days later, the Senate followed suit by a 78–21 margin. Marking one of the greatest foreign policy defeats of the Reagan administration, these two votes constituted the official death of the policy of constructive engagement.

The reasons for this setback in administration policy were basically fourfold. First, the rising electoral strength of African Americans was translated into effective political organizations capable of bringing pressure to bear on Congress.[149] The primary vehicle for this electoral voice outside of Congress was TransAfrica, the political lobby that effectively organized the protests at the South African Embassy beginning in 1984. Within the halls of Congress, not only had the Congressional Black Caucus grown in numbers (twenty-one members in 1986), but its members, such as Dellums and Gray, had also achieved greater seniority and positions of authority, and therefore were well poised to press for sanctions against South Africa. A second reason for the setback in administration policy, which derived from the growing electoral strength of African Americans, was rising Republican concern over the issue of race in US foreign policy. This factor was especially important because it contributed to divisiveness within the Republican Party in 1986 that was so crucial to the passage of sanctions legislation in the Republican-controlled Senate.

A third reason for the reversal of administration policy in South Africa was the steady growth of grassroots anti-apartheid organizations. National leadership for hundreds of such groups was provided by the American Committee on Africa (ACOA) and its Washington counterpart, the Washington Committee on Africa (WCOA), the Interfaith Center on Corporate Responsibility (ICCR), and the American Friends Service Committee (AFSC). These groups, which had been growing steadily in strength since the 1970s, increased significantly in influence after 1984.[150] Indeed, by 1986, 19 state governments, 68 cities and counties, and 131 colleges and universities had adopted various types of restrictions that affected nearly $220 billion of institutional assets related to pension and endowment funds.[151] In addition to promoting such divestment and disinvestment at the local and state levels, anti-apartheid organizations provided invaluable organizational support when the sanctions movement became a national phenomenon in 1986. These groups cooperated with liberal congressional allies, particularly those on the House Subcommittee on Africa, to seek passage of anti-apartheid legislation. Their contribution ranged from collecting data and providing witnesses crucial to congressional hearings to coordinating massive letter-writing campaigns to wavering congresspersons.[152]

The fourth and most important factor contributing to passage of the 1986 sanctions legislation was the unfolding of what came to be perceived among the US public as an extended crisis situation in South Africa. In the early stages of the crisis, Reagan was able to hold the line on sanctions by issuing an Executive Order. The short-lived success of this tactical move demonstrated how, even during short-term crises when an issue attracted the attention of a significant number of congresspersons, initial control of the policymaking process naturally flowed to the President and the bureaucracies of the executive branch. However, as the violence in South Africa continued to intensify, rising popular demands for the US government to "do something" to stop the unfolding tragedy in South Africa galvanized the anti-apartheid activities of African-American lobbying groups, Republican splinter groups, and grass-roots anti-apartheid organizations. These groups, in turn, placed pressure on vote-conscious congresspersons who recognized the popular political backlash that would accompany defeat of some sort of sanctions package. In hearings devoted to the question of sanctions, Representative Wolpe, chairperson of the House Subcommittee on Africa, dramatized the crucial relationship between events in South Africa and the US policymaking process: "Why are we so concerned with the passage [of sanctions legislation] at this point? The reason [is], very simply, because of the dramatic – very dramatic, I want to underscore that – deterioration of developments in South Africa."[153] The fact that these developments were linked to the politicization of the apartheid issue within US domestic politics was underscored by Senate Majority Leader Robert Dole (R-Kansas): "Let's face it, there's a lot of politics involved . . . .This has now become a civil rights issue."[154]

The override of Reagan's 1986 veto marked a historic turning point in US–South African relations as Congress reversed a policy strongly embraced by the executive branch. Although the legislation was still too mild for numerous anti-apartheid activists, its passage stood in stark contrast to the historical US tendency to rhetorically denounce South Africa's racial policies while simultaneously doing little to change the established status quo. The act now firmly matched US words with actions. Most significant, perhaps, was that large numbers of Republicans – most notably in the Republican-controlled Senate – abandoned a popular President of their own party during an election year. As Senator Simon, chairperson of the Senate Subcommittee on Africa, was to note: "Three years ago no one could have imagined that a Democratic House of Representatives and a Republican Senate would together repudiate the administration's policy, override a presidential veto, and forge a new direction for US policy in South Africa." He continued: "Congress seized the mantle of leadership, took a moral stand, and rejected a policy that compromised our commitment to individual rights and equivocated on our moral stand against apartheid."[155]

Absence of crisis and failed attempts at strengthening sanctions (November 1986–January 1989)

The passage of the Comprehensive Anti-Apartheid Act of 1986 did not end the highly politicized congressional-executive debate over economic sanctions against South Africa, but served as a new point of departure for congressional anti-apartheid activists who favored even stiffer measures against South Africa. For these members of Congress, the 1986 sanctions legislation, which comprised the milder "partial" sanctions of the Senate version, contained too many loopholes to ensure implementation of the will of Congress in the face of executive branch intransigence. "I firmly believe," explained Dellums, one of the moral barometers of the anti-apartheid movement within the House of Representatives, "that only full and comprehensive sanctions, implemented internationally, will cause the South African government to change its policies."[156]

Congressional critics initially focused on what they perceived as the administration's lax interpretation and implementation of various enforcement measures contained within the 1986 Anti-Apartheid Act.[157] For example, although Section 309(a) of the act banned the import of uranium ore or oxide from South Africa and Namibia, the administration's interpretation permitted such imports for reprocessing and reexport. Concerns were also raised that millions of dollars of South African iron and steel were allowed to illegally enter the US during 1987.[158] Congressional critics were especially concerned with the Reagan administration's unwillingness to adhere to the requirements of Section 401(b), which required the executive branch to "promptly" undertake multilateral negotiations – to be concluded "not later than 180 days" from the enactment of the 1986 act – to achieve "international cooperative agreements" designed to "bring about the complete dismantling of apartheid."[159] In the most blatant example of executive branch disregard for the spirit, if not the letter, of this particular clause of the 1986 Anti-Apartheid Act, the US in February 1987 vetoed a UN Security Council resolution calling for the imposition of international economic sanctions modeled after the 1986 US legislation. As aptly observed by one noted commentator of US–South African relations, the casting of this veto placed the US in the peculiar position of voting against the "spirit of its own law" within the international legal system.[160]

Apart from oversight hearings, the primary vehicle for demonstrating congressional unhappiness with the administration's track record was a renewed push for an "unambiguous, more easily enforced" set of sanctions against South Africa.[161] On March 12, 1987, Dellums introduced legislation (HR-1580) into the House of Representatives that streamlined the 1986 Anti-Apartheid Act into three comprehensive provisions: (1) the withdrawal of all US investments from South Africa; (2) the imposition of a complete ban on US–South African trade; and (3) a prohibition on any US military or intelligence cooperation with the South African government.[162] "The major thrust of this bill is to call for immediate divestment and total embargo against the government of South Africa," explained Dellums, "I call for comprehensive sanctions against South Africa," he continued, "not an incremental step, not a measured step, but an all-out, powerful and aggressive statement."[163]

The response of the national security bureaucracies was predictably and overwhelmingly negative. Crocker led the opposition by arguing that additional sanctions would make the white Afrikaner government more intransigent, and impede the diplomatic resolution of conflicts in southern Africa. Crocker was hopeful that, after an April 1987 meeting with Angolan officials in Brazzaville, the People's Republic of the Congo, the stalled regional talks on Namibian independence would be placed back on track. "At this delicate juncture in the diplomatic talks," explained Crocker, "carrots, not sticks, were the proper means of ensuring South African cooperation so crucial to Namibian independence."[164] Despite Crocker's support for minor changes in policy – such as the January 1987 meeting between Secretary of State George Shultz and ANC President Oliver Tambo – designed to compensate for past neglect of the black nationalist side of the political equation in South Africa, his arguments revealed the State Department's continued tilt toward the white Afrikaner government.

Speaking for the Pentagon, James L. Woods, Deputy Assistant Secretary of Defense for International Security Affairs, voiced opposition to that part of the sanctions legislation which would have outlawed the stationing of military attaché officers in South Africa. Reflecting the importance of bureaucratic missions in determining the policy stances of individual organizations, Woods asserted that the continued presence of defense attachés was "extremely valuable" due to their primary mission of reporting "politico-military intelligence."[165] In this regard, the Defense Department specifically was interested in maintaining access to South African intelligence concerning Soviet bloc involvement in the Angolan civil war.[166]

The CIA's bureaucratic missions similarly prompted it to oppose that portion of the sanctions bill which would have precluded intelligence cooperation with the South African government. As explained in Chapter 3, South Africa was an integral part of the CIA's covert paramilitary campaign in Angola after the repeal of the Clark Amendment in 1985. Constituting one of two paramilitary fronts (the other being Zaire), US–South African intelligence cooperation most likely was modeled after the de facto covert alliance indicative of the 1975–76 Angolan civil war and, at the very least, included the sharing of intelligence through third parties (such as Zaire). Indeed, there remain unresolved questions over the CIA's alleged illegal cooperation with the South African government in providing arms to the Nicaraguan contras, as well as to Jonas Savimbi's UNITA guerrilla forces in Angola.[167]

Congressional consideration of the Dellums bill (HR-1580) during 1987–89 demonstrated, however, that the executive branch had little to fear from anti-apartheid activists within both the House and the Senate. Although passing the House in 1988 by a large margin (244 to 132), the bill died on the floor of the Senate after being favorably voted out of the Foreign Relations Committee by the narrow margin of 10 to 9. Since bills do not carry over from one congress to another, the failure of the sanctions legislation at the end of the 100th congress meant that it had to be reintroduced during the first session of the 101st congress in 1989. Once again passing the House by a wide margin, the bill was unable to garner enough support to bring it to a vote on the full floor of the 101st Senate. In sharp contrast to the jubilation that accompanied passage of the 1986 sanctions legislation, anti-apartheid activists were forced to reassess their tactics and ponder the reasons for defeat.

The most important reason for the failure of more comprehensive sanctions legislation during 1987–89 was the lack of popular perceptions of an ongoing crisis in South Africa.[168] Although several factors – the electoral strength of African Americans, a coalition of race-conscious Republicans, and the steady growth of grass-roots anti-apartheid organizations – remained constant from the 1986 sanctions victory, popular opinion was no longer as closely focused on the issue of South Africa. In addition to the natural cycle of decreasing official and public interest once action had been taken (sanctions were imposed in 1986), the South African government's successful repression of dissent, particularly independent press accounts, contributed to declining numbers of nightly broadcasts of violence in South Africa.[169] This, in turn, translated into decreasing popular pressure for wavering congresspersons to vote against the wishes of a popular administration. As popular pressure subsided, traditional ideological splits, especially within the Senate, made passage of further sanctions difficult, if not impossible. For example, a significant number of conservative Senators began focusing on the concept of "black empowerment" – providing economic incentives to enhance the economic and, subsequently, political power of blacks in South Africa – as the preferable way of building on existing sanctions.[170] Even if the Senate had been able to garner the bare minimum number of votes necessary to pass the Dellums bill, there simply were not enough votes to overcome a certain presidential veto.[171] In short, the decline of popular pressures to "do something" contributed to the breakdown of the anti-apartheid coalition that existed in 1986.

Any hopes among congressional anti-apartheid activists of legislating further sanctions against South Africa effectively were precluded by the successful resolution of the diplomatic impasse over Namibian independence. On July 20, 1988, a US-mediated accord among Angola, Cuba, and South Africa was made public in which all three countries agreed in principle to work toward Namibian independence as the basis for a withdrawal of Cuban troops from Angola. On December 22, 1988, two agreements – the Namibia Accord and the Angola Accord – were signed that formalized these themes, ultimately leading to independence for Namibia on March 30, 1990.[172] In this atmosphere of diplomatic compromise in which the South African government finally agreed to relinquish political control over Namibia, even the most vehement opponents of constructive engagement were forced to acknowledge the significance of this achievement. Although Crocker's policy of constructive engagement was not exonerated by the dramatic diplomatic events in southern Africa, proponents within the national security bureaucracies of closer US–South African ties nonetheless were given ample ammunition to oppose any enhancement of sanctions against South Africa during the final months of the Reagan administration.

The sanctions debate amidst an altered Cold War environment (January 1989–January 1993)

The Bush administration entered office in January 1989 determined to avoid the bruising battles with Congress over South Africa so frequent during the Reagan years. Whereas Secretary of State James A. Baker III indicated in his confirmation hearings that the administration was seeking a bipartisan approach built on close consultation with Congress,[173] Bush sought to demonstrate his sympathy with the anti-apartheid movement by personally meeting with South African activists and publicly expressing his abhorrence of apartheid.[174]

"Reagan never succeeded in communicating his sympathy with the victims of apartheid," noted Herman Nickel, Ambassador to South Africa from 1982 to 1986, "So the Congress doubted whether his heart was in the right place on the issue of racial justice generally and South Africa in particular."[175] In this regard, the Bush administration won the cautious praise of influential congressional opponents of apartheid, such as Wolpe, who claimed to be "encouraged" by what seemed to be "a much more sensitive public posture toward the South African regime" and "more interest and emphasis on this critical question."[176]

Despite the willingness of Bush and his senior advisers to demonstrate that their "hearts were in the right places," US foreign policy toward South Africa in the early months of the Bush administration differed little, if at all, from the later years of the Reagan administration. Because of the preoccupation with the dramatic socio-political changes in the Soviet Union and Eastern Europe, as well as the reunification of Germany and the future of the NATO alliance, US–South African relations were relegated to the Africa specialists within the State Department. In congressional testimony strikingly reminiscent of Crocker's policy of constructive engagement, newly appointed Assistant Secretary of State for African Affairs Herman J. Cohen stressed that he perceived "new thinking" and a "new sense of realism" among the white Afrikaner elite. If supported by an active US stance of "dialogue, negotiation and compromise," explained Cohen, "a democratic solution may be achievable."[177] Although willing to concede that economic sanctions had been successful in forcing the Afrikaner elite to consider negotiations with the black majority, Cohen nonetheless emphasized the State Department's continuing opposition to further sanctions against South Africa. This stance also enjoyed broad support within the CIA and the Pentagon.

The opposition of the national security bureaucracies to further sanctions against South Africa stood in sharp contrast to the sentiments of congressional anti-apartheid activists. Led by the House Subcommittee on Africa and the Congressional Black Caucus, activists continued to favor the tightening of economic sanctions. At the very least, these members of Congress hoped that the Bush administration would support the multilateralization of sanctions, and were willing to concede the administration's unwillingness to advance beyond the sanctions legislation "currently on the books" in exchange for making that legislation the basis of a US-supported resolution within the UN Security Council – a step the Reagan administration was unwilling to take.[178] As demonstrated by South Africa's successful refinancing in October 1989 of a significant portion of its outstanding international loans, however, an ongoing congressional-executive stand-off favored continuation of the status quo. In this case, anti-apartheid activists sought White House intervention to prevent international banks from extending the grace period for nearly $8 billion in South African loans scheduled to fall due in June 1990. Congressional activists had hoped to precipitate a major financial crisis in South Africa similar to the one in 1985 when banks recalled nearly $14 billion in debt, the idea being to undermine apartheid further and force the Afrikaners to negotiate with the black opposition. Yet in the face of executive branch opposition and the inability of Congress to muster enough interest to force the issue, Washington stood on the sidelines as South Africa reached agreement with its creditors.[179]

Unable to force the executive branch to adopt more stringent economic sanctions, congressional activists from mid-1989 on were faced with a growing movement within the national security bureaucracies to repeal portions of the 1986 Comprehensive Anti-Apartheid Act as a result of far-reaching changes in South Africa's political system. At the forefront of these political changes was Frederik W. de Klerk, the national chairperson of the ruling National Party who in the September 1989 election emerged as the new President of South Africa. Adopting a reformist stance that in many respects paralleled the approach taken by Soviet leader Mikhail Gorbachev, de Klerk as early as June 1989 announced his intention to create a "new South Africa" in which the white minority would share power with the black majority.[180] In order to demonstrate his sincerity in seeking implementation of some type of power-sharing agreement, de Klerk in the months that followed initiated a series of political reforms that began with the September 1989 legalization of peaceful anti-government protests. In what surely will be recorded as one of the most historic moments in South African history, de Klerk four months later announced the unconditional release of Nelson Mandela, the world-renowned ANC leader who had spent nearly twenty-eight years in South African prisons.[181]

The evolving political events in South Africa contributed to a significant change in the sanctions debate within the US policymaking establishment, which broke down essentially into four major groups. The first group, comprising those portions of the policymaking establishment that had never supported the imposition of economic sanctions – the State Department, the Pentagon, and the CIA – broached the idea of partially lifting some of those measures. One of the primary concerns of this group was that the growing polarization of South African politics could lead to the downfall of de Klerk, a reformist leader who, like Gorbachev, was perceived as crucial to the reform process. Specifically, in order to forestall the rising electoral strength of right-wing forces in South Africa opposed to any changes in apartheid, this group argued that the judicious lifting of sanctions would strengthen the hand of de Klerk. This viewpoint became increasingly debated after British Prime Minister Margaret Thatcher on February 21, 1990, announced her government's intention unilaterally to lift a self-imposed ban on new investment in South Africa.[182]

The second group consisted of those congressional activists who favored holding the line on sanctions until it became clear that the reform process in South Africa was irreversible. In September 1989, for example, members of this group were questioning whether de Klerk represented "real change." Although he was perceived as much "smoother" than his predecessor and "better able to put a positive face on the tragedy of South Africa," congressional activists cautioned that this did not ensure a "fundamental change" in the structures of apartheid.[183] Even after a two-day fact-finding mission to South Africa in March 1990 in the aftermath of Mandela's release from prison, congressional activists, though hopeful, remained cautious. Describing the period as a "rare window of opportunity" for the creation of a non-racial democracy, congressional activists nonetheless noted that there remained significant obstacles to a lasting negotiated settlement.[184]

In addition to those groups favoring the partial lifting and maintenance of existing sanctions legislation – the dominant perspectives within the US policymaking establishment during 1990 – two other groups constituted fringe elements. Although having declined in numbers as a result of the evolution of political events in South Africa, a third group continued to call for the strengthening of sanctions measures. The most prominent supporters of such an approach were TransAfrica and other grass-roots anti-apartheid organizations. The final group included those conservative members of Congress, such as Helms, who favored the complete lifting of economic sanctions. Whereas the number of proponents of further sanctions declined due to the recognition that de Klerk deserved to "be given a chance," proponents of completely lifting sanctions became isolated by the realization among some conservatives that the 1986 legislation did, in fact, contribute to political change in South Africa.

The primary issue in the growing congressional-executive sanctions debate was South African compliance with the legal requirements of the Comprehensive Anti-Apartheid Act of 1986. According to Section 311 of the act, Bush was authorized to suspend or modify any of the sanctions measures if South Africa fulfilled the first and three out of the four remaining conditions listed below:

(1) The release of Nelson Mandela, as well as all other persons persecuted for their political beliefs or detained unduly without trial.

(2) Repeal of the state of emergency and release of all detainees held under such a state of emergency.

(3) Unban all democratic political parties and permit the free exercise by South Africans of all races of the right to form political parties, express political opinions, and otherwise participate in the political process.

(4) Repeal of the Group Areas Act and Population Registration Act and institution of no other measures with the same purposes.

(5) Agree to enter into good faith negotiations with truly representative members of the black majority without preconditions.

An Executive Order repealing sanctions would take effect thirty days after being issued unless Congress by a majority vote passed a joint resolution overturning the President's decision.

By June 1991, the reform process initiated by de Klerk (measured in terms of South African compliance with the preceding five major conditions of the legislation) had reached the point that the White House could seriously entertain the lifting of sanctions.[185] First, the Afrikaner government demonstrated its willingness to enter into good-faith negotiations (condition 5) through ongoing talks with the black majority that had resolved several thorny political issues; most notable was the ANC's August 1990 agreement to suspend its guerrilla struggle in favor of peaceful negotiations.[186] A second requirement (condition 4) was met when the two key legal foundations of the apartheid system – the Group Areas Act and the Population Registration Act – were repealed in June 1991.[187] Third, all previously banned political parties and organizations, most notably the ANC, were legalized (condition 3) as of February 2, 1990.[188] A fourth requirement (condition 2) was met when, in the aftermath of similar actions in the Transvaal, Cape Province, and the Orange Free State in June 1990, the state of emergency was lifted in the remaining province of Natal in November 1990.[189]

The only really contested requirement (condition 1) revolved around the US demand for the release of all political prisoners. In August 1990, the South African government agreed to the "phased release" of several categories of such prisoners by April 1991, as well as the return of more than 20,000 political exiles. This agreement, of course, followed on the heels of Mandela's dramatic release in February 1990, which was preceded by the release of seven prominent political prisoners in October 1989. A dispute arose, however, over who exactly constituted a political prisoner. Despite the amnesty granted to hundreds of individuals detained without trial or jailed for their political beliefs, the South African government initially refused to release prisoners who had committed "violent" crimes, even if those crimes were politically motivated. According to the Human Rights Commission, a monitoring group based in South Africa, approximately 800 such political prisoners were being held as of July 1991 in violation of the August 1990 agreement.[190] This interpretation was rejected by a State Department sponsored fact-finding mission that concluded in July 1991 that all political prisoners jailed for non-violent crimes – in essence an acceptance of the South African government's definition – had been released.

The State Department's certification of South African compliance with all five conditions of the 1986 anti-apartheid legislation was the culmination of a pro-repeal trend within the national security bureaucracies that ultimately required an executive decision by the White House. Having never agreed with his critics about the efficacy of the sanctions weapon in seeking an end to apartheid, Bush on July 10, 1991, underscored the "irreversible" nature of political change in South Africa and announced the lifting of all punitive measures associated with the 1986 anti-apartheid act.[191] "Since coming to office in 1989," he explained, "President de Klerk has repealed the legislative pillars of apartheid and opened up the political arena to prepare the way for constitutional negotiations, and as I've said on several occasions, I really firmly believe that this progress is irreversible."[192] As a result, bans were lifted on, among other things, trade in various products, the provision of bank loans to the South African government, and new investments by US companies.

The executive branch's decision to lift sanctions was not greeted warmly by those portions of the policymaking establishment that had been in the forefront of the sanctions campaign throughout the 1980s. Members of the House Subcommittee on Africa and the Congressional Black Caucus favored the continuation of sanctions until a new constitution guaranteeing the right to vote for South African blacks was in place, despite the fact that this was not one of the conditions of the 1986 legislation. For these critics, lifting sanctions before obtaining some sort of power-sharing agreement only invited intransigence on the part of the Afrikaner regime. "They will be removed, and it will be tragic," explained Gray on the day Bush announced his decision to repeal sanctions, "If you lift them too soon, you lock in apartheid."[193]

The proponents of maintaining sanctions were severely hampered by the simple reality that South Africa largely had met the conditions originally established by Congress in 1986. As aptly noted by Lugar, one of the original coauthors of the 1986 Anti-Apartheid Act who favored the lifting of sanctions, to change the conditions of the 1986 law to include some sort of power-sharing agreement was tantamount to changing the rules in the middle of a game.[194] Moreover, despite the continued existence of a broad constituency that at the very least wanted the Bush administration to hold off on repealing sanctions, the lack of popular perceptions of an ongoing crisis in South Africa ensured that traditional ideological splits within Congress would hamper any efforts at achieving the number of votes necessary to stop the White House. Indeed, even heightened township violence between Mandela's forces and those supportive of Chief Gatscha Buthelezi's Inkatha Freedom Party, which culminated in the Boipatong massacre of forty-two civilians in June 1992, and led to accusations that the violence was orchestrated by an Afrikaner government still pursuing divide-and-rule policies, was insufficient to alter the direction of US foreign policy toward South Africa.[195] "As long as there is continued, demonstrable progress in South Africa toward the removal of the obstacles," conceded Wolpe, one of the congressional leaders who felt that the Bush administration's embrace of South Africa was premature, "I think Congress will adopt a wait-and-see attitude."[196]

The general movement toward reform in South Africa which continued into January 1993 did not mean that the Bush administration had a free hand in reestablishing the close US–South African ties that existed prior to the mid-1970s. Despite such growing pressures within the national security bureaucracies, the anti-apartheid coalition was sufficiently strong to maintain other forms of sanctions legislation unassociated with the 1986 anti-apartheid act. In addition to a variety of legislation that remains in place at the local, city, and state levels, continued restrictions at the federal level include bans on exports to the South African military and police forces, and any form of intelligence sharing. Although Cohen indicated the possibility of seeking the prosecution of a "test case" in which local anti-apartheid legislation failed to comply with new federal realities, this approach seemed highly unlikely given the continued political concerns of the antiapartheid movement. Whereas the lifting of sanctions in accordance with legislatively mandated conditions was one thing, to seek the reversal of other forms of legislation before actual constitutional changes in South Africa was quite another. It is for this reason that the State Department's Africa Bureau sought to soften the potential domestic firestorm that could have accompanied the lifting of sanctions by ensuring that the decision was announced in consultation with Mandela in the aftermath of a major ANC conference during the first week of July 1990, at the same time giving notice of a doubling in the levels of US assistance (from $40 million to $80 million) devoted to housing, economic development, and education programs for black South Africans.[197]

The most notable foreign policy aspect of the ongoing process of reform in South Africa was that it essentially shifted the policy debate over sanctions within the US policymaking establishment. Prior to 1990, the national security bureaucracies sought to "hold the line" against congressional demands for stricter sanctions against South Africa. In 1990, these roles, in a sense, had shifted as congressional activists became confronted with the necessity of "holding the line" in the face of growing repeal pressures emanating from the national security bureaucracies. The critical element of both of these processes was the absence of crisis in which the national security bureaucracies were able to hold, and subsequently overturn, the sanctions efforts of a variety of governmental and non-governmental forces associated with the anti-apartheid movement. As long as the process of political reform continues to unfold, however slowly, the national security bureaucracies led by the State Department will continue to seek the incremental enhancement of US–South African ties.

Conclusion

The importance of the relationship between the nature of events within Africa and the operation of the US policymaking process is vividly portrayed by the evolution of US interventionist practices in South Africa during the post-World War II period. Since 1948 when the Afrikaner National Party formally institutionalized a pattern of political rule known as apartheid, policymakers were confronted with the dilemma of associating with a minority white-ruled government that discriminated on the basis of race against the majority of its population, and which was increasingly isolated within the international system. Yet the political stability of South Africa from 1948 to 1974 reinforced the historical tendency of both the White House and Congress to ignore South African issues. As a result, US policies toward the Afrikaner government were driven by the parochial, Cold War oriented missions of the State Department, the Pentagon, and the CIA. Although there were some minor shifts in policy during this period – such as the Kennedy administration's adoption of a voluntary arms embargo – they did not substantially deviate from the incrementalist pattern of seeking closer US–South African cooperation. Indeed, the tremendous gap between rhetoric and reality in the Kennedy administration's approach to South Africa clearly demonstrated how bureaucratic missions associated with the Cold War confounded the attempts of activist political appointees to fundamentally alter US–South African cooperation.

The first real assessment of US–South African cooperation at the highest levels of the policymaking establishment did not occur until 1974. During this year, the Portuguese *coup d'état* confronted the Nixon and Ford administrations with a major crisis in southern Africa. In a classic example of when a region of Africa received sustained White House attention, White House policymakers perceived a withdrawing colonial power unwilling to maintain stability in the face of Soviet–Cuban intervention. However, rather than serve as the basis for a significant departure in US foreign policy toward southern Africa, the *realpolitik* worldview of the Nixon–Ford administrations favored close cooperation with the South African government during 1974–76. This cooperation ranged from involvement in a paramilitary war in Angola to the diplomatic resolution of a growing guerrilla insurgency in Southern Rhodesia.

In the aftermath of this crisis, US policy, once again, was primarily driven by the organizational missions of the national security bureaucracies largely independent of either White House or congressional involvement. During the Carter administration, for example, there existed, similar to the Kennedy years, a growing gap between the anti-apartheid rhetoric of senior policymakers and the ongoing efforts of the national security bureaucracies to cooperate with the apartheid government. This gap occurred due to the perceived necessity of enlisting South African involvement in resolving conflicts in both Namibia and Southern Rhodesia. During the initial years of the Reagan administration, this gap was closed by Crocker's quiet pursuit of constructive engagement – a policy whose intellectual origins were derivative of the Nixon administration's policy of communication. Indeed, despite the growing politicization of the issue of apartheid during the late 1970s and early 1980s, especially in the immediate aftermath of the Soweto revolt of 1976, the Africa specialists within the State Department largely remained responsible for the formulation and implementation of US foreign policy toward South Africa.

The most striking aspect of the historical US–South African relationship, however, is its demonstration of the relationship between an extended crisis situation and the role of Congress in seizing the initiative from the executive branch and asserting its influence within the policymaking process. Despite the gradual rise from the 1960s to the 1980s of various anti-apartheid groupings both outside and within the US policymaking establishment committed to the imposition of economic sanctions against South Africa, US policies never went much beyond the more limited restrictions on US–South African military cooperation. It was not until the mid-1980s that, in the face of executive branch intransigence, Congress responded to the extended political crisis in South Africa and passed the Comprehensive Anti-Apartheid Act of 1986. A critical ingredient of this event was the US public's perception of a crisis in South Africa that, as time went by, prompted citizens to place pressure on their representatives in Congress to "do something." Yet once that something was done and the crisis in South Africa began to subside, the traditional partisan and ideological rivalries that hindered unified congressional action reemerged, and Congress was unable to pass further sanctions as policy once again fell under the realm of the national security bureaucracies.

The emerging issue of the post-1990 period was no longer whether to enhance sanctions, but rather *when* they should be repealed. Although the White House ultimately was credited with making the decision to lift sanctions, this action did not necessarily constitute the culmination of ongoing, high-level attention, and instead emerged as a result of rising pressures within the national security bureaucracies to respond positively to evolving political events in South Africa. For example, the State Department's Africa Bureau perceives South Africa as the key to regional economic growth and stability, especially once the thorny issue of black majority rule is resolved and the country becomes a "legitimate" actor within the southern African region. Similarly, the Defense Department looks forward to the day when its ships can routinely dock at South African ports.[198] This issue may become especially salient if deteriorating events in the Middle East once again make the oil route of the Cape of Good Hope of particular strategic importance to the West. Finally, members of the US intelligence community have noted that they look forward to the day when their organizations can renew official ties with what has always been considered to be one of the most efficient and friendly intelligence organizations on the African continent.[199] In short, bureaucratic pressures for

Table 5.1. *US economic and military aid to South Africa (bilateral loans and grants, millions of dollars)*

Program	1985	1986	1987	1988	1989	1990	1991	1992
I. Economic aid – total	–	0.5	7.4	22.4	20.0	22.9	40.0	75.5
A. Aid & predecessors	–	0.5	7.4	22.4	20.0	22.9	40.0	75.5
B. Food for peace	–	–	–	–	–	–	–	–
Title I – total	–	–	–	–	–	–	–	–
Repay. in $-loans	–	–	–	–	–	–	–	–
Pay. in for. curr.	–	–	–	–	–	–	–	–
Title II – total	–	–	–	–	–	–	–	–
Economic relief	–	–	–	–	–	–	–	–
Vol. relief agency	–	–	–	–	–	–	–	–
C. Other econ. grants	–	–	–	–	–	–	–	–
Peace corps	–	–	–	–	–	–	–	–
Other	–	–	–	–	–	–	–	–
D. Other econ. loans	–	–	–	–	–	–	–	–
Export–Import bank	–	–	–	–	–	–	–	–
All other	–	–	–	–	–	–	–	–
II. Military aid – total	–	–	–	–	–	–	–	–
A. MAP grants	–	–	–	–	–	–	–	–
B. Credit financing	–	–	–	–	–	–	–	–
C. IMET	–	–	–	–	–	–	–	–
D. Tran-excess stock	–	–	–	–	–	–	–	–
E. Other grants	–	–	–	–	–	–	–	–
III. ESF	–	13.8	9.2	3.4	13.3	10.0	10.0	–
IV. Total	–	14.3	16.6	25.8	33.3	32.9	50.0	75.5
Loans	–	–	–	–	–	–	–	–
Grants	–	14.3	16.6	25.8	33.3	32.9	50.0	75.5

Figures for 1985–1990 are derived from US Agency for International Development (USAID), *U.S. Overseas Loans and Grants. Series of Yearly Data (Volume IV. Africa). Obligations and Loan Authorizations. FY 1946-FY 1990.* Washington, DC: USAID, 1990.
Figures for 1991–2 were provided by USIA.
(–) no aid provided during the fiscal year
(*) less than $50,000 provided in aid during the fiscal year

the incremental strengthening of traditionally close US–South African ties most likely will multiply as long as the reform process in South Africa continues to unfold in a relatively peaceful manner.

6 US AFRICA POLICIES IN THE POST-COLD WAR ERA

When the elephants fight, the grass suffers.
> Swahili proverb of the 1950s

When the elephants make love, the grass suffers just as much.
> Swahili proverb of the 1990s

Introduction

For the duration of the Cold War, Africa was an arena, even a battle-ground, for East–West conflict, as both the United States and the former Soviet Union sought to win the allegiance of newly independent African countries. Rather than perceiving such competition as a blessing to Africa's future, African critics cited a traditional Swahili proverb – "When the elephants fight, the grass suffers" – to underscore the potential dangers of alignment with either superpower. The pessimistic tone of this proverb indicated that even if individual African countries profited in the short term by dealing with either of the superpowers, Africa as a whole would lose in the long term. When confronted with growing levels of US–Soviet cooperation at the end of the 1980s, African critics questioned exactly what this new form of East–West détente meant for the African continent. Whereas some optimists considered US–Soviet cooperation to be a catalyst for solving some of Africa's most challenging socio-economic and politico-military problems, skeptical observers indicated their views by giving the above-noted Swahili proverb a new twist: "When the elephants make love, the grass suffers just as much."[1]

Cold War rationales and US Africa policies

As demonstrated by the evolution of US foreign policy toward Ethiopia, Somalia, South Africa, and Zaire, the desire of US policymakers to stop the spread of communism and contain perceived Soviet

247

expansionism significantly influenced US interventionist practices on the African continent from the 1950s to the late 1980s. Two themes aptly illustrate Africa's place within the various strategies of containment initially outlined by the Truman administration and applied to Africa, albeit in varying forms, during the Cold War era.

(1) *Africa as a solution for non-African problems.* The most important feature of Washington's containment policies in Africa was an approach that looked upon the continent as a means of solving non-African problems. Rather than being regarded as important in their own right, African countries were perceived by US policymakers as a means of preventing the further advances of Soviet communism, and therefore US relationships with African regimes evolved according to their relative importance within an East–West framework. The US courted Haile Selassie from the 1940s to the 1970s, for example, due to Ethiopia's strategic location and partnership in a global telecommunications surveillance network directed against the Soviet Union. When the security relationship between the US and Ethiopia shattered during the 1970s, the US turned to Siad Barre because access to bases in Somalia could enhance the US military capability to counter any Soviet threats to Middle Eastern oil fields. Similarly, Washington policymakers viewed Mobutu Sese Seko and a host of Afrikaner governments positively because Zaire and South Africa could serve as regional bulwarks against communism. In each of these cases, an overriding US preoccupation with anti-communism led Washington to overlook the authoritarian excesses of these regimes in favor of their willingness to support US containment policies in Africa.

(2) *Africa as a proxy battlefield in East–West conflict.* The second major outcome of Washington's containment policies in Africa was the emergence of the continent as a battlefield for proxy wars as both the US and the Soviet Union became involved in regional conflicts. In almost every case, regional conflict was exacerbated by one superpower's reaction to the other's involvement in a particular crisis situation. Indeed, Soviet involvement, as well as merely the "threat" of Soviet involvement, was enough to capture White House attention, and usually provoke an escalation of the conflict. In the case of Zaire, the political instability of the early independence years, even when coupled with only relatively limited amounts of Soviet involvement, was enough to warrant presidentially authorized covert assassination attempts, as well as two military operations involving limited amounts of US troops and transport aircraft. During the 1975–76 Angolan civil war, Soviet–Cuban involvement led to a tacit US–South African–Zairian alliance in which Washington supported the direct involve-

ment of Zairian and, more onerous from the point of view of most African countries, South African troops. The Reagan administration continued in this tradition and seized upon the Ethiopian–Somali border conflict of 1982 to demonstrate renewed US resolve to stand by anti-communist allies who were threatened by Soviet-backed, communist regimes. In these and other cases, local conflicts having little, if anything, to do with the ideological concerns of communism or capitalism threatened to become East–West flashpoints in the face of growing US–Soviet involvement.

The Cold War foundations of US Africa policies were dramatically called into question by radical changes in the Soviet bloc introduced by Soviet President Mikhail Gorbachev. After emerging in 1985 as the undisputed leader of the Communist Party of the Soviet Union (CPSU), Gorbachev introduced a twofold plan to significantly alter Soviet economic and political structures that became known throughout the West as *perestroika* (economic restructuring) and *glasnost* (political openness). Of greatest interest to US policymakers was Gorbachev's desire to move beyond the confines of the Cold War and seek a form of international cooperation based on the concept of *novoye myslenye* (new political thinking). In the case of Eastern Europe, this policy led to Soviet tolerance of the fall of single-party communist states and a recognition of the need to allow the peoples of Eastern Europe to determine their own political paths independent of Soviet control. Throughout the various regions of the Third World, including Africa, the new political thinking entailed a rejection of revolutionary struggle, calling instead for political negotiations and compromise to resolve ongoing regional disputes and civil wars.[2]

The irony of Gorbachev's initiatives is that they unleashed a variety of forces that ultimately led in 1991 to the fragmentation of the Soviet Union into a collection of smaller independent and non-communist countries. Although the largest of these – the Russian Republic – pledged to seek further cooperation with the United States in a variety of realms – including the resolution of regional conflict in Africa – the reality of the fragmentation of the Soviet Union was a significant shift in the international balance of power as a former superpower ceased to exist. Most important, this event underscored the end of the Cold War and the irrelevance of its related anti-communist rationales. In a stunning example of how the foundations of Cold War policies had disappeared, US policymakers at the beginning of 1993 were embroiled in a fierce debate over how best to ensure future cooperation with Russia and the other newly independent countries of the former Soviet Union.

The post-Cold War era and the future of US Africa policies

As US–Russian cooperation continues to replace the former antagonistic relationship, Washington's Cold War driven policies have changed, and will continue to change, accordingly.[3] Specifically, six trends indicative of US Africa policies in the post-Cold War era have emerged and potentially will intensify in the years to come.

(1) *Reinforcement of the historical tendency to treat Africa as a "back-burner" issue.* Although many Africans are quick to note the tremendous negative impact of the Cold War on Africa, this struggle ironically did lead to greater US attention to the continent. In fact, African leaders often were able to use US–Soviet competition as a bargaining tool to obtain substantial increases in economic and military aid. However, as political changes in Eastern Europe and the newly independent countries of the former Soviet Union continue to dominate the agenda of the US policymaking establishment, Africans rightly have begun to question what this means in terms of future US attention. "The Soviet Union will attract a lot of resources from the Third World, especially Africa," lamented Wilson Ndolo Ayah, Foreign Minister of Kenya. "A lot of Western countries believe there is more profit to be made in Eastern Europe than in Africa, but there's also an ethnic or racial sympathy that doesn't apply to Africa."[4] As explained by B. A. Kiplagat, another member of Kenya's Ministry of Foreign Affairs, "Eastern Europe is the most sexy beautiful girl, and we are an old tattered lady." Capturing the mood of both the US policymaking establishment and the US public, Kiplagat sadly noted that "people are tired of Africa. So many countries, so many wars."[5]

Kiplagat and other diplomats and scholars have correctly discerned that the end of the Cold War has reinforced the tendency within the US policymaking establishment to ignore Africa in favor of other regions of greater concern, such as Western and Eastern Europe and, more recently, the Middle East. As succinctly noted by Michael Clough, Senior Fellow for Africa at the Council on Foreign Relations, this has resulted in a policy of "cynical disengagement" in which policymakers are guided by three principles. (1) "Do not spend much money unless Congress makes you." (2) "Do not let African issues complicate policy toward other, more important parts of the world." and (3) most important, "Do not take stands that might create political controversies in the United States."[6] Indeed, as noted by another observer of US Africa policies, Africa in a sense is becoming the "dark continent" again.[7] In the absence of the rallying points of Soviet

expansionism and anti-communism, the myriad of seemingly insuper-
able socio-economic and politico-military problems besetting the continent foster a tendency within the policymaking establishment to
relegate Africa to "other" countries that "surely know Africa better
than we do."[8]

(2) *Pressure to trim already reduced levels of economic and military aid.*
When combined with domestic pressures to trim the budget deficit
and enhance spending for domestic social programs, the perception
among US policymakers that Africa is less important relative to other
regions of the world in the post-Cold War era has led to significant
budgetary cutbacks in some program offices related to Africa. For
example, in order to staff growing numbers of consulates and embassies in Eastern Europe and the newly independent republics of the
former Soviet Union, the State Department has trimmed approximately seventy positions from its Bureau of African Affairs, and has
closed consulates and embassies in Cameroon, the Comoro Islands,
Kenya, and Nigeria.[9] The US Agency for International Development
(USAID) similarly has cut a variety of programs and staff positions
related to Africa, and reportedly only the "11th-hour intervention" of
the Congressional Black Caucus prevented the Foreign Affairs Committee of the House of Representatives from merging its subcommittees on African and Latin American affairs.[10] The significant drop in US
foreign assistance to the African continent during the 1980s and 1990s
constitutes one of the most vivid examples of Africa's declining fortunes relative to other regions of the world. From 1985 to 1990, for
example, cost-cutting measures associated with the 1986 Gramm-
Rudman-Hollings Deficit Reduction Act led to dramatic cuts in US
military aid to the African continent (minus the roughly $2 billion
annually given to Egypt) from $279.2 million to $11.39 million. Other
forms of security assistance, such as Economic Support Funds (ESF),
similarly dropped from $452.8 million to $58.9 million during this same
period. Although economic aid fared better, it nonetheless dropped
from over $1.14 billion in 1985 to approximately $1.06 billion in 1990.[11]
Most important, when compared with other regions of the world,
Africa's share of US foreign assistance dropped from roughly 10.3
percent ($1.87 billion) of an overall budget of $18.13 billion in 1985, to
approximately 7.5 percent ($1.18 billion) of the $15.73 billion budget for
1990.[12] Indeed, despite the African continent's dubious honor as host
to the largest number of impoverished countries, Central America in
1990 received thirty-four times more aid on a per capita basis.[13]

During the final two years of the Bush administration, Washington's
preoccupation with the end of the Cold War reinforced Africa's

traditional low standing within the aid hierarchy. In addition to responding to a growing sense among the US public that foreign assistance should be invested in a lackluster US economy, the Bush administration trimmed US foreign assistance to the African continent in order to free up funds to reward the transition to democracy in other regions of the world, as well as to pay for the enormous costs associated with the US military operation against Iraq in 1991 known as Operation Desert Storm. In a January 1990 budget address, for example, Bush informed Congress of the administration's intention to reduce aid to Africa specifically in order to free up larger amounts of aid for Poland.[14] Although the African Affairs contituency in Congress was somewhat successful in reversing Africa's marginalization within the aid hierarchy, most notably by increasing Africa's share to 7.6 percent ($1.2 billion) of the $15.8 billion foreign assistance budget for 1992, the policymaking establishment's growing concern with other regions and interests in an altered Cold War environment ensures that proponents will be hard-pressed to maintain, let alone increase, Africa's share of the foreign aid budget. As succinctly noted by Chester Crocker, former Assistant Secretary of State for African Affairs, "Africans could end up paying for the expanding frontiers of freedom everywhere else. That would be an obscene response to the African crisis."[15]

(3) *Continuing importance of the national security bureaucracies as the primary driving forces of US Africa policies.* The third most important outcome of the end of the Cold War has been the reinforcement of the roles of the national security bureaucracies as the primary driving forces of US Africa policies. In the absence of the high-level attention that inevitably resulted from the introduction of an East–West dimension into a particular conflict, the White House has increasingly deferred to the Africa specialists within the State Department, the Pentagon, and the CIA. Moreover, despite the growing watch-dog role of Congress, ongoing ideological and partisan splits within and between the House and the Senate strengthen the position of the Africa specialists within the national security bureaucracies. As a result, bureaucratic interpretations of the national interest as perceived through the parochial filters of bureaucratic missions will serve as the primary guides for the evolution of US Africa policies during the emerging post-Cold War era.

The US response to the escalating civil war in Liberia during 1990 demonstrates the importance of the national security bureaucracies in shaping the future evolution of US Africa policies.[16] Unlike its direct handling of more hardline military operations designed to oust Panamanian dictator Manuel Noriega and to expell Iraq from its illegal occupation of Kuwait – both of which initially were opposed by the State Department's Bureaus of Latin American Affairs and Near Eastern and South Asian Affairs, respectively – the White House deferred to the Africa Bureau's desire to remain relatively neutral in the civil war and seek the negotiated departure of Liberian dictator Samuel Doe.[17] Conscious of African concerns over unilateral super-power intervention on the African continent, the Africa Bureau managed to gain White House approval to seek the negotiated depart-ure of President Doe and, failing that, support of a multilateral occu-pation force led by Nigeria and solely comprised of African troops. Although the White House ultimately did send in the US Marines to ensure the safe departure of approximately 1,100 US civilians and diplomatic personnel residing in the country, their actions were solely limited to this humanitarian goal. At no point did US forces seek to militarily determine the outcome of fighting between government forces and two guerrilla factions vying for control.[18]

In other words, the White House deferred to the Africa Bureau's rec-ommendation to support African efforts to resolve what policymakers perceived as a uniquely African problem within an altered Cold War environment. Most important, the major impetus for bureaucratic interest in the special relationship that has existed since 1847, when Liberia was founded by freed American slaves, was Washington's anxiety not to jeopardize a number of valuable assets. Among these were unimpeded landing and refueling rights for all Pentagon aircraft and ships; the "Omega" navigation station, one of eight such instal-lations found throughout the world, that guide US ships and aircraft within the Atlantic Ocean; and two communications relay stations that carry nearly all US diplomatic and intelligence transmissions (inclusive of the Voice of America) throughout sub-Saharan Africa.

(4) *Rising perceptions of the threat posed by the spread of Islamic funda-mentalism.* A fourth significant outcome of the end of the Cold War is a growing perception within the policymaking establishment that Islamic fundamentalism is a threat to US interests on the African continent.[19] Many officials privately note that the decline of the Soviet Union and communism have created a power vacuum on the African continent that could easily be filled by "radical" forms of Islamic fundamentalism, particularly the "shia" variant espoused by Iran.[20] In a statement indicative of growing concern throughout the policymak-ing establishment, a senior-level Bush administration official noted that the "march of Islamic fundamentalism" was "the single most worrisome trend for policymakers."[21] In a sense, the anti-communist

logic of containment of the Soviet Union during the Cold War era may be in the process of being replaced by an anti-Islamic variant focused specifically on the variety of fundamentalist regimes in the Middle East and North Africa.

The growing concern with Islamic fundamentalism was clearly demonstrated by US foreign policy toward the Sudan at the beginning of 1992.[21] A close ally of the United States during the 1980s, Sudanese President Ja'faar al-Nimeiri was overthrown in a 1986 military *coup d'état*, an event leading to the intensification of a guerrilla war led by the Sudan People's Liberation Army (SPLA), and another successful military coup led by General Omar Hassan al-Bashir in 1989. Bashir's regime is buttressed by the strong support of the National Islamic Front (NIF), an extremely well-organized and vocal fundamentalist group led by Dr. Hassan al-Turabi. The Sudanese military regime earned the strong denunciations of the Bush administration due to Bashir's strict enforcement of sharia (Islamic law) and, most important, his apparent decision to allow for the creation of Iranian-sponsored bases reportedly designed to train Islamic militants for "terrorist" actions throughout Africa. "By January 1992, US officials were telling reporters that Sudan might become a base for exporting Islamic revolution across Africa," explains Raymond W. Copson, a researcher for the Foreign Affairs and National Defense Division of the Congressional Research Service, "although some nongovernment specialists doubted that troubled Sudan would prove very useful to the fundamentalist cause over the long term."[22]

US–Sudanese relations became especially strained in the aftermath of an incident in the southern town of Juba in which Andrew Tombe and Aboudoin Talle, two Sudanese AID employees, were executed by the Sudanese government in September 1992. According to Sudanese officials, the employees had commited treason by utilizing a USAID radio to direct shelling by the insurgent SPLA forces. And, in what one analyst regarded as "an astonishing insult" to the US government, the Sudan's Embassy in London announced that it had "given the US government the benefit of the doubt, assuming that it did not have any knowledge of its employee's illegal activities nor condoned them.[23] Despite official protests by the US Embassy in Khartoum, including a statement by the State Department that the Bashir regime should be condemned for its "clear violation of international legal standards," not only were the executions carried out, but Sudanese authorities refused to provide the whereabouts of other local USAID employees in Juba, and hindered the travel of US diplomats in the southern portion of the country.[24]

(5) *Great power involvement in the resolution of regional conflicts.* An extremely fruitful outcome of the end of the Cold War has been Great Power involvement in the resolution of regional conflicts in Africa.[25] The most dramatic example of what such cooperation can yield was demonstrated by the US–brokered accords of 1988 which linked South Africa's withdrawal from Namibia and independence for that country to the withdrawal of Cuban troops from Angola. In an event of historic proportions, Namibia on March 21, 1990, achieved independence under the leadership of African nationalist Sam Nujoma as one of the few multiracial, multiparty democracies on the African continent. Two important ingredients which facilitated the resolution of this long-standing regional conflict were the efforts of Assistant Secretary of State for African Affairs Chester Crocker to make the US a peace-broker in the negotiating process, and the willingness of the former Soviet Union to pressure its Angolan and Cuban allies to accept a negotiated settlement.[26] Both of these ingredients – which built upon the desires of regional African participants to seek a negotiated settlement – obviously were by-products of a decline in Cold War tensions beginning in the late 1980s.

A highly favorable outgrowth of US–Soviet cooperation in facilitating Namibia's independence was discussion of other conflicts that had been internationalized due to East–West conflict. For example, the issue of US–Soviet cooperation in resolving the various conflicts in the Horn of Africa was raised at a June 1989 meeting between Assistant Secretary of State for African Affairs Herman Cohen and Soviet Deputy Foreign Minister Anatoly Adamishin, and continued well into the aftermath of the overthrow of both the Mengistu and Siad regimes in the first half of 1991. Similarly, the US and the former Soviet Union demonstrated a willingness to facilitate a negotiated settlement of civil wars in Mozambique and Angola, as well as to work together in fostering a peaceful solution to the problem of apartheid in South Africa. Although the fragmentation of the Soviet Union in 1991 and continuing economic and political crisis in its largest successor country (Russia) at the beginning of 1993 effectively preclude any significant involvement for the time being by this former superpower, the US along with the other Great Powers (such as Japan and the former colonial powers) can nonetheless work together as "facilitators" of resolving regional conflict in Africa.[27]

However, a significant constraint on US efforts at resolving regional conflict is the historical neglect of Africa by both the White House and Congress. In order to be successful, US efforts ideally require the interest and support for activist measures at the highest levels of the policymaking establishment. In the case of southern Africa, Crocker's interest in seeking the independence of Namibia was supported at the highest levels of the State Department and, in the aftermath of the Reagan–Gorbachev summits, the White House during the last two years of the Reagan administration. Indeed, resolving issues such as the intensifying civil war in Somalia would be extremely difficult even if the White House made peace in the Horn of Africa its number one priority. Unfortunately, at least from the viewpoint of conflict resolution in Africa, the highest levels of the US policymaking establishment remain primarily concerned with Western and Eastern Europe, the newly independent countries of the former Soviet Union, and flashpoints in the Third World, most notably the Middle East.

One alternative to *direct* US involvement in the resolution of regional conflicts in Africa was the Bush administration's growing reliance on regional and international organizations. Although this trend was indicative of the Bush administration's approach to all the regions of the Third World, one could argue that the lack of high-level interest in the African continent relative to other regions of the world perhaps makes Africa an even more apt candidate for such multilateral diplomacy.[28] In the case of the Liberian civil war, the Bush administration supported the intervention of Nigeria under the auspices of the Economic Community of West African States (ECOWAS), an economic organization that, under Nigeria's leadership, may assume a more proactive security role in the region. As discussed in Chapter 4, the Bush administration similarly sought to make the UN primarily responsible for resolving the intensification of civil conflict and famine in Somalia. Moreover, although the Bush administration eventually authorized US military intervention in Somalia to facilitate famine relief operations, the White House sought and received the support of the UN Security Council, and made it clear that the UN was to assume primary responsibility for political reconstruction. In short, US involvement in the resolution of regional conflicts in Africa during the post-Cold War era may increasingly benefit from closer cooperation with regional and international organizations, such as ECOWAS and the UN.[29]

(6) *Rising debate over making multiparty democracy a precondition of closer US ties.* A final trend of US Africa relations during the emerging post-Cold War era has been a growing, albeit still small, debate over the establishment of multiparty democracy in Africa as a precondition for the improvement of economic and political relations with Washington.[30] Specifically, the downfall of single-party regimes throughout Eastern Europe and the former Soviet Union – the intellectual heart-

land of single-party rule – has raised important questions concerning the viability of this model in Africa. Most important, just as political democratization became a precondition for dramatically expanding levels of US aid to Eastern Europe and the newly independent countries which once comprised the Soviet Union, this concept has filtered through the various other regional bureaus of the State Department, including the Africa Bureau. In Kenya, US Ambassador Smith Hempstone enraged the Kenyan government of President Daniel Arap Moi by publicly calling for the scrapping of Kenya's single-party system. This view was also advanced by Donald K. Petterson, former US Ambassador to Somalia (1978–82) and Tanzania (1986–89), who wrote an editorial in which he argued for greater consideration of tieing development aid to political reforms in Africa.[31]

Policymakers who are seeking to encourage democratization in Africa by making an explicit link between this process and the possibility of closer US relations (particularly in the form of increased levels of US foreign assistance) are confronted with two major contradictions. The first is related to the already cited decline in US foreign assistance to the African continent. Whereas Eastern Europe and the former Soviet Union have been the principal foci of attention within the US policymaking establishment during the last forty years, and therefore the targets of a tremendous growth in US economic and humanitarian aid during the 1990s, African countries, even if they do adopt political reforms, are unlikely to receive greater amounts of resources from a foreign aid budget that places Africa last relative to other regions of the world. Moreover, the majority of US Ambassadors in Africa, as well as the Africa specialists within the national security bureaucracies, are usually less inclined to push for a link between political reforms and economic aid. These individuals often not only wish to avoid offending those they perceive as valuable African clients, but also realize that promises of further economic aid most likely will not materialize even if political reforms are adopted. It is for this reason, for example, that Assistant Secretary of State for African Affairs Cohen consistently emphasized the importance of "sound economic policies" as the basis for non-aid related economic initiatives, such as debt relief.[32] Similar to the position adopted by his predecessors within the Africa Bureau, Cohen emphasized the necessity of African countries finding their own political paths. "While the United States favors a multi-party system," he explained, "who are we to say it is good for everybody?"[33]

A second and more serious contradiction of linking democratization to closer US ties derives from the already cited growing perception within the policymaking establishment that Islamic fundamentalism is a threat to US interests on the African continent. Specifically, a tension has always existed between the often-stated preference for democracy in Africa and perceived national security interests. For example, when during the Cold War era the ideal of democracy clashed with the national security objective of containing communism on the African continent, containment prevailed at the expense of democracy. It is for this reason that a succession of US administrations were willing to downplay the internal shortcomings of a variety of US allies on the African continent – such as Ethiopia's Haile Selassie, Somalia's Siad, Zaire's Mobutu, and a host of Afrikaner regimes in South Africa – in favor of their strong support for US policies of anti-communism and containment.

Although expectations initially were high among US policy analysts and academics that Washington could focus on the normative goal of promoting democracy and human rights in the emerging post-Cold War international system, the US response to events in Algeria in 1991 seemed to indicate that containment of Islamic fundamentalism had replaced anti-communism as at least one security objective that over-rode preferences for democratization. In sharp contrast to rising US denunciations of authoritarianism in other regions of Africa, the poli-cymaking establishment remained surprisingly silent when the Algerian army annulled the first multiparty elections in Algeria since independence and assumed control of the country in a military *coup d'état*. The reason for US silence was not a firm belief in the Algerian generals as guarantors of democracy, but rather was due to the fact that an Islamic fundamentalist party – the Islamic Salvation Front (FIS) – which, among other campaign promises, had called for the strict enforcement of sharia, was on the verge of taking power through the ballot box.[34]

Conclusion

The emergence of the post-Cold War era thus entails both drawbacks and opportunities for the African continent. The downside is that Africa risks sinking even lower in the consciousness of academics, policymakers, and the general public. For better or for worse, the Cold War succeeded in making Africa an integral part of US containment policies and elevated several countries to positions of preeminence at the levels of the national security bureaucracies, the White House, and Congress. Although established bureaucratic missions and the per-ceived threat of Islamic fundamentalism may serve as important constraints on the further deterioration of US ties with the African continent, low levels of economic and military aid and a desire to have regional and international organizations take the lead in conflict resolution suggest Africa's potential marginalization within the policy-making establishment.

In a positive sense, the decline of the Cold War suggests decreasing amounts of US covert and military intervention on the African continent, as well as less foreign assistance for authoritarian clients who used the threat of Soviet expansionism to attract White House attention and support. Moreover, the possibilities are also good for continued cooperation among the Great Powers in resolving African conflicts. Even if the US and other major powers of the world only adopt neutral stances, as opposed to more activist positions either in favor of cooperation or conflict, the stage may be set for African solutions to African problems.

APPENDIX A: NOTE ON METHOD

An important dilemma confronting scholars in the fields of international relations theory and comparative foreign policy is the critique of policymakers that much of the research in academia either lacks policy relevance or is presented in such a fashion as to be "undigestable" to the policymaker attempting to deal with the day-to-day routine of foreign policy management. For example, whereas policymakers often underscore the need for policy-relevant case studies that recognize that no two cases are exactly alike, and therefore must be informed by the rich detail of history, political scientists, particularly those associated with the behavioral revolution in the social sciences, seek the construction and cumulation of theories which identify pertinent variables and causal patterns, and therefore transcend individual cases and time periods. In short, there exists what has been referred to as a "policy-relevance gap" between the needs of policymakers and the research carried out in academia.

This book seeks to bridge the policy-relevance gap by offering an analysis of US intervention in Africa that responds to the needs and interests of both policymakers within the foreign policy establishment and theorists within the broad fields of comparative foreign policy and international relations theory. The most appropriate method that responds to the policy-relevance gap is that of "structured, focused comparison" of a selected number of well-chosen case studies. As explained by Alexander L. George, such a method is "focused" in the sense that it seeks to deal selectively with only certain aspects of the case studies in question.[1] It is "structured" in the sense that it utilizes general questions to guide the data collection and analysis of those cases. This method combines the historian's eye for providing "detailed and discriminating explanations of single historical outcomes" with the political scientist's specialization in "techniques for generalizing from and explaining the variance among historical outcomes."[2] "In other words," explains George, "the task is to convert 'lessons of history' into a comprehensive *theory* that encompasses the complexity of the phenomenon or activity in question."[3] Such an approach recognizes both the unique aspects of individual historical cases, as well as the generalized patterns and relationships which emerge from these cases, which subsequently can "contribute to an orderly, cumulative development of knowledge and theory about the phenomenon in question."[4]

As the method of structured, focused comparison can be applied to a host of differing approaches to case analysis, the specific type of case analysis adopted in this study is that known as "disciplined-configurative."[5] The four basic elements or "rules" of this approach have been summarized as follows:

1. The researcher recognizes the necessity for case-specific knowledge that only detailed case research can provide, yet concomitantly also sees the difficulties in generalizations from such unique case analyses. Thus, it becomes necessary to examine cases through an "analytical/inductive" framework that focuses the research into generalizable factors or variables that are utilized to examine a specific class of behavior.
2. An inductive element is introduced in that the researcher is intellectually aware not only of the behavior to be studied but of its general patterns across cases and of the salient factors that appear important. Consequently, variables are pre-selected based in part on prior theoretical work and also on pre-case work to examine assumptions and hypotheses.
3. The hypotheses and assumptions regarding the interplay of these variables and their effects are stated prior to the research so they can be evaluated against the weight of evidence.
4. Finally, the framework is amenable to adaptation based on the introduction of new knowledge from the subsequent case analyses.[6]

The disciplined-configurative case study approach is applied to three case studies: Zaire (Chapter 3), Ethiopia–Somalia (Chapter 4), and South Africa (Chapter 5). The case studies were chosen with two important criteria in mind. First, cases were chosen that witnessed extensive levels of US involvement during the entire post-World War II period. This was deemed important in order to fully understand the evolution of US Africa policies, particularly as concerned the changes (or lack of changes) in policies as different administrations assumed office in Washingtion. Second, as a result of prior research, cases were chosen that seemingly reflected, and therefore provided the best tests of, the three patterns more fully explained in Chapter 2. Toward this end, each of the case studies is representative of a dominant pattern of US Africa policies (although each, of course, embodies elements of all three patterns). The dominant pattern of each case study is as follows: routine situations and bureaucratic politics (Ethiopia–Somalia); crisis situations and presidential politics (Zaire); and extended crisis situations and congressional politics (South Africa). The analysis focuses on the similarities and differences among, as well as longitudinally between various time periods within, each case study.

APPENDIX B: NOTE ON
INTERVIEW TECHNIQUES

A fascinating aspect of the research process was interviewing approximately 100 individuals who, as either current or past members of the US policymaking establishment, contributed to the framing of the various policies described in this volume. It is the remembrances of these individuals that provided a context and tone for the various periods examined which were simply impossible to obtain from written sources. Rather than provide a laundry list of interview techniques which have been examined exhaustively by other researchers in the field,[1] I simply wish to note four issues of the interview process which were of particular relevance to this study.

The first issue revolved around whether to use a standardized set of questions or a more open-ended interview technique. Due to the historical nature of the project which focused on US foreign policies toward four African countries during a period spanning more than fifty years, interviews were used as an important means of filling in controversial gaps in the historical record. For example, as discussed in Chapter 4, interviews were crucial in determining the extremely controversial role of the CIA in successfully promoting certain Somali candidates in that country's 1967 parliamentary elections. As a result, each interview inevitably required the formulation of questions unique to that country or historical period. However, this open-ended interview technique usually was complemented by a brief series of questions that sought to obtain individual perceptions of the three major patterns of the policymaking process described in Chapter 2. Specifically, these questions were designed to explore the relationship between routine situations and bureaucratic politics, crisis situations and presidential politics, and extended crisis situations and domestic politics.

A second issue revolved around whether the interviewer should begin at the "top" or at the lower rungs of the policymaking establishment. In the case of the State Department, for example, should one begin with the Assistant Secretaries of State for African Affairs or the

Desk Officers for individual African countries? My approach, which was particularly fruitful as concerned the State Department, was to begin at the top and work my way downward. The obvious advantages to such an approach, if one is successful, is that lower-level bureaucrats are much more willing to talk and provide detail if they are made aware of the fact that one already has had one or two interviews with their superiors. In this regard, it is advantageous to first start with a senior-level official (such as an Assistant Secretary of State for African Affairs) who no longer is serving in an official capacity within the policymaking establishment. Once achieving this interview, this diplomatically can be mentioned to enormous benefit when seeking access to current officials at the same level.

Another issue revolved around whether or not to use a tape recorder. The most important advantage of using a tape recorder – my first choice in all interview settings – is that it frees up the interviewer from the necessity of taking notes, a process which can often impede a more natural, relaxed conversation, particularly as concerns eye contact and the reading of body language. A problem with using tape recorders, however, is that their creation of an oral record of sensitive issues may actually inhibit a free exchange of ideas, even when the interviewee has been guaranteed strict confidentiality. In this regard, I found that members of Congress, as well as current members of the CIA and the Defense Department, especially were prone to reject the use of the tape recorder. In these cases, note-taking was kept to a minimum and restricted to simply capturing key words and phrases. In order not to lose the flavor of these interviews, I immediately retired to a quiet spot following the session in order to write a brief summary of each of the key words and phrases marked during the interview. In short, what may be clear immediately following the interview may not necessarily be the case several months down the road when one is attempting to synthesize dozens of interviews into a coherent argument.

A final issue revolves around the importance of internships or some other means of working within the policymaking establishment in order to gain access. I was pleasantly surprised that my three-month stint during 1987 as a State Department intern at the US Embassy in Djibouti City, Djibouti, was invaluable in opening up a variety of doors throughout the policymaking establishment. Beginning with the individuals that I had met while working at the Embassy, these interviews resulted in phone calls and letters that subsequently contributed to the opening of further doors within the various bureaucracies back in Washington, DC. The primary lesson of this brief point is that, if one is seeking privileged access to certain portions of the policymaking establishment, almost any job, however brief, within that realm can be crucial in opening doors that are usually closed to the outsider.

See the endnotes section of each chapter for the name, title, and date of interview of those individuals willing to make their comments for the public record. In addition to these individuals, approximately seventy other people were interviewed but requested strict confidentiality. They are listed in the endnotes sections as follows: Confidential interview no. **. Unless otherwise noted, each individual was interviewed in Washington, DC.

NOTES

1 An introduction to US foreign policy toward Africa

1 Henry F. Jackson, *From the Congo to Soweto: US Foreign Policy Toward Africa Since 1960* (New York: Quill, 1984), p. 18.

2 Richard M. Nixon, "The Emergence of Africa, Report to President Eisenhower by Vice President Nixon," *Department of State Bulletin* 36, 930 (April 22, 1957): 640.

3 John F. Kennedy, "The Challenge of Imperialism: Algeria," in Theodore C. Sorensen, *"Let the Word Go Forth": The Speeches, Statements, and Writings of John F. Kennedy* (New York: Delacorte Press, 1988), pp. 331–37.

4 John F. Kennedy, "The New Nations of Africa," in Theodore C. Sorensen, *"Let the Word Go Forth"*, pp. 365, 368.

5 Quoted in Helen Kitchen, "The Making of US Policy Toward Africa," in Robert I. Rotberg, ed., *Africa in the 1990s and Beyond: US Policy Opportunities and Choices* (Algonac, MI: Reference Publications, 1988), p. 14.

6 Peter Duignan and L. H. Gann, *The United States and Africa: A History* (Cambridge: Cambridge University Press, 1984), p. 9.

7 A note is in order concerning the adoption throughout this book of the title "African American" – a term that has not received complete acceptance within the black community – whenever referring to US citizens whose cultural heritage is the African continent. For a discussion of the term's origins and some of the controversy surrounding its adoption, see Ben L. Martin, "From Negro to Black to African American," *Political Science Quarterly*, 106, 1 (Spring 1991): 83–108.

8 See, for example, Immanuel Wallerstein, *Africa and the Modern World* (Trenton, NJ: Africa World Press, 1986), p. 80.

9 "Putting Djibouti on the Map for Senator Jesse Helms," *New York Times*, April 24, 1987, p. A14.

10 Qaddafi promotes a "third" path of development based upon Islamic values as outlined in his three-volume *Green Book*. For a detailed analysis of Qaddafi's rule, see René Lemarchand, ed., *The Green and the Black: Qadhafi's Policies in Africa* (Bloomington: Indiana University Press, 1988).

11 For examples of Somali rhetoric, see Republic of Somalia, *Somali National Development Plan: 1982–1986* (Mogadishu: Government Printing Office, 1982). For a detailed discussion of Somalia's evolution from support for "scientific socialism" to strong adherence to International Monetary Fund directives for a capitalist, export-run economy, see David D. Laitin and Said

S. Samatar, *Somalia: Nation in Search of a State* (Boulder: Westview, 1987), esp. ch. 5.

12 These observations result from reactions to lectures given by the author to first year university students at the University of South Carolina (Columbia) and Loyola University of Chicago.

13 For analyses of media programming about Africa, see "Capturing the Continent: US Media Coverage of Africa," *Africa News Special Report* (Durham, NC: Africa News, 1990); Paul Harrison and Robin Palmer, *News Out of Africa: Biafra to Band Aid* (London: Hillary Shipman, 1986); and Mary Anne Fitzgerald, "The News Hole: Reporting Africa," *Africa Report* (July–August 1989): 59–61.

14 Quoted in Michael Paul Maren, "Assignment Africa," *Africa Report* 32, 2 (March–April 1987): 68.

15 *Ibid.*

16 Helen Kitchen, *US Interests in Africa* (New York: Praeger, 1983), p. 9. See also Kitchen, "Still on Safari," in L. Carl Brown, ed., *Centerstage: American Diplomacy Since World War Two* (New York: Holmes and Meier, 1990), pp. 171–92.

17 Maren, "Assignment Africa," p. 68.

18 For analyses of the relationship between academics and the policymaking establishment in the formulation of US Africa policies, see Larry W. Bowman, "Government Officials, Academics, and the Process of Formulating US National Security Policy Toward Africa," *Issue* 19, 1 (Winter 1990): 5–20; Michael Bratton, "Academic Analysis and US Economic Assistance Policy on Africa," *Issue* 19, 1 (Winter 1990): 21–37; David S. Wiley, "The United States Congress and Africanist Scholars," *Issue* 19, 2 (Summer 1991): 4–13; Michael Bratton, Reinhard Heinisch, and David S. Wiley, "How Africanists View US Policy: Results of a Survey," *Issue* 19, 2 (Summer 1991): 14–30; "Appendix; Questionnaire: Africanist Scholarship and US Policy Making on Africa," *Issue* 19, 2 (Summer 1991): 31–37; and David S. Wiley, "Academic Analysis and US Policy-Making on Africa: Reflections and Conclusions," *Issue* 19, 2 (Summer 1991): 38–48. See also Martin Staniland, *American Intellectuals and African Nationalists, 1955–1970* (New Haven: Yale University Press, 1991).

19 Crawford Young, "United States Foreign Policy Toward Africa: Silver Anniversary Reflections," *African Studies Review* 27, 3 (September 1984): 14.

20 N. Brian Winchester, "United States Policy Toward Africa," *Current History* 87, 529 (May 1988): 193.

21 Michael Clough, *Free at Last? US Policy Toward Africa and the End of the Cold War* (New York: Council on Foreign Relations Press, 1992), p. 2.

22 Richard H. Mahoney, *JFK: Ordeal in Africa* (New York: Oxford University Press, 1983), p. 244.

23 See Peter J. Schraeder, "The Faulty Assumptions of US Foreign Policy in the Third World," in Ted Galen Carpenter, ed., *Collective Defense or Strategic Independence? Alternative Strategies for the Future* (Washington, DC: Cato Institute; and Lexington, Massachusetts: Lexington Books, 1989), pp. 151–74.

24 See, for example, Pauline H. Baker, "United States Foreign Policy in Southern Africa," *Current History* 86, 520 (May 1987): 193–96, 225–27.

25 Young, "United States Foreign Policy," p. 21.

26 See John Marcum, "The Politics of Indifference: Portugal and Africa, a Case Study in American Foreign Policy," *Issue* 2, 3 (Fall 1972): 9–17.
27 See David D. Laitin, "Security, Ideology, and Development on Africa's Horn," in Rotberg, ed., *Africa in the 1990s and Beyond*, pp. 206–9.
28 Young, "United States Foreign Policy," p. 1.
29 For a discussion of this point, from which this paragraph was drawn, see Peter J. Schraeder, ed., *Intervention into the 1990s: US Foreign Policy in the Third World* (Boulder: Lynne Rienner Publishers, 1992), pp. 1–2.
30 David A. Korn, *Ethiopia, the United States and the Soviet Union* (Carbondale and Edwardsville: Southern Illinois University Press, 1986).

2 Pattern and process in US foreign policy toward Africa

1 Donald J. Puchala, "Of Blind Men, Elephants and International Integration," *Journal of Common Market Studies* 10, 3 (March 1972): 267.
2 Of course, unlike the story of the blind men and the elephant, many analysts consciously *choose* to center on one part of the elephant.
3 Quoted in Theodore C. Sorensen, *Decision-Making in the White House: The Olive Branch or the Arrows* (New York: Columbia University Press, 1963).
4 *Ibid.*
5 Although Kennedy also portrayed a vigorous interest in Africa, this must be viewed in relative terms to his interest in all the emerging areas of the Third World, others of which commanded much more attention. See Arthur M. Schlesinger, Jr., *A Thousand Days: John F. Kennedy in the White House* (Greenwich, CT: Fawcett Publications, 1967), esp. ch. 21.
6 Jimmy Carter, *Keeping Faith: Memoirs of a President* (New York: Bantam Books, 1982), pp. xiii–xiv.
7 See Steven Metz, "American Attitudes Toward Decolonization in Africa," *Political Science Quarterly* 99, 3 (Fall 1984): 521.
8 Waldemar A. Nielson, *The Great Powers and Africa* (New York: Praeger, 1969), p. 302.
9 See John Marcum, "The Politics of Indifference: Portugal and Africa, a Case Study in American Foreign Policy," *Issue* 2, 3 (Fall 1972): 9–17.
10 George Ball, *The Disciples of Power* (Boston: Little, Brown, 1968), p. 240.
11 US Department of State, "Guidelines for Policy and Operations, Africa," March 1962, p. 1. Declassified document from the Kennedy Library. Reproduced in microfiche series produced by University Publications of America, *Africa: National Security Files, 1961–1963*, Reel no. 1.
12 For an overview of US containment efforts in Africa, see F. Ugboaja Ohaegbulam, "Containment in Africa: From Truman to Reagan," *Trans-Africa Forum* 6, 1 (Fall 1988): 7–34.
13 Statement by Francis Kornegay, Jr., chairperson of a panel, "Great Power Relations After Perestroika," 31st Annual Meeting of the African Studies Association, McCormick Center Hotel, Chicago, IL, October 28–31, 1988.
14 See James C. Thomson, Jr., "How Could Vietnam Happen? An Autopsy," *The Atlantic* (1968): 47–53.
15 See Morton H. Halperin, *Bureaucratic Politics & Foreign Policy* (Washington, DC: The Brookings Institution, 1974).

16 African issues previously were handled by State's Bureau of Near Eastern and African Affairs, which itself was preceded by the Bureau of Near Eastern, South Asian and African Affairs.

17 This line of reasoning also holds true for the politically appointed Assistant Secretaries of State for African Affairs, including Crocker. As one author noted, "In previous administrations [to that of Reagan], the Africa Bureau generally held a perspective more accommodating to African interests than other power centers within the government. Although its political spectrum was shifted considerably to the right, the Reagan administration was no exception to this general rule – its ideological center of gravity has been to Crocker's right." See William Minter, "Destructive Engagement: The United States and South Africa in the Reagan Era," in Phyllis Johnson and David Martin, eds., *Frontline Southern Africa: Destructive Engagement* (New York: Four Walls Eight Windows, 1988), p. 397.

18 See Bowman, "Government Officials, Academics."

19 Previous to that date, the region of Africa within the DDO was divided between the CIA's European and Middle Eastern Divisions. The DDI, however, still combines Africa with Latin America under the Office of African and Latin American Analysis. For a critical anthology of CIA activities in Africa, see Ellen Ray, William Schaap, Karl Van Meter, and Louis Wolf, eds., *Dirty Work 2: The CIA in Africa* (Secaucus, NJ: Lyle Stuart, 1979).

20 The centrality of the Soviet threat is best summarized by a former CIA case officer: "The Soviet Union was the enemy, and the 'Soviet target' our intelligence mission. We were professionally and emotionally committed to a single purpose. We felt ourselves as much a part of the American crusade against Stalin as we had against Hitler." See Harry Rositzke, *The CIA's Secret Operations* (New York: Reader's Digest Press, 1977), p. 13.

21 See Daniel Volman, "Africa's Rising Status in American Defense Policy," *Journal of Modern African Studies* 22, 1 (1984): 143–51.

22 African issues were handled prior to 1982 by the Deputy Assistant Secretary of Defense for the Near East, Africa, and South Asia.

23 Also involved in a very minor way are the varying (but limited) sized security detachments of the US Marines that guard US Embassies in Africa. For a variety of Pentagon perspectives on US Africa policies, see the papers presented at a panel, "US Defense Perspectives on Sub-Saharan Africa," 32nd Annual Meeting of the African Studies Association, Hyatt Regency Hotel, Atlanta, Georgia, November 3, 1989: Gregory H. Bradford, "The Importance of Defense Interests in US Foreign Policy in Africa"; Bryant P. Shaw, "Internal and External Threats to US Interests in Africa"; Bernd McConnell, "US Security Assistance in Africa: A Traditional View"; and Vincent D. Kern, "Synergy: Non-Traditional Security Assistance in Africa." See also William J. Foltz, "Africa in Great-Power Strategy," in William J. Foltz and Henry S. Bienen, eds., *Arms and the African: Military Influences on Africa's International Relations* (New Haven and London: Yale University Press, 1985), esp. pp. 21–22.

24 For a critical view of USAID's activities in Africa, see Sean Gervasi, Ann Seidman, Immanuel Wallerstein, and David Wiley, "Why We Said No to A.I.D." *Issue* 7, 4 (Winter 1977): 35–38.

25 For an overview of USIA's role in Africa, see Donald Culverson, "The US Information Agency in Africa," *TransAfrica Forum* 6, 2 (Winter 1989): 61–80.
26 The observations in this paragraph are based on my internship with the State Department's Bureau of African Affairs at the US Embassy in Djibouti during the summer and fall of 1987.
27 Quotes from John Stockwell, *In Search of Enemies: A CIA Story* (New York: W. W. Norton, 1978), p. 63.
28 The following account is based on Michael Brown, Gary Freeman, and Kay Miller, *Passing By: The United States and Genocide in Burundi, 1972* (Washington, DC: Carnegie Endowment for International Peace, c. 1972). See also the account by Thomas Patrick Melady, the US Ambassador to Burundi from 1969 to 1972: *Burundi: The Tragic Years* (New York: Orbis Books, 1974).
29 Brown, Freeman, and Miller, *Passing By*, p. 12.
30 *Ibid.*
31 For a discussion of these and other factors, see John R. Oneal, *Foreign Policy Making in Times of Crisis* (Columbus: Ohio State University Press, 1982). See also John D. Steinbruner, *The Cybernetic Theory of Decision: New Dimensions of Political Analysis* (Princeton: Princeton University Press, 1974); and Graham T. Allison, *The Essence of Decision: Explaining the Cuban Missile Crisis* (Boston: Little, Brown, 1971).
32 Halperin, *Bureaucratic Politics & Foreign Policy*, p. 99.
33 See Hedrick Smith, *The Power Game: How Washington Works* (New York: Random House, 1988), esp. chs. 8 and 15.
34 For more detail, see Richard D. Mahoney, *JFK: Ordeal in Africa* (New York and Oxford: Oxford University Press, 1983), pp. 189–90, 195–97, 204–6.
35 *Ibid.*, pp. 209, 215.
36 Dean Acheson, *Grapes from Thorns* (New York: W. W. Norton, 1969), p. 187. See also Douglas Brinkley and G. E. Thomas, "Dean Acheson's Opposition to African Liberation," *TransAfrica Forum* 5, 4 (Summer 1988): 63–83.
37 Schlesinger, *A Thousand Days*, pp. 536–37.
38 For a discussion of the incrementalist approach compared to the more classic "rationalist" approach, see David Nachmias and David H. Rosenbloom, *Bureaucratic Government USA* (New York: St. Martin's, 1980), pp. 24–28.
39 Confidential interview no. 31.
40 Confidential interview no. 32.
41 *Ibid.*
42 US Agency for International Development (USAID), *US Overseas Loans and Grants, Series of Yearly Data (Volume IV, Africa), Obligations and Loan Authorizations, FY 1946–FY 1987* (Washington, DC: USAID, 1990).
43 Quoted in Halperin, *Bureaucratic Politics & Foreign Policy*, p. 292. See also Frederick C. Mosher, W. David Clinton, and Daniel G. Lang, *Presidential Transitions and Foreign Affairs* (Baton Rouge and London: Louisiana State University Press, 1987).
44 The study of crisis has enjoyed a rich history which can essentially be divided into two basic approaches – systemic and decisionmaking – both of which fundamentally orient the type of definition adopted. For an overview of these approaches, see Charles F. Hermann, "International Crisis as

a Situational Variable," in James N. Rosenau, ed., *International Politics and Foreign Policy* (New York: The Free Press, 1969). For an application of the concept of crisis within an African context, see Gerald J. Bender, James S. Coleman, and Richard L. Sklar, eds., *African Crisis Areas and US Foreign Policy* (Berkeley: University of California Press, 1985).

45 Interview with Richard Moose, Assistant Secretary of State for African Affairs under the Carter administration, Washington, DC, June 26, 1989.

46 Quoted in J. Gus Liebenow, *African Politics: Crises and Challenges* (Bloomington and Indianapolis: Indiana University Press, 1986), p. 272.

47 For more detail, see F. Chidozie Ogene, *Interest Groups and the Shaping of Foreign Policy: Four Case Studies of United States Africa Policy* (New York: St. Martin's, 1983). See also John J. Stremlau, *The International Politics of the Nigerian Civil War 1967–1970* (Princeton: Princeton University Press, 1977).

48 Ogene, *Interest Groups*, p. 84.

49 For more detail, see Kevin Danaher, *The Political Economy of US Policy Toward South Africa* (Westview: Boulder, 1985), p. 109.

50 For a discussion of this concept, see Gabriel Kolko, *Confronting the Third World: United States Foreign Policy 1945–1980* (New York: Pantheon, 1988).

51 Brown, Freeman, and Miller, *Passing By*, p. 13.

52 Included were the bureaus of African Affairs, European and Canadian Affairs, Policy Planning, and Intelligence and Research.

53 For an analysis of this topic, from which the discussion throughout the remainder of this chapter is based, see Gerald J. Bender, "Kissinger in Angola: Anatomy of Failure," in René Lemarchand, ed., *American Policy in Southern Africa: The Stakes and the Stance* (Lanham, MD: University Press of America, 1981). See also Nathaniel Davis, "The Angola Decision of 1975: A Personal Memoir," *Foreign Affairs* 57, 1 (Fall 1978): 109–24; and William Hyland, *Mortal Rivals* (New York: Random House, 1987).

54 Stockwell, *In Search of Enemies*, p. 41.

55 Quoted in Bender, "Kissinger in Angola," p. 105.

56 *Ibid.*

57 Marcum, "The Politics of Indifference," p. 10.

58 Schlesinger, *A Thousand Days*, pp. 536–37.

59 Oneal, *Foreign Policy Making*, p. 42.

60 See Harry S. Truman, *Memoirs*, 2 vols. (Garden City: Doubleday, 1955, 1956); and Dean Acheson, *Present at the Creation: My Years in the State Department* (New York: W. W. Norton, 1969). For an overview of Acheson's beliefs on Africa, see Brinkley and Thomas, "Dean Acheson's Opposition to African Liberation."

61 In a speech before a joint session of Congress on March 12, 1947, Truman invoked this premise by painting the Greek civil war as a contest between Soviet-supplied communists and Western democratic forces of freedom, subsequently calling upon the American people "to support free peoples who are resisting attempted subjugation by armed minorities or by outside pressures." See Ronald J. Stupak, *American Foreign Policy: Assumptions, Processes and Projections* (New York: Harper & Row, 1976), p. 188.

62 For example, the now famous National Security Council Memorandum no. 68 (NSC-68) portrayed the Soviet Union "as indistinguishable from a

world-wide Communist revolutionary movement, newly capable of initiating a war against the West and intent on world domination." Quoted in Richard A. Melanson, *Writing History and Making Policy: The Cold War, Vietnam, and Revisionism* (Lanham, MD: University Press of America, 1983), p. 13.

63 See Dwight D. Eisenhower, *Peace with Justice* (New York: Columbia University Press, 1961); and Eisenhower, *Waging Peace, 1956–1961* (Garden City: Doubleday, 1965).

64 Quoted in John Foster Dulles, "The Cost of Peace," *Department of State Bulletin* (June 18, 1956): 999–1004.

65 See Madeleine G. Kalb, *The Congo Cables: The Cold War in Africa – From Eisenhower to Kennedy* (New York: Macmillan, 1982), esp. ch. 9; and Stephen R. Weissman, *American Foreign Policy in the Congo: 1960–1964* (Ithaca and London: Cornell University Press, 1974), esp. ch. 4.

66 See Thomas J. Schoenbaum, *Waging Peace and War: Dean Rusk in the Truman, Kennedy, and Johnson Years* (New York: Simon & Schuster, 1988), p. 413. For Johnson's personal narrative, see *The Vantage Point: Perspectives on the Presidency, 1963–1969* (New York: Holt, Rinehart and Winston, 1971).

67 For Nixon's personal account, see *RN: The Memoirs of Richard Nixon*, 2 vols. (New York: Warner Books, 1978). For Gerald Ford's personal account, see *A Time to Heal: The Autobiography of Gerald R. Ford* (New York: Harper & Row, 1979). For Kissinger's perspective, see *White House Years* (Boston: Little Brown, 1979); and *Years of Upheaval* (Boston: Little Brown, 1982). For a critical assessment, see Roger Morris, *Uncertain Greatness: Henry Kissinger and American Foreign Policy* (New York: Harper & Row, 1977).

68 Carter, for example, in a now famous speech at Notre Dame University in 1977, noted: "Being confident of our own future, we are now free of that inordinate fear of communism which once led us to embrace any dictator who joined us in that fear . . . .This approach failed, with Vietnam the best example of its intellectual and moral poverty." See Jimmy Carter, "A Foreign Policy Based on America's Essential Character," *Department of State Bulletin* (June 13, 1977): 621–22.

69 See Carter, *Keeping Faith: Memoirs of a President*; Zbigniew Brzezinski, *Power and Principle: Memoirs of the National Security Adviser 1977–1981* (New York: Farrar, Straus, Giroux, 1983); and Cyrus Vance, *Hard Choices: Critical Years in America's Foreign Policy* (New York: Simon & Schuster, 1983).

70 See Anthony Lake, "Africa in a Global Perspective," *Department of State Bulletin* (December 12, 1977): 843.

71 For a variety of insider's accounts, see William Niskanen, *Reaganomics: An Insider's Account of the Policies and the People* (New York: Oxford University Press, 1988); Nancy Reagan, *My Turn: The Memoirs of Nancy Reagan* (New York: Random House, 1989); Donald Regan, *For the Record: From Wall Street to Washington* (San Diego: Harcourt, Brace, Jovanovich, 1988); Larry Speakes, with Robert Pack, *Speaking Out: The Reagan White House* (New York: Charles Scribner's Sons, 1988); and David Stockman, *The Triumph of Politics: Why the Reagan Revolution Failed* (New York: Harper & Row, 1986).

72 Quoted in Arthur Schlesinger, Jr., "Foreign Policy and the American Character," *Foreign Affairs* 62, 1 (Fall 1983): 5.

73 Reagan himself chided this conflict within his administration in 1981: "Sometimes my right hand doesn't know what my far right hand is doing." Quoted in Laurence I. Barrett, *Gambling With History: Reagan in the White House* (Harmondsworth: Penguin, 1984), p. 61.

74 For discussion, see Charles W. Kegley, Jr., "The Bush Administration and the Future of American Foreign Policy: Pragmatism, or Procrastination?" *Presidential Studies Quarterly* 12 (1989): 717–31; and Charles W. Kegley, Jr. and Eugene R. Wittkopf, *American Foreign Policy: Pattern and Process* (New York: St. Martin's Press, 1991), pp. 544–60. For an analysis specifically related to Africa, see Donald Rothchild and John Ravenhill, "Retreat From Globalism: US Policy Toward Africa in the 1990s," in Kenneth A. Oye, Robert J. Lieber, Donald Rothchild, eds., *Eagle in a New World: American Grand Strategy in the Post-Cold War Era* (New York: Harper Collins, 1991).

75 Quoted in Don Oberdorfer, "Bush Finds Theme of Foreign Policy: 'Beyond Containment'," *The Washington Post*, May 28, 1989, p. A30.

76 The following two paragraphs are based on Bender, "Kissinger in Angola."

77 Quotes on the Angolan civil war are taken from Kissinger's testimony before the Africa Subcommittee of the Senate Foreign Relations Committee, January 29, 1976. See Henry Kissinger, "Implications of Angola for Future US Foreign Policy," *Department of State Bulletin* 74, 1912 (February 16, 1976): 174–82. See also Ford's letter to Congress, which reiterates the main points that Kissinger makes in his testimony, as reproduced in the same issue under the title, "President Ford Reiterates US Objective in Angola" (pp. 182–83).

78 For an overview of congressional influence in US foreign policy, see Jerel A. Rosati, "Congressional Influence in American Foreign Policy: Addressing the Controversy," *Journal of Political and Military Sociology* 12 (Fall 1984): 311–33. For a summary of congressional activities related to Africa at the beginning of the 1990s, see "Congress and Africa: New Realities in a New Decade," *Washington Notes on Africa* (Spring 1991).

79 Danaher, *The Political Economy of US Policy Toward South Africa*, p. 49.

80 Confidential interview no. 45.

81 Danaher, *The Political Economy of US Policy Toward South Africa*, p. 61.

82 Chester A. Crocker, "The US Policy Process and South Africa," in Alfred O. Hero, Jr. and John Barratt, eds., *The American People and South Africa: Publics, Elites, and Policymaking Processes* (Lexington: Lexington Books, 1981), p. 49.

83 Interview with Charles C. Diggs, former chairperson of the House Subcommittee on Africa, Washington, DC, June 13, 1989.

84 See John Joseph Seiler, "The Formulation of US Policy Toward Southern Africa, 1957–1976: The Failure of Good Intentions," Ph.D. dissertation, University of Connecticut, 1976, p. 275. Prior to 1959, the Senate Foreign Relations Committee had no permanent subcommittees. Other chairs of the subcommittee have included John F. Kennedy (1959–60), Albert Gore (1961–63), Mike Mansfield (1963–64), Frank J. Lausche (1965–66), Eugene J. McCarthy (1967–69), Gale W. McGee (1969–72), Hubert H. Humphrey (1973–74), Dick Clark (1975–78), George McGovern (1979–80), Nancy Kassebaum (1981–86), and Paul Simon (1987-).

85 Francis A. Kornegay, Jr., *Washington and Africa: Reagan, Congress, and an*

African Affairs Constituency in Transition (Washington, DC: African Bibliographic Center, 1982), p. 14.

86 Confidential interviews with individuals associated with the House Subcommittee on Africa and the Congressional Black Caucus.

87 Prior to 1959, the House Foreign Affairs Committee placed responsibility for Africa under the Near Eastern and Africa Subcommittee. The chairpersons of the House Subcommittee on Africa include Barratt O'Hara (1959–68), Charles C. Diggs (1969–78), Stephen J. Solarz (1979–82), Howard Wolpe (1981–91), Mervyn Dymally (1991-93), and Harry Johnson (1993–).

88 Howard Wolpe, "Africa and the US House of Representatives," *Africa Report* 29, 4 (July–August 1984): 68.

89 For a discussion of the role of Congress in allocating aid to Africa, see Carol Lancaster, "US Aid to Africa: Who Gets What, When, and How?" *CSIS Africa Notes* 25 (March 31, 1984); and Carol Lancaster, *US Aid to Sub-Saharan Africa: Challenges, Constraints, and Change* (Washington, DC: CSIS, 1988).

90 For a discussion of US aid policies in Africa, see Jeffrey Herbst, *US Economic Policy Toward Africa* (New York: Council on Foreign Relations Press, 1992). For a comparative analysis of US economic and military aid in the Third World by region, see Doug Bandow, "Economic and Military Aid," in Schraeder, *Intervention into the 1990s*, pp. 75–96. See also John W. Sewell and Anthony W. Gambino, "Is the International Community Keeping its Promise to Africa? *TransAfrica Forum* 5, 3 (Spring 1988): 3–16, esp. pp. 10–12.

91 US House, Committee on Foreign Affairs, *Background Materials on Foreign Assistance: Report of the Task Force on Foreign Assistance to the Committee on Foreign Affairs, US House of Representatives*, 101st Cong., 1st Sess. (Washington, DC: GPO, 1989), p. 257.

92 For an historical overview of US–Southern Rhodesian relations prior to 1973, see Anthony Lake, *The "Tar Baby" Option: American Policy Toward Southern Rhodesia* (New York: Columbia University Press, 1976). For an overview of congressional debate over sanctions, see a special issue, "Controversy Over United States Policy Toward Rhodesia: Pro & Con," of *Congressional Digest* (February 1973).

93 Lake, *The "Tar Baby" Option*, pp. 61, 239, 237.

94 Interview with Stephen R. Weissman, former staff director of the House Subcommittee on Africa, Washington, DC, May 17, 1989. The quote is taken from an article Weissman wrote with Johnnie Carson, "Economic Sanctions Against Rhodesia," in John Spanier and Joseph Nogee, eds., *Congress, the Presidency and American Foreign Policy* (New York: Pergamon, 1981), p. 134.

95 As Lake, *The "Tar Baby" Option*, p. 226, notes: "To anyone concerned with the Rhodesian issue, the performance of the White House would seem to indicate cynical and covert support for the Byrd Amendment. This misses the point. In fact, the White House was mostly indifferent about the issue, and decided to duck it for reasons unrelated to events in southern Africa. As an official at Foote Mineral [a company that lobbied for appeal] puts it, 'I don't think the White House cared one way or the other – they just didn't want to be forced to take a stand.'"

96 Barry B. Hughes, *The Domestic Context of American Foreign Policy* (San Francisco: W. H. Freeman, 1978), p. 153.

97 For an overview, see Norman J. Ornstein, "Interest Groups, Congress, and American Foreign Policy," in David P. Forsythe, ed., *American Foreign Policy in an Uncertain World* (Lincoln: University of Nebraska Press, 1984), pp. 49–64. For a listing of the variety of organizations seeking to enhance US ties with Africa, see Kevin Danaher, *Beyond Safaris: A Guide to Building People-to-People Ties With Africa* (Trenton, NJ: Africa World Press, 1991).

98 Lake, *The "Tar Baby" Option*, p. 285.

99 Crocker, "The US Policy Process," pp. 155–56.

100 See Herschelle Sullivan Challenor, "The Influence of Black Americans on US Foreign Policy Toward Africa," in Abdul Aziz Said, ed., *Ethnicity and US Foreign Policy* (New York: Praeger, 1981), pp. 143–81. See also Ronald J. Walters, "African-American Influence in US Foreign Policy Toward South Africa," in Mohammed E. Ahair, ed., *Ethnic Groups and US Foreign Policy* (New York: Greenwood, 1987), p. 72. For the comprehensive analysis of the impact of African Americans on US foreign policy toward Africa, see Elliott P. Skinner, *African Americans and US Policy Toward Africa 1850–1924* (Washington, DC: Howard University Press, 1992).

101 Martin Weil, "Can the Blacks do for Africa What the Jews Did For Israel?" *Foreign Policy*, no. 15 (Summer 1974): 109–30. See also Willard R. Johnson, "Afro-American and African Links: Cooperation For Our Long-Term Economic Empowerment," *TransAfrica Forum* 1, 4 (Spring 1983): 81–92; TransAfrica Forum Conference, "African-Americans in International Affairs," *TransAfrica Forum* 6, 3–4 (Spring–Summer 1989): 53–66; and Brenda Gayle Plummer, "Evolution of the Black Foreign Policy Constituency," *TransAfrica Forum* 6, 3–4 (Spring–Summer 1989): 67–82.

102 Interview with Bob Brauer, Special Counsel to Representative Ronald V. Dellums, Washington, DC, May 25, 1989.

103 *Ibid.*

104 Quoted in Anthony J. Hughes, "Randall Robinson: Executive Director of TransAfrica," *Africa Report* 25, 1 (January–February 1980): 9.

105 For an overview of recent electoral advances by the African-American community, see a series of brief articles under the title "Black Electoral Success in 1989," *PS: Political Science & Politics* 23, 2 (June 1990): 141–62.

106 Interview with Weissman (May 17, 1989).

107 For an overview, see Weissman and Carson, "Economic Sanctions Against Rhodesia."

108 Anne Forrester Holloway, "Congressional Initiatives on South Africa," in Bender, Coleman, and Sklar, eds., *African Crisis Areas*, p. 90.

109 The Biafra example is based on Ogene, *Interest Groups*, pp. 62–101. For a general discussion of US foreign policy toward Nigeria, see Robert B. Shephard, *Nigeria, Africa and the United States from Kennedy to Reagan* (Bloomington: Indiana University Press, 1991).

110 *Ibid.*, p. 93.

111 Discussion is based on Bender, "Kissinger in Angola."

112 The "40 committee", a four-person subcommittee of the NSC, reviewed funding proposals for covert intervention. The four members included Kissinger, Deputy Secretary of Defense William Clement, CIA Director

William Colby, and General George S. Brown (chairperson of the Joint Chiefs of Staff).

113 Bender, "Kissinger in Angola," p. 99.

114 *Ibid.*

115 *Ibid.*, p. 100.

116 This anti-interventionist consensus, however, potentially is in the process of being reversed by a string of US military interventions in Grenada, Panama, and Iraq. It is notable that, in the aftermath of the 1991 Persian Gulf War, the US public increasingly seems to believe, once again, that the US is capable of successfully intervening throughout the globe and that such intervention should be easy.

117 See US Senate, Select Committee to Study Governmental Operations, *Alleged Assassination Plots Involving Foreign Leaders: An Interim Report of the Select Committee to Study Governmental Operations With Respect to Intelligence Activities*, 94th Cong., 1st Sess. (Washington, DC: GPO, 1975).

118 For example, see Robert Parry and Peter Kornbluh, "Iran–Contra's Untold Story," *Foreign Policy*, no. 72 (Fall 1988): 3–30.

119 For discussion, see Jerel A. Rosati, *The Politics of US Foreign Policy* (Dallas, TX: Holt, Rinehart & Winston, 1993).

3 US foreign policy toward Zaire

1 Press release obtained from the White House, Office of the Press Secretary.

2 Any historical analysis of US–Zairian relations which goes beyond the period of the 1960s confronts the dilemma of whether one should adopt the original Belgian or the currently accepted names of Zairian cities, many of which were only changed at the beginning of the 1970s. In this chapter, the original Belgian names will be noted first, followed by the currently accepted version in parentheses. Except for quotes dating back to the pre-1971 period, usage will then follow the current version (e.g., Leopold-ville will be referred to as Kinshasa).

3 Press release obtained from the White House, Office of the Press Secretary.

4 National Security Council (NSC) 6001, "US Policy Toward South, Central and East Africa," January 19, 1960, pp. 2, 3. Document obtained from the National Security Archive.

5 See Stephen R. Weissman, *American Foreign Policy in the Congo: 1960–1964* (Ithaca: Cornell University Press, 1974), p. 44.

6 Dwight D. Eisenhower, "Message to President Kasavubu on the Occasion of the Independence of the Republic of the Congo. June 30, 1960." In *Public Papers of the Presidents of the United States, Dwight D. Eisenhower, 1960–61* (Washington, DC: GPO, 1961), p. 544.

7 For an overview of Zairian politics during this period, see Crawford Young, *Politics in the Congo: Decolonization and Independence* (Princeton: Princeton University Press, 1965); Herbert F. Weiss, *Political Protest in the Congo: The Parti Solidaire Africain During the Independence Period* (Princeton: Princeton University Press, 1967); and Jules Gérard-Libois and Benoit Verhaegen, eds., *Congo 1960*, 3 vols. (Brussels: Centre de Recherche et d'Information Socio-Politiques (CRISP), 1960).

8 These were made on July 10 and 12. See Ernest Lefever, *Uncertain Mandate: Politics of the UN Congo Operation* (Baltimore: NP, 1967), pp. 224–25.

9 Quoted in Madeleine G. Kalb, *The Congo Cables: The Cold War in Africa – From Eisenhower to Kennedy* (New York: Macmillan, 1982), p. 7.

10 Weissman, *American Foreign Policy*, p. 54.

11 Kalb, *The Congo Cables*, p. 36.

12 *Ibid.*, p. 26.

13 *Ibid.*

14 Quoted in US Senate, Select Committee to Study Governmental Operations, *Alleged Assassination Plots Involving Foreign Leaders: An Interim Report of the Select Committee to Study Governmental Operations With Respect to Intelligence Activities*, 94th Cong., 1st Sess. (Washington, DC: GPO, 1975), p. 53.

15 *Ibid.*

16 *Ibid.*, p. 58.

17 For an economically informed interpretation of the Eisenhower (and subsequent) administration's actions in Zaire, see David N. Gibbs, *The Political Economy of Third World Intervention: Mines, Money, and US Policy in the Congo Crisis* (Chicago: University of Chicago Press, 1991).

18 This group consisted of four NSC standing members: Director of Central Intelligence (Allen Dulles); Special Assistant to the President for National Security Affairs (Gordon Gray); Under Secretary of State for Political Affairs (Livingston Merchant); and Assistant Secretary of Defense (John N. Irwin, II).

19 See US Senate, *Alleged Assassination Plots*, p. 60.

20 According to one account, Kasavubu willingly sought the support of the US and "sat at the feet of … CIA men … who reminded him that it was within his realm of responsibility to depose Lumumba and form a new government." Andrew Tully, *CIA: The Inside Story* (New York: William Morrow, 1962), p. 221.

21 Devlin originally met Mobutu in Brussels just prior to Zaire's independence, and maintained excellent contacts with the soon-to-be leader during his tenure as Chief of Station in Zaire.

22 US Senate, *Alleged Assassination Plots*, p. 18.

23 Kalb, *The Congo Cables*, pp. 144–49.

24 Quoted in US Senate, *Alleged Assassination Plots*, p. 62.

25 The day after Lumumba left UN custody, CIA Chief of Station Devlin cabled Washington that he was "working with" the Zairian government "to get roads blocked and troops alerted" to block any "possible escape route." *Ibid.*

26 Quoted in *ibid.*, pp. 48–50.

27 William Minter, "The Limits of Liberal Africa Policy: Lessons from the Congo Crisis," *TransAfrica Forum* 2, 3 (Fall 1984): 34.

28 See Roger Hilsman, *To Move a Nation: The Politics of Foreign Policy in the Administration of John F. Kennedy* (Garden City: Doubleday, 1967).

29 Weissman, *American Foreign Policy*, p. 141; Kalb, *The Congo Cables*, p. 228.

30 Quoted in *Public Papers of the Presidents of the United States, John F. Kennedy, 1961* (Washington, DC: GPO, 1962), p. 92. See also Arthur M. Schlesinger, Jr.,

A Thousand Days: John F. Kennedy in the White House (Greenwich, CT: Fawcett Crest, 1967), p. 530.

31 For more discussion, see Kalb, *Congo Cables*, pp. 260–61.

32 For a summary of CIA actions at this conference, see Richard H. Mahoney, *JFK: Ordeal in Africa* (New York and Oxford: Oxford University Press, 1983), pp. 85–88.

33 The importance of the CIA effort was summarized in the second of a five-part series of articles on the CIA written primarily by correspondents Tom Wicker, John W. Finney, Max Frankel, and E. W. Kenworthy. See "How CIA Put 'Instant Air Force' into Congo," *New York Times*, April 26, 1966, p. A30.

34 Henry Tanner, "Congo's Parliament in Session; Early Vote on Regime Planned," *New York Times*, July 28, 1966, p. A6.

35 Correspondence from Crawford Young, June 11, 1990. For a compilation of documents relevant to this period, see Benoit Verhaegen, ed., *Congo 1961* (Brussels: CRISP, 1961).

36 Michael Streulens, a Belgian public relations specialist, opened the Katangan Information Office in October 1960 in New York as the official registered agent of the Tshombe secessionist regime, marking the beginning of the so-called Katanga Lobby. For a good overview of the lobby's efforts, see F. Chidozie Ogene, *Interest Groups and the Shaping of Foreign Policy: Four Case Studies of United States African Policy* (New York: St. Martin's, 1983), pp. 19–61.

37 Other influential congressional supporters included Senators Richard Russell, Strom Thurmond, Minority Leader Everett M. Dirksen, Bourke B. Kickenlooper, and Barry B. Goldwater.

38 According to Weissman, *American Foreign Policy*, pp. 23–24, "The mining industry produced 22 percent of the Congo's gross national product and 60 percent of its exports. Of this production, 75 percent came from Katanga [Shaba]. More than half of the total mining production, and 70 percent of Katanga's, consisted of copper – of which Union Minière had a monopoly. It was estimated that half of the Congo's budgetary receipts and the majority of its foreign exchange came from Katanga."

39 Mahoney, *JFK*, pp. 105–6.

40 The two military operations reportedly were carried out without prior notification of the Kennedy administration. Both Kennedy and Rusk were "extremely upset" over the lack of prior consultation and had urged Hammarskjold to find a diplomatic way to bring Adoula and Tshombe together. Weissman, *American Foreign Policy*, p. 158.

41 "In fact, many officials indicate that the Africanists were not above exploiting what seemed to them to be a bonafide Communist threat. Experience in the State Department and in earlier intra-administration wrangling on the Congo had taught them the uses of anti-Communist rhetoric." Quoted in *ibid.*, p. 163.

42 Mahoney, *JFK*, p. 114.

43 In nearly 100 flights over a period of two weeks (December 6–21), the US transported 3 battalions of UN troops (roughly 1,600 soldiers), 12 armored cars, and approximately 100 tons of cargo. See Weissman, *American Foreign Policy*, pp. 165–67.

44 Mahoney, *JFK*, p. 117.
45 Senator Dodd, for example, upon returning from Zaire where he had attempted to intercede with Tshombe on the behalf of Kennedy, attacked the administration's support for the UN military action. W. Granger Blair, "Bomboko Scores Tshombe and Asks Congo Unity," *New York Times*, December 8, 1961, p. A2.
46 See *New York Times*, December 14, 1961, p. A49. The advertisement appeared in at least nineteen other newspapers and generated over $25,000 in contributions from roughly 3,000 contributors in two weeks. For a summary of the committee's activities, as well as those of the Katanga Lobby, see Weissman, *American Foreign Policy*, pp. 168–72.
47 Mahoney, *JFK*, p. 135, notes that "even Senator George D. Aiken, no lover of the Congo operation, told Rusk that despite his previous doubts about Adoula, he was now '100 percent behind him.'"
48 Policy perspectives are derived from Mahoney, *JFK*, pp. 144–49; Kalb, *Congo Cables*, pp. 338–52; and Schlesinger, Jr., *A Thousand Days*, pp. 532–33.
49 The vote was fifty in favor and forty-eight opposed, with two abstaining. See Weissman, *American Foreign Policy*, p. 185.
50 Kalb, *Congo Cables*, p. 355.
51 The greatest switch in position, which was said to be "singularly consequential" in swaying the opinions of other bureaucratic players (most notably the Joint Chiefs of Staff) was that of the staunch Europeanist George Ball (who had been arguing for disengagement). Ball noted in a telephone conference with McGeorge Bundy on December 12, 1962, "that after much thought he felt that we had no choice but to resort to force." Mahoney, *JFK*, p. 152. Roger Hilsman, chief of the State Department's Bureau of Intelligence and Research who personally briefed Ball at the time, noted that the reason for the change was the severity of the communist threat: "the notion of getting out was tempting, he said, but when you thought it all through the risk was just too great." Hilsman further notes that the Europeanists (most notably the European Bureau), who were "the most reluctant of all to abandon current policy," were swayed by Spaak's endorsement of action. See Hilsman, *To Move a Nation*, p. 266.
52 The requested equipment included ten US aircraft (six F-86s and four Mustangs), thirty-two army trucks, six armored cars, and a Bailey bridging unit. Mahoney, *JFK*, p. 295, fn. 133.
53 The Greene Plan was the result of a field mission led by US Colonel Michael J. Greene in Zaire during July 1962. Greene's mission was to assess the quality and capabilities of the Zairian Army and recommend a program for turning it into a quality force capable of maintaining both internal and external security for the Zairian nation.
54 Weissman, *American Foreign Policy*, p. 213.
55 Mahoney, *JFK*, pp. 226–27.
56 Memorandum for Mr. McGeorge Bundy. From: William P. Bundy, Deputy Assistant Secretary of Defense for International Security Affairs, May 16, 1963. Subject: Presidential Meeting with Major General Mobutu, Commander in Chief, CNA [Congolese National Army]. Biographic Data – Republic

of the Congo, April 29, 1963. Document obtained from the National Security Files of the White House, John F. Kennedy Library.

57 Memorandum of Conversation between President Kennedy and General Mobutu, Commander in Chief of the Congolese National Army, May 31, 1963. Document obtained from the John F. Kennedy Library.

58 For an analysis, see Catherine Coquery-Vidrovitch, Alain Forest, and Herbert Weiss, eds., *Rébellions-Révolution au Zaire, 1963–1965*, 2 vols. (Paris: L'Harmattan, 1987); and Georges Nzongola-Ntalaja, "The Second Independence Movement in Congo-Kinshasa," in Peter Anyang' Nyong'o, ed., *Popular Struggles for Democracy in Africa* (London and New York: The United Nations University and Zed Books, 1988), pp. 113–41.

59 See Stephen R. Weissman, "The CIA and US Policy in Zaire and Angola," in Ellen Ray et al., eds., *Dirty Work 2: The CIA in Africa* (Secaucus, NJ: Lyle Stuart, 1979), pp. 89–190.

60 Interview with Donald O. Clark, Carlisle, Pennsylvania, June 28, 1989. Clark was a US army officer who served at Strike Command (STRIKECOM) from 1964 to 1966 and was involved in the intelligence planning for Operation Red Dragon.

61 Minter, "The Limits of Liberal Africa Policy," p. 41.

62 Weissman, *American Foreign Policy*, p. 235.

63 See Thomas Powers, *The Man Who Kept the Secrets: Richard Helms and the CIA* (New York: Alfred Knopf, 1979), pp. 122–23.

64 State Department cable from Rusk to the US Embassy in Brussels (for delivery to Foreign Minister Paul-Henri Spaak), August 6, 1964. Reproduced in Minter, "Candid Cables: Some Reflections on the US Response to the Congo Rebellions, 1964" in Georges Nzongola-Ntalaja, ed., *The Crisis in Zaire: Myths and Realities* (Trenton, NJ: Africa World Press, 1986, pp. 265–87.

65 See Fred E. Wagoner, *Dragon Rouge: The Rescue of Hostages in the Congo* (Washington, DC: GPO, 1980), p. 22.

66 Weissman, *American Foreign Policy*, p. 239.

67 Correspondence from Crawford Young, June 11, 1990.

68 See Roger Morris and Richard Mauzy, "Following the Scenario: Reflections on Five Case Histories in the Mode and Aftermath of CIA Intervention," in Robert L. Borosage and John Marks, eds., *The CIA File* (New York: Grossman Publishers, 1976), pp. 28–45.

69 See Wagoner, *Dragon Rouge*, pp. 54–57.

70 Quoted in M. S. Handler, "Revolt in Congo Termed 'Serious' by US Officials," *New York Times*, August 15, 1964, p. A1.

71 Wagoner, *Dragon Rouge*, p. 77.

72 *Ibid.*, pp. 86–87, 123–24.

73 The bureaucratic positions and quotes of relevant officials in this paragraph were derived from Weissman, *American Foreign Policy*, p. 249.

74 For details of both operations, see Wagoner, *Dragon Rouge*, pp. 130–88. See also Major Thomas P. Odom, *Dragon Operations: Hostage Rescues in the Congo, 1964–1965* (Fort Leavenworth, KS: Combat Studies Institute, US Army Command and General Staff College, 1988).

75 See *ibid.*, pp. 189–92, 197–98. For a summary of administration responses to criticism in the aftermath of the military operations (including a statement

by Johnson on November 28), see "United States Cooperates with Belgium in Rescue of Hostages From the Congo," *Department of State Bulletin* 51, 1329 (December 14, 1964): 838–46.

76 CIA memorandum, "The Congo: Assessment and Prospects" (December 31, 1964), p. 1. Document obtained from the National Security Archive.

77 Tshombe's CONACO party, along with political allies, "won two-thirds of the 166 national deputy seats and gained 'control' of a majority of the 21 provincial assemblies." See CIA, Office of Current Intelligence, Intelligence Memorandum, "Situation in the Congo" (August 26, 1965), p. 2. Document obtained from the National Security Archive.

78 Quoted in National Security Adviser McGeorge Bundy, "Memorandum for the President" (August 25, 1965), p. 1. Document obtained from the National Security Archive.

79 *Ibid.*, pp. 1, 4–5.

80 For discussion, see Jules Gérard-Libois and Jean Van Lierde, eds., *Congo 1965* (Brussels: CRISP, 1966).

81 Weissman, "The CIA and US Policy," p. 191.

82 Although the question of CIA involvement has not been proven through archival research, one scholar notes that "Every informant on Zaire (based on sixty-one interviews with US policymakers) assumes that the CIA backed his [Mobutu's] coup and as far back as his meeting with Kennedy in May 1963, a coup was considered inevitable by the Americans." See Elise Forbes Pachter, "Our Man in Kinshasa: US Relations With Mobutu, 1970–1983; Patron–Client Relations in the International Sphere," Ph.D. dissertation, The Johns Hopkins University, 1987, p. 107. Similarly, Weissman, "The CIA and US Policy," p. 191, claims that three "informed" individuals that he interviewed verified CIA involvement in the coup: "a US official then in Washington, a Western diplomatic Congo specialist, and an American businessman who talked with the returned CIA man Devlin."

83 Confidential interview no. 5. This corresponds with a similar statement made by Cyrus Vance, a member of the NSC's Special Group, before the Senate Select Intelligence Committee. See Weissman, "The CIA and US Policy," p. 191.

84 CIA, Directorate of Intelligence, "Mobutu and the Congo" (Special Report, Weekly Review, June 23, 1967), p. 1. Reproduced in microfiche series produced by University Publications of America, *CIA Research Reports (Africa 1946-1976)*, reel 2.

85 Henry Tanner, "Congolese Hail US Planes' Role," *New York Times*, July 20, 1967, p. A5.

86 For a discussion of the factors surrounding this event, see Jules Gérard-Libois, ed., *Congo 1967* (Brussels: CRISP, 1968).

87 Department of State, Memorandum from Eugene V. Rostow to President Johnson, "C-130s for the Congo" (July 6, 1967), pp. 1–2. Document obtained from the National Security Archive.

88 The discussion is based on a chronology of the episode as pieced together with supporting documents by Roger Morris (on file at the Lyndon B. Johnson Library and obtained from the National Security Archive); and a cable (no. 1540) from Ambassador McBride, US Embassy Kinshasa, to

Washington, D.C. (July 6, 1967). Document obtained from the National Security Archive.

89 See Felix Belair, Jr., "Senators Assail US Aid to Congo: Democrats and Republicans Call Dispatch of 3 Planes Immoral Intervention," *New York Times*, July 11, 1967, pp. A1, A4. Letter dated July 27, 1967 from thirteen Republican Senators to Johnson. Document obtained from the National Security Archive.

90 Statement dated July 10, 1967. Document obtained from National Security Archive.

91 Statement dated July 10, 1967. Document obtained from National Security Archive.

92 See Anthony Lake, *The "Tar Baby" Option: American Policy Toward Southern Rhodesia* (New York: Columbia University Press, 1976), p. 120. Johnson's characterization of Zaire, indicative of his approach to Africa as a whole, was noted in correspondence from Crawford Young, June 11, 1990.

93 An internal memorandum titled "The Situation in the Congo" (July 13, 1967) noted that, as of July 13, there was no "immediate threat to Mobutu's position as head of the central government, although there is always a possibility of unrest in a number of quarters while Mobutu is preoccupied with the mercenaries" (p. 1). The memorandum further noted (p. 2) that the mercenaries were apparently interested "mainly in getting out of the Congo." Indeed, after only eight days, the back of the rebellion had been broken. Document obtained from the National Security Archive.

94 See Benjamin Wells, "US Aid to Congo Termed Success: Planes Said to Have Helped Save Regime in Uprising," *New York Times*, December 11, 1967, p. A16.

95 This terminology is drawn from the title of Pachter, *Our Man in Kinshasa*.

96 This sentiment was disclosed in a memorandum for President Johnson. From: Eugene V. Rostow, July 6, 1967. Subject: C-130s for the Congo, p. 2. Document obtained from the National Security Archive.

97 Remarks made by President Mobutu on August 4, 1970 while visiting the United States. See "Remarks of Welcome to President Joseph Désiré Mobutu of the Democratic Republic of the Congo," *Public Papers of the Presidents of the US, President Nixon, 1970* (Washington, DC: GPO, 1971), p. 645.

98 For a discussion of this theme, see Michael G. Schatzberg, *Mobutu or Chaos? The United States and Zaire, 1960–1990* (Lanham, MD: University Press of America, 1991).

99 See Memorandum for the President. From: The Secretary of Defense. Subject: Visit of Zaire's President Mobutu. Date: October 4, 1973. pp. 1–2. Document obtained from the National Security Archive.

100 Although the CIA was more inclined to support Portugal's continued presence on the African continent, links were maintained with the anti-communist Roberto as an insurance policy against the possible disintegration of Portuguese control. During the early 1970s, for example, CIA payments to Roberto averaged only $10,000 a year for "intelligence collection" purposes. For an overview of the CIA's relationship with Portugal and Angola prior to 1974, see Weissman, "The CIA and US Policy," pp. 192–97.

101 *Ibid.*, pp. 191–92.

102 See Sheldon B. Vance (with contributions by Jean Vance), "American Foreign Policy: The Glory Years – and Now What? An Insider Look at the Foreign Service," unpublished manuscript, pp. 200–5.

103 See Crawford Young, "The Zairian Crisis and American Foreign Policy," in Gerald J. Bender, James S. Coleman, and Richard L. Sklar, eds., *African Crisis Areas and US Foreign Policy* (Berkeley: University of California Press, 1985), pp. 214–19.

104 As Pachter, *Our Man in Kinshasa*, p. 107, observed: "Interviews held with Zairians in 1983 confirmed what a number of sources have claimed: even today [1987], much of what remains of Mobutu's support by his people stems from his role in saving the country from endless rounds of internecine and sectional strife."

105 The discussion is based on an interview with David Newsom, Assistant Secretary of State for African Affairs under the Nixon administration, Washington, DC, June 13, 1989. Newsom was present at the meeting in which Kissinger expressed his displeasure with Mobutu's actions.

106 *Ibid.*

107 *Ibid.*

108 Copper prices dropped from a peak of $1.40 per pound in April 1974 to as low as $0.53 per pound in late 1975. This price stabilized at around $0.65 per pound in 1976. See Thomas M. Callaghy, "Zaire: The Ritual Dance of the Debt Game," *Africa Report* 29, 5 (September-October 1984): 22. For a discussion of Mobutu's "radicalization" campaign, see Michael G. Schatzberg, "The State and the Economy: The 'Radicalization of the Revolution' in Mobutu's Zaire," *Canadian Journal of African Studies* 14, 2 (1980): 239–57.

109 Pachter, *Our Man in Kinshasa*, pp. 216–20. However, the State Department did facilitate Mobutu's access to loan relief (primarily in the shape of Import-Export Bank loans). Loan amounts secured (in millions of dollars) included $53.3 in 1973, $122.2 in 1974, and $60.6 in 1975.

110 John Stockwell, *In Search of Enemies: A CIA Story* (New York: W. W. Norton, 1978), p. 67.

111 *Ibid.*, p. 52.

112 For example, Tom Killoran, the US consul-general in Luanda, was said to believe that the "MPLA was the best qualified to run Angola and that its leaders sincerely wanted a peaceful relationship with the United States. SWISH [CIA cryptonym for Killoran] had worked with all three movements and found the MPLA better organized and easier for him to see. They were the best educated up and down the line, from leaders who had taken doctorates at European universities to cadres of urban dwellers, civil servants, and technicians." See *ibid.*, p. 64.

113 Interview with Walter L. Cutler, US Ambassador to Zaire (1975–79), Washington, DC, June 27, 1989. Quote taken from Pachter, *Our Man in Kinshasa*, p. 224.

114 Stockwell, *In Search of Enemies*, p. 44.

115 See Vance, "An Insider Look at the Foreign Service," ch. 12.

116 Interview with Cutler (June 27, 1989).

117 For a discussion, see US Senate, Committee on Foreign Relations, Subcom-

mittee on Africa, *Security Supporting Assistance for Zaire*, Hearings, October 24, 1975, 94th Cong., 1st Sess. (Washington, DC: GPO, 1975).

118 Interview with Newsom (June 13, 1989).

119 Pachter, *Our Man in Kinshasa*, p. 239.

120 A history of the exploits of the FLNC could constitute a book in itself. Originally forming the core of Tshombe's secessionist Shaba forces from 1960 to 1963, the Zairian exiles fled to Angola when that movement was defeated in 1963. Returning to Zaire when Tshombe was named Prime Minister in 1963, many once again fled to Angola in 1965 when Mobutu assumed power through a military *coup d'état*. Many of those who remained took part in the mercenary uprising against Mobutu in 1967, similarly seeking shelter in Angola when that movement was defeated. In 1968, these disparate forces regrouped under the banner of the FNLC and committed their movement to the overthrow of Mobutu. Armed and trained by the Portuguese colonial government, the FLNC fought against the Mobutu-supported FNLA prior to the Portuguese *coup d'état* in 1974. Subsequently armed and trained by Cuban soldiers, the FLNC fought alongside the MPLA (and against the Zairian-backed FNLA) during the ensuing 1975–76 Angolan civil war. For discussion, see "Contribution à l'étude des mouvements d'opposition au Zaire: le F.L.N.C.," *Cahiers du CEDAF*, no. 6 (1980).

121 See Galen Hull, "Internationalizing the Shaba Conflict," *Africa Report* 22, 4 (July–August 1977): 4–9.

122 See Cyrus Vance, *Hard Choices: Critical Years in American Foreign Policy* (New York: Simon & Schuster, 1983), pp. 70–71. For a complete listing of the *matériel* provided by the US government, see US House, Committee on Foreign Relations, Subcommittee on Africa, *Foreign Assistance Legislation For Fiscal Year 1978* (Part 3) *Economic and Military Assistance Programs in Africa*, Hearings and Markup, March 17, 18, 23, 28, 29, and April 28, 1977, 95th Cong., 1st Sess. (Washington, DC: GPO, 1977), pp. 196–97. (Hereinafter *House Foreign Assistance FY 1978*.)

123 Arnaud de Borchgrave, "Mobutu Speaks Out," *Newsweek* (April 18, 1977): 50

124 See Anthony J. Hughes, "Interview: Umba Di Lutete, Zairian Ambassador to the United Nations," *Africa Report* 22, 4 (July–August 1977): 11.

125 Adelman, "Old Foes and New Friends," p. 9.7

126 Interview with Cutler (June 27, 1989).

127 For a variety of overviews of the authoritarian nature of the Mobutu regime, see Thomas M. Callaghy, *The State-Society Struggle: Zaire in Comparative Perspective* (New York: Columbia University Press, 1984); David J. Gould, *Bureaucratic Corruption and Underdevelopment in the Third World: The Case of Zaire* (Elmsford, New York: Pergamon Press, 1980); Georges Nzongola-Ntalaja, ed., *The Crisis in Zaire: Myths and Realities* (Trenton, NJ: Africa World Press, 1986); and Michael G. Schatzberg, *The Dialectics of Oppression in Zaire* (Bloomington: Indiana University Press, 1988).

127 *House Foreign Assistance FY 1978*, p. 143.

129 Vance, *Hard Choices*, p. 70.

130 Interview with Cutler (June 27, 1989).

131 Testimony of Deputy Assistant Secretary of State for African Affairs Lannon Walker before the House Subcommittee on Africa, March 2, 1978, as found in US House, Committee on International Relations, Subcommittee on Africa, *Foreign Assistance Legislation for Fiscal Year 1979* (Part 3) *Economic and Military Assistance Programs in Africa*, Hearings and Markup, February 7, 8, 14, 28; March 1 and 2, 1978, 95th Cong., 2nd Sess. (Washington, DC: GPO, 1978), p. 193. (Hereinafter *House Foreign Assistance FY 1979*.)

132 Although the majority opposed human rights initiatives, some "were deeply offended by the Mobutu regime and were happy to see an administration take a stand on human rights in foreign policy." Interview with Moose (June 26, 1989).

133 Other political reforms included the creation of the position of prime minister and the reinvigoration of dormant urban councils at the local level.

134 *House Foreign Assistance FY 1979*, p. 193.

135 *Ibid.*, p. 192.

136 Martin Schram, "A Storm Over Cuba Role in Zaire," *Newsday* (August 31, 1978): 6.

137 See US House, Committee on International Relations, Subcommittee on International Security and Scientific Affairs, *Congressional Oversight of War Powers Compliance: Zaire Airlift*, Hearing, August 10, 1978, 95th Cong., 2nd Sess. (Washington, DC: GPO, 1978).

138 Press conference by Carter in Chicago, IL, May 25, 1977, as recorded in "News Conferences, May 4 and 25 (Excerpts)," *Department of State Bulletin* 78, 2016 (July 1978): 18.

139 Schram, "A Storm," p. 43.

140 Press conference by Carter on June 14, 1977, as recorded in "The President: News Conferences, June 14 and 26 (Excerpts)," *Department of State Bulletin* 78, 2017 (August 1978): 6.

141 Quoted in Martin Schram, "Out of the Tumult, One Voice," *Newsday* (September 1, 1978): 6, 41. For full statement, see "Meet the Press," *Department of State Bulletin* 78, 2016 (July 1978): 26.

142 Kenneth L. Adelman, "Zaire: Old Foes and New Friends," *Africa Report* 23, 1 (January–February 1978), p. 8. See also Vance, *Hard Choices*, p. 92.

143 Interview with Moose (June 26, 1989).

144 See Zbigniew Brzezinski, *Power and Principle: Memoirs of the National Security Adviser 1977–1981* (New York: Farrar, Straus, Giroux, 1983).

145 Interview with Moose (June 26, 1989).

146 Confidential interview no. 10.

147 Speech by Vance in Atlantic City, June 20, 1978. "The Secretary: US Relations with Africa," *Department of State Bulletin* 78, 2017 (August 1978): 10.

148 Congressional testimony of Robert Remole before the House Subcommittee on Africa, March 5, 1980. See US House, Committee on Foreign Affairs, Subcommittee on Africa, *Foreign Assistance Legislation for Fiscal Year 1981* (Part 7) *Economic and Security Assistance Programs in Africa*, Hearings and Markup, February 7, 12, 13, 20, 25, 26, 27, 28; March 5 and 6, 1980, 96th

Cong., 2nd Sess. (Washington, DC: GPO, 1980), p. 563. (Hereinafter *House Foreign Assistance FY 1980.*)

149 *Ibid.*, p. 565.
150 Pachter, *Our Man in Kinshasa*, p. 300.
151 *Ibid.*, p. 300.
152 Interview with Moose (June 26, 1985).
153 Lannon Walker, "US Policy Toward Zaire," *Department of State Bulletin* 80, 2041 (August 1980): 46.
154 *Ibid.*
155 *Ibid.*, p. 48.
156 Quoted in US House, Committee on Foreign Affairs, Subcommittee on Africa, *Foreign Assistance Legislation for Fiscal Years 1980–81* (Part 6) *Economic and Military Assistance Programs in Africa*, Hearings and Markup, February 13, 14, 21, 22, 27, 28; March 5, 6, 7, and 12, 1979, 96th Cong., 1st Sess. (Washington, DC: GPO, 1979), p. 351. (Hereinafter *House Foreign Assistance FY 1980.*)
157 Although Nguza's testimony caused quite a stir, it is important to remember that he afterwards returned to Zaire and accepted a position with the Mobutu regime. In fact, he was even posted in Washington as Zaire's Ambassador to the US in the aftermath of his resignation (and testimony before the House Subcommittee on Africa). For the text of his testimony, see US House, Committee on Foreign Affairs, Subcommittee on Africa, *Political and Economic Situation in Zaire – Fall 1981*, Hearing, September 15, 1981, 97th Cong., 1st Sess. (Washington, DC: GPO, 1982).
158 Quoted in *House Foreign Assistance FY 1980*, p. 351.
159 Among the examples often cited of such a trend (besides Iran) are Cuba (1959), Ethiopia (1974), Vietnam (1975), and Nicaragua (1978).
160 Confidential interview no. 78.
161 Interview with Peter Dalton Constable, US Ambassador to Zaire (1982-84), Washington, DC, June 20, 1989.
162 *Ibid.*
163 Interview with Brandon Hambright Grove, Jr., US Ambassador to Zaire (1984–87), Washington, DC, June 29, 1989.
164 The House repealed Clark by a vote of 236 to 185, despite the strong opposition of the House Subcommittee on Africa, the Congressional Black Caucus, and TransAfrica. The Senate previously had repealed Clark by a vote of sixty-three to thirty-four, including seventeen Democrats who voted in favor. See US House, Committee on Foreign Affairs, Subcommittee on Africa, *Legislation to Require That Any United States Government Support For Military or Paramilitary Operations in Angola be Openly Acknowledged and Publicly Debated* (H.R. 4276), Hearings and Markup, April 22 and 23, 1986, 99th Cong., 1st Sess. (Washington, DC: GPO, 1986).
165 See J. Stephen Morrison, "Mr Savimbi Goes to Washington," *Africa Report* 33, 5 (September–October 1988): 55–58.
166 Confidential interview no. 20.
167 James Brooke, "C.I.A. Said to Send Weapons via Zaire to Angola Rebels," *New York Times*, February 1, 1987, p. 12.
168 Confidential interview no. 15.

169 Confidential interview no. 20.
170 *Ibid.*
171 John B. Cushman, Jr., "US Seeking Agreement to Use Air Base in Zaire," *New York Times*, February 22, 1987, p. A9.
172 Confidential interview no. 25.
173 For a brief exchange between the House Subcommittee on Africa and Crocker over this issue, see US House, Committee on Foreign Affairs, Subcommittee on Africa, *Foreign Assistance Legislation for Fiscal Years 1988–89* (Part 6), Hearings and Markup, March 4, 10, 18, and 19, 1987, 100th Cong., 1st Sess. (Washington, DC: GPO, 1987), pp. xvi–xvii, 138–43.
174 For a description, see "Zaire–US Military Co-operation," *Africa Research Bulletin, Political Series* 24, 3 (April 15, 1987): 8451–52; and "Zaire-US Military Exercises," *Africa Research Bulletin, Political Series* 25, 5 (June 15, 1988): 8895.
175 See David B. Ottaway, "US Hails Angolan Talks as 'Watershed'," *Washington Post*, June 24, 1989, pp. A18, A22.
176 Interview with Jack Aubert, Desk Officer for Zaire in the State Department's Africa Bureau, Washington, DC, June 8, 1989.
177 Bush, "Remarks by the President," p. 1.4
178 Quoted in Margaret A. Novicki, "Interview: Herman J. Cohen: Forging a Bipartisan Policy," *Africa Report* 34, 5 (September-October 1989): 19.
179 See Robert Pear, "Congress Gives African Leaders the Human Rights Test," *New York Times*, July 2, 1989, p. E2. For a brief overview of Mobutu's efforts at countering this trend, see Edward T. Pound, "Congo Drums: With Dictators Falling, Zaire's Mobutu Hires Lobbyists to Make Sure He Retains American Aid," *Wall Street Journal*, March 7, 1990.
180 Robert Pear, "Mobutu, on Visit, Lauded and Chided," *New York Times*, June 30, 1989, p. A3.
181 Pear, "Congress Gives," p. E2.
182 Interview with Weissman (May 17, 1989). This figure – advanced by Mike Wallace on Sixty Minutes in 1984 – also was contained in a leaked classified briefing paper prepared for Reagan by the State Department's Africa Bureau just prior to his December 1986 meeting with Mobutu. See William Claiborne, "Mobutu Refurbishing Image Tainted by Corruption Charge," *Washington Post*, June 30, 1989, p. A32.
183 Quoted in Clifford Krauss, "House Democrats Challenge Bush by Seeking to Reduce Aid to Zaire," *New York Times*, April 11, 1990, p. A2.
184 For a discussion of this event, see Jean-Claude Willame, "Zaire, Années 90: Volume I," *Les Cahiers du CEDAF–ASDOC*, series 2, nos. 5–6, 1991. For an overview of human rights violations in Zaire, see Lawyers Committee for Human Rights, *Zaire: Repression as Policy, A Human Rights Report* (New York: Lawyers Committee for Human Rights, 1990). See also Amnesty International, *The Republic of Zaire: Outside the Law – Security Force Repression of Government Opponents, 1988–1990* (New York: Amnesty International Publications, September 1990).
185 Quoted in Clifford Krauss, "US Cuts Aid to Zaire, Setting Off a Policy Debate," *New York Times*, November 4, 1990, p. A7.

186 See Schatzberg, *Mobutu or Chaos?*.
187 See Krauss, "House Democrats Challenge Bush," p. A2.
188 Confidential interview no. 96.
189 Quoted in Clifford Krauss, "US Cuts Aid to Zaire, Setting Off Policy Debate," *New York Times*, November 4, 1990.
190 Confidential interview no. 83.
191 See Neil Henry, "France, Belgium Send Troops to Zaire," *Washington Post*, September 25, 1991, p. A19.
192 Quoted in "Rioting Subsides in Zaire: Foreign Troops Lead Evacuations to Congo," *Washington Post*, September 26, 1991, p. A31.
193 For an overview, see Vicki R. Finkel, "Angola: Violence and the Vote," *Africa Report* 37, 4 (July-August 1992): 52–54.
194 Confidential interview no. 100.
195 Quoted in Kenneth B. Noble, "Zaire Coalition Ends 26 Years of Dictatorship," *New York Times*, September 30, 1991, p. A1. See also Mark Huband, "Zaire: The Revolving Door," *Africa Report* 37, 1 (January–February 1992): 25–28.
196 Quoted in Mark Huband, "Zaire: Pressure from Abroad," *Africa Report* 37, 2 (March–April 1992): 43.
197 *Ibid.*
198 Quoted in Keith B. Richburg, "Mobutu: A Rich Man in Poor Standing," *Washington Post*, October 3, 1991, p. A1.

4 US foreign policy toward Ethiopia and Somalia

1 Quoted in Raymond L. Thurston, "The United States, Somalia and the Crisis in the Horn," *Horn of Africa* (April–June 1978): 20.
2 Chester Crocker, "US Interests in Regional Conflicts in the Horn of Africa," address before the Washington World Affairs Council, Washington, DC, November 13, 1985, p. 3.
3 For an introduction to these themes, see I. M. Lewis, ed., *Nationalism & Self-Determination in the Horn of Africa* (London: Ithaca Press, 1983).
4 The study of superpower intervention in the Horn of Africa has generated a tremendous amount of scholarship. In addition to the more specialized works on US foreign policy which are cited throughout the volume, see James Dougherty, *The Horn of Africa: A Map of Political-Strategic Conflict* (Cambridge, MA: Institute for Foreign Policy Analysis, 1982); Tom J. Farer, *War Clouds on the Horn of Africa: The Widening Storm* (New York: Carnegie Endowment for International Peace, 1979); Robert F. Gorman, *Political Conflict on the Horn of Africa* (New York: Praeger, 1981); Paul B. Henze, *The Horn of Africa: From War to Peace* (London and New York: Macmillan and St. Martin's, 1991); Samuel M. Makinda, *Superpower Diplomacy in the Horn of Africa* (New York: St. Martin's, 1987); Marina Ottaway, *Soviet and American Influence in the Horn of Africa* (New York: Praeger, 1982); and Bereket Habte Selassie, *Conflict and Intervention in the Horn of Africa* (New York: Monthly Review Press, 1980).
5 For an even earlier account by an official who led the first US diplomatic mission to Ethiopia, see Robert P. Skinner, *Abyssinia of Today: An Account of*

the First Mission Sent by the American Government to the Court of the King of Kings (1903–1904) (London: Edward Arnold, 1906). See also William McE. Dye, *Moslem Egypt, Christian Abyssinia, or Military Service Under the Khedive, in His Provinces and Beyond Their Borders, as Experienced by the American Staff* (New York: Negro Universities Press, 1968); and David Shinn, "A Survey of American-Ethiopian Relations Prior to the Italian Occupation of Ethiopia," *Ethiopia Observer* 14, 4 (1971).

6 John R. Rasmuson, *A History of Kagnew Station and American Forces in Eritrea* (Arlington, VA: US Army Security Agency, Information division, 1973), p. 22.

7 *Ibid.*, pp. 28–29

8 Harold G. Marcus, *Ethiopia, Great Britain, and the United States, 1941-1974: The Politics of Empire* (Berkeley: University of California Press, 1983), p. 12.

9 For a history, see Rasmuson, *A History of Kagnew Station.*

10 Quoted in Afeworki Paulos, "Superpower–Small State Interaction: The Case of US–Ethiopian Relations, 1945–1986," Ph. D. dissertation, The George Washington University, Washington, 1987, p. 84.

11 See Robert L. Hess, *Italian Colonialism in Somalia* (Chicago: University of Chicago Press, 1966), p. 191.

12 See Marcus, *Ethiopia, Great Britain, and the United States,* p. 83.

13 Quoted in Paulos, *Superpower–Small State Interaction,* p. 80.

14 *Ibid.*, p. 81.

15 *Ibid.*

16 *Ibid.*, p. 86.

17 Marcus, *Ethiopia, Great Britain, and the United States,* p. 83.

18 *Ibid.*, p. 84.

19 *Ibid.*, p. 83.

20 Quoted in *ibid.*, p. 84.

21 For an overview of Haile Selassie's early actions in this regard, see John H. Spencer, *Ethiopia at Bay: A Personal Account of the Haile Selassie Years* (Algonac, MI: Reference Publications, 1987), esp. chs. 6–9.

22 *Ibid.*, p. 102.

23 For discussion, see Marcus, *Ethiopia, Great Britain, and the United States,* p. 86.

24 For a more in-depth discussion of the negotiations that led to the agreement, see Jeffrey A. Lefebvre, *Arms for the Horn: US Security Policy in Ethiopia and Somalia 1953–1991* (Pittsburgh: University of Pittsburgh Press, 1991), pp. 55–74.

25 For a more detailed discussion, see Spencer, *Ethiopia at Bay,* pp. 261–68; and Marcus, *Ethiopia, Great Britain, and the United States,* pp. 88–90.

26 Spencer, *Ethiopia at Bay,* p. 270.

27 Confidential interview no. 35.

28 Confidential interview no. 65.

29 See NSC, "US Foreign Policy Toward Ethiopia," NSC 5615, October 23, 1956. Reproduced in microfiche series produced by University Publications of America, *Africa: National Security Files, 1961–1963.* (Hereinafter NSC 5615.

30 *Ibid.*

31 *Ibid.*

32 NSC, Operations Coordinating Board Report, "US Policy Toward the Horn of Africa," NSC 5903, July 13, 1960, p. 1. Reproduced in microfiche series produced by University Publications of America, *Africa: National Security Files, 1961–1963.* (Hereinafter NSC 5903.)

33 For a discussion of this theme, see Saadia Touval, *Somali Nationalism: International Politics and the Drive for Unity in the Horn* (Cambridge, MA: Harvard University Press, 1963), pp. 49–50; I. M. Lewis, *A Modern History of Somalia: Nation and State in the Horn in Africa* (Boulder: Westview, 1988); and David D. Laitin and Said S. Samatar, *Somalia: Nation in Search of a State* (Boulder: Westview, 1987).

34 NSC 5615, p. 2.

35 NSC 5903, pp. 2–3.

36 Spencer, *Ethiopia at Bay*, p. 294.

37 Marcus, *Ethiopia, Great Britain, and the United States*, p. 112.

38 NSC 5903, pp. 2–3.

39 Quoted in Marcus, *Ethiopia, Great Britain, and the United States*, p. 110.

40 For discussion, see Lefebvre, *Arms for the Horn*, pp. 94–110.

41 US Senate, Committee on Foreign Relations, Subcommittee on United States Security Agreements and Commitments Abroad, *United States Security Agreements and Commitments Abroad* (Volume 2, Part 8) *Ethiopia*, Hearing, June 1, 1970, 91st Cong., 2nd Sess. (Washington, DC: GPO, 1971), p. 1905.

42 The following description of US involvement is largely derived from two chronologies written by the US Embassy and the US MAAG. See "Attempted Coup d'Etat," US Embassy, Addis Ababa, Despatch no. 198, December 29, 1960 (Hereinafter "Richards Report"), and "Army Attaché's Report on Attempted Coup d'Etat," US Embassy, Addis Ababa, Despatch no. 217, January 13, 1961 (Hereinafter "Crosson Report"). Reproduced in microfiche series produced by University Publications of America, *Africa: National Security Files, 1961-1963.*

43 "Crosson Report," p. 18.

44 *Ibid.*

45 *Ibid.*, p. 23.

46 "Richards Report," pp. 4–6.

47 US Embassy, Addis Ababa, to Washington, Telegram no. 557, December 17, 1960. Document obtained from the National Security Archive.

48 "Richards Report," p. 7.

49 "Crosson Report," p. 20.

50 For a good introduction to the early conflicts generated by Somali nationalism, see Catherine Hoskyns, ed., *Case Studies in African Diplomacy (II): The Ethiopia-Somalia-Kenya Dispute; 1960–1967* (Dar es Salaam, Tanzania: Oxford University Press for the Institute of Public Administration, 1969); and John Drysdale, *The Somali Dispute* (London: Pall Mall Press, 1964).

51 NSC, "US Foreign Policy on the Horn of Africa," NSC 6028, December 30, 1960, p. 5. Document reproduced in University Microfilm International.

52 For a summation of the Africa Bureau's position concerning US foreign policy toward the Ogaden, see a working paper written by David D. Newsom, "US Policy Toward the Ogaden," August 26, 1963. Reproduced

in microfiche series produced by University Publications of America, *Africa: National Security Files, 1961–1963*.

53 For a discussion of these requests, see Farer, *War Clouds on the Horn of Africa*, pp. 115–16.

54 For a comprehensive analysis of Somalia's claims to Kenya's Northern Frontier District, see Korwa Gombe Adar, "The Significance of the Legal Principle of 'Territorial Integrity' as the Modal Determinant of Relations: A Case Study of Kenya's Foreign Policy Towards Somalia, 1963–1983", Ph.D. dissertation, University of South Carolina, Columbia, SC, 1986.

55 Interview with Horace G. Torbert, Jr., US Ambassador to Somalia (1963–65), Washington, DC, June 21, 1989.

56 *Ibid.*

57 For discussion, see John Markakis, *National and Class Conflict in the Horn of Africa* (Cambridge: Cambridge University Press, 1987), pp. 169–81.

58 See Baffour Agyeman-Duah, "United States Military Assistance Relationship With Ethiopia, 1953–77: Historical and Theoretical Analysis," Ph.D. dissertation, University of Denver, Denver, CO, 1984, p. 192.

59 See Spencer, *Ethiopia at Bay*, p. 320; and the congressional testimony of Ambassador Korry in US Senate, Committee on Foreign Relations, Subcommittee on African Affairs, *Ethiopia and the Horn of Africa*, Hearings, August 4, 5 and 6, 94th Cong., 2nd Sess. (Washington, DC: GPO, 1976), p. 46.

60 G. Mennen Williams, "Promising Trends in Africa," *Department of State Bulletin* 50, 1289 (March 9, 1964), p. 371.

61 Quoted in Agyeman-Duah, *United States Military Assistance Relationship with Ethiopia*, p. 161.

62 Interview with David Newsom, Assistant Secretary of State for African Affairs under the Nixon administration, Washington, DC, June 13, 1989. At the time of the Ogaden conflict, Newsom was the Office Director for the Bureau of African Affairs.

63 Interview with Torbert (June 21, 1982).

62 US Senate, *Ethiopia and the Horn of Africa*, p. 35.

65 Confidential interview no. 38.

66 See Lefebvre, *Arms for the Horn*, p. 122. See also Rasmuson, *A History of Kagnew Station*, pp. 55–62.

67 US House, Committee on Foreign Affairs, *The Middle East, Africa, and Inter-American Affairs* (volume 16) *Selected Executive Session Hearings of the Committee on Foreign Affairs, 1951–56* (Washington, DC: GPO, 1980), pp. 335–36.

68 US Senate, *Ethiopia and the Horn of Africa*, p. 35.

69 *Ibid.*, p. 36.

70 US Senate, *United States Security Agreements and Commitments Abroad*, p. 1907. For discussion, see Jeffrey A. Lefebvre, "Donor Dependency and American Arms Transfers to the Horn of Africa: The F-5 Legacy," *The Journal of Modern African Studies* 25, 3 (1987): 473.

71 Testimony of George Bader, Office of the Assistant Secretary for International Security Affairs, Department of Defense, US Senate, *United States Security Agreements and Commitments Abroad*, pp. 1935–37.

72 See the testimony of Assistant Secretary of State for African Affairs David

D. Newsom in US Senate, *United States Security Agreements and Commitments Abroad*, p. 1911.

73 For a more extensive analysis of these three trends, see Paulos, *Superpower–Small State Interaction*, pp. 210–14. For a discussion of Diego Garcia's evolution as a base, see Joel Larus, "Diego Garcia: The Military and Legal Limitations of America's Pivotal Base in the Indian Ocean," in William Dowdy and Russell Trood, eds., *The Indian Ocean: Perspectives on a Strategic Arena* (Durham, NC: Duke University Press, 1985), pp. 435–51.

74 Quoted in Marcus, *Ethiopia, Great Britain, and the United States*, p. 188.

75 Newsom, "US Policy Toward the Ogaden," p. 2.

76 Confidential interview no. 1.

77 For an overview written by a former US Ambassador to Somalia, see Raymond L. Thurston, "Détente in the Horn," *Africa Report* 14, 2 (February 1969): 6–13.

78 Confidential interview no. 36. According to several sources, Egal's appointment was facilitated by a small-scale CIA political action campaign designed to strengthen pro-Western elements in the Somali Youth League just prior to the 1967 presidential elections. See Roger Morris and Richard Mauzey, "Following the Scenario: Reflections on Five Case Histories in the Mode and Aftermath of CIA Intervention," in Robert L. Borosage and John Marks, eds., *The CIA File* (New York: Grossman Publishers, 1976).

79 Thurston, "The United States," p. 14.

80 Confidential interview no. 36.

81 *Ibid.*

82 For discussion, see I. M. Lewis, "The Politics of the 1969 Coup," *Journal of Modern African Studies* 10, 3 (1972): 383–408. See also Gary Payton, "The Somali Coup of 1969: The Case for Soviet Complicity," *Journal of Modern African Studies* 18, 3 (1980): 11–20.

83 Confidential interview no. 36. For a discussion of this theme, see I. M. Lewis, *A Pastoral Democracy: A Study of Pastoralism and Politics Among the Northern Somali of the Horn of Africa* (New York: Africana Publishing, 1982).

84 Interview with Fred L. Hadsel, US Ambassador to Somalia (1969–71), Atlanta, GA, November 4, 1989.

85 *Ibid.*

86 According to Thurston, "The United States" (p. 16), this practice "had benefited the Somali treasury and, no doubt, sticky-handed Somali officials personally for several years."

87 *Ibid.*

88 Interview with Hadsel (November 4, 1989).

89 US Senate, *Ethiopia and the Horn of Africa*, p. 45.

90 See US Senate, *United States Security Agreements and Commitments Abroad*.

91 *Ibid.*, p. 1922.

92 For example, as of July 1, 1970, the US MAAG numbered forty-eight officers, fifty-three enlisted men, and six authorized civilian personnel. Of this total, three each were stationed in Asmara, Massawa, and Harar. See *ibid.*, pp. 1914, 1947.

93 See Rasmuson, *A History of Kagnew Station*, pp. 63–70.

94 See Spencer, *Ethiopia at Bay*, p. 324; and Lefebvre, *Arms for the Horn*, pp. 131–48

95 Spencer, *Ethiopia at Bay*, p. 323.

96 For example, see "Donald E. Paradis Presents Paper on Urgent Need for Governmental Reforms to Emperor," US Embassy, Addis Ababa, Despatch no. 223, January 18, 1961, Enclosure: "Memorandum to His Imperial Majesty," Donald E. Paradis, US legal adviser to the Ethiopian goverment, to Emperor Selassie, January 18, 1961; "Politico-Military Assessment," US Embassy, Addis Ababa, Despatch no. 21, July 18, 1961; and "The Attempted Coup d'Etat-Nine Months Later," US Embassy, Addis Ababa, Despatch no. 51, August 15, 1961, esp. pp. 7–9. Reproduced in microfiche series produced by University Publications of America, *Africa: National Security Files, 1961–1963*.

97 Confidential interview no. 2.

98 Much of what is contained in the remainder of this section is based on two accounts written by US diplomats who served in the region: David A. Korn, *Ethiopia, the United States and the Soviet Union* (Carbondale: Southern Illinois University Press, 1986); and Donald K. Petterson, "Ethiopia Abandoned? An American Perspective," *International Affairs* 62, 4 (Autumn 1986): 627–45. Korn was the US Chargé d'Affaires in Ethiopia from 1982 to 1985. Petterson was the US Ambassador to Somalia from 1978 to 1982.

99 Quoted in Petterson, "Ethiopia Abandoned?" p. 630.

100 For a variety of interpretations of the causes and evolution of the Ethiopian revolution, see Christopher Clapham, *Transformation and Continuity in Revolutionary Ethiopia* (Cambridge: Cambridge University Press, 1988); Fred Halliday and Maxime Molyneux, *The Ethiopian Revolution* (London: Verso Publications, 1981); John W. Harbeson, *The Ethiopian Transformation: The Quest for the Post-Imperial State* (Boulder: Westview, 1988); Edmond J. Keller, *Revolutionary Ethiopia: From Empire to People's Republic* (Bloomington: Indiana University Press, 1988); René Lefort, *Ethiopia: A Heretical Revolution?* (London: Zed Press, 1983); John Markakis and Nega Ayele, *Class and Revolution in Ethiopia* (Nottingham: Spokesman Press, 1978); and Marina and David Ottaway, *Ethiopia: Empire in Revolution* (London: Africana Publishing Company, 1978).

101 For a discussion of the Africanist-Arabist split, see Lefebvre, *Arms for the Horn*, pp. 155–56.

102 For example, see two editorials carried in the *Chicago Tribune*, March 12, 1975, sec. 3, p. 2.

103 See US House, Committee on Foreign Affairs, Subcommittee on International Political and Military Affairs, *US Policy and Request for Sale of Arms to Ethiopia*, Hearing, March 5, 1975, 94th Cong., 1st Sess. (Washington, DC: GPO, 1975).

104 Interview with Arthur W. Hummel, Jr., US Ambassador to Ethiopia (1975-76), Washington, DC, June 28, 1989.

105 In addition, the administration is said to have "deliberately delayed acting on the request so as to avoid any impression that it was taking sides in the struggle between the Ethiopian government and the Eritrean rebels." For discussion, see Petterson, "Ethiopia Abandoned?" p. 632–34.

106 *Ibid.*, p. 635.

107 Quoted in Korn, *Ethiopia, the United States and the Soviet Union*, p. 17.

108 See US Senate, *Ethiopia and the Horn of Africa.*
109 Quoted in Korn, *Ethiopia, the United States and the Soviet Union*, p. 20. See also US Senate, *Ethiopia and the Horn of Africa*, p. 114.
110 Confidential interview no. 65.
111 See Korn, *Ethiopia, the United States and the Soviet Union*, p. 26.
112 Interview with Richard Moose, Assistant Secretary of State for African Affairs under the Carter administration, Washington, DC, June 26, 1989.
113 See US House, Committee on Foreign Relations, Subcommittee on Africa, *Foreign Assistance Legislation for Fiscal Year 1978* (Part 3) *Economic and Military Assistance Programs in Africa*, Hearings and Markup, March 17, 18, 23, 28, 29, and April 28, 1977, 95th Cong., 1st Sess. (Washington, DC, GPO, 1977), p. 193.
114 Korn, *Ethiopia, the United States and the Soviet Union*, p. 28.
115 Quoted in Lefebvre, *Arms for the Horn*, p. 153.
116 Korn, *Ethiopia*, 1986, p. 32.
117 For discussion, see Lefebvre, *Arms for the Horn*, pp. 175–96.
118 Confidential interview no. 13.
119 This statement reportedly was made in the presence of a reporter who was spending the day with the president. See Stanley Cloud, "With Jimmy from Dawn to Midnight," *Time* (April 18, 1977), p. 15.
120 See Cyrus Vance, *Hard Choices: Critical Years in America's Foreign Policy* (New York: Simon & Schuster, 1983), p. 73.
121 Confidential interview no. 13.
122 Quoted in Korn, *Ethiopia, the United States and the Soviet Union*, p. 36. See also Petterson, "Ethiopia Abandoned?" p. 639.
123 Nelson P. Valdés, "Cuba's Involvement in the Horn of Africa: The Ethiopian–Somali War and the Eritrean Conflict," *Cuban Studies/Estudios Cubanos* 10, 1 (January 1980): 55.
124 For discussion of US and Soviet involvement in the Ogaden War, see Larry C. Napper, "The Ogaden War: Some Implications for Crisis Prevention," in Alexander L. George, ed., *Managing US–Soviet Rivalry: Problems of Crisis Prevention* (Boulder: Westview, 1983), pp. 225–53; and I. William Zartman, *Ripe for Resolution: Conflict and Intervention in Africa* (New York and Oxford: Oxford University Press, 1985), pp. 71–117.
125 See Vance, *Hard Choices*, pp. 73–74.
126 See US House, Committee on International Relations, *War in the Horn of Africa: A Firsthand Report on the Challenges For United States Policy*, 95th Cong., 1st Sess. (Washington, DC: GPO, 1978).
127 Jimmy Carter, "Foreign Policy Address of 19 January 1978." In *Public Papers of the Presidents of the United States, Jimmy Carter* (vol. 1) (Washington, DC: GPO, 1979).
128 Quoted in Zbigniew Brzezinski, *Power and Principle: Memoirs of the National Security Adviser 1977–1981* (New York: Farrar, Straus, Giroux, 1983), p. 182.
129 *Ibid.*, p. 183.
130 *Ibid.*, p. 180. One example of this effort was a front page story published by the *New York Times* on November 17, 1977 that detailed the scope of Soviet–Cuban involvement on the African continent.
131 The term "arc of crisis" was publicly stated for the first time by Brzezinski

in a December 20, 1978 address to a foreign policy association. See Bernard Gwertzman, "The Crescent of Crisis: Iran and a Region of Rising Instability," *Time* (January 15, 1979), p. 18. See also George Lenczowski, "The Arc of Crisis: Its Central Sector," *Foreign Affairs* 57 (Spring 1979): 796–820.

132 Jimmy Carter, "A Foreign Policy Based on America's Essential Character," *Department of State Bulletin* 76, 1981 (June 13, 1977): 621.

133 Jimmy Carter, "State of the Union," *Department of State Bulletin* (February 1978).

134 Korn, *Ethiopia, the United States and the Soviet Union*, p. 44.

135 Brzezinski, *Power and Principle*, p. 183.

136 Vance, *Hard Choices*, p. 86.

137 Quoted in Brzezinski, *Power and Principle*, p. 182.

138 For discussion, see "Top Carter Aides Seen in Discord on How to React to Soviet Actions; Brzezinski Appears Tougher than Vance – President Leans Toward National Security Adviser," *New York Times*, May 1–2, 1978. For Carter's statement, see "The President: News Conferences of February 17, March 2 and 9 (Excerpts)," *State Department Bulletin*, vol. 78 (1978), pp. 20–21. See also Brzezinski, *Power and Principle*, pp. 184–90; and Vance, *Hard Choices*, pp. 84-88.

139 Vance, *Hard Choices*, p. 88.

140 Interview with Frederic L. Chapin, US Ambassador to Ethiopia (1978–80), Washington, DC, June 28, 1989.

141 See US House, Committee on Foreign Affairs, Subcommittee on Africa, *Foreign Assistance Legislation for Fiscal Years 1980–81* (Part 6) *Economic and Military Assistance Programs in Africa*, Hearings and Markup, February 13, 14, 21, 22, 27, 28; March 5, 6, 7, and 12, 1979, 96th Cong., 1st Sess. (Washington, DC: GPO, 1979), p. 338. (Hereinafter *House Foreign Assistance FYs 1980–81.*)

142 For a list of other claimants, see US House, Committee on Foreign Affairs, Subcommittee on Africa, *Foreign Assistance Legislation for Fiscal Year 1981* (Part 7) *Economic and Security Assistance Programs in Africa*, Hearings and Markup, February 7, 12, 13, 20, 25, 26, 27, 28; March 5 and 6, 1980, 96th Cong., 2nd Sess. (Washington, DC: GPO, 1980), pp. 333–34. (Hereinafter *House Foreign Assistance FY 1981.*)

143 Interview with Chapin (June 28, 1989).

144 Confidential interview no. 66.

145 For discussion, see *House Foreign Assistance FYs 1980–81*, pp. 443–78.

146 Interview with Chapin (June 28, 1989).

147 For discussion, see Lefebvre, *Arms for the Horn*, pp. 197–219.

148 Petterson, "Ethiopia Abandoned?" p. 642.

149 Donald K. Petterson, "Somalia and the United States, 1977–1983: The New Relationship," in Gerald J. Bender, James S. Coleman, and Richard L. Sklar, eds., *African Crisis Areas and US Foreign Policy* (Berkeley: University of California Press, 1985), p. 199.

150 See, for example, Matthew Nimitz, "Somalia and the US Security Framework," *Department of State Bulletin* 80, 2045 (December 1980): 22–26.

151 Jimmy Carter, "State of the Union," *Department of State Bulletin* (February 1980).

152 Petterson, "Somalia and the United States," p. 201.
153 Confidential interview no. 45.
154 Confidential interview no. 16.
155 Petterson, "Ethiopia Abandoned?" p. 643.
156 For congressional debate over the issues of military access and aid to Somalia, see *House Foreign Assistance FY 1981*, pp. 304–36.
157 Quoted in Juan de Onis, "US–Somalia Pact Drawing Opposition," *New York Times*, August 29, 1980.
158 Dougherty, *The Horn of Africa*, p. 60.
159 For discussion, see US House, Committee on Foreign Affairs, Subcommittee on Africa, *Foreign Assistance Legislation for Fiscal Year 1982* (Part 8) *Economic and Security Assistance Programs in Africa*, Hearings and Markup, March 19, 24, 26, 31; April 1, 2, and 27, 1981, 97th Cong., 1st Sess. (Washington, DC: GPO, 1981), pp. 347–434. (Hereinafter *House Foreign Assistance FY 1982*.)
160 One scholar noted that the Reagan administration's foreign policies toward the Horn of Africa had a "Carteresque" ring. For discussion, see David D. Laitin, "Security, Ideology and Development on Africa's Horn: United States Policy – Reagan and the Future," in Robert I. Rotberg, ed., *Africa in the 1990s and Beyond: US Policy Opportunities and Choices* (Algonac, MI: Reference Publications, 1988), pp. 204–19.
161 Confidential interview no. 3.
162 See Korn, *Ethiopia, the United States and the Soviet Union*, pp. 56–57.
163 *Ibid.* For an extended discussion, see Lefebvre, *Arms for the Horn*, 220–40.
164 Confidential interviews no. 16 and no. 25.
165 Korn, *Ethiopia, the United States and the Soviet Union*, pp. 77–78.
166 Confidential interview no. 30.
167 Confidential interview no. 4.
168 For a summary of early House Subcommittee concerns over Somalia's continuing involvement in the Ogaden region, see US House, Committee on Foreign Affairs, Subcommittee on Africa, *Foreign Assistance Legislation for Fiscal Year 1983* (Part 7) *Economic and Security Assistance Programs for Africa*, Hearings and Markup, April 20, 21, and 29, 1982, 97th Cong., 2nd Sess. (Washington, DC: GPO, 1982), pp. xxii–xxiii. For a summary of concerns over human rights abuses in Somalia, see US House, Committee on Foreign Affairs, Subcommittee on Africa, *Foreign Assistance Legislation for Fiscal Years 1988-89* (Part 6) *Economic and Security Assistance Programs for Africa*, Hearings and Markup, March 4, 10, 18, and 19, 1987, 100th Cong., 1st Sess. (Washington, DC: GPO, 1987), pp. xxx, 256–62. See also US House, Committee on Foreign Affairs, Subcommittee on Human Rights and International Organizations, Subcommittee on Africa, *The Human Rights Situation in South Africa, Zaire, the Horn of Africa, and Uganda*, Hearings, June 21; August 9, 1984, 98th Cong., 2nd Sess. (Washington, DC: GPO, 1985).
169 Jack Shephard, "The Politics of Food Aid," *Africa Report* 30, 2 (March-April 1985): 52.
170 *Ibid.*
171 *Ibid.*
172 See US House, Committee on Foreign Affairs, *The Impact of US Foreign*

> *Policy on Seven African Countries: Report of a Congressional Study Mission to Ethiopia, Zaire, Zimbabwe, Ivory Coast, Algeria, and Morocco, August 6–25, 1985 and a Staff Study Mission to Tunisia, August 24–27, 1983*, 98th Cong., 2nd Sess. (Washington, DC: GPO, 1984).

173 "Ethiopia's Drought and Famine Crisis," *Africa Report*, 30, 1 (January–February 1985): 47.

174 For a discussion of this legislation, see Jack Shephard, "Congress and the White House at Odds," *Africa Report* 30, 3 (May–June 1985): 25–28.

175 For a useful breakdown of all US famine relief distributed during FYs 1984–85, see Korn, *Ethiopia, the United States and the Soviet Union*, pp. 186–89.

176 See Shephard, "Congress and the White House at Odds."

177 Interview with Jennifer White, former legislative staff assistant to Toby Roth, Washington, DC, June 16, 1989.

178 H.R. 588, "A Bill to Express the Opposition of the United States to Oppression in Ethiopia, to Promote the Development of Democracy in Ethiopia, and for Other Purposes," pp. 2–3.

179 For the debate over H.R. 588, see US House, Committee on Foreign Affairs, Subcommittees on International Economic Policy and Trade, and on Africa, *Proposed Economic Sanctions Against South Africa*, Hearings and Markup, March 22, 23; April 20, 28; and May 3, 1988, 100th Cong., 2nd Sess. (Washington, DC: GPO, 1988), pp. 467–85.

180 For a description of the evolution of these guerrilla groups, see Daniel Compagnon, "The Somali Opposition Fronts: Some Comments and Questions," *Horn of Africa* 13, 1–2 (January–March, April–June 1990): 29–54.

181 For a discussion of these and other guerrilla conflicts in the Horn of Africa, see Markakis, *National and Class Conflict in the Horn of Africa*. See also a special edition of *Africa Today*, "Eritrea: An Emerging New Nation in Africa's Troubled Horn," 38, 2 (1992); as well as Georges Nzongola-Ntalaja, *Conflict in the Horn of Africa* (Atlanta, GA: African Studies Association Press, 1991).

182 Robert Gersony, *Why Somalis Flee: Synthesis of Accounts of Conflict Experience in Northern Somalia by Somali Refugees, Displaced Persons and Others* (Washington, DC: Bureau for Refugee Programs, Department of State, August 1989), pp. 60–62. See also Africa Watch, *Somalia: A Government at War With Its Own People; Testimonies About the Killings and the Conflict in the North* (London: Africa Watch, 1990).

183 US General Accounting Office (GAO), *Somalia: Observations Regarding the Northern Conflict and Resulting Conditions* (Washington, DC: GAO, May 1989), pp 7–9.

184 Confidential interview no. 19.

185 Quoted in US House, Committee on Foreign Affairs, Subcommittee on Africa, *Reported Massacres and Indiscriminate Killings in Somalia*, Hearing, July 14, 1988, 100th Cong., 2nd Sess. (Washington, DC: GPO, 1989), p. 2.

186 Confidential interview no. 30.

187 Confidential interview no. 19.

188 Countries in Africa subject to notification requirements during FYs 1990 and 1991 were Burundi, Liberia, Somalia, and Sudan.

189 Confidential interviews nos. 30 and 7.

190 In order of publication, see Amnesty International, *Somalia: A Long-Term Human Rights Crisis* (London: Amnesty International Publications, September 1988); GAO, *Somalia*; Gersony, *Why Somalis Flee*; and Africa Watch, *Somalia: A Government at War With its Own People*.

191 Confidential interview no. 15.

192 Confidential interview no. 7.

193 Quoted in US House, Committee on Foreign Affairs, Subcommittees on International Economic Policy and Trade, and on Africa, *Proposed Economic Sanctions Against South Africa*, Hearings and Markup, March 22, 23; April 20, 28; and May 3, 1988, 100th Cong., 2nd Sess. (Washington, DC: GPO, 1988), pp. 467–85.

194 Quoted in US House, Committee on Foreign Affairs, Subcommittees on Human Rights and International Organizations and on Africa, *Update on the Recent Developments in Ethiopia: The Famine Crisis*, Hearing, April 21, 1988, 100th Cong., 2nd Sess. (Washington, DC: GPO, 1988), p. 6.

195 Quoted in Jane Perlez, "Ethiopian Government Fights for Life," *New York Times*, April 17, 1990, p. A4.

196 For an analysis of Israel's role in the Horn, see Lefebvre, *Arms for the Horn*, pp. 42–43, 133, 161–63, 261, 263. See also Victor Levine, "The African–Israeli Connection 40 Years Later," *Middle East Review* 21 (Fall 1988): 12–17; and Mitchell Bard, "The Evolution of Israel's Africa Policy," *Middle East Review* 21 (Winter 1988/89): 21–28.

197 For a general overview, see David Kessler, *The Falashas: The Forgotten Jews of Ethiopia* (New York: Schocken Books, 1982). For a discussion of Operation Moses, see Tudor Parfit, *Operation Moses: The Story of the Exodus of the Falasha Jews From Ethiopia* (London: Stein and Day, 1985).

198 Quoted in Flora Lewis, "Ethiopia Peers West," *New York Times*, January 30, 1990, p. A15.

199 Confidential interview no. 60.

200 Tom Hundley, "These Days, It's Ethiopian Jews Who Feel Passed Over," *Chicago Tribune*, July 15, 1990, sec. 1, p. 17. See also Jane Hunter, "Israel and Ethiopia: Cluster Bombs and Falashas," *Middle East International*, no. 368 (February 2, 1990): 11–12.

201 Quoted in *ibid*.

202 Richard Greenfield, "Somalia: Siad's Sad Legacy," *Africa Report* (March–April 1991): 13–18.

203 French helicopters took part in another rescue mission in which forty-seven people were evacuated to a French frigate from the town of Merca.

204 For a discussion of this theme, see Maina Kiai, "Perestroika's Impact on US Policy Toward Somalia," *TransAfrica Forum* 7, 1 (Spring 1990): 17–24.

205 Quoted in Jane Perlez, "Heavy Fighting Erupts in Somali Capital," *New York Times*, January 1, 1991, p. A3.

206 Confidential interview no. 88.

207 For example, see Peter J. Schraeder and Jerel A. Rosati, "Policy Dilemmas in the Horn of Africa: Contradictions in the US–Somalia Relationship," *Northeast African Studies* 9, 3 (1987): 19–42.

208 Quoted in Perlez, "Somalia, Abandoned," p. E2.

209 *Ibid*.

210 See Said S. Samatar, *Somalia: A Nation in Turmoil* (London: The Minority Rights Group, 1991).
211 Confidential Interview no. 101.
212 Confidential interview no. 90. As of March 1992, for example, the US owed $400 million in unpaid dues (including $140 million in peace-keeping costs). Moreover, Baker reportedly received a "frosty reception" when he requested an extra $810 million (above the $107 million already approved by Congress) to pay for peace-keeping operations (not including Somalia) envisioned for 1992 and 1993. See Paul Lewis, "Security Council Weighs Role in Somali Civil War," *New York Times*, March 18, 1992, p. A9.
213 Confidential interview no. 89.
214 See Gayle Smith, "Test of US Africa Policy: Birth Pains of a New Ethiopia," *The Nation*, July 1, 1991, pp. 1, 18–20.
215 Quoted in Terrence Lyons, "The Transition in Ethiopia," *CSIS Africa Notes*, no. 127 (August 27, 1991): 5.
216 Quoted in Clifford Krauss, "Ethiopia and Rebels Near Peace Talks," *New York Times*, May 14, 1991, p. A7.
217 See, for example, congressional testimony by Cohen, US House, Committee on Foreign Affairs, Subcommittee on Africa, *The Political Crisis in Ethiopia and the Role of the United States*, Hearing, June 18, 1991, 102nd Cong., 1st Sess. (Washington, DC: GPO, 1992).
218 Quoted in Clifford Krauss, "Ethiopia's Leader Agrees to Give Up Capital to Rebels," *New York Times*, May 28, 1991, p. A1.
219 Quoted in Jane Perlez, "Reversal on Ethiopia: Plight of Jews and the Prospects for Chaos Aroused US Interest in a Mediation Role," *New York Times*, May 31, 1991, p. A1.
220 See, for example, US House, Committee on Foreign Affairs, Subcommittee on Africa, and Select Committee on Hunger, International Task Force, *Famine in Ethiopia*, Joint Hearing, February 28, 1990, 101st Cong., 2nd Sess. (Washington, DC: GPO, 1990); and US House, Committee on Foreign Affairs, Subcommittee on Africa, and Select Committee on Hunger, International Task Force, *Conflict and Famine in the Horn of Africa*, Hearing, May 30, 1991, 102nd Cong., 1st Sess. (Washington, DC: GPO, 1991).
221 For a discussion of this operation and the politics of Falasha emigration, see Teshome G. Wagaw, "The International Political Ramifications of Falasha Emigration," *Journal of Modern African Studies* 29, 4 (1991): 557–82.
222 See Steve McDonald, "Ethiopia: Learning a Lesson," *Africa Report* 37, 5 (September–October 1992): 27–29.
223 *Ibid.*, p. 29.
224 See Cameron McWhirter and Gur Melamede, "Ethiopia: The Ethnicity Factor," *Africa Report* 37, 5 (September–October 1992): 30–33.
225 Confidential interview no. 98.
226 See Michael R. Gordon, "Pentagon to Fly Food to Somalia to Fight Hunger," *New York Times*, August 15, 1992, pp. A1, A2.
227 Quoted in address reproduced in "Bush's Talk on Somalia: US Must 'Do It Right,'" *New York Times*, December 5, 1992, p. A4.
228 For a good summary of the background to US intervention, including a

chronology, see Walter S. Clarke, *Somalia: Background Information For Operation Restore Hope 1992–93* (Carlisle, PA: Department of National Security and Strategy, US Army War College, Carlisle Barracks, December 1992) (Special Report of the Strategic Studies Institute, US Army War College). For a critique, see Jeffrey Clark, "Debacle in Somalia," *Foreign Affairs* 72, 1 (1992–93): 109–23.

229 See Jane Perlez, "Bush Meets Victims of the Famine in Somalia," *New York Times*, January 1, 1993, pp. A1, A4.

230 For example, see Michael R. Gordon, "Somali Aid Plan is Called Most Ambitious Option," *New York Times*, November 28, 1992, p. A4.

231 See Elaine Scielino, "Bush Offered Troops to Aid Somalis Despite C.I.A.'s Doubts," *New York Times*, December 3, 1992, p. A8.

232 Quoted in Michael R. Gordon, "Envoy Asserts Intervention in Somalia is Risky and Not in Interests of US," *New York Times*, December 6, 1992, p. A12.

233 *Ibid.*, For another critique, see Alex de Waal and Rakiya Omaar, "Somalia: the Lessons of Famine," *Africa Report* 37, 6 (November–December 1992): 62–64.

234 Quoted in Jane Perlez, "Somali Warlord Agrees to Allow U.N. to Protect its Relief Supplies," *New York Times*, August 13, 1992, p. A1.

235 See Walter Goodman, "Re Somalia: How Much Did TV Shape Policy?" *New York Times*, December 8, 1992, p. B4. For a critical analysis of the role of the media in the Somali crisis, see Jane Perlez, "Life and Times," *The New York Times Magazine*, January 24, 1993, p. 54.

236 For example, see Leslie H. Gelb, "Shoot to Feed Somalia," *New York Times*, November 19, 1992, p. A17. See also Anthony Lewis, "Action or Death," *New York Times*, November 20, 1992, p. A15.

237 For an earlier statement co-authored by Simon and Kassebaum, see "Save Somalia From Itself," *New York Times*, January 2, 1992, p. A11.

238 For figures and analysis, see Peter Applebome, "Seared by Faces of Need, Americans Say, 'How Could We Not Do This?'" *New York Times*, December 13, 1992, p. A8.

239 See Michael Wines, "Aides Say US Role in Somalia Gives Bush a Way to Exist in Glory," *New York Times*, December 6, 1992, p. A12.

240 *Ibid.*

241 *Ibid.*

242 Thomas L. Friedman, "In Somalia, New Criteria for US Role," *New York Times*, December 5, 1992, p. A1.

243 Quoted in "Bush's Talk on Somalia," p. A4.

244 See Alison Mitchell, "First Marines Leave Somalia, a Signal to the U.N.," *New York Times*, January 20, 1993, p. A3.

245 Quoted in "Bush's Talk on Somalia," p. A4.

246 See, for example, Update Section, "US Commits Force to Somalia, But For How Long?" *Africa Report* 38, 1 (January–February 1993): 5–6, 11.

247 See Alison Mitchell, "US Legislator Says U.N. Delays Steps to Take Over Somalia Roles," *New York Times*, January 11, 1993, p. A4.

248 See Francis A. Kornegay, Jr., "Africa in the New World Order," *Africa Report* 38, 1 (January–February 1993): 13–17.

5 US foreign policy toward South Africa

1 Quoted in Anthony Lake, "Caution and Concern: The Making of American Policy Toward South Africa, 1946–1971," Ph.D. dissertation, Princeton, NJ, Princeton University, 1974, p. 74.

2 Quoted in William Minter, *King Solomon's Mines Revisited: Western Interests and the Burdened History of Southern Africa* (New York: Basic Books, 1986), p. 137.

3 Quoted in Sheridan Johns and R. Hunt Davis, Jr., eds. *Mandela, Tambo, and the African National Congress: The Struggle Against Apartheid, 1948–1990* (New York and Oxford: Oxford University Press, 1991), p. 103.

4 For a comprehensive listing of materials related to US relations with South Africa, see Y. G.-M. Lulat, *US Relations With South Africa: An Annotated Bibliography* 2 vols. (Boulder: Westview, 1991).

5 Quote taken from a letter from Roosevelt to Henry White, New York, March 30, 1896. Reproduced in Elting G. Morison, ed., *The Letters of Theodore Roosevelt*, vol. 1 (Cambridge: Harvard University Press, 1951), p. 523. For several overviews of US foreign policy toward South Africa prior to 1948, see John H. Ferguson, *American Diplomacy and the Boer War* (Philadelphia: University Press, 1939); Myra S. Goldstein, "The Genesis of Modern American Relations With South Africa," Ph.D. dissertation, Buffalo, NY, State University of New York at Buffalo, 1972; Clement T. Keto, "American Involvement in South Africa, 1870–1915," Ph.D. dissertation, Washington, DC, Georgetown University, 1972; Thomas J. Noer, *Briton, Boer, and Yankee: The United States and South Africa 1870–1914* (Kent, Ohio: Kent State University Press, 1978); and Ward Anthony Spooner, "United States Foreign Policy Toward South Africa, 1919–1941: Political and Economic Aspects," Ph.D. dissertation, St. Johns University, 1979.

6 See Kevin Danaher, *The Political Economy of US Policy Toward South Africa* (Boulder: Westview, 1985), pp. 24–26; and Noer, *Britain, Boer, and Yankee*, pp. 74–76.

7 See Thomas J. Noer, *Cold War and Black Liberation: The United States and White Rule in Africa, 1948–1968* (Columbia, MO: University of Missouri Press, 1985), p. 18.

8 Lake, "Caution and Concern," p. 49.

9 Noer, *Cold War and Black Liberation*, pp. 18–19.

10 Consider, for example, a 1942 statement by B. J. Vorster, future Prime Minister of South Africa: "We stand for Christian Nationalism, which is an ally of Nazism." Quoted in John Laurence, *Race Propaganda and South Africa* (London: Victor Gollancz Ltd., 1979), p. 141.

11 Quoted in *ibid.*, p. 20.

12 Whereas the agreement guaranteeing Indian rights was known as the Capetown Agreement, the legislation which restricted those same rights was entitled the Asiatic Land Tenure and Indian Representation Act of 1946.

13 For discussion, see Lake, "Caution and Concern," pp. 56–60.

14 *Ibid.*, p. 63.

15 Interview with William B. Edmondson, US Ambassador to South Africa (1978–81), Washington, DC, June 18, 1989.

16 *Ibid.*

17 Quoted in Noer, *Cold War and Black Liberation*, pp. 24-25.

18 However, South Africa initially refused to join the US-led effort in Korea, presumably at least partially out of disdain for contributing forces under a UN umbrella. "Only after our strong representations (and opposition criticism within the country)," noted one assessment of US foreign policy toward South Africa, "did the South African government agree to give help." See William R. Duggan, Policy Planning Council, and Waldemar B. Campbell, Bureau of African Affairs, Department of State, *National Strategy Series: South Africa* (intermediate draft), p. 202. Reproduced in microfiche series produced by University Publications of America, *Africa: National Security Files, 1961-1963.*

19 See Noer, *Cold War and Black Liberation*, pp. 38-40.

20 Quoted in Danaher, *The Political Economy of US Policy Toward South Africa*, p. 68.

21 Quoted in *ibid.*, p. 69.

22 Quoted in *ibid.*, p. 68.

23 See Noer, *Cold War and Black Liberation*, pp. 24-225.

24 For discussion, see Danaher, *The Political Economy of US Policy Toward South Africa*, p. 68. See also US House, Committee on Foreign Affairs, Subcommittee on Africa, *US Business Involvement in Southern Africa* (Part II) Hearings, May-December 1971, 92nd Cong., 1st Sess. (Washington, DC: GPO, 1972), pp. 40-76.

25 Danaher, *The Political Economy of US Policy Toward South Africa*, p. 68.

26 Noer, *Cold War and Black Liberation*, p. 51. See Mary-Louise Hopper, "The Johannesburg Bus Boycott," *Africa Today*, no. 4 (November-December 1957): 13-16.

27 Noer, *Cold War and Black Liberation*, p. 52.

28 See Study Commission on US Policy Toward South Africa, *South Africa: Time Running Out* (Berkeley: University of California Press and Foreign Policy Study Foundation, 1981), pp. 173-76, 187-88.

29 *Ibid.*, pp. 54-55.

30 *New York Times*, March 23, 1960.

31 Secretary of State Herter, who was particularly incensed at apparent US support for protests in a friendly country, apparently "disowned" the press release in a memo to Andrew Goodpaster, staff secretary to Eisenhower. See Noer, *Cold War and Black Liberation*, p. 55.

32 For statements made by Henry Cabot Lodge, US Ambassador to the UN, as well as the text of the Security Council resolution adopted on April 1, 1960, see "Security Council Calls for Adherence to U.N. Principles in South Africa," *Department of State Bulletin* 17, 1087 (April 25, 1960): 667-69.

33 Minter, *King Soloman's Mines Revisited*, p. 135.

34 The tracking stations are described in NSC, "Briefing for NSC Standing Group. Subject: South Africa and South West Africa," March 10, 1964, pp. 11-12. Document obtained from the National Security Archive.

35 Consider, for example, the following NSC assessment: "Continued use of these stations, or use of new alternative stations in the same geographic region including a variety of possible locations outside South Africa, is

essential to accomplishment of the space and missile programs to which the US is already committed in this decade. NASA has need for at least one additional station now and other increments may be necessary before 1970." Quoted in *ibid.*, p. 11.

36 See, for example, the following speeches by Williams: "South Africa in Transition," *Department of State Bulletin* (October 16, 1961): 638–42; and "The Three 'A's' of Africa: Algeria, Angola, and Apartheid," *Department of State Bulletin* (November 27, 1961): 280–88.

37 Francis Plimpton, *Department of State Bulletin* (April 24, 1961).

38 Confidential interview no. 36.

39 *Ibid.*

40 See Department of State, "Republic of South Africa: Guidelines for Policy and Operations," May 1962, p. 2. Reproduced in microfiche series produced by University Publications of America, *Africa: National Security Files, 1961–1963*.

41 See NSC, "Briefing for NSC Standing Group. Subject: South Africa and South West Africa," March 10, 1964, p. 11; and Department of State. "Republic of South Africa: Guidelines for Policy and Operations," May 1962, p. 7. Documents obtained from the National Security Archive.

42 Confidential interview no. 36.

43 Joseph Albright and Marcia Kunstel, "CIA Tip Led to '62 Arrest of Mandela: Ex-Official Tells of US 'Coup' to Aid S. Africa," *The Atlanta Constitution*, June 10, 1990, p. A14.

44 See, for example, CIA, Office of Current Intelligence, "Special Report: Subversive Movements in South Africa," May 10, 1963. Document obtained from the National Security Archive.

45 See US Embassy, Pretoria, "Country Internal Defense Plan: South Africa," December 18, 1962, p. 2. Document obtained from the National Security Archive.

46 Quoted in Albright and Kunstel, "CIA Tip," p. A14. For discussion of Mandela's role, see US Embassy, Pretoria, "Country Internal Defense Plan," pp. 3–4.

47 See Albright and Kunstel, "CIA Tip," p. A14.

48 Among the types of sanctions sought were expulsion from international organizations (political), a ban on trade with both countries (economic), and the cessation of all military cooperation (military).

49 Quoted in Arthur M. Schlesinger, Jr., *A Thousand Days: John F. Kennedy in the White House* (Greenwich, CT: Fawcett Publications, 1967), p. 535.

50 Letter from Stevenson to Kennedy, June 26, 1963. Document obtained from the National Security Archive.

51 Confidential interview no. 33.

52 For an overview of pro-sanctions arguments, see *ibid.* See also a memorandum from Williams entitled, "US Position in the Security Council on the Question of Portuguese Territories and Apartheid," July 11, 1963. For an overview of why sanctions would threaten bureaucratic interests in Portuguese Africa and South Africa, see Maxwell Taylor, Chairman of the Joint Chiefs of Staff, memorandum for the Secretary of Defense, "US Policy Toward Portugal and the Republic of South Africa," July 11, 1963. All

documents obtained from the National Security Archive. For an overview of domestic political considerations, see Schlesinger, *A Thousand Days*, pp. 534–38.

53 Schlesinger, *A Thousand Days*, p. 537.

54 After arguing that any joint resolution against Portugal and South Africa should be separated into separate discussions in order to permit "more rational consideration," the Joint Chiefs of Staff claimed that Washington should "resist the institution of strong measures against Portugal." In the case of South Africa, the Joint Chiefs of Staff merely noted that any UN effort should be "examined upon its merits." The greater importance attached to Portugal was further noted in an accompanying letter signed by McNamara in which he explained that there was "no truly satisfactory alternative" to US facilities in the Azores, and continued access to the missile tracking station in South Africa was described as "important" although "not vital." See Maxwell D. Taylor, Chairman, Joint Chiefs of Staff, memorandum for the Secretary of Defense, "US Policy Toward Portugal and the Republic of South Africa," July 10, 1963; and a letter from McNamara to Rusk concerning the US position on a possible UN Security Council resolution calling for severe measures against Portugal and the Republic of South Africa, July 11, 1963. Documents obtained from the National Security Archive.

55 See collection of statements, including that of Ambassador Stevenson on August 2, 1963, as contained in "Security Council Calls for Ban on Sale of Arms to South Africa," *Department of State Bulletin*, vol. 49, no. 1261 (August 26, 1963): 333–39. Quoted portion found on p. 335.

56 *Ibid.*, p. 335.

57 Among the bureaucratic interests cited by Sloan were US–South African cooperation in annual anti-submarine warfare exercises (CAPEX) in the region, the use of South Africa as a "provisioning point" for military operations, and continued access to the missile tracking station. Letter from Deputy Assistant Secretary of Defense Frank R. Sloan to Deputy Under Secretary for Political Affairs U. Alexis Johnson, January 31, 1964. Document obtained from the National Security Archive.

58 Cable from Stevenson to Rusk, "US Arms Policy Re South Africa," September 13, 1963. For an overview of the debate, see NSC, Bill Brubeck, memorandum for McGeorge Bundy, "Proposed Lockheed Sale to South Africa," September 22, 1964. Documents obtained from the National Security Archive.

59 Confidential interview no. 33.

60 NSC, Bill Brubeck, memorandum to NSC Director McGeorge Bundy, "Proposed Lockheed Sale to South Africa," September 22, 1964, p. 4. Document obtained from the National Security Archive.

61 Secretary of Defense, Robert S. McNamara, memorandum to President Lyndon B. Johnson, November 20, 1964. Document obtained from the National Security Archive.

62 As explained by Lake, "Caution and Concern," pp. 105–6, the Johnson administration generally refused to sell items that were of immediate military value. Among these were a 1965 request for single-engine Cessna

aircraft hosting "special equipment" of value to the South African military, a 1965 request for a marine patrol aircraft (the Atlantic 1150) developed in conjunction with NATO, and a 1966 request for three French Mystère 20 fighters that included US-made engines. However, the administration did allow for the sale of light aircraft, transport aircraft, and helicopters to civilian purchasers in South Africa, even though they "could serve as military transport in a future crisis." The numbers of aircraft sold ranged from 194 in 1963 to 284 in 1969, the first and last full years of the Johnson administration (p. 137).

63 For a summary, see *ibid.*, pp. 372–81.

64 *Ibid.*

65 Department of State, J. Wayne Fredericks, cable to US Consulate General, Cape Town, "Cape Town," February 14, 1967. Document obtained from the National Security Archive.

66 Confidential interview no 36.

67 For the unabridged text of NSSM 39, as well as an analysis placing the document in perspective, see Mohamed A. El-Khawas and Barry Cohen, eds., *The Kissinger Study of Southern Africa: National Security Study Memorandum 39* (Westport, CT: Lawrence Hill & Company, 1976). For an intriguing insider's analysis as written by the NSC Africa specialist who drafted the final NSSM 39 document, see Roger Morris, *Uncertain Greatness: Henry Kissinger and American Foreign Policy* (New York: Harper & Row, 1977), pp. 107–22.

68 The CIA was the most fervent supporter of this point of view. Consider, for example, the following passage by NSC Africa specialist Roger Morris who sat in on the meetings in which the various approaches were debated: "So transparently pro-white was the CIA presentation, so disdainful of black African opposition, so reflective of the views of the white security services on whose reports CIA analysis was based, that at one point even the cynical Kissinger passed a puzzled note to an aide, 'Why is he doing this?' At the one-word reply, 'Clients,' he gave a knowing scowl. Southern Africa was one in a train of NSC briefings, intelligence estimates, and field reports during 1969 that convinced Kissinger of the Agency's preoccupation with its established role and sources, and of [CIA Director] Helms's basic inability or unwillingness to control the resulting bias." See Morris, *Uncertain Greatness*, p. 115. For further discussion of option no. 1, see El-Khawas and Cohen, *The Kissinger Study of Southern Africa*, pp. 103–5.

69 For further discussion, see El-Khawas and Cohen, *The Kissinger Study of Southern Africa*, 103–5.

70 For a comprehensive discussion of the "tar baby" option as applied to US foreign policy toward Southern Rhodesia (Zimbabwe), see Anthony Lake, *The "Tar Baby" Option: American Policy Toward Southern Rhodesia* (New York: Columbia University Press, 1976).

71 For further discussion, see El-Khawas and Cohen, *The Kissinger Study of Southern Africa*, pp. 109–11.

72 For further discussion, see *ibid.*, pp. 111–14.

73 Clyde Fergusson and William Cotter, "South Africa: What is to be Done?" *Foreign Affairs* 56, 2 (1978): 266–67.

74 For further discussion, see El-Khawas and Cohen, *The Kissinger Study of Southern Africa*, pp. 114–16.

75 Lake, "Caution and Concern," p. 173.

76 Morris, *Uncertain Greatness*, p. 107.

77 BOSS was created on May 1, 1969 to "assume overall planning and direction of all South African security police and intelligence operations." For a critical account of the CIA's early relationship with this organization, see Stephen Talbot, "The CIA and BOSS: Thick as Thieves," in Ellen Ray, William Schapp, Karl van Meter, and Louis Wolf, eds., *Dirty Work 2: The CIA in Africa* (Secaucus, NJ: Lyle Stuart, 1979), pp. 266–75. The level of cooperation between the US and South African intelligence services was marked by the close relationship between General Hendrik van den Bergh, the director of BOSS, and George Bush who, during the 1970s, was the director of the CIA. See Danaher, *The Political Economy of US Policy Toward South Africa*, p. 97.

78 For a comparative analysis of the implementation of the US arms embargo against Portugal and South Africa during the Kennedy, Johnson, and Nixon administrations, see US House, Committee on Foreign Affairs, Subcommittee on Africa, *Implementation of the US Arms Embargo (Against Portugal and South Africa, and Related Issues)*, Hearings, March 20, 22; April 6, 1973, 93rd Cong., 1st Sess. (Washington, DC: GPO, 1973).

79 "In spite of the technical justifications produced by NASA," explained Diggs, "it is obvious that they have in fact responded to pressures by myself, Congressman Rangel of New York, and the Congressional Black Caucus, and our friends in the Senate, particularly Senator Edward Kennedy." Quoted in Steven Metz, "The Anti-Apartheid Movement and the Formulation of American Policy Toward South Africa 1969–1981," Ph.D. dissertation, Baltimore, MD, Johns Hopkins University, 1985, p. 198.

80 For an assessment of the impacts of "communication" on US–South African relations, see Minter, *King Soloman's Mines Revisited*, pp. 222–25.

81 See, for example, US House, Committee on Foreign Affairs, Subcommittee on Africa, *South Africa and United States Foreign Policy*, Hearings, April 2 and 15, 1969, 91st Cong., 1st Sess. (Washington, DC: GPO, 1969).

82 For a more complete analysis of the efforts of Diggs and the CBC during this period, see John Joseph Seiler, "The Formulation of US Policy Toward Southern Africa, 1957–1976: The Failure of Good Intentions," Ph.D. dissertation, The University of Connecticut, 1976, pp. 278–89.

83 *Ibid.*, p. 291.

84 Interview with Charles C. Diggs, former chairperson of the House Subcommittee on Africa, Washington, DC, June 13, 1989.

85 For a review of congressional efforts to end South Africa's sugar quota in 1971, see F. Chidozie Ogene, *Interest Groups and the Shaping of Foreign Policy: Four Case Studies of United States African Policy* (New York: St. Martin's Press, 1983), pp. 147–90.

86 John Stockwell, *In Search of Enemies: A CIA Story* (New York: W. W. Norton, 1978), p. 187.

87 "Quietly South African planes and trucks turned up throughout Angola with just the gasoline or ammunition needed for an impending mission,"

explained Stockwell. "On October 20, after a flurry of cables between headquarters and Kinshasa [Zaire]," he continued, "two South African C-130 airplanes, similar to those used by the Israelis in their raid on Entebbe, feathered into Ndjili Airport at night to meet a CIA C-141 flight and whisk its load of arms down to Silva Porto [Angola]." *Ibid.*

88 Methven is referred to as Victor St. Martin (his pseudonym) throughout Stockwell, *In Search of Enemies*. His real name is disclosed in Talbot, "The CIA and BOSS," p. 267.

89 *Ibid.*

90 For an insider's account, see Nathaniel Davis, "The Angolan Decision of 1975: A Personal Memoir," *Foreign Affairs* 57 (1978): 109–24.

91 Stockwell, *In Search of Enemies*, pp. 188–89.

92 Quoted in "Henry Kissinger on the US and Rhodesia," *Washington Post*, July 3, 1979.

93 See Henry Kissinger, "United States Policy on Southern Africa," *Department of State Bulletin* 74, 1927 (May 31, 1976): 672–79.

94 Confidential interview no. 60.

95 In a step calculated to placate South African desires for international acceptance, for example, Kissinger broke with the US diplomatic tradition of avoiding public contacts with high-level South African officials and held several meetings with Prime Minister Johannes Vorster. Among other benefits granted to the Afrikaner goverment were an invitation to send a South African naval vessel to the US bicentennial celebrations, as well as Washington's willingness to seek over $400 million in International Monetary Fund credits during 1976–77. See Danaher, *The Political Economy of US Policy Toward South Africa*, pp. 122–23.

96 For a summary, see Study Commission on US Policy Toward South Africa, *South Africa*, pp. 168–69, 183–88. The words "at least" are used to describe the number of wounded and killed in that these are official South African government totals, and therefore possibly on the conservative side.

97 For the text of the platform devoted to Africa, see Colin Legum, ed., *Africa Contemporary Record, 1976–77* (London: Rex Collings, 1977), p. C163.

98 *Washington Notes on Africa* (Summer 1977): 6.

99 *Africa News* (April 10, 1978).

100 Secretary of State Cyrus Vance, "US Policy Toward Africa," July 1, 1977; quoted in Danaher, *The Political Economy of U.S. Policy toward South Africa*, p. 164.

101 Confidential interview no. 36.

102 Confidential interview no. 40.

103 For discussion, see *Africa News* (July 11, 1977): 2–3; and *Africa Confidential* (August 19, 1977): 1–2.

104 Interview published in the *Financial Mail*, November 5, 1976, p. 501.

105 Consider, for example, a statement of President Carter prior to the 1980 presidential elections: "This administration neither encourages nor discourages US investment in South Africa and continues to believe that US firms, by adopting fair employment practices in their South African subsidiaries, can play a positive, if limited, role in introducing social change to

South Africa." Quoted in Richard Deutsch, "Interview: President Jimmy Carter," *Africa Report* (July–August 1980): 10.

106 For an overview of the evolution of the US anti-apartheid movement, particularly during the Carter administration, see Metz, "The Anti-Apartheid Movement."

107 *Ibid.*, p. 415.

108 For a discussion of Biko and his movement, see Donald Woods, *Biko* (New York: Vintage Books, 1979).

109 See Carlyle Murphy, "Young Personally Favors Sanctions Against South Africa," *Washington Post*, October 25, 1977, pp. A1, A14.

110 US House, Committee on Banking, Finance, and Urban Affairs, Subcommittee on International Trade, Investment, and Monetary Policy, *Export–Import Bank and Trade With Africa*, Hearings, 1978, 95th Cong., 2nd Sess. (Washington, DC: GPO, 1978), p. 28.

111 For a listing of other anti-apartheid resolutions and bills initiated within the House, see Ronald W. Walters, *US–South Africa Relations: A Legislative Review* (Washington, DC: Howard University, 1985). For a summary of opposing viewpoints within the US policymaking establishment as concerns US–South African relations in 1980, see US House, Committee on Foreign Affairs, Subcommittees on International Economic Policy and Trade, on Africa, and on International Organizations, *US Policy Toward South Africa*, Hearings, April 30; May 6, 8, 13, 15, 20, 22; and June 10, 1980, 96th Cong., 2nd Sess. (Washington, DC: GPO, 1980).

112 See "House Censures 'Repressive' South African Tactics," *Washington Post*, November 1, 1977. For discussion, see US House, Committee on International Relations, Subcommittees on Africa and on International Organizations, *United States Foreign Policy Toward South Africa*, Hearing, January 31, 1978, 95th Cong., 2nd Sess. (Washington, DC: GPO, 1978).

113 For a discussion of the political debate that surrounded this piece of legislation, see Metz, "The Anti-Apartheid Movement," pp. 412–25.

114 See Zbigniew Brzezinski, *Power and Principle: Memoirs of the National Security Adviser 1977–1981* (New York: Farrar, Straus, Giroux, 1983), pp. 139-45.

115 Moose, for example, claims that the Carter administration never consciously went easy on South Africa in order to seek concessions in other, more pressing areas. After reflection, however, he noted that this, "de facto, may have happened." Interview (June 26, 1989).

116 Confidential interview no. 45. For a critical account of the Carter administration's policies as written by a South African, see Daan Prinsloo, *United States Foreign Policy and the Republic of South Africa* (Pretoria, South Africa: Foreign Affairs Association, 1978).

117 Quoted in Pauline H. Baker, *The United States and South Africa: The Reagan Years* (New York: Ford Foundation and the Foreign Policy Association, 1989), p. 25.

118 Confidential interview no. 43.

119 Crocker noted, for example, that Shultz was influential in ensuring a great deal of autonomy as concerns US Africa policies. "A man of infinite integrity who supported his people," explained Crocker. "Didn't want me coming every thirty minutes. Autonomy was a function of competence

and credibility with his top people." Interview with Chester Crocker, Assistant Secretary of State for African Affairs under the Reagan administration, Washington, DC, June 13, 1989.

120 Interview with Crocker (June 13, 1989). For Crocker's distinction between types of Marxist countries in Africa, see "Memorandum of Conversation" (April 15/16, 1981), a leaked State Department document reproduced in "New US Policy on South Africa: State Department Documents Uncover Developing Alliance," *TransAfrica News Report*, 1, 10 (August 1981). (Hereinafter referred to as *TransAfrica News Report*.)

121 For a discussion of this concept as written by Crocker prior to his appointment as Assistant Secretary of State for African Affairs, see Chester Crocker, "South Africa: Strategy for Change," *Foreign Affairs* 59, 2 (Winter 1980–81); and Chester Crocker, *High Noon in Southern Africa: Making Peace in a Rough Neighborhood* (New York: W. W. Norton, 1992). See also Christopher Coker, *The United States and South Africa, 1968–1985: Constructive Engagement and its Critics* (Durham, NC: Duke University Press, 1986).

122 *Ibid.*, p. 337.

123 Crocker to Haig, "Your Meeting with South African Foreign Minister Botha, 11:00 A.M., May 14, at the Department – *Scope Paper.*" Document reproduced in *TransAfrica News Report*.

124 *Ibid.*

125 *Ibid.*

126 Confidential interview no. 49.

127 For other examples, see Danaher, *The Political Economy of US Policy Toward South Africa*, p. 193.

128 Confidential interview no. 32.

129 Interview with Crocker (June 13, 1989).

130 Confidential interview no. 8.

131 Interview with Gil Kulick, former desk officer (South Africa) in the State Department's Africa Bureau, Washington, DC, June 15, 1989.

132 Confidential interview no. 12.

133 Baker, *The United States and South Africa*, p. 14.

134 For an overview of South Africa's regional destabilization policies, see Joseph Hanlon, *Beggar Your Neighbours: Apartheid Power in South Africa* (Bloomington: Indiana University Press, 1986). See also Robert S. Jaster, *South Africa and its Regional Neighbors: The Dynamics of Regional Conflict* (London: International Institute for Strategic Studies, 1986).

135 For an overview of the early stages of the political violence, see US House, Committee on Foreign Affairs, Subcommittee on Africa, *The Current Crisis in South Africa*, Hearing, December 4, 1984, 98th Cong., 2nd Sess. (Washington, DC: GPO, 1985). For a general review of black politics during the 1980s, see Tom Lodge and Bill Nasson, *All, Here, and Now: Black Politics in South Africa in the 1980s* (New York: Ford Foundation and The Foreign Policy Association, 1991).

136 Quoted in US House, Committee on Foreign Affairs, Subcommittee on Africa, *US Policy on South Africa*, Hearing, September 26, 1984, 98th Cong., 2nd Sess. (Washington, DC: GPO, 1985), p. 9.

137 *Ibid.*, p. 27. For a sharp critique of the policy of constructive engagement,

see Kevin Danaher, *South Africa: A New US Policy for the 1990s* (San Francisco: The Institute for Food and Development Policy, April 1988).

138 "Sanctions: The Time Has Come!" *The Washington Notes on Africa* (Summer 1985).

139 A more comprehensive sanctions bill was proposed by Representative Dellums. Dellums unsuccessfully sought to attach an amendment to HR 1460 that would have banned all US trade with and mandated complete corporate divestment from South Africa. This amendment failed by a vote of 340 to 80.

140 Two other sanctions bills introduced into the Senate were S-1235 and S-1020. Introduced by Senators Edward Kennnedy (D-Massachusetts) and Lowell Weicker (R-Connecticut), S-1235 was the Senate equivalent of HR–1460. Introduced by Senators William Roth (R-Delaware) and Mitchell McConnell (R-Kentucky), S-1020 included provisions that were amended onto S-995 (ban on bank loans to South Africa and restrictions on the export of computer and nuclear products to South Africa).

141 Confidential interview no. 26.

142 For a copy of this order and Reagan's remarks prior to its signing, see "South Africa: Presidential Actions," *Department of State Bulletin* 85, 2103 (October 1985): 1–8.

143 See US House, Committee on Foreign Affairs, Subcommittee on Africa, *Developments in South Africa: United States Policy Responses*, Hearing, March 12, 1986, 99th Cong., 2nd Sess. (Washington, DC: GPO, 1986), p. 6.

144 Interview with Stephen Weissman, former Staff Director of the House Subcommittee on Africa, Washington, DC, May 17, 1989.

145 The final bill reflected adoption of the Dellums amendment that had been defeated in 1985. This amendment replaced sanctions legislation originally submitted by Gray. Among the components of the Dellums bill were bans on new investment, bank loans to the South African government, and coal, steel, and uranium imports from South Africa; divestment from the South African computer market; and withdrawal of US landing rights for South African Airways. See Ronald V. Dellums, "The Need for Comprehensive Sanctions," *Washington Notes on Africa* (Summer 1986).

146 S-2701 was originally proposed by Lugar, chairperson of the Senate Foreign Relations Committee. Three other major bills were introduced into the Senate for consideration. Senator Nancy Kassebaum (R-Kansas), chairperson of the Senate Subcommittee on Africa, introduced S-2636, which included a ban on new US investment in South Africa. Senator Alan Cranston (D-California) introduced the Senate equivalent of the final version of HR-4868. Senator Edward Kennedy (D-Massachusetts) introduced S-2498, which was the Senate equivalent of the original, milder version of HR-4868.

147 For various statements by Reagan concerning this veto, see "Economic Sanctions Against South Africa," *Department of State Bulletin* 86, 2117 (December 1986): 35–37.

148 Ronald Reagan, "Ending Apartheid in South Africa," address reproduced in Baker, *The United States and South Africa*.

149 Baker, *The United States and South Africa*, pp. 31–32.

150 *Ibid.*, p. 31.
151 *Ibid.*
152 See, for example, Janice Love, *The Anti-Apartheid Movement: Local Activism in Global Politics* (New York: Praeger, 1985).
153 Quoted in US House, Committee on Foreign Affairs, Subcommittees on International Economic Policy and Trade, and on Africa, *Legislative Options and United States Policy Toward South Africa*, Hearings and Markup, April 9, 16; June 4, 5, 1986, 99th Cong., 2nd Sess. (Washington, DC: GPO, 1987), p. 246.
154 Quoted in Pauline H. Baker, "The Sanctions Vote: A G.O.P. Milestone," *New York Times*, August 26, 1986.
155 Paul Simon, "The Senate's New African Agenda," *Africa Report* 32, 3 (May–June 1987): 14.
156 Quoted in US House, Committee on Foreign Affairs, Subcommittees on International Economic Policy and Trade, and on Africa, *Proposed Economic Sanctions Against South Africa*, Hearings and Markup, March 22, 23; April 20, 28; and May 3, 1988, 100th Cong., 2nd Sess. (Washington, DC: GPO, 1988), p. 41.
157 For an overview of congressional oversight, see US House, Committee on Foreign Affairs, Subcommittees on International Economic Policy and Trade, and on Africa, *Oversight of the Administration's Implementation of the Comprehensive Antiapartheid Act of 1986 (Public Law 99–440) and an Assessment of Recent South African Political and Economic Developments*, Hearing, June 16, 1987, 100th Cong., 1st Sess. (Washington, DC: GPO, 1988). See also US House, Committee on Foreign Affairs, Subcommittees on International Economic Policy and Trade, and on Africa, *The President's Report on Progress Toward Ending Apartheid in South Africa and the Question of Future Sanctions*, Hearing, November 5, 1987, 100th Cong., 1st Sess. (Washington, DC: GPO, 1988).
158 US House, *Proposed Economic Sanctions Against South Africa*, p. 41.
159 *Ibid.*
160 Baker, *The United States and South Africa*, p. 53.
161 US House, *Proposed Economic Sanctions Against South Africa*, p. 41.
162 For the complete text of this bill, see *ibid.*, pp. 698–718. Four other bills were also debated by the House. Representative Mickey Leland (D-Texas) introduced legislation (HR-3328) which sought to prohibit South African mining interests from investing in US capital markets. Representative Mervyn M. Dymally (D-California) presented a bill (HR-1051) that sought to ban imports of all South African diamonds. Gray's legislation (HR-2443) focused on prohibiting all US–South African cooperation in the military and intelligence fields. Finally, Representative Robert E. Wise (D-West Virginia) introduced a bill (HR-3317) that would have outlawed US investment in the South African oil industry. For a discussion of these bills, see *ibid.*, pp. 63–91.
163 *Ibid.*, p. 39.
164 Interview with Crocker (June 13, 1989).
165 Quoted in US House, *Oversight of the Administration's Implementation of the Comprehensive Antiapartheid Act of 1986*, p. 65.

166 Confidential interview no. 16.
167 For congressional inquiries into these topics, see *ibid*, pp. 64–69, 284–85. See also US House, Committee on Foreign Affairs, Subcommittee on Africa, *Possible Violation or Circumvention of the Clark Amendment*, Hearing, July 1, 1987, 100th Cong., 1st Sess. (Washington, DC: GPO, 1987); and US House, Committee on Foreign Affairs, Subcommittee on Africa, *Legislation to Require that Any United States Government Support for Military or Paramilitary Operations in Angola be Openly Acknowledged and Publicly Debated*, Hearings and Markup, April 22 and 23, 1986, 99th Cong., 1st Sess. (Washington, DC: GPO, 1986).
168 This statement was largely supported by every individual interviewed as part of this project. Indeed, one prominent anti-apartheid activist noted that the passage of more comprehensive sanctions "depended" on the South African government doing something "stupid" that would inflame international and US public opinion. "Its almost a requirement of their system," he continued, "The way they are forced to react to a majority of their population, they will do something to somebody." Confidential interview no. 50.
169 See US House, Committee on Foreign Affairs, Subcommittee on Africa, *Media Restrictions in South Africa*, Hearings, March 15 and 16, 1988, 100th Cong., 2nd Sess. (Washington, DC: GPO, 1988).
170 This concept constituted the core of legislation that Representative Dan Burton (R-Indiana) offered as an alternative to sanctions legislation from 1986 to 1989. For brief descriptions of this approach, see the following articles published in the *Washington Post*: William Raspberry, "Sanctions – or Strikes?" June 16, 1988; Helen Suzman, "A Wrecked Economy Won't End Apartheid," June 15, 1988; and William Claiborne, "Inside South Africa's Quiet Townships, Blacks See New Leverage in Economic Muscle," June 12, 1988.
171 Interview with Bob Brauer, Special Counsel to Representative Ronald V. Dellums, Washington, DC, May 25, 1989.
172 For texts of these accords, see *New York Times*, December 23, 1988, p. A5.
173 Quoted in Robert Pear, "US Putting Hope in South African," *New York Times*, September 6, 1989, p. A3.
174 For example, Bush met with Albertina "Mama" Sisulu, the co-president of the United Democratic Front and wife of Walter Sisulu, one of the most prominent leaders of the ANC, in June 1989. One month earlier, Bush met with South African Archbishop Desmond Tutu, who noted that the President had a "warm openness" to taking the "moral leadership" in the dismantling of apartheid. See Bernard Weinraub, "Bush Meets Tutu and Vows to Press Pretoria," *New York Times*, May 19, 1989, p. A8.
175 Quoted in *ibid*.
176 *Ibid*.
177 Quoted in David B. Ottaway, "State Nominee Stresses Peace in Africa," *Washington Post*, May 4, 1989, p. A21.
178 Interview with Bob Brauer (May 25, 1989).
179 Quoted in Christopher S. Wren, "Pretoria and Banks Reach Pact," *New York Times*, October 20, 1989, p. B34.

180 William Claiborne, "Pretoria's Power-Sharing Plan Modeled on Swiss Federal System," *New York Times*, June 30, 1989, p. A5.

181 For an overview of the evolution of the idea of reform within the white community, see Robert Schrire, *Adapt or Die: The End of White Politics in South Africa* (New York: Ford Foundation and The Foreign Policy Association, 1991).

182 See "Britain Breaks European Ranks to Ease South Africa Sanctions," *New York Times*, February 21, 1990, pp. A1, A4.

183 The quotes are those of Howard Wolpe, quoted in "US Putting Hope," 1989, p. A3.

184 See David B. Ottaway, "US Panel Hails S. African 'Dynamic'," *Washington Post*, March 5, 1990.

185 For a brief summary, see "South African Sanctions: Go Slow," *New York Times*, July 5, 1991, p. A10. For an earlier discussion of South Africa's compliance with the conditions of the 1986 act, see Robert Pear, "Bush Invites Mandela to the White House," *New York Times*, February 12, 1990, p. A12. For the administration's interpretation of South African compliance, see the annual "Report of the Congress Pursuant to Section 501 of the Comprehensive Anti-Apartheid Act of 1986."

186 See Christopher S. Wren, "De Klerk Announces New Round of Talks with Mandela Aides," *New York Times*, July 21, 1990, p. A3; and Alan Cowell, "African National Congress Suspends its Guerrilla War," *New York Times*, August 7, 1990, p. A2.

187 See Christopher S. Wren, "South Africa Scraps Law Defining People by Race: The Legal Foundation of Apartheid System is Eliminated," *New York Times*, June 19, 1991, p. A1.

188 See the numerous articles contained in the February 3, 1990 edition of the *New York Times* which carried the headline: "South Africa's President Ends 30-Year Ban on Mandela Group; Says it is Time for Negotiation."

189 See Christopher S. Wren, "De Klerk Lifts Emergency Rule in Natal Province," *New York Times*, October 19, 1990, p. A3; "South Africa Lifting State of Emergency," *Chicago Tribune*, June 8, 1990, sec. 1, pp. 1, 24; Alan Cowell, "African National Congress Suspends its Guerrilla War," *New York Times*, August 7, 1990, p. A2; and "In South Africa: The Nightmare Ends," *New York Times*, August 8, 1990, p. A14.

190 See Christopher S. Wren, "Dispute on Pretoria's Stance on Prisoners Persists," *New York Times*, July 13, 1991, p. A3.

191 Thomas L. Friedman, "Bush Lifts Ban on Economic Ties to South Africa: Calls Apartheid's End 'Irreversible' and Cites Prisoner Releases," *New York Times*, July 11, 1991, p. A1, A6.

192 "Excerpts from Bush's Remarks on Sanctions: 'This Progress is Irreversible'," *New York Times*, July 11, 1991, p. A6.

193 Quoted in Keith Bradsher, "Support for Pretoria Sanctions Weak," *New York Times*, July 10, 1991, p. A3.

194 Neil A. Lewis, "Administration Hoping to Lift US Sanctions," *New York Times*, June 18, 1991, p. A6.

195 Anne Shepherd, "South Africa: Fanning the Flames," *Africa Report* 37, 5 (September–October 1992): 57–60.

196 Keith Bradsher, "Support for Pretoria Sanctions Weak," *New York Times*, July 10, 1991, p. A3. For a good overview of congressional attitudes just prior to the administration's lifting of sanctions, see US House, Committee on Foreign Affairs, Subcommittee on International Economic Policy and Trade and Subcommittee on Africa, *The Status of United States Sanctions Against South Africa*, Hearing, April 30, 1991, 102nd Cong., 1st Sess. (Washington, DC: GPO, 1991).

197 Freidman, "Bush Lifts a Ban on Economic Ties to South Africa," p. A6.

198 This point was noted by almost every official interviewed that was connected with the Defense Department.

199 Almost every member of the intelligence community who was interviewed for this project expressed this opinion.

6 US Africa policies in the post-Cold War era

1 The proverb was noted by Francis A. Kornegay, Jr., chair of a panel, "Great Power Relations After Perestroika," 31st Annual Meeting of the African Studies Association, Chicago, October 28–31, 1988. For an optimistic outlook, see Anatoly A. Gromyko and C. S. Whitaker, *Agenda for Action: African–Soviet–US Cooperation* (Boulder; London: Lynne Rienner Publishers, 1990). For a more pessimistic interpretation, see Martin Lowenkopf, "If the Cold War is Over in Africa, Will the United States Still Care?" *CSIS Africa Notes* 98 (May 30, 1989). For a general analysis comparing and contrasting the actions of both the US and the former Soviet Union, see Zaki Laidi (translated by Patricia Baudoin), *The Superpowers and Africa: The Constraints of a Rivalry 1960–1990* (Chicago: University of Chicago Press, 1990).

2 See Mark Webber, "Soviet Policy in Sub-Saharan Africa: The Final Phase," *Journal of Modern African Studies* 30, 1 (1992): 1–30.

3 See, for example, Michael Clough, *Free at Last? US Policy Toward Africa and the End of the Cold War* (New York: Council on Foreign Relations Press, 1992). See also Jeffrey Herbst, "The United States and Africa: Issues for the Future," in John W. Harbeson and Donald Rothchild, eds., *Africa in World Politics* (Boulder: Westview, 1991); F. Ugboaja Ohaegbulam, "The United States and Africa After the Cold War," *Africa Today*, 39, 4 (1992): 19–34 and Donald Rothchild and John Ravenhill, "Retreat From Globalism: US Policy Toward Africa in the 1990s," in Kenneth A. Oye, Robert J. Lieber, and Donald Rothchild, eds., *Eagle in a New World: American Grand Strategy in the Post-Cold War Era* (New York: Harper Collins, 1991).

4 Quoted in Liz Sly, "Africa Fears Ranking Last in World Order," *Chicago Tribune*, October 20, 1991, sec. 4. p. 1.

5 Quoted in Jane Perlez, "Africans Fear Their Needs Will be Placed on the Back Burner," *New York Times*, December 27, 1989, p. A4.

6 See Michael Clough, "The United States and Africa: The Policy of Cynical Disengagement," *Current History* 91, 565 (May 1992): 193–98.

7 Flora Lewis, "Tide Reaching Africa," *New York Times*, April 21, 1990, p. A15.

8 Interview with Stephen R. Weissman, former Staff Director of the House Subcommittee on Africa, Washington, DC, May 17, 1989.

9 See Steven A. Holmes, "Africa, From The Cold War to Cold Shoulders," *New York Times*, March 7, 1993, p. E4.

10 *Ibid.*

11 Figures derived from US Agency for International Development (USAID), *U.S. Overseas Loans and Grants and Assistance from International Organizations: Obligations and Loan Authorizations. July 1, 1945–September 30, 1991* (Washington, DC: USAID, 1992). For a general discussion of US foreign assistance to Africa, see Jeffrey Herbst, *US Economic Policy Toward Africa* (New York: Council on Foreign Relations Press, 1992).

12 *Ibid.* Figures for 1992 obtained from the House Subcommittee on Africa.

13 "A Longing for Liberty," *Newsweek*, July 23, 1990, p. 27.

14 See Robert Pear, "Poland is Big Winner as Administration Lists Shifts in US Foreign Aid," *New York Times*, February 1, 1990, p. A7.

15 Quoted in "A Longing for Liberty," *Newsweek*, July 23, 1990, p. 27.

16 For an overview of the US position at the early stages of the conflict, see US House, Committee on Foreign Affairs, Subcommittee on Africa, *US Policy and the Crisis in Liberia*, Hearing, June 19, 1990, 101st Cong., 2nd Sess. (Washington, DC: GPO, 1990). For an overview of the US–Liberian relationship, see Hassan B. Sisay, *Big Powers and Small Nations: A Case Study of United States–Liberian Relations* (Lanham, MD: University Press of America, 1985). See also J. Gus Liebenow, *Liberia: The Quest for Democracy* (Bloomington: Indiana University Press, 1987).

17 For an overview, see Holly Burkhalter and Rakiya Omaar, "Failures of State," *Africa Report* (November–December 1990): 27–29.

18 For an overview written by a member of the US Embassy in Monrovia at the time, see Richard A. Bienia, "Meanwhile, One Continent Away ... in Africa ... Another War, in Liberia, Makes Life Hazardous for Embassy People," *State: The Newsletter*, no. 341 (February 1991): 2–7.

19 See Leon T. Hadar, "The 'Green Peril': Creating the Islamic Fundamentalist Threat," *Cato Institute Policy Analysis*, no. 177, August 27, 1992.

20 For a discussion of the spread of fundamentalist movements throughout North Africa, see Gary Abramson, "Rise of the Crescent," *Africa Report* 37, 2 (March–April 1992): 18–21.

21 Quoted in Barbara Crossette, "US Aide Calls Muslim Militants Concern to the World," *New York Times*, January 1, 1992, p. A3.

22 For a good overview of US policy toward Sudan, see US House, Committee on Foreign Affairs, Subcommittee on Africa; and Select Committee on Hunger, International Task Force, *War and Famine in the Sudan*, Joint Hearing, March 15, 1990, 101st Cong., 2nd Sess. (Washington, DC: GPO, 1991).

23 Raymond W. Copson, "Sudan: Foreign Assistance Facts," *CRS Issue Brief*, February 18, 1992.

24 Quoted in Nick Cater, "Sudan: At War with its People," *Africa Report* 37, 6 (November–December 1992): 66.

25 *Ibid.*

26 See Francis M. Deng and I. William Zartman, eds., *Conflict Resolution in Africa* (Washington, DC: The Brookings Institution, 1991); and I. William Zartman, *Ripe For Resolution: Conflict and Intervention in Africa* (New York: Oxford University Press, 1989).

27 For an insider's account, see Chester A. Crocker, "Peacemaking in Southern Africa: The Namibia–Angola Settlement of 1988," in David D. Newsom, ed., *The Diplomatic Record 1989–1990* (Washington, DC: Institute for the Study of Diplomacy, Georgetown University; Boulder: Westview, 1991).

28 See Donald Rothchild, "Regional Peacemaking in Africa: The Role of the Great Powers as Facilitators," in John W. Harbeson and Donald Rothchild, eds., *Africa in World Politics* (Boulder: Westview, 1991), pp. 284–306.

29 For an overview of UN efforts, see United Nations, *The Blue Helmets: A Review of United Nations Peace-Keeping* (New York: United Nations, 1991).

30 For a discussion as to how the US could better work within a UN framework as concerns US Africa policies, see Francis A. Kornegay, Jr., "US Policy: Africa in The New World Order," *Africa Report* 38, 1 (January–February 1993): 13–17.

31 See Herbst, *US Economic Policy Toward Africa*, esp. pp. 66–68.

32 Donald K. Petterson, "Democracy Can Take Hold in Africa," *New York Times*, May 19, 1990, p. A15.

33 Quoted in press release, US Embassy, Mogadishu, Somalia, "Winds of Change in Africa," June 7, 1990. For further discussion, see Carol Lancaster and Sergei Shatalov, "A Joint Approach to Africa's Debt," *Africa Report* (May–June 1989): 42–45; and Colleen Lowe Morna, "A New Development Compact?" *Africa Report* (March–April 1990): 50-53.

34 Quoted in Burkhalter and Omaar, "Failures of State," p. 27.

35 See, for example, Alfred Hermida, "Algeria: Democracy Derailed," *Africa Report* 37, 2 (March–April 1992): 13–17.

Appendix A A note on method

1 See Alexander L. George, "Case Studies and Theory Development: The Method of Structured, Focused Comparison," in Paul Gordon Lauren, ed., *Diplomacy: New Approaches in History, Theory, and Policy* (New York: The Free Press, 1979), pp. 43–68. For two applications of this method, see Alexander L. George and Richard Smoke, *Deterrence in American Foreign Policy: Theory and Practice* (New York: Columbia University Press, 1974), and Richard Smoke, *War: Controlling Escalation* (Cambridge: Harvard University Press, 1977).

2 George, "Case Studies and Theory Development," p. 44.

3 *Ibid.*, p. 43.

4 *Ibid.*, p. 62.

5 For an overview of various types of case study analysis, see Harry Eckstein, "Case Study and Theory in Political Science," in Fred I. Greenstein and Nelson W. Polsby, eds., *Handbook of Political Science*, vol. 7 (Reading, Massachusetts: Addison-Wesley, 1975), pp. 79–138.

6 Mark Owen Lombardi, "Superpower Intervention in Sub-Saharan Africa: A Framework for Analyzing Third World Conflicts," Paper presented at the 30th Annual Meeting of the International Studies Association, St. Louis, MO, March 29–April 2, 1988.

Appendix B A note on interview techniques

1 One of the most cited sources is the appendix, "Notes on Method: Participant Observation," in Richard E. Fenno, Jr., *Home Style: House Members in
Their Districts* (Boston: Little, Brown, 1978), pp. 249–95. For a more recent
analysis, see Robert L. Peabody et al., "Interviewing Political Elites," *PS:
Political Science & Politics* 23, 3 (September 1990): 451–54. See also Lewis A.
Dexter, *Elite and Specialized Interviewing* (Evanston, IL: Northwestern University Press, 1970).

SELECT BIBLIOGRAPHY

This bibliography is only inclusive of the books, scholarly articles, congressional documents, unpublished conference papers, and doctoral dissertations which are cited throughout the volume. For the variety of other sources utilized in the study, the interested reader is directed to the endnotes section of individual chapters. For a review of the literature related to U.S. Africa policies, as well as the major personalities and organizations involved in those policies throughout history, see David Shavit, *The United States and Africa: A Historical Dictionary* (Westport, CT: Greenwood Press, 1989), especially the section, "Bibliographical Essay" (pp. 275–78). See also the historiographical essay written by Thomas J. Noer, "'Non-Benign Neglect': The United States and Black Africa in the Twentieth Century," in Gerald K. Haines and J. Samuel Walker, eds, *American Foreign Relations: A Historiographical Review* (Westport, CT: Greenwood Press, 1981), pp. 271–92.

Abramson, Gary. "Rise of the Crescent." *Africa Report* 37, 2 (March–April 1992): 18–21.

Acheson, Dean. *Grapes from Thorns*. New York: W. W. Norton, 1972.

—— *Present at the Creation: My Years in the State Department*. New York: W. W. Norton, 1969.

Adar, Korwa Gombe. "The Significance of the Legal Principle of 'Territorial Integrity' as the Modal Determinant of Relations: A Case Study of Kenya's Foreign Policy Towards Somalia, 1963–1983." Ph.D. dissertation, University of South Carolina, Columbia, SC, 1986.

Africa Watch. *Somalia: A Government at War With its Own People: Testimonies About the Killings and the Conflict in the North*. London: Africa Watch, 1990.

Agyeman-Duah, Baffour. "United States Military Assistance Relationship With Ethiopia, 1953–77: Historical and Theoretical Analysis". Ph.D. dissertation, University of Denver, Denver, CO, 1984.

Allison, Graham T. *Essence of Decision: Explaining the Cuban Missile Crisis*. Boston: Little, Brown, 1971.

Amnesty International. *The Republic of Zaire: Outside the Law – Security Force Repression of Government Opponents, 1988–1990*. London: Amnesty International Publications, September 1990.

—— *Somalia: A Long-Term Human Rights Crisis*. London: Amnesty International Publications, September 1988.

"Appendix; Questionnaire: Africanist Scholarship and US Policy Making on Africa." *Issue* 19, 2 (Summer 1991): 31–37.

Baker, Pauline H. *The United States and South Africa: The Reagan Years*. New York: Ford Foundation and the Foreign Policy Association, 1989.

"United States Foreign Policy in Southern Africa." *Current History* 86, 520 (May 1987): 193–96, 225–27.

Ball, George. *The Disciples of Power*. Boston: Little, Brown, 1968.

Bandow, Doug. "Economic and Military Aid." In Peter J. Schraeder, ed. *Intervention into the 1990s: US Foreign Policy in the Third World*. Boulder: Lynne Rienner Publishers, 1992, pp. 75–96.

Bard, Mitchell. "The Evolution of Israel's Africa Policy." *Middle East Review* 21 (Winter 1988/89): 21–28.

Barrett, Laurence I. *Gambling with History: Reagan in the White House*. Harmondsworth: Penguin, 1984.

Bender, Gerald J. "Kissinger in Angola: Anatomy of Failure." In René Lemarchand, ed. *American Policy in Southern Africa: The Stakes and the Stance*. Lanham, MD: University Press of America, 1981, pp. 63–144.

Bender, Gerald J., James S. Coleman, and Richard L. Sklar, eds. *African Crisis Areas and US Foreign Policy*. Berkeley; Los Angeles: University of California Press, 1985.

"Black Electoral Success in 1989." *PS: Political Science & Politics* 23, 2 (June 1990): 141–62.

Bowman, Larry W. "Government Officials, Academics, and the Process of Formulating US National Security Policy Towards Africa." *Issue* 19, 1 (Winter 1990): 5–20.

Bradford, Gregory H. "The Importance of Defense Interests in US Foreign Policy in Africa." Paper presented at the 32nd Annual Meeting of the African Studies Association, Hyatt Regency Hotel, Atlanta, GA, November 3, 1989.

Bratton, Michael. "Academic Analysis and US Economic Assistance Policy on Africa." *Issue* 19, 1 (Winter 1990): 21–37.

Bratton, Michael, Reinhard Heinisch, and David S. Wiley. "How Africanists View US Policy: Results of a Survey." *Issue* 19, 2 (Summer 1991): 14–30.

Brinkley, Douglas, and G. E. Thomas. "Dean Acheson's Opposition to African Liberation." *TransAfrica Forum* 5, 4 (Summer 1988): 63–81.

Brown, Michael, Gary Freeman, and Kay Miller. *Passing By: The United States and Genocide in Burundi, 1972*. Washington, DC: Carnegie Endowment for International Peace, c. 1972.

Brzezinski, Zbigniew. *Power and Principle: Memoirs of the National Security Adviser 1977–1981*. New York: Farrar, Straus, Giroux, 1983.

Burkhalter, Holly, and Rakiya Omaar. "Failures of State." *Africa Report* (November–December 1990): 27–29.

Bush, George. "The US and Africa: The Republican Platform." *Africa Report* 33, 4 (July–August 1988): 13–16.

Callaghy, Thomas M. "Zaire: The Ritual Dance of the Debt Game." *Africa Report* 29, 5 (September–October 1984): 22–26.

The State–Society Struggle: Zaire in Comparative Perspective. New York: Columbia University Press, 1984.

"Capturing the Continent: US Media Coverage of Africa." *Africa News Special Report*. Durham, NC: Africa News, 1990.

Carter, Jimmy. *Keeping Faith: Memoirs of a President*. New York: Bantam Books, 1982.

Challenor, Herschelle Sullivan. "The Influence of Black Americans on US Foreign Policy Toward Africa." In Abdul Aziz Said, ed. *Ethnicity and US Foreign Policy*. New York: Praeger, 1981.

Clapham, Christopher. *Transformation and Continuity in Revolutionary Ethiopia*. Cambridge: Cambridge University Press, 1988.

Clark, Jeffrey. "Debacle in Somalia," *Foreign Affairs* 72, 1 (1992–93): 109–23.

Clough, Michael. *Free at Last? US Policy Toward Africa and the End of the Cold War* (New York: Council on Foreign Relations Press, 1992).

"The United States and South Africa: The Policy of Cynical Disengagement." *Current History* 91, 565 (May 1992): 193–98.

Coker, Christopher. *The United States and South Africa, 1968–1985: Constructive Engagement and its Critics*. Durham NC: Duke University Press, 1986.

Compagnon, Daniel. "The Somali Opposition Fronts: Some Comments and Questions," *Horn of Africa* 13, 1–2 (January–March, April–June, 1990): 29–54.

"Congress and Africa: New Realities in a New Decade." *Washington Notes on Africa* (Spring 1991).

"Contribution à l'étude des mouvements d'opposition au Zaire: Le F.L.N.C." *Cahiers du CEDAF*, no. 6 (1980).

"Controversy over United States Policy Toward Rhodesia: Pro & Con." Special issue of *Congressional Digest* 52, 2 (February 1973).

Coquery-Vidrovitch, Catherine, Alain Forest and Herbert Weiss, eds. *Rébellions-Révolution au Zaire. 1963–1965*. 2 volumes. Paris: L'Harmattan, 1987.

Crocker, Chester. *High Noon in Southern Africa: Making Peace in a Rough Neighborhood*. New York: W. W. Norton, 1992.

"Peacemaking in Southern Africa: The Namibia–Angola Settlement of 1988." In David D. Newsom, ed. *The Diplomatic Record 1989–1990*. Boulder: Westview, 1991, pp. 9–34.

"South Africa: Strategy for Change." *Foreign Affairs* 59, 2 (Winter 1980–81): 323–51.

"The US Policy Process and South Africa." In Alfred O. Hero, Jr. and John Barratt, eds. *The American People and South Africa: Publics, Elites, and Policymaking Processes*. Lexington: Lexington Books, 1981, pp. 139–62.

Culverson, Donald. "The US Information Agency in Africa." *TransAfrica Forum* 6, 2 (Winter 1989): 61–80.

Danaher, Kevin. *Beyond Safaris: A Guide to Building People-to-People Ties With Africa*. Trenton, NJ: Africa World Press, 1991.

The Political Economy of US Policy Toward South Africa. Washington, DC: Institute for the Study of Diplomacy, Georgetown University: Westview: Boulder, 1985.

South Africa: A New US Policy for the 1990s. San Francisco: The Institute for Food and Development Policy, 1988.

Davis, Nathaniel. "The Angolan Decision of 1975: A Personal Memoir." *Foreign Affairs* 57, 1 (Fall 1978): 109–24.

Deng, Francis M., and I. William Zartman, eds. *Conflict Resolution in Africa*. Washington, DC: The Brookings Institution, 1991.

320

Deutsch, Richard. "Interview: President Jimmy Carter." *Africa Report* (July–August 1980): 8–10.

Dexter, Lewis A. *Elite and Specialized Interviewing*. Evanston, IL: Northwestern University Press, 1970.

Dougherty, James. *The Horn of Africa: A Map of Political-Strategic Conflict*. Cambridge, MA: Institute for Foreign Policy Analysis, 1982.

Drysdale, John. *The Somali Dispute*. London, Pall Mall Press, 1964.

Duignan, Peter, and L. H. Gann. *The United States and Africa: A History*. Cambridge: Cambridge University Press, 1984.

Dye, William McE. *Moslem Egypt, Christian Abyssinia, or Military Service Under the Khedive, in His Provinces and Beyond Their Borders, as Experienced by the American Staff*. New York: Negro Universities Press, 1968.

Eckstein, Harry. "Case Study and Theory in Political Science." In Fred I. Greenstein and Nelson W. Polsby, eds., *Handbook of Political Science*. vol. 7. Reading, MA: Addison-Wesley Publishing Company, 1975, pp. 79–138.

Eisenhower, Dwight D. *Peace With Justice*. New York: Columbia University Press, 1961.

Waging Peace, 1956–1961. Garden City: Doubleday, 1965.

El-Khawas, Mohamed A., and Barry Cohen, eds. *The Kissinger Study of Southern Africa: National Security Study Memorandum 39*. Westport, CT: Lawrence Hill & Company, 1976.

"Eritrea: An Emerging New Nation in Africa's Troubled Horn." Special edition of *Africa Today*, 38, 2 (1992).

Farer, Tom J. *War Clouds on the Horn of Africa: The Widening Storm*. New York: Carnegie Endowment for International Peace, 1979.

Fenno, Jr., Richard E. *Home Style: House Members in their Districts*. Boston: Little, Brown, 1978.

Ferguson, John H. *American Diplomacy and the Boer War*. Philadelphia: University Press, 1939.

Fergusson, Clyde, and William Cotter. "South Africa: What is to be Done?" *Foreign Affairs* 56, 2 (January 1978): 266–67.

Finkel, Vicki R. "Angola: Violence and the Vote." *Africa Report* 37, 4 (July–August 1992): 52–54.

Fitzgerald, Mary Anne. "The News Hole: Reporting Africa." *Africa Report* (July–August 1989): 59–61.

Foltz, William J. "Africa in Great-Power Strategy." In William J. Foltz and Henry S. Bienen, eds., *Arms and the African: Military Influences on Africa's International Relations*. New Haven and London: Yale University Press, 1985, pp. 1–28.

Ford, Gerald R. *A Time to Heal: The Autobiography of Gerald R. Ford*. New York: Harper & Row, 1979.

George, Alexander L. "Case Studies and Theory Development: The Method of Structured, Focused Comparison." In Paul Gordon Lauren, ed., *Diplomacy: New Approaches in History, Theory, and Policy*. New York: The Free Press, 1979, pp. 43–68.

George, Alexander L., and Richard Smoke. *Deterrence in American Foreign Policy: Theory and Practice*. New York: Columbia University Press, 1974.

Gérard-Libois, Jules, ed. *Congo 1967.* Brussels: Centre de Recherche et d'Information Socio-Politiques (CRISP), 1968.

Gérard-Libois, Jules and Jean Van Lierde, eds. *Congo 1965.* Brussels: Centre de Recherche et d'Information Socio-Politiques (CRISP), 1966.

Gérard-Libois, Jules and Benoit Verhaegen, eds. *Congo 1960.* 3 volumes. Brussels: Centre de Recherche et d'Information Socio-Politiques (CRISP), 1960.

Gersony, Robert. *Why Somalis Flee: Synthesis of Accounts of Conflict Experience in Northern Somalia by Somali Refugees, Displaced Persons and Others.* Washington, DC: Bureau for Refugee Programs, Department of State, August 1989.

Gervasi, Sean, Anne Seidman, Immanuel Wallerstein, and David Wiley. "Why We Said No to A.I.D." *Issue* 7, 4 (Winter 1977): 35–38.

Gibbs, David N. *The Political Economy of Third World Intervention: Mines, Money, and US Policy in the Congo Crisis.* Chicago: University of Chicago Press, 1991.

Goldstein, Myra S. "The Genesis of Modern American Relations With South Africa." Ph.D. dissertation, Buffalo, NY, State University of New York at Buffalo, 1972.

Gorman, Robert F. *Political Conflict on the Horn of Africa.* New York: Praeger, 1981.

Gould, David J. *Bureaucratic Corruption and Underdevelopment in the Third World: The Case of Zaire.* Elmsford, New York: Pergamon Press, 1980.

Greenfield, Richard. "Somalia: Siad's Sad Legacy." *Africa Report* (March–April 1991): 13–18.

Gromyko, Anatoly A., and C. S. Whitaker. *Agenda For Action: African–Soviet–US Cooperation.* Boulder: Lynne Rienner Publishers, 1990.

Hadar, Leon T. "The 'Green Peril': Creating the Islamic Fundamentalist Threat." *Cato Institute Policy Analysis,* no. 177, August 27, 1992.

Halliday, Fred, and Maxime Molyneux. *The Ethiopian Revolution.* London, Verso Publications, 1981.

Halperin, Morton H. *Bureaucratic Politics & Foreign Policy.* Washington, DC: The Brookings Institution, 1974.

Hanlon, Joseph. *Beggar Your Neighbours: Apartheid Power in South Africa.* Bloomington: Indiana University Press, 1986.

Harbeson, John W. *The Ethiopian Transformation: The Quest for the Post-Imperial State.* Boulder: Westview, 1988.

Harrison, Paul, and Robin Palmer. *News Out of Africa: Biafra to Band Aid* London: Hilary Shipman, 1986.

Henze, Paul B. *The Horn of Africa: From War to Peace.* London and New York: Macmillan and St. Martin's, 1991.

Herbst, Jeffrey. "The United States and Africa: Issues for the Future." In John W. Harbeson and Donald Rothchild, eds. *Africa in World Politics.* Boulder: Westview, 1991.

US Economic Policy Toward Africa. New York: Council on Foreign Relations Press, 1992.

Hermann, Charles F. "International Crisis as a Situational Variable." In James N. Rosenau, ed. *International Politics and Foreign Policy.* New York: The Free Press, 1969.

Hermida, Alfred. "Algeria: Democracy Derailed." *Africa Report* 37, 2 (March–April 1992): 13–17.

Hess, Rogert L. *Italian Colonialism in Somalia.* Chicago: University of Chicago Press, 1966.

Hilsman, Roger. *To Move a Nation: The Politics of Foreign Policy in the Administration of John F. Kennedy.* Garden City, New York: Doubleday, 1967.

Holloway, Anne Forrester. "Congressional Initiatives on South Africa." In Gerald J. Bender, James S. Coleman and Richard L. Sklar, eds. *African Crisis Areas and US Foreign Policy.* Berkeley and Los Angeles: University of California Press, 1985, pp. 89–94.

Hopper, Mary-Louise. "The Johannesburg Bus Boycott." *Africa Today,* no. 4 (November–December 1957): 13–16.

Hoskyns, Catherine, ed. *Case Studies in African Diplomacy (II) The Ethiopia–Somalia–Kenya Dispute: 1960–1967.* Dar es Salaam, Tanzania: Oxford University Press for the Institute of Public Administration, 1969.

Huband, Mark. "Zaire: Pressure from Abroad." *Africa Report* 37, 2 (March–April 1992): 41–44.

Hughes, Anthony J. "Interview: Umba Di Lutete, Zairian Ambassador to the United Nations." *Africa Report* 22, 4 (July–August 1977): 10–13.

"Randall Robinson: Executive Director of TransAfrica." *Africa Report* 25, 1 (January–February 1980): 9–15.

Hughes, Barry B. *The Domestic Context of American Foreign Policy.* San Francisco: W. H. Freeman and Company, 1978.

Hull, Galen. "Internationalizing the Shaba Conflict." *Africa Report* 22, 4 (July–August 1977): 4–9.

Hyland, William. *Mortal Rivals.* New York: Random House, 1987.

Jackson, Henry F. *From the Congo to Soweto: US Foreign Policy Toward Africa Since 1960.* New York: Quill, 1984.

Jaster, Robert S. *South Africa and its Regional Neighbors: The Dynamics of Regional Conflict.* London: International Institute for Strategic Studies, 1986.

Johns, Sheridan, and R. Hunt Davis, Jr., eds. *Mandela, Tambo, and the African National Congress: The Struggle Against Apartheid, 1948–1990.* New York and Oxford: Oxford University Press, 1991.

Johnson, Lyndon B. *The Vantage Point: Perspectives on the Presidency, 1963–1969.* New York: Holt, Rinehart and Winston, 1971.

Johnson, Willard R. "Afro-Americans and African Links: Cooperation for Our Long Term Economic Empowerment." *TransAfrica Forum* 1, 4 (Spring 1983): 81–92.

"A Joint Approach to Africa's Debt." *Africa Report* (May–June 1989): 42–45.

Kalb, Madeleine G. *The Congo Cables: The Cold War in Africa – From Eisenhower to Kennedy.* New York: Macmillan, 1982.

Kegley, Jr., Charles W. "The Bush Administration and the Future of American Foreign Policy: Pragmatism, or Procrastination?" *Presidential Studies Quarterly* 12 (1989): 717–31.

Kegley, Charles W., Jr., and Eugene R. Wittkopf. *American Foreign Policy: Pattern and Process.* New York: St. Martin's Press, 1991.

Keller, Edmond J. *Revolutionary Ethiopia: From Empire to People's Republic.* Bloomington: Indiana University Press, 1988.

Kennedy, John F. "The Challenge of Imperialism: Algeria." In Theodore C. Sorensen. *"Let the Word go Forth": The Speeches, Statements, and Writings of John F. Kennedy.* New York: Delacorte Press, 1988.

"The New Nations of Africa." In Theodore C. Sorenson. *"Let the Word go Forth": The Speeches, Statements, and Writings of John F. Kennedy.* New York: Delacorte Press, 1988.

Kern, Vincent D. "Synergy: Non-Traditional Security Assistance in Africa." Paper presented at the 32nd Annual Meeting of the African Studies Association, Hyatt Regency Hotel, Atlanta, GA, November 3, 1989.

Kessler, David. *The Falashas: The Forgotten Jews of Israel.* New York: Schocken Books, 1982.

Keto, Clement T. "American Involvement in South Africa, 1870–1915." Ph.D. dissertation, Washington, DC, Georgetown University, 1972.

Kiai, Maina. "Perestroika's Impact on US Policy Toward Somalia." *TransAfrica Forum* 7, 1 (Spring 1990): 17–24.

Kissinger, Henry A. *White House Years.* Boston: Little Brown, 1979.

Years of Upheaval. Boston: Little Brown, 1982.

Kitchen, Helen. *Footnotes to the Congo Story: An "Africa Report" Anthology.* New York: Walker and Company, 1967.

US Interests in Africa. New York: Praeger, 1983.

"The Making of US Policy Toward Africa." In Robert I. Rotberg, ed. *Africa in the 1990s and Beyond: US Policy Opportunities and Choices.* Algonac, MI: Reference Publications, 1988, pp. 14–27.

"Still on Safari." In L. Carl Brown, ed. *Centerstage: American Diplomacy Since World War Two.* New York: Holmes and Meier, 1990, pp. 171–92.

Klare, Michael T. "The Development of Low-Intensity Conflict Doctrine." In Peter J. Schraeder, ed. *Intervention into the 1990s: US Foreign Policy in the Third World.* Boulder: Lynne Rienner Publishers, 1992, pp. 31–44.

Kolko, Gabriel. *Confronting the Third World: United States Foreign Policy 1945–1980.* New York: Pantheon, 1988.

Korn, David A. *Ethiopia, the United States and the Soviet Union.* Carbondale: Southern Illinois University Press, 1986.

Kornegay, Jr., Francis A. "Africa in the New World Order." *Africa Report* 38, 1 (January–February 1993): 13–17.

Washington and Africa: Reagan, Congress, and an African Affairs Constituency in Transition. Washington, DC: African Bibliographic Center, 1982.

Laidi, Zaki (translated by Patricia Baudoin). *The Superpowers and Africa: The Constraints of a Rivalry 1960–1990.* Chicago: University of Chicago Press, 1990.

Laitin, David D. "Security, Ideology, and Development on Africa's Horn: United States Policy – Reagan and the Future." In Robert I. Rotberg, ed. *Africa in the 1990s and Beyond: US Policy Opportunities and Choices.* Algonac, MI: Reference Publications, 1988. pp. 204–19.

Laitin, David D. and Said S. Samatar. *Somalia: Nation in Search of a State.* Boulder: Westview, 1987.

Lake, Anthony. "Caution and Concern: The Making of American Policy Toward South Africa, 1946–1971." Ph.D. dissertation, Princeton, NJ, Princeton University, 1974.

The "Tar Baby" Option: American Policy Toward Southern Rhodesia. New York: Columbia University Press, 1976.

Lancaster, Carol. "US Aid to Africa: Who Gets What, When, and How?" *CSIS Africa Notes* 25 (March 31, 1984): 1–6.

US Aid to Sub-Saharan Africa: Challenges, Constraints, and Change. Washington, DC: CSIS, 1988.

Larus, Joel. "Diego Garcia: The Military and Legal Limitations of America's Pivotal Base in the Indian Ocean." In William Dowdy and Russell Trood, eds. *The Indian Ocean: Perspectives on a Strategic Arena*. Durham, NC: Duke University Press, 1985.

Laurence, John. *Race Propaganda and South Africa*. London: Victor Gollancz Ltd., 1979.

Lawyers Committee for Human Rights. *Zaire: Repression as Policy. A Human Rights Report*. New York: Lawyers Committee for Human Rights, 1990.

Lefebvre, Jeffrey A. *Arms for the Horn: US Security Policy in Ethiopia and Somalia 1953–1991*. Pittsburgh: University of Pittsburgh Press, 1991.

"Donor Dependency and American Arms Transfers to the Horn of Africa: The F–5 Legacy." *The Journal of Modern African Studies* 25, 3 (1987): 465–88.

Lefever, Ernest. *Uncertain Mandate: Politics of the U.N. Congo Operation*. Baltimore: 1967.

Lefort, René. *Ethiopia: A Heretical Revolution?* London: Zed Press, 1983.

Lemarchand, René. "Burundi: The Killing Fields Revisited." *Issue* 18, 1 (Winter 1989): 22–28.

Lemarchand, René, ed. *The Green and the Black: Qadhafi's Policies in Africa*. Bloomington: Indiana University Press, 1988.

Lenczowski, George. "The Arc of Crisis: Its Central Sector." *Foreign Affairs* 57 (Spring 1979): 796–820.

Levine, Victor. "The African–Israeli Connection 40 Years Later." *Middle East Review* 21 (Fall 1988): 12–17.

Lewis, I. M. *A Modern History of Somalia: Nation and State in the Horn of Africa*. Boulder; London: Westview, 1988.

A Pastoral Democracy: A Study of Pastoralism and Politics Among the Northern Somali of the Horn of Africa. New York: Africana Publishing, 1982.

"The Politics of the 1969 Coup." *Journal of Modern African Studies* 10, 3 (1972): 383–408.

Lewis, I. M., ed. *Nationalism and Self-Determination in the Horn of Africa*. London: Ithaca Press, 1983.

Liebenow, J. Gus. *African Politics: Crises and Challenges*. Bloomington; Indianapolis: Indiana University Press, 1986.

Liberia: The Quest for Democracy. Bloomington: Indiana University Press, 1987.

Lodge, Tom, and Bill Nasson. *All, Here, and Now: Black Politics in South Africa in the 1990s*. New York: Ford Foundation and the Foreign Policy Association, 1991.

Lombardi, Mark Owen. "Superpower Intervention in Sub-Saharan Africa: A Framework for Analyzing Third World Conflicts." Paper presented at the 30th Annual Meeting of the International Studies Association, St. Louis, MO, March 29–April 2, 1988.

Love, Janice. *The Anti-Apartheid Movement: Local Activism in Global Politics.* New York: Praeger, 1985.

Lulat, Y. G.-M. *US Relations With South Africa: An Annotated Bibliography.* 2 vols. Boulder: Westview, 1991.

McConnell, Bernd. "US Security Assistance in Africa: A Traditional View." Paper presented at the 32nd Annual Meeting of the African Studies Association, Hyatt Regency Hotel, Atlanta, GA, November 3, 1989.

McDonald, Steve. "Ethiopia: Learning a Lesson." *Africa Report* 37, 5 (September–October 1992): 27–29.

McWhirter, Cameron, and Gur Melamede. "Ethiopia: The Ethnicity Factor." *Africa Report* 37, 5 (September–October 1992): 30–33.

Mahoney, Richard H. *JFK: Ordeal in Africa.* New York: Oxford University Press, 1983.

Makinda, Samuel M. *Superpower Diplomacy in the Horn of Africa.* New York: St. Martin's Press, 1987.

Marcum, John. "The Politics of Indifference: Portugal and Africa, a Case Study in American Foreign Policy." *Issue* 2, 3 (Fall 1972): 9–17.

Marcus, Harold G. *Ethiopia, Great Britain and the United States, 1941–1974: The Politics of Empire.* Berkeley: University of California Press, 1983.

Maren, Michael Paul. "Assignment Africa." *Africa Report* 32, 2 (March–April 1987): 68–69.

Markakis, John. *National and Class Conflict in the Horn of Africa.* Cambridge: Cambridge University Press, 1987.

Markakis, John, and Nega Ayele. *Class and Revolution in Ethiopia.* Nottingham: Spokesman Press, 1978.

Martin, Ben L. "From Negro to Black to African American." *Political Science Quarterly*, 106, 1 (Spring 1991): 83–108.

Melady, Thomas Patrick. *Burundi: The Tragic Years.* New York: Orbis Books, 1974.

Melanson, Richard A. *Writing History and Making Policy: The Cold War, Vietnam, and Revisionism.* Lanham, MD: University Press of America, 1983.

Metz, Steven. "American Attitudes Toward Decolonization in Africa." *Political Science Quarterly* 99, 3 (Fall 1984): 515–33.

"The Anti-Apartheid Movement and the Formulation of American Policy Toward South Africa 1969–1981." Ph.D. dissertation, Baltimore, MD, Johns Hopkins University, 1985.

Minter, William. "Destructive Engagement: The United States and South Africa in the Reagan Era." In Phyllis Johnson and David Martin, eds. *Frontline Southern Africa: Destructive Engagement.* New York: Four Walls Eight Windows, 1988.

King Solomon's Mines Revisited: Western Interests and the Burdened History of Southern Africa. New York: Basic Books, 1986, pp. 387–440.

"The Limits of Liberal Africa Policy: Lessons From the Congo Crisis." *Trans-Africa Forum* 2, 3 (Fall 1984): 27–47.

Morison, Elting G., ed. *The Letters of Theodore Roosevelt.* 7 volumes. Cambridge: Harvard University Press, 1951–54.

Morna, Colleen Lowe. "A New Development Compact?" *Africa Report* (March–April 1990): 50–53.

Morris, Roger. *Uncertain Greatness: Henry Kissinger and American Foreign Policy.* New York: Harper & Row, 1977.

Morris, Roger, and Richard Mauzey. "Following the Scenario: Reflections on Five Case Histories in the Mode and Aftermath of CIA Intervention." In Robert L. Borosage and John Marks, eds. *The CIA File.* New York: Grossman Publishers, 1976. pp. 28–45.

Mosher, Frederick C., W. David Clinton, and Daniel G. Lang. *Presidential Transitions and Foreign Affairs.* Baton Rouge and London: Louisiana State University Press, 1987.

Nachmias, David, and David H. Rosenbloom. *Bureaucratic Government USA.* New York: St. Martin's Press, 1980.

Napper, Larry C. "The Ogaden War: Some Implications for Crisis Prevention." In Alexander L. George, ed. *Managing US–Soviet Rivalry: Problems of Crisis Prevention.* Boulder: Westview, 1983, pp. 225–54.

Nielson, Waldemar A. *The Great Powers and Africa.* New York: Praeger, 1969.

Niskanen, William. *Reaganomics: An Insider's Account of the Policies and the People.* New York: Oxford University Press, 1988.

Nixon, Richard M. *RN: The Memoirs of Richard Nixon.* 2 vols. New York: Warner Books, 1978.

Noer, Thomas J. *Briton, Boer, and Yankee: The United States and South Africa 1870–1914.* Kent, OH: Kent State University Press, 1978.

Cold War and Black Liberation: The United States and White Rule in Africa, 1948–1968. Columbia, MO: University of Missouri Press, 1985.

Novicki, Margaret A. "Interview: Herman J. Cohen: Forging a Bipartisan Policy." *Africa Report* 34, 5 (September–October 1989): 13–20.

Nzongola-Ntalaja, Georges, ed. *Conflict in the Horn of Africa.* Atlanta, GA: African Studies Association Press, 1991.

The Crisis in Zaire: Myths and Realities, Trenton, NJ: Africa World Press, 1986.

Odom, Major Thomas P. *Dragon Operations: Hostage Rescues in the Congo, 1964–1965.* Fort Leavenworth, KS: Combat Studies Institute, US Army Command and General Staff College, 1988.

Ogene, F. Chidozie. *Interest Groups and the Shaping of Foreign Policy: Four Case Studies of United States African Policy.* New York: St. Martin's Press, 1983.

Ohaegbulam, F. Ugboaja. "Containment in Africa: From Truman to Reagan." *TransAfrica Forum* 6, 1 (Fall 1988): 7–34.

"The United States and Africa After the Cold War," *Africa Today* 39, 4 (1992): 19–34.

Oneal, John R. *Foreign Policy Making in Times of Crisis.* Columbus, OH: State University Press, 1982.

Ornstein, Norman J. "Interest Groups, Congress, and American Foreign Policy." In David P. Forsythe, ed. *American Foreign Policy in an Uncertain World.* Lincoln, Nebraska: University of Nebraska Press, 1984, pp. 49–64.

Ottaway, Marina. *Soviet and American Influence in the Horn of Africa.* New York: Praeger, 1982.

Ottaway, Marina, and David Ottaway. *Ethiopia: Empire in Revolution.* London: Africana Publishing Company, 1978.

Pachter, Elise Forbes. "Our Man in Kinshasa: US Relations With Mobutu,

1970–1983; Patron Client Relations in the International Sphere." Ph.D. dissertation, Baltimore, MD, The Johns Hopkins University, 1987.

Parfit, Tudor. *Operation Moses: The Story of the Exodus of the Falasha Jews From Ethiopia*. London: Stein and Day, 1985.

Parry, Robert, and Peter Kornbluh. "Iran–Contra's Untold Story." *Foreign Policy* no. 72 (Fall 1988): 3–30.

Patman, Robert G. *The Soviet Union and the Horn of Africa: The Diplomacy of Intervention and Disengagement*. Cambridge: Cambridge University Press, 1990.

Pateman, Roy. "Intelligence Agencies in Africa: A Preliminary Assessment." *Journal of Modern African Studies* 30, 4 (1992): 569–85.

Paulos, Afeworki. "Superpower-Small State Interaction: The Case of US–Ethiopian Relations, 1945–1986." Ph.D. dissertation, Washington, DC, The George Washington University, 1987.

Payton, Gary. "The Somali Coup of 1969: The Case for Soviet Complicity." *Journal of Modern African Studies* 18, 3 (1980): 11–20.

Peabody, Robert L., Susan Webb-Hammond, Jean Torcom, Lynne P. Brown, Carolyn Thompson, Robin Kolodny. "Interviewing Political Elites." *PS: Political Science & Politics* 23, 3 (September 1990): 451–54.

Petterson, Donald K. "Ethiopia Abandoned? An American Perspective." *International Affairs* 62, 4 (Autumn 1986): 627–45.

"Somalia and the United States, 1977–1983: The New Relationship." In Gerald J. Bender, James S. Coleman, and Richard L. Sklar, eds. *African Crisis Areas and US Foreign Policy*. Berkeley: University of California Press, 1985.

Plummer, Brenda Gayle. "Evolution of the Black Foreign Policy Constituency." *TransAfrica Forum* 6, 3–4 (Spring–Summer 1989): 67–82.

Powers, Thomas. *The Man Who Kept the Secrets: Richard Helms and the CIA*. New York: Alfred Knopf, 1979.

Prinsloo, Daan. *United States Foreign Policy and the Republic of South Africa*. Pretoria, South Africa: Foreign Affairs Association, 1978.

Puchala, Donald J. "Of Blind Men, Elephants and International Integration." *Journal of Common Market Studies* 10, 3 (March 1972): 267–84.

Rasmuson, John R. *A History of Kagnew Station and American Forces in Eritrea*. Arlington, VA: US Army Security Agency, Information Division, 1973.

Ray, Ellen, William Schaap, Karl Van Meter, and Louis Wolf, eds. *Dirty Work 2: The CIA in Africa*. Secaucus, NJ: Lyle Stuart, 1979.

Reagan, Nancy. *My Turn: The Memoirs of Nancy Reagan*. New York: Random House, 1989.

Regan, Donald. *For the Record: From Wall Street to Washington*. San Diego: Harcourt, Brace, Jovanovich, 1988.

Rosati, Jerel A. *The Carter Administration's Quest for Global Community: Beliefs and Their Impact on Behavior*. Columbia: University of South Carolina Press, 1987.

"Congressional Influence in American Foreign Policy: Addressing the Controversy." *Journal of Political and Military Sociology* 12 (Fall 1984): 311–33.

"The Impact of Beliefs on Behavior: The Foreign Policy of the Carter Administration." In Donald Sylvan and Steve Chan, eds., *Foreign Policy Decision-Making*. New York: Praeger, 1984.

The Politics of US Foreign Policy. Dallas, TX: Holt, Rinehart & Winston, 1993.

Rositzke, Harry. *The CIA's Secret Operations.* New York: Reader's Digest Press, 1977.

Rothchild, Donald. "Regional Peacemaking in Africa: The Role of the Great Powers as Facilitators." In John W. Harbeson and Donald Rothchild, eds., *Africa in World Politics.* Boulder: Westview, 1991, pp. 284–306.

Rothchild, Donald, and John Ravenhill. "Retreat From Globalism: US Policy Toward Africa in the 1990s." In: Kenneth A. Oye, Robert J. Lieber, and Donald Rothchild, eds. *Eagle in a New World: American Grand Strategy in the Post-Cold War Era.* New York: Harper Collins, 1991, pp. 389–415.

Samatar, Said S. *Somalia: A Nation in Turmoil.* London: The Minority Rights Group, 1991.

Schatzberg, Michael G. *The Dialectics of Oppression in Zaire.* Bloomington: Indiana University Press, 1988.

Mobutu or Chaos? The United States and Zaire, 1960–1990. Lanham, MD: University Press of America, Philadelphia: Foreign Policy Research Institute, 1991.

"The State and the Economy: The 'Radicalization of the Revolution' in Mobutu's Zaire." *Canadian Journal of African Studies* 14, 2 (1980): 239–57.

Schlesinger, Jr., Arthur M. "Foreign Policy and the American Character." *Foreign Affairs* 62, 1 (Fall 1983): 1–16.

A Thousand Days: John F. Kennedy in the White House. Greenwich, CT: Fawcett Publications, 1967.

Schoenbaum, Thomas J. *Waging Peace and War: Dean Rusk in the Truman, Kennedy, and Johnson Years.* New York: Simon & Schuster, 1988.

Schraeder, Peter J. "The Faulty Assumptions of US Foreign Policy in the Third World." In Ted Galen Carpenter, ed. *Collective Defense or Strategic Independence? Alternative Strategies for the Future.* Washington, DC: Cato Institute; Lexington, MA: Lexington Books, 1989.

Schraeder, Peter J., ed. *Intervention into the 1990s: US Foreign Policy in the Third World.* Boulder: Lynne Rienner Publishers, 1992.

Schraeder, Peter J., and Jerel A. Rosati. "Policy Dilemmas in the Horn of Africa: Contradictions in the US–Somalia Relationship." *Northeast African Studies* 9, 3 (1987): 19–42.

Schrire, Robert. *Adapt or Die: The End of White Politics in South Africa.* New York: Ford Foundation and the Foreign Policy Association, 1991.

Seiler, John Joseph. "The Formulation of US Policy Toward Southern Africa, 1957–1976: The Failure of Good Intentions." Ph.D. dissertation, University of Connecticut, 1976.

Selassie, Bereket Habte. *Conflict and Intervention in the Horn of Africa.* New York: Monthly Review Press, 1980.

Sewell, John W., and Anthony W. Gambino. "Is the International Community Keeping its Promise to Africa?" *TransAfrica Forum* 5, 3 (Spring 1988): 3–16.

Shaw, Bryant P. "Internal and External Threats to US Interests in Africa." Paper presented at the 32nd Annual Meeting of the African Studies Association, Hyatt Regency Hotel, Atlanta, GA, November 3, 1989.

Shepard, Robert B. *Nigeria, Africa, and the United States from Kennedy to Reagan.* Bloomington: Indiana University Press, 1991.

329

Shephard, Jack. "Congress and the White House at Odds." *Africa Report* 30, 3 (May–June 1985): 25–28.

"The Politics of Food Aid." *Africa Report* 30, 2 (March–April 1985): 51–54.

Shinn, David. "A Survey of American-Ethiopian Relations Prior to the Italian Occupation of Ethiopia." *Ethiopia Observer* 14, 4 (1971).

Simon, Paul. "The Senate's New African Agenda." *Africa Report* 32, 3 (May–June 1987): 14–16.

Sisay, Hasan B. *Big Powers and Small Nations: A Case Study of United States-Liberian Relations.* Lanham, MD: University Press of America, 1985.

Skinner, Elliott P. *African Americans and US Policy Toward Africa 1850–1924.* Washington, DC: Howard University Press, 1992.

Skinner, Robert P. *Abyssinia of Today: An Account of the First Mission Sent by the American Government to the Court of the King of Kings (1903–1904).* London: Edward Arnold, 1906.

Smith, Hedrick. *The Power Game: How Washington Works.* New York: Random House, 1988.

Smoke, Richard. *Controlling Escalation.* Cambridge: Cambridge University Press, 1977.

Sorensen, Theodore C. *Decision-Making in the White House: The Olive Branch or the Arrows.* New York: Columbia University Press, 1963.

Speakes, Larry, with Robert Pack. *Speaking Out: The Reagan White House.* New York: Charles Scribner's Sons, 1988.

Spencer, John H. *Ethiopia at Bay: A Personal Account of the Haile Selassie Years.* Algonac, MI: Reference Publications, 1987.

Spooner, Ward Anthony. "United States Foreign Policy Toward South Africa, 1919–1941: Political and Economic Aspects." Ph.D. dissertation, St. John's University, 1979.

Staniland, Martin. *American Intellectuals and African Nationalists, 1955–1970.* New Haven: Yale University Press, 1991.

Steinbruner, John D. *The Cybernetic Theory of Decision: New Dimensions of Political Analysis.* Princeton: Princeton University Press, 1974.

Stockman, David. *The Triumph of Politics: Why the Reagan Revolution Failed.* New York: Harper & Row, 1986.

Stockwell, John. *In Search of Enemies: A CIA Story.* New York: W. W. Norton, 1978.

Stremlau, John J. *The International Politics of the Nigerian Civil War 1967–1970.* Princeton: Princeton University Press, 1977.

Study Commission on US Policy Toward South Africa. *South Africa: Time Running Out.* Berkeley: University of California Press, 1981.

Stupak, Ronald J. *American Foreign Policy: Assumptions, Processes and Projections.* New York: Harper & Row, 1976.

Talbot, Stephen. "The CIA and BOSS: Thick as Thieves." In Ellen Ray, William Schapp, Karl Van Meter, and Louis Wolf, eds. *Dirty Work 2: The CIA in Africa.* Secaucus, NJ: Lyle Stuart, 1979, pp. 266–75.

Thurston, Raymond L. "Détente in the Horn." *Africa Report* 14, 2 (February 1969): 6–13.

"The United States, Somalia and the Crisis in the Horn." *Horn of Africa* (April–June 1978): 11–20.

Touval, Saadia. *Somali Nationalism: International Politics and the Drive for Unity in the Horn.* Cambridge, MA: Harvard University Press, 1963.

TransAfrica Forum Conference. "African-Americans in International Affairs." *TransAfrica Forum* 6, 3–4 (Spring–Summer 1989): 53–66.

Truman, Harry S. *Memoirs.* 2 vols. Garden City: Doubleday, 1955 & 1956.

Tully, Andrew. *CIA: The Inside Story.* New York: William Morrow, 1962.

United Nations. *The Blue Helmets: A Review of United Nations Peace-Keeping.* New York: United Nations, 1991.

US Agency for International Development (USAID). *US Overseas Loans and Grants, Series of Yearly Data (Volume IV, Africa), Obligations and Loan Authorizations, FY 1946–FY 1990.* Washington, DC: USAID, 1990.

US General Accounting Office (GAO). *Somalia: Observations Regarding the Northern Conflict and Resulting Conditions.* Washington, DC: GPO, May 1989.

US House. *The Middle East, Africa, and Inter-American Affairs* (volume 16) *Selected Executive Session Hearings of the Committee on Foreign Affairs, 1951–56.* Washington, DC: GPO, 1980.

US House. Committee on Banking, Finance, and Urban Affairs. Subcommittee on International Trade, Investment, and Monetary Policy. *Export-Import Bank and Trade With Africa,* Hearings, 1978, 95th Cong., 2nd Sess., Washington, DC: GPO, 1978.

US House. Committee on Foreign Affairs. *Background Materials on Foreign Assistance: Report of the Task Force on Foreign Assistance to the Committee on Foreign Affairs, US House of Representatives,* 101st Cong., 1st Sess., Washington, DC: GPO, 1989.

US House. Committee on Foreign Affairs. *The Impact of US Foreign Policy on Seven African Countries: Report of a Congressional Study Mission to Ethiopia, Zaire, Zimbabwe, Ivory Coast, Algeria, and Morocco, August 6–25, 1985 and a Staff Study Mission to Tunisia, August 24–27, 1983,* 98th Cong., 2nd Sess., Washington, DC: GPO, 1984.

US House. Committee on Foreign Affairs. Subcommittee on Africa. *The Current Crisis in South Africa,* Hearing, December 4, 1984, 98th Cong., 2nd Sess., Washington, DC: GPO, 1985.

US House. Committee on Foreign Affairs. Subcommittee on Africa. *Developments in South Africa: United States Policy Responses,* Hearing, March 12, 1986, 99th Cong., 2nd Sess., Washington, DC: GPO, 1986.

US House. Committee on Foreign Affairs. Subcommittee on Africa. *Foreign Assistance Legislation for Fiscal Year 1978* (Part 3) *Economic and Military Assistance Programs in Africa,* Hearings and Markup, March 17, 18, 23, 28, 29, and April 28, 1977, 95th Cong., 1st Sess., Washington, DC: GPO, 1977.

US House. Committee on Foreign Affairs. Subcommittee on Africa. *Foreign Assistance Legislation for Fiscal Year 1980–81* (Part 6) *Economic and Military Assistance Programs in Africa,* Hearings and Markup, February 13, 14, 21, 22, 27, 28; March 5, 6, 7, and 12, 1979, 96th Cong., 1st Sess., Washington, DC: GPO, 1979.

US House. Committee on Foreign Affairs. Subcommittee on Africa. *Foreign Assistance Legislation for Fiscal Year 1981* (Part 7) *Economic and Military Assistance Programs in Africa,* Hearings and Markup, February 7, 12, 13, 20,

25, 26, 27, 28; March 5 and 6, 1980, 96th Cong., 2st Sess., Washington, DC: GPO, 1980.

US House. Committee on Foreign Affairs. Subcommittee on Africa. *Foreign Assistance Legislation for Fiscal Year 1982* (Part 8) *Economic and Military Assistance Programs in Africa*, Hearings and Markup, March 19, 24, 26, 31; April 1, 2, and 27, 1981, 97th Cong., 1st Sess., Washington, DC: GPO, 1981.

US House. Committee on Foreign Affairs. Subcommittee on Africa. *Foreign Assistance Legislation for Fiscal Year 1983* (Part 7) *Economic and Military Assistance Programs in Africa*, Hearings and Markup, April 20, 21, and 29, 1982, 97th Cong., 2nd Sess., Washington, DC: GPO, 1982.

US House. Committee on Foreign Affairs. Subcommittee on Africa. *Foreign Assistance Legislation for Fiscal Year 1988–89* (Part 6) *Economic and Military Assistance Programs in Africa*, Hearings and Markup, March 4, 10, 18, and 19, 1987, 100th Cong., 1st Sess., Washington, DC: GPO, 1987.

US House. Committee on Foreign Affairs. Subcommittee on Africa. *Implementation of the US Arms Embargo (Against Portugal and South Africa, and Related Issues)*, Hearings, March 20, 22; April 6, 1973, 93rd Cong., 1st Sess., Washington, DC: GPO, 1973.

US House. Committee on Foreign Affairs. Subcommittee on Africa. *Legislation to Require that Any United States Government Support for Military or Paramilitary Operations in Angola be Openly Acknowledged and Publicly Debated*, Hearings and Markup, April 22 and 23, 1986, 99th Cong., 1st Sess., Washington, DC: GPO, 1986.

US House. Committee on Foreign Affairs. Subcommittee on Africa. *Media Restrictions in South Africa*, Hearings, March 15 and 16, 1988, 100th Cong., 2nd Sess., Washington, DC: GPO, 1988.

US House. Committee on Foreign Affairs. Subcommittee on Africa. *Political and Economic Situation in Zaire – Fall 1981*, Hearing, September 15, 1981, 97th Cong., 1st Sess., Washington, DC: GPO, 1982.

US House. Committee on Foreign Affairs. Subcommittee on Africa. *The Political Crisis in Ethiopia and the Role of the United States*, Hearing, June 18, 1991, 102 Cong., 1st Sess., Washington, DC: GPO, 1992.

US House. Committee on Foreign Affairs. Subcommittee on Africa. *Possible Violation or Circumvention of the Clark Amendment*, Hearing, July 1, 1987, Washington, DC: GPO: 1987.

US House. Committee on Foreign Affairs. Subcommittee on Africa. *Reported Massacres and Indiscriminate Killings in Somalia*, Hearing, July 14, 1988, 100th Cong., 2nd Sess., Washington, DC: GPO, 1989.

US House. Committee on Foreign Affairs. Subcommittee on Africa. *South Africa and United States Foreign Policy*, Hearings, April 2 and 15, 1969, 91st Cong., 1st Sess., Washington, DC: GPO, 1969.

US House. Committee on Foreign Affairs. Subcommittee on Africa. *US Business Involvement in Southern Africa* (Part 2), Hearings, May–December 1971, 92nd Cong., 1st Sess., Washington, DC: GPO, 1972.

US House. Committee on Foreign Affairs. Subcommittee on Africa. *US Policy and the Crisis in Liberia*, Hearing, June 19, 1990, 101st Cong., 2nd Sess., Washington, DC: GPO, 1990.

US House. Committee on Foreign Affairs. Subcommittee on Africa. *US Policy* on *South Africa*, Hearing, September 26, 1984, 98th Cong., 2nd Sess., Washington, DC: GPO, 1985.

US House. Committee on Foreign Affairs. Subcommittee on Africa; and Select Committee on Hunger, International Task Force. *Conflict and Famine in the Horn of Africa*, Hearing, May 30, 1991, 102nd Cong., 1st Sess., Washington, DC: GPO, 1991.

US House. Committee on Foreign Affairs. Subcommittee on Africa; and Select Committee on Hunger, International Task Force. *Famine in Ethiopia*, Joint Hearing, February 28, 1990, 101st Cong., 2nd Sess., Washington, DC: GPO, 1990.

US House. Committee on Foreign Affairs. Subcommittee on Africa; and Select Committee on Hunger, International Task Force. *War and Famine in the Sudan*, Joint Hearing, March 15, 1990, 101st Cong., 2nd Sess., Washington, DC: GPO, 1990.

US House. Committee on Foreign Affairs. Subcommittee on Human Rights and International Organizations. Subcommittee on Africa. *The Human Rights Situation in South Africa, Zaire, the Horn of Africa, and Uganda*, Hearings, June 21; August 9, 1984, 98th Cong., 2nd Sess., Washington, DC: GPO, 1985.

US House. Committee on Foreign Affairs. Subcommittees on Human Rights and International Organizations and on Africa. *Update on the Recent Developments in Ethiopia: The Famine Crisis*, Hearing, April 21, 1988, 100th Cong., 2nd Sess., Washington, DC: GPO, 1988.

US House. Committee on Foreign Affairs. Subcommittees on International Economic Policy and Trade, and on Africa. *Legislative Options and United States Policy Toward South Africa*, Hearings and Markup, April 9, 16; June 4, 5, 1986, 99th Cong., 2nd Sess., Washington, DC: GPO, 1987.

US House. Committee on Foreign Affairs. Subcommittees on International Economic Policy and Trade, and on Africa. *Oversight of the Administration's Implementation of the Comprehensive Anti-Apartheid Act of 1986 (Public Law 99–440) and an Assessment of Recent South African Political and Economic Developments*, Hearing, June 16, 1987, 100th Cong., 1st Sess., Washington, DC: GPO, 1988.

US House. Committee on Foreign Affairs. Subcommittees on International Economic Policy and Trade, and on Africa. *The President's Report on Progress Toward Ending Apartheid in South Africa and the Question of Future Sanctions*, Hearing, November 5, 1987, 100th Cong., 1st Sess., Washington, DC: GPO, 1988.

US House. Committee on Foreign Affairs. Subcommittees on International Economic Policy and Trade, and on Africa. *Proposed Economic Sanctions Against South Africa*, Hearings and Markup, March 22, 23; April 20, 28; and May 3, 1988, 100th Cong., 2nd Sess., Washington, DC: GPO, 1988.

US House. Committee on Foreign Affairs. Subcommittees on International Economic Policy and Trade, and on Africa. *The Status of United States Sanctions Against South Africa*, Hearing, April 30, 1991, 102nd Cong., 1st Sess., Washington, DC: GPO, 1991.

US House. Committee on Foreign Affairs. Subcommittees on International Economic Policy and Trade, on Africa, and on International Organizations. *US Policy Toward South Africa*, Hearings, April 30; May 6, 8, 13, 15, 20, 22; and June 10, 1980, 96th Cong., 2nd Sess., Washington, DC: GPO, 1980.

US House. Committee on Foreign Affairs. Subcommittee on International Political and Military Affairs. *US Policy and Request for Sale of Arms to Ethiopia*, Hearing, March 5, 1975, 94th Cong., 1st Sess., Washington, DC: GPO, 1975.

US House. Committee on International Relations. *War in the Horn of Africa: A Firsthand Report on the Challenges for United States Policy*. 95th Cong., 1st Sess., Washington, DC: GPO, 1978.

US House. Committee on International Relations. Subcommittee on Africa. *Foreign Assistance Legislation for Fiscal Year 1979* (Part 3) *Economic and Military Assistance Programs in Africa*, Hearings and Markup, February 7, 8, 14, 28; March 1 and 2, 1978, 95th Cong., 2nd Sess., Washington, DC: GPO, 1978.

US House. Committee on International Relations. Subcommittees on Africa and on International Organizations. *United States Foreign Policy Toward South Africa*, Hearing, January 31, 1978, 95th Cong., 2nd Sess., Washington, DC: GPO, 1978.

US House. Committee on International Relations. Subcommittee on International Security and Scientific Affairs, *Congressional Oversight of War Powers Compliance: Zaire Airlift*, Hearing, August 10, 1978, 95th Cong., 2nd Sess, Washington, DC: GPO, 1978.

US Senate. Committee on Foreign Relations. Subcommittee on Africa. *Ethiopia and the Horn of Africa*, Hearings, August 4, 5, and 6, 1976. 94th Cong. 2nd Sess. Washington, DC: GPO, 1976.

US Senate. Committee on Foreign Relations. Subcommittee on Africa. *Security Supporting Assistance for Zaire*, Hearing, October 24, 1975, 94th Cong., 1st Sess., Washington, DC: GPO, 1975.

US Senate. Committee on Foreign Relations. Subcommittee on United States Security Agreements and Commitments Abroad. *United States Security Agreements and Commitments Abroad* (Volume 2, Part 8) *Ethiopia*, Hearing, June 1, 1970, 91st Cong., 2nd Sess., Washington, DC: GPO, 1971.

US Senate. Select Committee to Study Governmental Operations. *Alleged Assassination Plots Involving Foreign Leaders: An Interim Report of the Select Committee to Study Governmental Operations With Respect to Intelligence Activities*, 94th Cong., 1st Sess., Washington, DC, GPO, 1975.

Valdés, Nelson P. "Cuba's Involvement in the Horn of Africa: The Ethiopian–Somali War and the Eritrean Conflict." *Cuban Studies/Estudios Cubanos* 10, 1 (January 1980): 49–79.

Vance, Cyrus. *Hard Choices: Critical Years in American Foreign Policy*. New York: Simon & Schuster, 1983.

Vance, Sheldon B. "American Foreign Policy: The Glory Years – and Now What? An Insider Look at the Foreign Service" (with contributions by Jean Vance). Unpublished manuscript.

Verhaegen, Benoit ed. *Congo 1961*. Brussels: Centre de Recherche et d'Information Socio-Politiques (CRISP), 1961.

Volman, Daniel. "Africa's Rising Status in American Defense Policy." *Journal of Modern African Studies* 22,1 (1984): 143–51.

de Waal, Alex, and Rikiya Omaar. "Somalia. The Lessons of Famine." *Africa Report* 37, 6 (November–December 1992): 62–64.

Wagaw, Teshome G. "The International Political Ramifications of Falasha Emigration." *Journal of Modern African Studies* 29, 4 (1991): 557–82.

Wagoner, Fred E. *Dragon Rouge: The Rescue of Hostages in the Congo.* Washington, DC: GPO, 1980.

Wallerstein, Immanuel. *Africa and the Modern World.* Trenton, NJ: Africa World Press, 1986.

Walters, Ronald J. *US–South Africa Relations: A Legislative Review.* Washington, DC: Howard University, 1985.

Walters, Ronald J. "African-American Influence in US Foreign Policy Toward South Africa." In Mohammed E. Ahrair, ed. *Ethnic Groups and US Foreign Policy.* New York: Greenwood, 1987, pp. 65–82

Webber, Mark. "Soviet Policy in Sub-Saharan Africa: The Final Phase." *Journal of Modern African Studies* 30, 1 (1992): 1–30.

Weil, Martin. "Can the Blacks Do For Africa What the Jews Did for Israel?" *Foreign Policy*, no. 15 (Summer 1974): 109–30.

Weiss, Herbert F. *Political Protest in the Congo: The Parti Solidaire Africain During the Independence Period.* Princeton: Princeton University Press, 1967.

Weissman, Stephen R. *American Foreign Policy in the Congo: 1960–1964.* Ithaca: Cornell University Press, 1974.

"The CIA and US Policy in Zaire and Angola." In Ellen Ray, William Schaap, Karl Van Meter, and Louis Wolf, eds. *Dirty Work 2: The CIA in Africa.* Secaucus, NJ: Lyle Stuart, 1979, pp. 89–190.

Weissman, Stephen R., and Johnnie Carson. "Economic Sanctions Against Rhodesia." In John Spanier and Joseph Nogee, eds. *Congress, the Presidency and American Foreign Policy.* New York: Pergamon, 1981.

Wiley, David S. "Academic Analysis and U.S. Policy-Making on Africa: Reflections and Conclusions." *Issue* 19, 2 (Summer 1991): 38–48.

"The United States Congress and Africanist Scholars." *Issue* 19, 2 (Summer 1991): 4–13.

Willame, Jean-Claude. "Zaire, Années 90: Volume I." *Les Cahiers du CEDAF–ASDOC*, series 2, nos. 5–6, 1991.

Winchester, N. Brian. "United States Policy Toward Africa." *Current History* 87, 529 (May 1988): 193–96, 232–34.

Wolpe, Howard. "Africa and the U.S. House of Representatives." *Africa Report* 29, 4 (July–August 1984): 67–71.

Woods, Donald. *Biko.* New York: Vintage Books, 1979.

Young, Crawford. *Politics in the Congo: Decolonization and Independence.* Princeton: Princeton University Press, 1965.

"United States Foreign Policy Toward Africa: Silver Anniversary Reflections." *African Studies Review* 27, 3 (September 1984): 1–17.

"The Zairian Crisis and American Foreign Policy." In Gerald J. Bender, James S. Coleman, and Richard L. Sklar, eds. *African Crisis Areas and U.S. Foreign Policy.* Berkeley: University of California Press, 1985, pp. 214–19.

Zartman, I. William. *Ripe for Resolution: Conflict and Intervention in Africa.* New York; Oxford: Oxford University Press, 1985.

INDEX

CAMBRIDGE STUDIES IN INTERNATIONAL RELATIONS